Effective DevOps with AWS

Ship faster, scale better, and deliver incredible productivity

Nathaniel Felsen

BIRMINGHAM - MUMBAI

Effective DevOps with AWS

First published: July 2017

Production reference: 1310717

Published by Packt Publishing Ltd.
Livery Place
35 Livery Street
Birmingham
B3 2PB, UK.
ISBN 978-1-78646-681-5

www.packtpub.com

Credits

Author
Nathaniel Felsen

Reviewer
Sanjeev Kumar Jaiswal

Commissioning Editor
David Barnes

Acquisition Editor
Vijin Boricha

Content Development Editor
Mamata Walkar

Technical Editor
Sayali Thanekar

Copy Editor
Safis Editing

Project Coordinator
Kinjal Bari

Proofreader
Safis Editing

Indexer
Pratik Shirodkar

Graphics
Abhinash Sahu

Production Coordinator
Shantanu Zagade

About the Author

Nathaniel Felsen is a DevOps engineer who started working on DevOps engineering concepts over 10 years ago, before the term was even coined. He worked in several companies ranging from small start-ups to enterprises, including Qualys, Square, and more recently, Medium.

Outside of work, Nathaniel lives a fabulous life where he enjoys running after his very active kids and spending a fortune on occasional date nights with his wife. Although Nathaniel is French, he prefers exploring local stout beers with friends than drinking wine. He holds a MS degree in system, network, and security from Ecole Pour l'Informatique et les Techniques Avancées (EPITA), a top CS engineering school in France.

I would like to thank the team of editors and reviewers at Packt Publishing for this book and, in particular, Mamata Walkar, Sayali Thanekar, Mehvash Fatima, Usha Iyer, and David Barnes.

I also want to thank all my friends who have supported me unconditionally throughout the writing of this book, but more than anything, I would like to thank Matine, Bernard, Eunsil, Hanna, Leo, and Oceane for their patience, love, and support.

About the Reviewer

Sanjeev Kumar Jaiswal is a computer graduate with 8 years of industry experience. He uses Perl, Python, and GNU/Linux for his day-to-day activities. He is currently working on projects involving penetration testing, source code review, and security design and implementations. He is mostly involved in the web and cloud security projects.

He is currently learning NodeJS and React Native as well. Sanjeev loves teaching engineering students and IT professionals. He has been teaching for the last 8 years in his leisure time.

He founded Alien Coders, based on the learning through sharing principle, for computer science students and IT professionals in 2010, which became a huge hit in India among engineering students. You can follow him on Twitter at `@aliencoders`.

He has written *Instant PageSpeed Optimization* and co-authored *Learning Django Web Development* with Packt Publishing. He has reviewed more than seven books for Packt Publishing and looks forward to authoring and reviewing more books for Packt and other publishers.

www.PacktPub.com

For support files and downloads related to your book, please visit www.PacktPub.com. Did you know that Packt offers eBook versions of every book published, with PDF and ePub files available? You can upgrade to the eBook version at www.PacktPub.comand as a print book customer, you are entitled to a discount on the eBook copy. Get in touch with us at service@packtpub.com for more details. At www.PacktPub.com, you can also read a collection of free technical articles, sign up for a range of free newsletters and receive exclusive discounts and offers on Packt books and eBooks.

https://www.packtpub.com/mapt

Get the most in-demand software skills with Mapt. Mapt gives you full access to all Packt books and video courses, as well as industry-leading tools to help you plan your personal development and advance your career.

Why subscribe?

- Fully searchable across every book published by Packt
- Copy and paste, print, and bookmark content
- On demand and accessible via a web browser

Customer Feedback

Thanks for purchasing this Packt book. At Packt, quality is at the heart of our editorial process. To help us improve, please leave us an honest review on this book's Amazon page at https://www.amazon.com/dp/1786466813.

If you'd like to join our team of regular reviewers, you can e-mail us at customerreviews@packtpub.com. We award our regular reviewers with free eBooks and videos in exchange for their valuable feedback. Help us be relentless in improving our products!

Table of Contents

Preface

AWS provides a huge range of managed services. While each is well-documented, figuring out how to use them together to build a business infrastructure is less clear. In this book, you'll see how the most successful tech start-ups launch and scale their services on AWS, and how you can do it too. Thanks to the implementation of this new philosophy, high performers such as Amazon, Netflix, and Airbnb have been able to break down the silos surrounding developers and operations teams, gaining tremendous agility and the ability to deliver new code quickly and reliably. This book is a comprehensive guide to AWS that will help readers understand AWS in a step-by-step manner.

What this book covers

Chapter 1, *The Cloud and the DevOps Revolution*, states that adopting a DevOps culture means first and foremost changing the way traditional engineering and operations teams operate.

Chapter 2, *Deploying Your First Web Application*, introduces AWS and its most notorious service, EC2. After signing up for AWS, we will configure our environment in such a way that we can create a virtual server using the command-line interface.

Chapter 3, *Treating Your Infrastructure As Code*, covers a good production environment ready to host any application. We will see how to architect it and monitor our servers.

Chapter 4, *Adding Continuous Integration and Continuous Deployment*, improves the developer's productivity. To that effect, we will build a continuous integration pipeline.

Chapter 5, *Scaling Your Infrastructure*, shows how to break the monolith into a service-oriented architecture and other AWS managed services, such as ALB, SQS, and Kinesis, for better load balancing and better service-to-service communication.

Chapter 6, *Running Containers in AWS*, explains the concept of containers using Docker and ECS, and the basics of how Docker works. It shows how to create a container for our application.

Chapter 7, *Monitoring and Alerting,* explains several ways to add monitoring and alerting to our application and infrastructure. We can do it reasonably well by taking advantage of some of the services AWS provides, including CloudWatch, ElasticSearch, and SNS.

Chapter 8, *Hardening the Security of Your AWS Environment,* covers one of the more complex aspect of a cloud infrastructure, its security, and different ways to audit and assess the security of our infrastructure.

What you need for this book

You will need a recent web browser, a Terminal application, and an SSH. For this book, you will also need Git, Python, and Ansible. You can use either a Windows, Mac, or Linux operating system.

Who this book is for

This book is for developers, operations, and DevOps people who want to build and use AWS for their software infrastructure. Basic computer science knowledge is required for this book.

Conventions

In this book, you will find a number of text styles that distinguish between different kinds of information. Here are some examples of these styles and an explanation of their meaning.

Code words in text, database table names, folder names, filenames, file extensions, pathnames, dummy URLs, user input, and Twitter handles are shown as follows:

"The tool is more interactive than the classic awscli command."

A block of code is set as follows:

```
- name: Import Jenkins GPG key
  rpm_key:
    state: present
    key: http://pkg.jenkins-ci.org/redhat/jenkins-ci.org.key
```

When we wish to draw your attention to a particular part of a code block, the relevant lines or items are set in bold:

```
describe('main page', function() {
  before(function() {
    this.browser = new Browser({ site: 'http://localhost:3000' });
  });

  it('should say hello world');
});
```

Any command-line input or output is written as follows:

```
$ npm install zombie
```

New terms and **important words** are shown in bold. Words that you see on the screen, for example, in menus or dialog boxes, appear in the text like this:

"Click on **Create pull request** and follow the steps to create a pull request. "

 Warnings or important notes appear like this.

 Tips and tricks appear like this.

Reader feedback

Feedback from our readers is always welcome. Let us know what you think about this book-what you liked or disliked. Reader feedback is important for us as it helps us develop titles that you will really get the most out of. To send us general feedback, simply email feedback@packtpub.com, and mention the book's title in the subject of your message. If there is a topic that you have expertise in and you are interested in either writing or contributing to a book, see our author guide at www.packtpub.com/authors.

Customer support

Now that you are the proud owner of a Packt book, we have a number of things to help you to get the most from your purchase.

Downloading the example code

You can download the example code files for this book from your account at `http://www.p acktpub.com`. If you purchased this book elsewhere, you can visit `http://www.packtpub.c om/support`and register to have the files emailed directly to you. You can download the code files by following these steps:

1. Log in or register to our website using your email address and password.
2. Hover the mouse pointer on the **SUPPORT** tab at the top.
3. Click on **Code Downloads & Errata**.
4. Enter the name of the book in the **Search** box.
5. Select the book for which you're looking to download the code files.
6. Choose from the drop-down menu where you purchased this book from.
7. Click on **Code Download**.

Once the file is downloaded, please make sure that you unzip or extract the folder using the latest version of:

- WinRAR / 7-Zip for Windows
- Zipeg / iZip / UnRarX for Mac
- 7-Zip / PeaZip for Linux

The code bundle for the book is also hosted on GitHub at `https://github.com/PacktPubl ishing/Effective-DevOps-with-AWS`. We also have other code bundles from our rich catalog of books and videos available at `https://github.com/PacktPublishing/`. Check them out!

Downloading the color images of this book

We also provide you with a PDF file that has color images of the screenshots/diagrams used in this book. The color images will help you better understand the changes in the output. You can download this file from `https://www.packtpub.com/sites/default/files/down loads/EffectiveDevOpswithAWS_ColorImages.pdf`.

Errata

Although we have taken every care to ensure the accuracy of our content, mistakes do happen. If you find a mistake in one of our books-maybe a mistake in the text or the code-we would be grateful if you could report this to us. By doing so, you can save other readers from frustration and help us improve subsequent versions of this book. If you find any errata, please report them by visiting http://www.packtpub.com/submit-errata, selecting your book, clicking on the **Errata Submission Form** link, and entering the details of your errata. Once your errata are verified, your submission will be accepted and the errata will be uploaded to our website or added to any list of existing errata under the Errata section of that title. To view the previously submitted errata, go to https://www.packtpub.com/books/content/supportand enter the name of the book in the search field. The required information will appear under the **Errata** section.

Piracy

Piracy of copyrighted material on the internet is an ongoing problem across all media. At Packt, we take the protection of our copyright and licenses very seriously. If you come across any illegal copies of our works in any form on the internet, please provide us with the location address or website name immediately so that we can pursue a remedy. Please contact us at copyright@packtpub.com with a link to the suspected pirated material. We appreciate your help in protecting our authors and our ability to bring you valuable content.

Questions

If you have a problem with any aspect of this book, you can contact us at questions@packtpub.com, and we will do our best to address the problem.

1
The Cloud and the DevOps Revolution

The tech industry is constantly changing. The internet was born only a quarter of a century ago but has already transformed the way we live. *"Every day, over a billion people visit Facebook[1]; every hour, approximately 18,000 hours of videos are uploaded on YouTube[2]; and every second, Google processes approximately 40,000 search queries[3]."* (Refer to this websites `https://www.facebook.com/zuck/posts/10102329188394581`, `https://fortunelords.com/youtube-statistics,` and `http://www.internetlivestats.com/google-search-statistics`) Being able to handle such a staggering scale isn't easy. Thanks to this book, you will have a practical guide to adopting a similar philosophy, tooling, and best practices to these companies. Through the use of **Amazon Web Services** (**AWS**), you will be able to build the key principles to efficiently manage and scale your infrastructure, your engineering processes and your applications with minimal cost and effort.

This first chapter will explain in detail the new paradigms of:

- Thinking in terms of cloud and not infrastructure
- Adopting a DevOps culture
- Deploying in AWS following DevOps best practices

Thinking in terms of cloud and not infrastructure

The day I discovered that noise can damage hard drives.

In December 2011, sometime between Christmas and new Year's Eve, I received dozens of alerts from OnLive's (my employer then) monitoring system. Apparently, we had just lost connectivity to our European data center in Luxembourg. I rushed to the **network operations center** (**NOC**) hoping that it's only a small glitch in our monitoring system, maybe just a joke after all; with so much redundancy, how can everything go offline? Unfortunately, when I got into the room, the big monitoring monitors were all red, not a good sign. This was just the beginning of a very long nightmare. An electrician working in our data center mistakenly triggered the fire alarm; within seconds, the fire suppression system set off and released its aragonite on top of our server racks. Unfortunately, this kind of fire suppression system made so much noise when it released its gas that sound waves instantly killed hundreds and hundreds of hard drives, effectively shutting down our only European facility. It took months for us to be back on our feet.

Where is the cloud when you need it!

Charles Philips said it best, "*Friends don't let friends build a data center.*"

Deploying your own hardware versus in the cloud

It wasn't long ago that tech companies, small and large, had to have a proper technical operations organization able to build out infrastructures.

The process went a little bit like this:

1. Fly to the location you want to set up your infrastructure in; take a tour of different data centers and their facilities. Look at the floor considerations, power considerations, HVAC (Heating, Ventilating, and Air Conditioning), fire prevention systems, physical security, and so on.
2. Shop for an internet provider; ultimately, you are talking about servers and a lot more bandwidth but the process is the same: you want to get internet connectivity for your servers.

3. Once this is done, it's time to buy your hardware. Make the right decisions because you will probably spend a big portion of your company's money on buying servers, switches, routers, firewalls, storage, UPS (for when you have a power outage), KVM, network cables, the dear to every system administrator's heart labeler and a bunch of spare parts, hard drives, raid controllers, memory, power cables, and much more.

4. At this point, once the hardware is bought and shipped to the data center location, you can rack everything, wire all the servers, and power everything. Your network team can kick in and establish connectivity to the new data center using various links, configuring the edge routers, switches, top of the racks switches, KVM, and firewalls (sometimes). Your storage team is next and will provide the much needed **Network Attached Storage (NAS)** or **Storage Area Network (SAN)**; next, comes your sysops team, who will image the servers, sometimes upgrade the BIOS, configure hardware raid, and finally put an OS on these servers.

Not only is this a full-time job for a big team, but it also takes a lot of time and money to even get there.

As you will see in this book, getting new servers up and running with AWS will take us minutes. In fact, more than just providing a server within minutes, you will soon see how to deploy and run a service in minutes and just when you need it.

Cost analysis

From a cost standpoint, deploying in a cloud infrastructure such as AWS usually ends up being a lot cheaper than buying your own hardware. If you want to deploy your own hardware, you have to pay upfront for all the hardware mentioned previously (servers, network equipment, and so on) and sometimes licensed software as well. In a cloud environment, you pay as you go. You can add or remove servers in no time and only be charged for the duration the servers were running for. Also, if you take advantage of PaaS and SaaS applications, you usually end up saving even more money by lowering your operating costs as you don't need as many staff to administrate your database, storage, and so on. Most cloud providers, AWS included, also offer tiered pricing and volume discount. As your service gets bigger and bigger, you end up paying less for each unit of storage, bandwidth, and so on.

Just-in-time infrastructure

As you just saw, when deploying in the cloud, you only pay for the resources you provision. Most cloud companies use this to their advantage to scale their infrastructure up or down as the traffic to their site changes.

This ability to add or remove new servers and services in no time and on demand is one of the main differentiators of an effective cloud infrastructure. In the example below, we can see the amount of traffic hitting `Amazon.com` during the month of November. Thanks to Black Friday and Cyber Monday, the traffic triples at the end of the month:

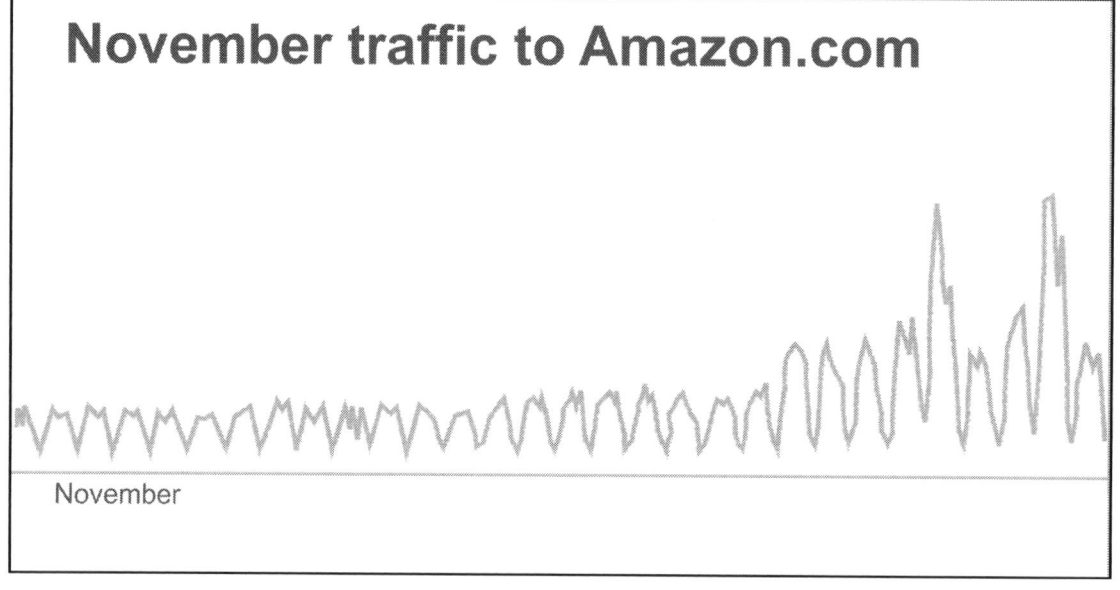

If the company was hosting their service in an old-fashioned way, they would need to have enough servers provisioned to handle this traffic such that only 24% of their infrastructure used on an average during the month:

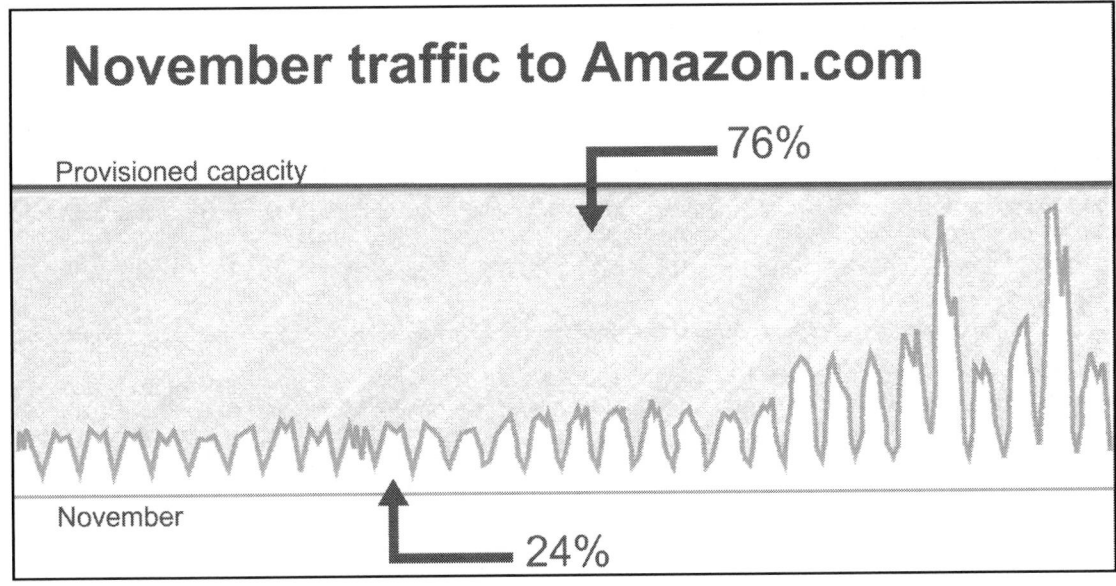

however, thanks to being able to scale dynamically, they are able to provide only what they really need and dynamically absorb the spikes in traffic that Black Friday and Cyber Monday trigger:

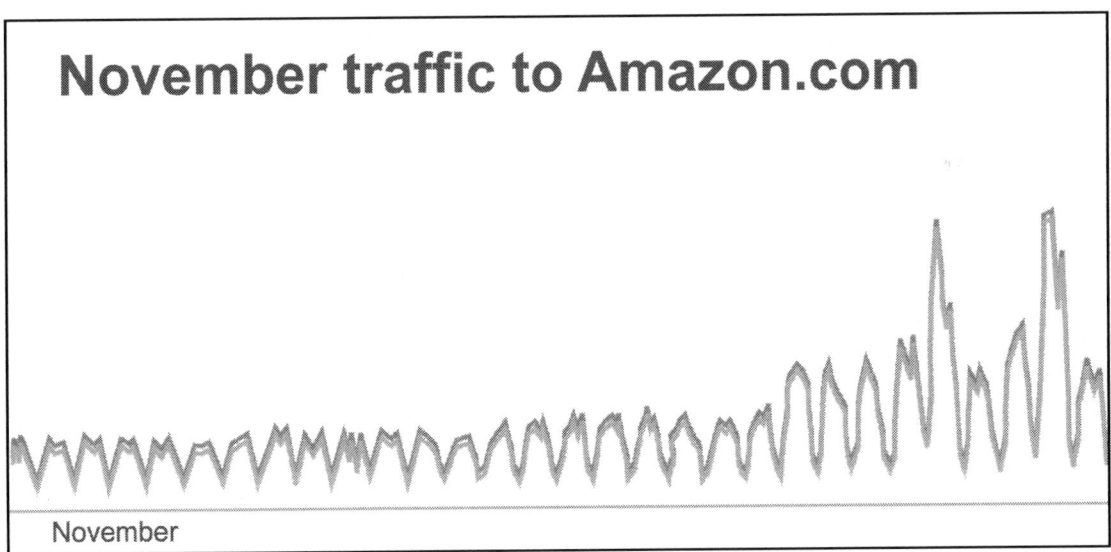

Here at Medium, you also see, on a very regular basis, the benefits of having fast auto-scaling capabilities. Very often, stories become viral and the amount of traffic going on Medium drastically changes. On January 21, 2015, to our surprise, the White House posted a transcript of the State of the Union minutes before President Obama started his speech:

```
http://bit.ly/2sDvseP
```

As you can see in the following graph, thanks to being in the cloud and having auto-scaling capabilities, our platform was able to absorb five times the instant spike of traffic that the announcement made by doubling the number of servers our front service used. Later, as the traffic started to drain naturally, you automatically removed some hosts from our fleet:

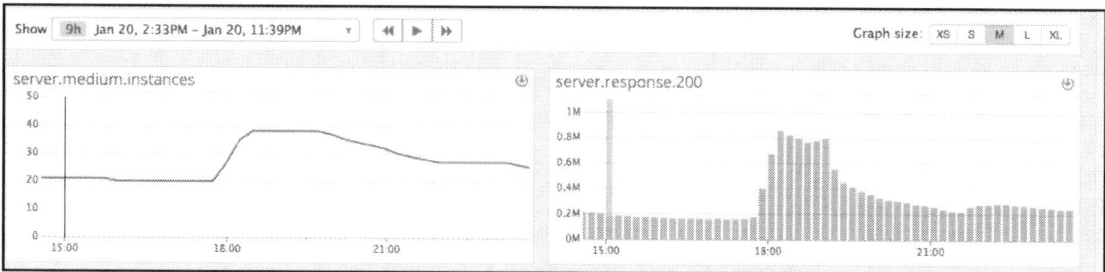

The different layers of building a cloud

Cloud computing is often broken down into three different types of services, as follows:

- **Infrastructure as a Service (IaaS)**: This is the fundamental block on top of which everything cloud is built upon. IaaS is usually a computing resource in a virtualized environment. It offers a combination of processing power, memory, storage, and network. The most common IaaS entities you will find are **virtual machines (VM)**, network equipment, such as load balancers or virtual Ethernet interfaces, and storage such as block devices. This layer is very close to the hardware and gives you the full flexibility that you would get deploying your software outside of a cloud. If you have any physical knowledge about data centers, it will also mostly apply to this layer.

- **Platform as a Service (PaaS)**: This layer is where things start to get really interesting with the cloud. When building an application, you will likely need a certain number of common components, such as a data store and a queue. The PaaS layer provides a number of ready-to-use applications to help you build your own services without worrying about administrating and operating those third-party services such as database servers.

- **Software as a Service (SaaS)**: This layer is the icing on the cake. Similar to the PaaS layer, you get access to managed services, but this time these services are a complete solution dedicated to certain purposes, such as management or monitoring tools.

This book covers a fair amount of services of PaaS and SaaS types. When building an application, relying on these services make a big difference when compared to the more traditional environment outside of the cloud.

Another key element to success when deploying or migrating to a new infrastructure is to adopt a DevOps mindset.

Adopting a DevOps culture

Running a company with a DevOps culture is all about adopting the right culture for developers and the operations team to work together. For that, DevOps culture preconizes implementing several engineering best practices by relying on tools and technologies that you will discover through out the book.

The origin of DevOps

DevOps is a new movement that officially started in 2009 in Belgium, when a group of people met at the first DevOpsDays conference, organized by Patrick Debois, to talk about how to apply some agile concepts to infrastructure.

Agile methodologies transformed the way software is developed. In a traditional waterfall model, a product team would come up with specifications, a design team would then create and define a certain user experience and user interface, the engineering team would then start implementing the requested product or feature and hand off the code to a QA team, who would test and make sure that the code behaves correctly according to the design specifications. Once all the bugs are fixed, a release team would package the final code that would be handed off to the technical operations team, who would deploy the code and monitor the service over time:

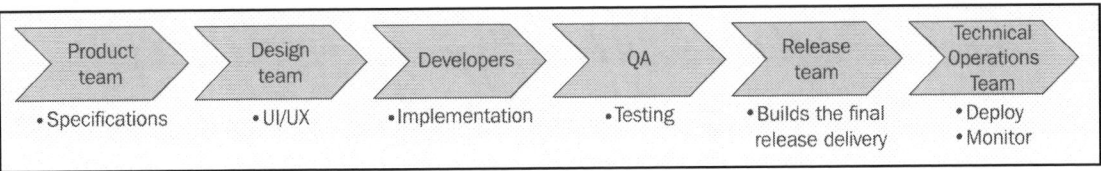

The increasing complexity of developing certain software and technologies showed some limitations with this traditional waterfall pipeline.

The agile transformation addressed some of these issues, allowing for more interaction between the designers, developers, and testers. This change increased the overall quality of the product as these teams now had the opportunity to iterate more on product development; but apart from this, you would still be in a very classical waterfall pipeline:

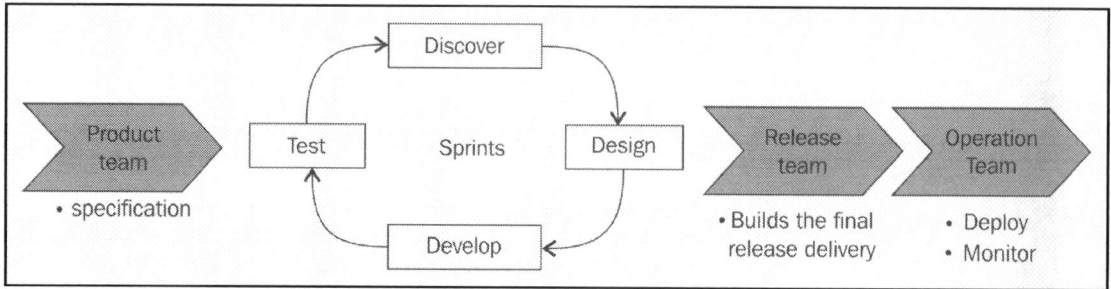

All the agility added by this new process didn't extend past the QA cycles, and it was time to modernize this aspect of the software development life cycle. This foundational change with the agile process, which allows for more collaboration between the designers, developers, and QA teams, is what DevOps was initially after, but very quickly the DevOps movement started rethinking how developers and operations team could work together.

The developers versus operations dilemma

In a non-DevOps culture, developers are in charge of developing new products and features and maintaining the existing code, but ultimately they are rewarded when their code is shipped. The incentive is to deliver as fast as possible.

On the other hand, the operations team, in general, have the responsibility to maintain the uptime of the production environments. For these teams, "change is evil." New features and services increase the risk of having an outage, and therefore it is important to move with caution.

To minimize the risks of having outages, operations team usually need to schedule any deployment ahead of time so that they can stage and test any production deployment and maximize their chances of success. It is also very common for the enterprise type of software companies to schedule maintenance windows and, in these cases, this means production changes can only be done a few times a quarter.

Unfortunately, a lot of time deployments won't succeed, and there are many possible reasons for that.

Too much code changing at once

There is a certain correlation that can be made between the size of the change and the risk of introducing critical bugs in the product, as follows:

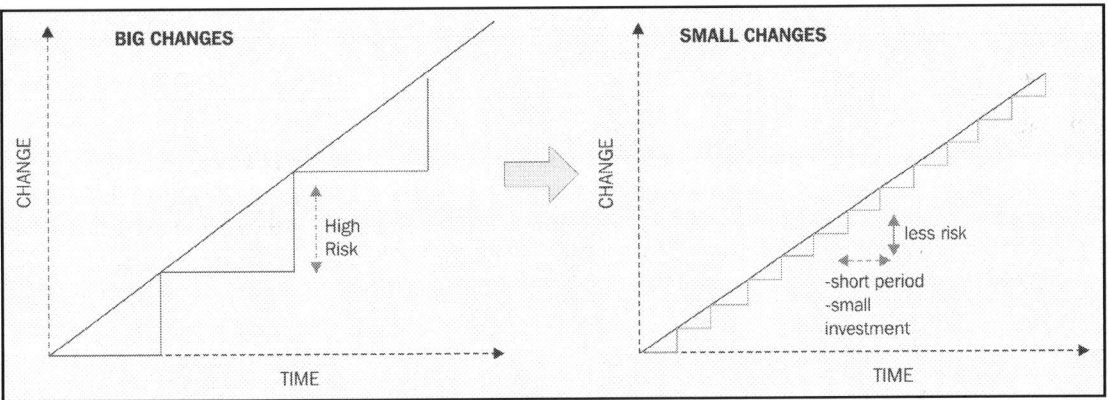

Differences in the production environment

It is often the case that the code produced by developers works fine in a development environment but not in production. A lot of the time, it's because the production environment might be very different from other environments and some unforeseen errors occurred. The common mistakes are that in a development environment, services are collocated on the same servers or there isn't the same level of security, so services can communicate with one another in development but not in production. Another issue is that the development environment might not run the same versions of a certain library, and therefore the interface to communicate with them might differ. The development environment may be running a newer version of a service that has new features production doesn't have yet, or it's simply a question of scale. The dataset used in development isn't as big as production, and scaling issues might crop up once the new code is out in production.

Communication

The last dilemma relates to bad communication.

As Melvin Conway said (in what is now called the Conway's Law), "*Organizations which design systems are constrained to produce designs which are copies of the communication structures of these organizations.*"

In other words, the product you are building reflects the communication of your organization. A lot of time, problems don't come from the technology but from the people and organization surrounding this technology. If there is any dysfunction among your developers and operations in the organization, this will show.

In a DevOps culture, developers and operations have a different mindset. They help to break down the silos that surround those teams by sharing responsibilities and adopting similar methodologies to improve productivity. They automate everything and use metrics to measure their success.

Key characteristics of a DevOps culture

As we just said, a DevOps culture relies on a certain number of principles: source control everything, automate everything, and measure everything.

Source control everything

Revision control software has been around for many decades now, but too often only the product code is checked in. When practicing DevOps, not only is the application code checked but also its configuration, tests, documentation, and all the infrastructure automation needed to deploy the application in all environments, and everything goes through the regular review process.

Automate testing

Automated software testing predates the history of DevOps, but it is a good starting point. Too often, developers focus on implementing features and forget to add a test to their code. In a DevOps environment, developers are responsible for adding proper testing to their code. QA teams can still exist; however, similar to other engineering teams, they work on building automation around testing.

This topic could deserve its own book, but in a nutshell, when developing code, keep in mind that there are four levels of testing automation to focus on to successfully implement DevOps:

- **Unit test**: This is to test the functionality of each code block and function.
- **Integration testing**: This is to make sure that services and components work together.
- **User interface testing**: This is often the most challenging one to successfully implement.
- **System testing**: This is end-to-end testing. Let's take an example of a photo-sharing application. Here, the end-to-end testing could be open the homepage, sign in, upload a photo, add a caption, publish the photo, and then sign out.

Automate infrastructure provisioning and configuration

In the last few decades, the size of the average infrastructure and complexity of the stack has skyrocketed. Managing infrastructure on an ad-hoc basis, as it was once possible, is very error-prone. In a DevOps culture, the provisioning and configuration of servers, networks, and services in general are all done through automation. Configuration management is often what the DevOps movement is known for; however, as you all know now, it is just a small piece of a big puzzle.

Automate deployment

As you now know, it is easier to write software in small chunks and deploy these new chunks as soon as possible to make sure that they are working. To get there, companies practicing DevOps rely on continuous integration and continuous deployment pipelines.

Whenever a new chunk of code is ready, the continuous integration pipeline kicks off. Through an automated testing system, the new code is run through all the relevant tests available. If the new code shows no obvious regression, the code is considered valid and can be merged to the main code base. At that point, without further involvement from the developer, a new version of the service (or application) that includes those new changes will be created and handed off to a system called a continuous deployment system.

The continuous deployment system will take the new builds and automatically deploy them to the different environments available. Depending on the complexity of the deployment pipeline, this might include a staging environment, an integration environment, sometimes a pre-production environment but ultimately, if everything goes as planned without any manual intervention, this new build will get deployed to production.

One misunderstood aspect about practicing continuous integration and continuous deployment is that new features don't have to be accessible to users as soon as they are developed. In this paradigm, developers rely heavily on feature flagging and dark launches. Essentially, whenever you develop new code and want to hide it from the end users, you set a flag in your service configuration to describe who gets access to the new feature and how. At the engineering level, by dark launching a new feature that way, you can send production traffic to the service but hide it from the UI to see the impact it has on your database, or on performance, for example. At the product level, you can decide to enable the new feature for only a small percentage of your users to see if the new feature is working correctly and if the users who have access to the new feature are more engaged than the control group, for example.

Measure everything

Measure everything is the last major principle that DevOps-driven companies adopt. As Edwards Deming said, *"You can't improve what you can't measure."* DevOps is an ever-evolving process that feeds off of those metrics to assess and improve the overall quality of the product and the team working on it.

From a tooling and operating standpoint, here are some of the metrics most organizations look at:

- Check how many builds a day are pushed to production
- Check how often do you need to roll back production in your production environment (this indicated when your testing didn't catch an important issue)
- The percentage of code coverage
- Frequency of alerts resulting in paging the on-call engineers for immediate attention
- Frequency of outages
- Application performance
- **Mean Time to Resolution (MTTR)** which is the speed at which an outage or a performance issue can be fixed

At the organizational level, it is also interesting to measure the impact of shifting to a DevOps culture. While it is a lot harder to measure, you can consider the following points:

- The amount of collaboration across teams
- Team autonomy
- Cross-functional work and team efforts
- Fluidity in the product
- Happiness among engineers
- Attitude toward automation
- Obsession with metrics

As you just saw, having a DevOps culture means, first of all, changing the traditional mindset that developers and operations are two separate silos and make both teams collaborate more during all phases of the software development life cycle.

In addition to a new mindset, DevOps culture requires a specific set of tools geared toward automation, deployment, and monitoring:

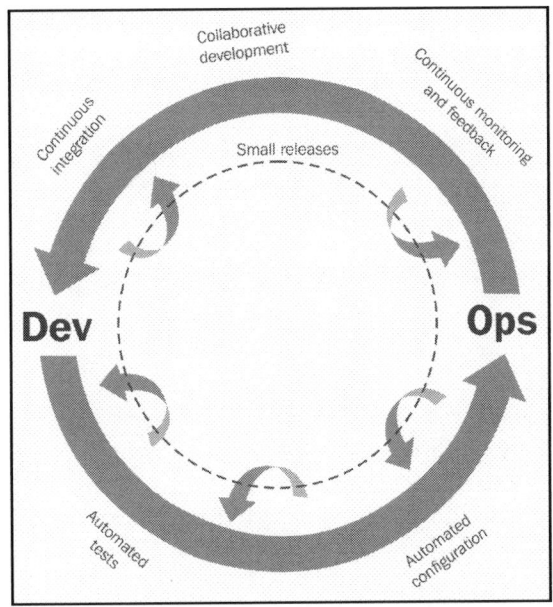

http://www.pwc.com/us/en/technology-forecast/2013/issue2/features/cios-agility-stability-paradox.html

Amazon with AWS offers a number of services of PaaS and SaaS types that will let us do just that.

Deploying in AWS

AWS is at the forefront of cloud providers. Launched in 2006 with SQS and EC2, Amazon quickly became the biggest IaaS provider.

They have the biggest infrastructure, the biggest ecosystem, and constantly add new features and release new services. In 2015, they passed 1 million active customers. Over the last few years, they have managed to change people's mindset about the cloud, and now deploying new services to the cloud is the new normal.

Using AWS's managed tools and services is a drastic way to improve your productivity and keep your team lean.

Amazon continually listens to its customer's feedback and looks at the market trends. Therefore, as the DevOps movement started to get established, Amazon released a number of new services tailored toward implementing some DevOps best practices. In this book, you will also see how these services synergize with the DevOps culture.

How to best take advantage of the AWS ecosystem

Amazon services are like Lego pieces. If you can picture your final product, then you can explore the different services and start combining them the way you would assemble a Lego, in order to build the supporting stack needed to quickly and efficiently build your product. Of course, in this case, the "if" is a big if, and unlike Lego, understanding what each piece can do is a lot less visual and colorful than Lego pieces. This is why this book is written in a very practical way; throughout the different chapters, we are going to take a web application and deploy it like it's our core product. We will see how to scale the infrastructure supporting it so that millions of people can use it and finally make it more secure. And, of course, we will do this following DevOps best practices.

By going through that exercise, you will learn how AWS provides a number of managed services and systems to perform a number of common tasks such as computing, networking, load balancing, storing data, monitoring, programmatically managing infrastructure and deployment, caching, and queueing.

How AWS synergizes with a DevOps culture

As you saw earlier in this chapter, having a DevOps culture is about rethinking how engineering teams work together by breaking these development and operations silos and bringing a new set of new tools to implement the best practices.

AWS helps in many different ways to accomplish this. For some developers, the world of operations can be scary and confusing, but if you want better cooperation between engineers, it is important to expose every aspect of running a service to the entire engineering organization. As an operations engineer, you can't have a gatekeeper mentality toward developers; instead, it's better to make them comfortable accessing production and working on the different components of the platform. A good way to get started with this in the AWS console:

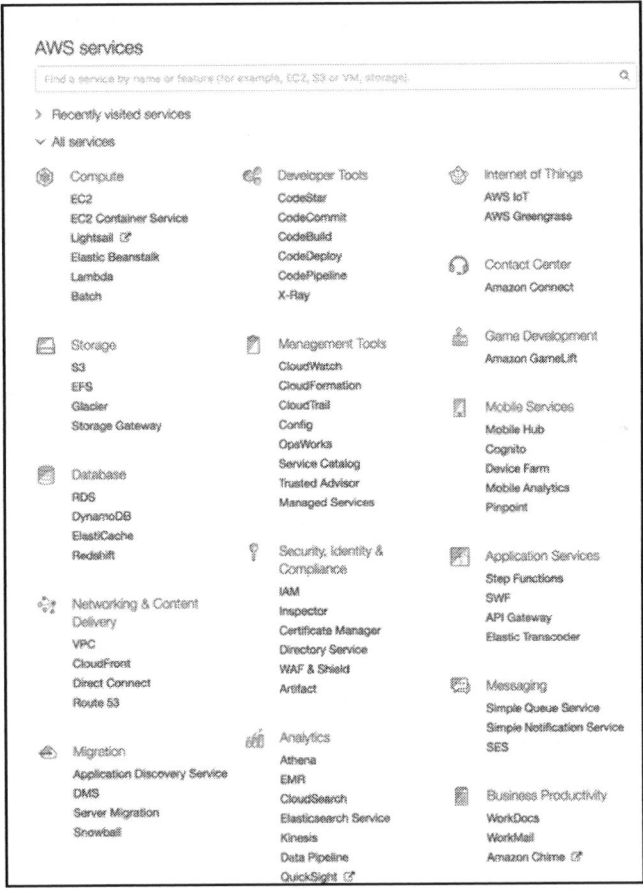

While a bit overwhelming, it is still a much better experience for people not familiar with this world to navigate this web interface than referring to constantly out-of-date documentation, using SSH and random plays, to discover the topology and configuration of the service.

Of course, as your expertise grows and your application becomes more complex, the need to operate it faster increases, and the web interface starts to show some weaknesses. To get around this issue, AWS provides a very DevOps-friendly alternative: an API. Accessible through a command-line tool and a number of SDKs (which include Java, JavaScript, Python, .NET, PHP, Ruby Go, and C++), the SDKs let you administrate and use the managed services.

Finally, as you have seen a bit in the previous section, AWS offers a number of services that fits DevOps methodologies and will ultimately allow us to implement complex solutions in no time.

Some of the major services you will use are, at the compute level, **EC2**, the service to create virtual servers. Later, as you start looking into how to scale our infrastructure, you will discover Auto Scaling Groups, a service that let you scale pools on EC2 instances to handle traffic spikes and host failure. You will also explore the concept of containers with **Docker** via **ECS**. Lastly, you will create serverless functions via **Lambda** to run custom code without having to host it on our servers.

To implement our continuous integration and continuous deployment system, you will rely on four services: **S3**, the object store service that will allow us to store our artifacts; **CodeBuild**,which will let us test our code; **CodeDeploy**, which will let us deploy artifacts to our EC2 instances; and finally **CodePipeline**, which will let you orchestrate how our code is built, tested, and deployed across environments.

To monitor and measure everything, you will rely on **CloudWatch** and later **ElasticSearch/Kibana** to collect, index, and visualize metrics and logs. To stream some of our data to these services, you will rely on **AWS Kinesis**. To send email and SMS alerts, you will use the **SNS** service.

For infrastructure management, you will heavily rely on **CloudFormation,** which provides the ability to create templates of infrastructure.

In the end, as you explore ways to better secure our infrastructure, you will encounter **Inspector** and **Trusted Advisor**, and explore in more detail the **IAM** and the **VPC service**.

Summary

In this chapter, you learned that adopting a DevOps culture means first and foremost changing the way traditional engineering and operations teams operate. Instead of being two isolated teams with opposing goals and responsibilities, companies with a DevOps culture take advantage of the complementary domain of expertise to collaborate better through converging processes and using a new set of tools.

These new processes and tools include not only automating everything from testing to deployment through infrastructure management, but also measuring everything so that you can improve each process over time.

When it comes to cloud services, AWS is leading the effort, with more services than any other cloud provider. All these services are usable via APIs and SDKs, which is good for automation; in addition, AWS has tools and services for each key characteristic of the DevOps culture.

In Chapter 2, *Deploying Your First Web Application*, you are finally going to get our feet wet and start using AWS. The final goal of the chapter will be to have a hello world application accessible to anyone on the internet.

2
Deploying Your First Web Application

In Chapter 1, *The Cloud and the DevOps Revolution*, we covered a general introduction to the Cloud, its benefits, and what having a DevOps philosophy meant. AWS offers a number of services all easily accessible through the web interface, command-line interface, various SDKs, and API. In this chapter, we will take advantage of the web interface and command-line interface to create and configure our account and create a web server to host a simple Hello World application, all in a matter of minutes.

In this chapter, we will go through the following topics:

- Creating and configuring your account
- Spinning up your first web server

Creating and configuring your account

In case you haven't signed up for AWS yet, it is time to do so.

Signing up

This step is, of course, fairly simple and self-explanatory. In order to sign up, if you haven't done so yet, open `https://portal.aws.amazon.com/gp/aws/developer/registration/` in your browser and follow the steps. You will need an email address and your credit card information.

There are two exceptions to this process, as follows:

- If you plan on deploying servers in China, then you need to create your account on `https://www.amazonaws.cn/`.
- AWS has a special facility called **GovCloud** for specific regulatory needs of United States federal, state, and local agencies. To sign up for this, use the link `https://aws.amazon.com/govcloud-us/contact/`.

 In this book, we will use servers located in Northern Virginia so you will need to sign up using the standard registration process.

Amazon runs a free tier program for new users. It's designed to help you discover their services free of cost. Amazon gives free credit on most services. It is likely that over time the offer will change, so this book isn't going to cover the specificity of this offer, but the details are available at `https://aws.amazon.com/free/`.

Once you're done with the sign-up process, you will land on the AWS Management Console landing page. This screen can be a bit overwhelming as Amazon now has a lot of services, but you will quickly get used to it. If you are a fan of bookmarks, this page is definitely a prime candidate:

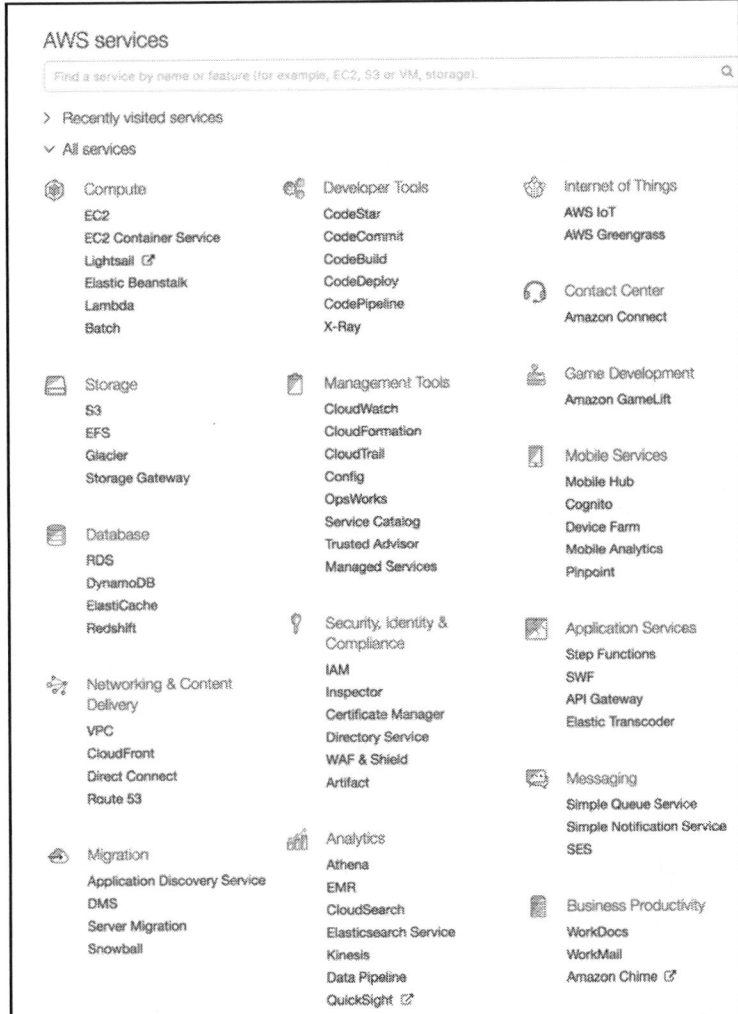

The account you just created is called a root account. This account will always have full access to all your resources. Because of this, make sure to keep your password in a safe place. The best practice is to use the root account only to create the initial user through the IAM service that we will discover shortly. In addition, it is strongly recommended to switch to multi-factor authentication and use the identity service (IAM) to manage user accounts, so pick a relatively complex password.

Enabling multi-factor authentication on the root account

In order to avoid any kind of issues, the first thing we need to do once we sign up is to enable multi-factor authentication. In case you haven't seen or heard of this before, multi-factor authentication is a security system that requires more than one method of authentication from independent categories of credentials to verify the user's identity to log in. In practice, once enabled, in order to log into your root account, you will need the password previously set when you signed up but also another code provided from a different source. That second source can be provided through a physical device such as the SafeNet ID Prone available on amazon.com (`http://amzn.to/2u4K1rR`), an SMS on your phone, or an application installed on your smartphone. We will use the third option which is completely free:

1. Go to your App Store, Google Play Store or App Market place and install an application called "Google Authenticator" (or any other equivalent such as Authy).
2. In the AWS Management Console, in the top-right corner, open the **My Security Credentials** page:

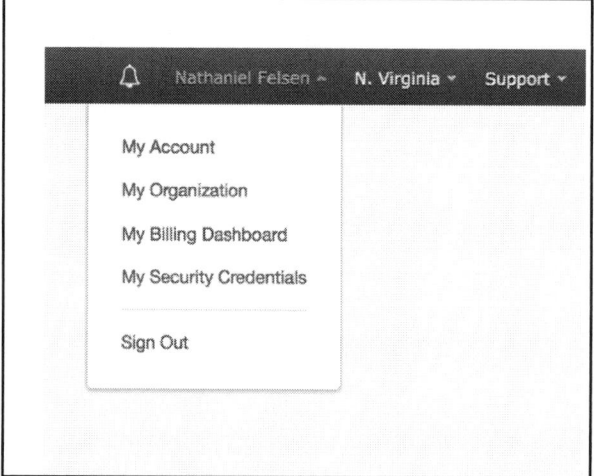

3. If prompted for **Creating** and using AWS Identity and Access Management users with limited permissions, click on **Continue to Security Credentials**. (We will explore the IAM system in Chapter 3, Treating Your Infrastructure As Code. Expand the **multi-factor authentication** (**MFA**) section on the page.

4. Pick Virtual MFA and follow the instructions to sync Google Authentication with your root account (note that the **scan the QR code** option is the easiest one to pair the device).

From this point on, you will need your password and the token displayed on the MFA application to log in as root in the AWS console.

Two general tips for managing your passwords and MFA
There are a number of good applications to manage passwords, such as 1Password (https://agilebits.com/onepassword) or Dashlane (https://www.dashlane.com).
For multi-factor authentication, I really like Authy (https://www.authy.com). It works like Google Authenticator but also has a centralized server allowing it to work across multiple devices (including desktop applications), so if you lose your phone you won't lose access to AWS.

As we have seen earlier, the root account usage should be limited to a bare minimum. So in order to create virtual servers, configure services, and so on, we will rely on the IAM service that will let us have granular control over permissions for each user.

Creating a new user in IAM

In this section, we will create and configure accounts for different individuals who need access to AWS. For now, we will keep things simple and only create an account for ourselves, as follows:

1. Navigate to the **Identity and Access Management** menu in the AWS console (https://console.aws.amazon.com/iam/).
2. Choose **Users** from the navigation pane.
3. Create a new user (for you), and make sure to keep the **Generate an access key for each user** checkbox checked.
4. On the next screen, click on **Download Credentials** and then close.
5. Back in the **Users** menu, click on your user to access the **Details** page.
6. In the **Permissions** tab, click on **Attach Policy**.

7. Select the checkbox next to **AdministratorAccess**. Then, click on **Attach Policy**. You will end up with a screen looking like this:

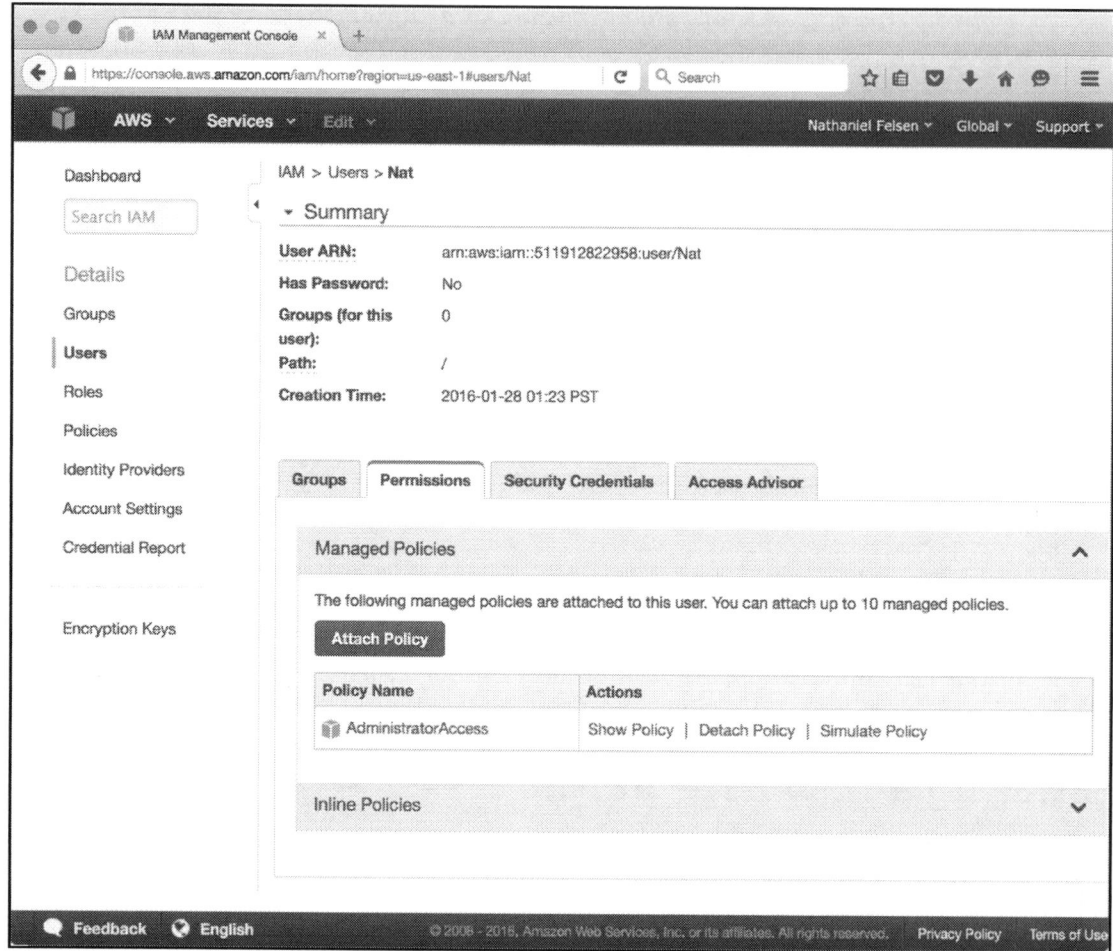

The last thing we need to do is add a password and turn on multi-factor authentication for this account, as follows:

8. Navigate to the **Security Credentials** tab.
9. Click on **Manage Password** and follow the instructions.
10. Once you're done adding a password, click on **Manage MFA Device**.
11. Select **A Virtual MFA Device** and follow the remaining instructions in order to turn on multi-factor authentication on your newly created account.

At this point, you are ready to start using the newly created user account. The important thing to note is that signing in with an IAM user account is different from the root account. The main difference is that you sign in using a different URL:

12. Navigate to `https://console.aws.amazon.com/iam/home#home` or click on **Dashboard** in the **Identity and Access Management** menu.
13. You will see your unique sign-in URL under **IAM users sign-in link**. Feel free to also customize the link. Save this new URL in your bookmarks, and from now on, use this link to sign into the AWS console.
14. **Sign out** from the root account.
15. Sign back in, but this time, using your IAM user account (`https://AWS-account-ID-or-alias.signin.aws.amazon.com/console`).

Do not share your access key and secret key
By going through those steps, we enforced the use of MFA to access the AWS console with our IAM user. We now need two factors (the password and the MFA token) to access the console. That said we also created an access key which is far less secure. Anyone in possession of the secret key and access key (both present in the `credentials.csv`) will have full administrative access to the AWS account. Make sure to never share these credentials online. In `Chapter 8`, *Hardening the Security of Your AWS Environment*, we will make a few changes to better protect this key and require the use of MFA to gain administrator privileges.

The next step in configuring our account is to configure our computers to interact with AWS using the command-line interface.

Installing and configuring the command-line interface (CLI)

Using Amazon's web interface is usually a great way to explore new services. The problem is that when you just want to go fast, want to create more repeatable steps, or want to create good documentation, having simple commands to execute becomes efficient. Amazon provides a great and easy-to-use command-line interface. The tool is written in Python and therefore is cross-platform (Windows, Mac, and Linux).

We will install the tool on our laptop/desktop such that we can interact with AWS using bash commands. Linux and Mac OS X come natively with bash. If you use one of these operating systems you can skip the next section. On Windows, we first need to install a feature called Windows Subsystem for Linux which will give us the ability to run bash commands very similar to what you get on Ubuntu Linux.

Installing Windows Subsystem for Linux (Windows only)

Nowadays, Linux and Mac OS X are among the most predominant Operating Systems used by developers. Windows recently released through a partnership with Canonical, the company behind one of the most popular Linux distribution, support for Bash and most of the common Linux packages. By installing this tool on Windows, we will be able to more efficiently interact with our servers which will also be running Linux:

1. Click on the **start** button and search for settings, then open the **Settings** application:

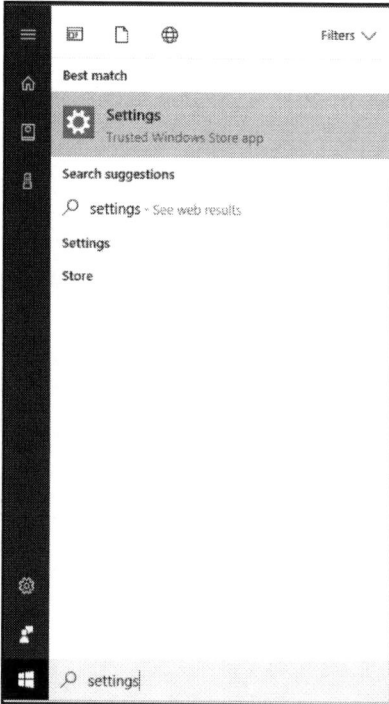

2. This will lead you to the following window where you the **Windows Update Settings**. Open the **Windows Update Settings** menu:

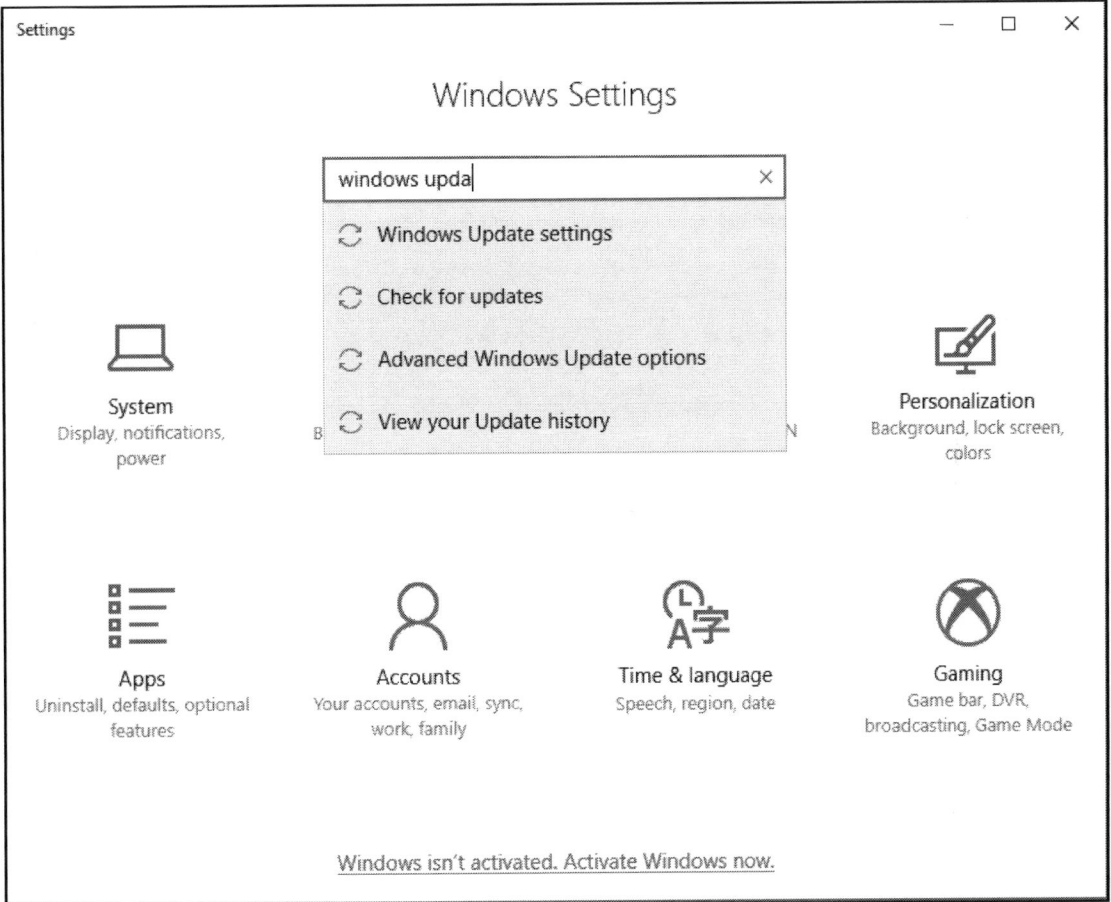

3. In the left-hand side menu of the **Windows Update Settings**, click on **For developers** and turn on the **Developer mode**.

4. Once your **Developer mode** is turned on, search in the search bar on the left hand-side menu for the **Control Panel**:

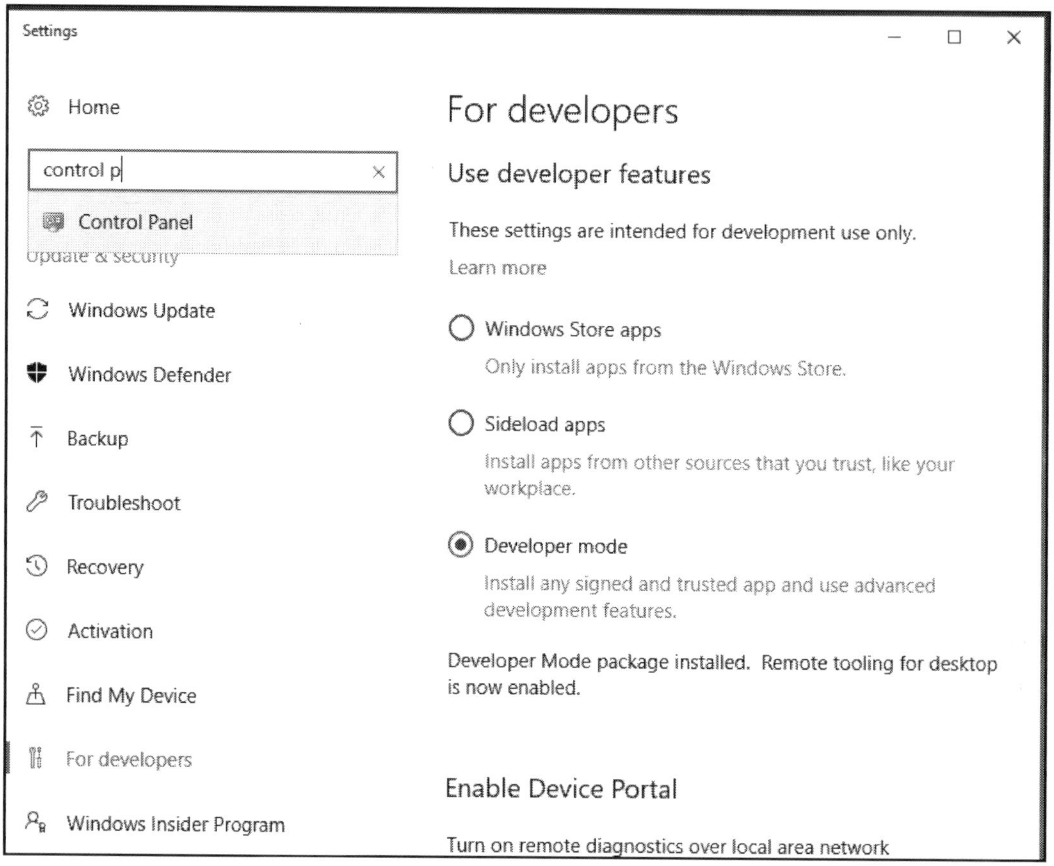

5. In the **Control Panel**, use the search bar at the top to find the menu called **Programs and Features**:

6. In this menu, find the feature called **Windows Subsystem for Linux (Beta)**, check the on the **OK** button:

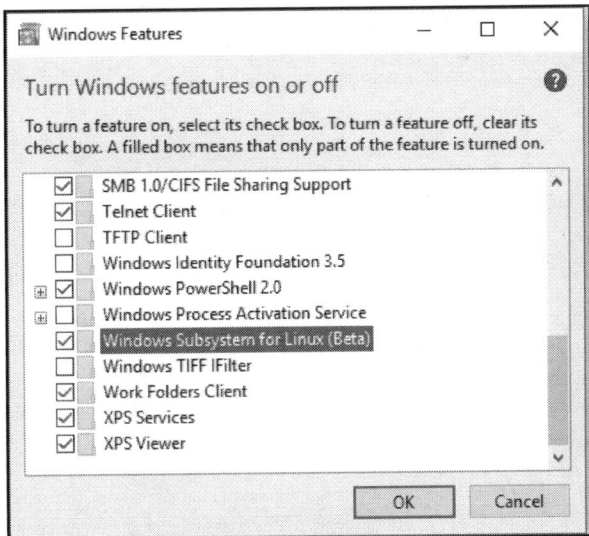

This will install the feature and ask you to restart your computer.

7. Once you are back in Windows, click the **Start** button again, search for **Bash** and start the **Bash** on Ubuntu on Windows application:

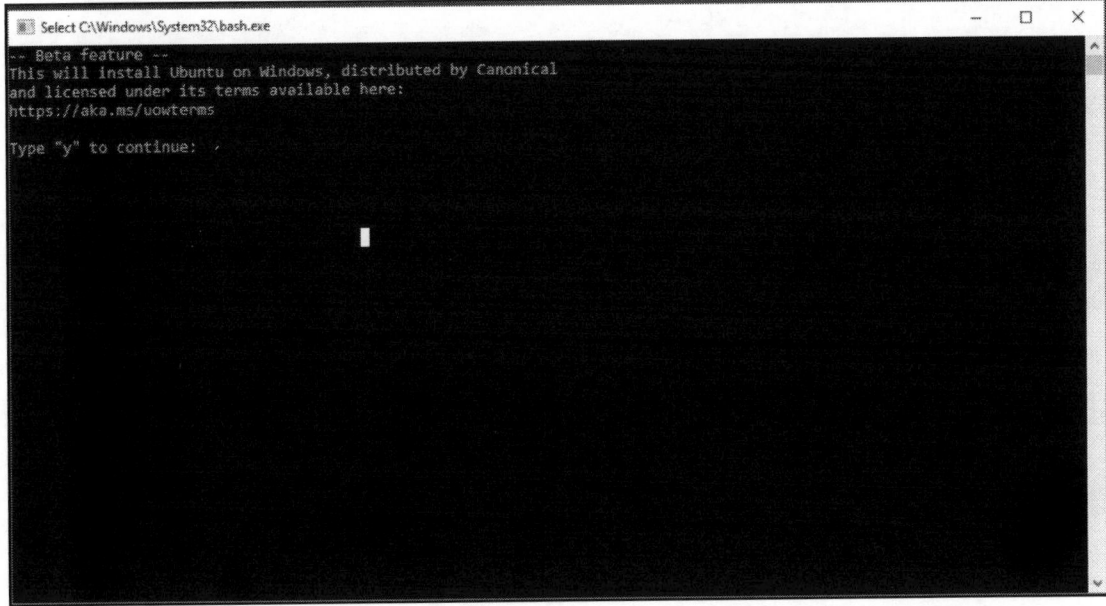

8. After a few initialization steps, you will be able to use Bash on Windows in the same way you would on Linux.

From that point on, use the bash application to run the commands present in the book.

Installing the AWS CLI package

As mentioned before, this utility is written in Python. While there are several ways to install it, we will use PyPA, the Python Package manager, to install the tool.

To install PyPA, depending on your OS you will need to run the following command.

On Windows:

```
$ sudo apt install python-pip
```

On Mac OS X:

```
$ sudo easy_install pip
```

On Debian based Linux distribution:

```
$ sudo apt-get install python-pip python-dev build-essential
```

On Redhat based Linux distribution:

```
$ sudo yum -y install python-pip
```

Once PyPA is installed, you will get access to the command `pip`.

Lastly, to install the AWS CLI using the `pip` command, you simply need to run the following command:

```
$ sudo pip install --upgrade --user awscli
```

Configuring the AWS CLI

To do this, you will need to extract the `Access Key` and `Secret Access Key` from the file downloaded in step 4 of the section creating a new user in IAM:

```
$ more credentials.csv
User Name,Access Key Id,Secret Access Key
"Nat",AKIACZ6HA,f6hoyLgExmoq/V4VQjf3nB
```

We will run the following command to configure our AWS account as follows:

```
$ aws configure
AWS Access Key ID [None]: AKIACZ6HA
AWS Secret Access Key [None]: f6hoyLgExmoq/V4VQjf3nB
Default region name [None]: us-east-1
Default output format [None]:
```

At this point, we are ready to start using the CLI. We can quickly verify that everything is working by listing the user accounts, as follows:

```
$ aws iam list-users
{
    "Users": [
        {
            "UserName": "Nat",
            "PasswordLastUsed": "2017-07-30T03:11:30Z",
            "CreateDate": "2017-07-28T09:23:50Z",
            "UserId": "AKIACZ6HA",
            "Path": "/",
            "Arn": "arn:aws:iam::511912822959:user/Nat"
        }
    ]
}
```

> **AWS aws-shell**
> Amazon has a second CLI tool called aws-shell. The tool is more interactive than the classic `awscli` command. It offers out-of-the-box auto completion and a split-screen view that let you access the documentation as you type your commands. If you are a new AWS user, give it a shot (`pip install aws-shell`).

Creating our first web server

Now that we have our environment set up, we are finally ready to launch our first EC2 instance. There are a couple of ways to do that. Since we just installed and configured awscli and we want to see effective ways of managing infrastructures, we will demonstrate how to do this using the command-line interface.

Launching a virtual server requires having a certain amount of information ahead of time. We will use the `aws ec2 run-instances` command, but we need to supply it with:

- An AMI ID
- An instance type
- A security group
- An SSH key-pair

AMI

An **Amazon Machine Image** (**AMI**) is a package that contains, among other things, the root filesystem with the operating system (for example, Linux, Unix, or Windows) and additional software required to start up the system. To find the proper AMI, we will use the `aws ec2 describe-images`. By default, the describe-image command will list all the public AMI available which is way over 3 million by now. To get the best out of that command, it is important to combine it with the filter option to only include the AMI we would like to use. In our case, we want to use the following to filter our AMI:

- We want the name to be Amazon Linux AMI which designates the Linux distribution officially supported by AWS. Amazon Linux is based off Redhat/CentOS but includes a few extra packages to make the integration with other AWS services easy to do. You can read more about AWS Linux at `http://amzn.to/2uFT13F`.
- We want to use `x84_64` bits version of it to match the architecture we will use.
- The virtualization type should be HVM which stands for hardware virtual machine. This is the newest and best-performing type of virtualization.
- With GP2 support which will let us use the newest generation of instances that don't come with "instance store" meaning that the servers that power our instances will be different from the servers that store our data.

In addition, we will sort the output by age and only look at the most recent AMI released:

```
$ aws ec2 describe-images --filters "Name=description,Values=Amazon Linux
AMI * x86_64 HVM GP2"  --query 'Images[*].[CreationDate, Description,
ImageId]' --output text | sort -k 1 | tail
2017-01-26T14:04:52.000Z        Amazon Linux AMI 2016.09.1.20161221 x86_64
HVM GP2     ami-6cb4477a
2017-03-02T21:35:49.000Z        Amazon Linux AMI 2016.09.1.20161221 x86_64
HVM GP2     ami-1f70a809
2017-03-20T09:30:49.000Z        Amazon Linux AMI 2017.03.rc-0.20170320 x86_64
HVM GP2     ami-5b94234d
2017-03-28T01:56:01.000Z        Amazon Linux AMI 2017.03.rc-1.20170327 x86_64
HVM GP2     ami-a672ccb0
2017-04-02T05:53:05.000Z        Amazon Linux AMI 2017.03.0.20170401 x86_64
HVM GP2     ami-22ce4934
2017-04-17T08:14:59.000Z        Amazon Linux AMI 2017.03.0.20170417 x86_64
HVM GP2     ami-c58c1dd3
2017-04-25T20:53:03.000Z        Amazon Linux AMI 2016.09.1.20161221 x86_64
HVM GP2     ami-d8d64cce
2017-05-12T00:45:32.000Z        Amazon Linux AMI 2017.03.0.20170417 x86_64
HVM GP2     ami-ab9aebbd
2017-06-17T21:56:53.000Z        Amazon Linux AMI 2017.03.1.20170617 x86_64
HVM GP2     ami-643b1972
2017-06-23T23:35:49.000Z        Amazon Linux AMI 2017.03.1.20170623 x86_64
HVM GP2     ami-a4c7edb2
```

As you can see, at this time, the most recent AMI ID is `ami-a4c7edb2`. This might differ by the time you execute the same command, as Amazon vendors included regularly update their OS.

Using the `aws cli --query` **option**

On certain commands, the output can be very consequential. Taking the preceding example, if we only care about a subset of information, we can supplement the commands with `--query` option to filter in only the information we want. This option uses the `JMESPath` query language.

Instance type

In this section, we will select the virtual hardware to use for our virtual server. AWS provides a number of options best described <in their documentation `https://aws.amazon.com/ec2/instance-types/`. We will talk more in detail about instance type in `Chapter 5`, *Scaling Your Infrastructure.*

For now, we will select the t2.micro instance type as it is eligible for the AWS free usage tier.

Security group

Security groups work a bit like firewalls. All EC2 instances have a set of security groups assigned to them. Each security group contains rules to allow traffic to flow inbound (ingress) and/or outbound (egress).

For this exercise, we will create a small web application running on port TCP/3000. In addition, we want to be able to ssh into the instance, so we also need to allow inbound traffic to the port TCP/22. We will create a simple security group to allow this, using the following steps:

1. First, we need to find out our default **virtual private cloud** (**VPC**) ID. VPC stands for Virtual Private Cloud. Despite being in a Cloud environment, where the physical resources are shared by all AWS customers, there is still a strong emphasis on security. AWS segmented their virtual infrastructure using a concept of virtual private cloud; you can imagine it as being a virtual datacenter with its own network. The security groups which protect our EC2 instances are tied subnets which in turn are tied to the network that the VPC provide:

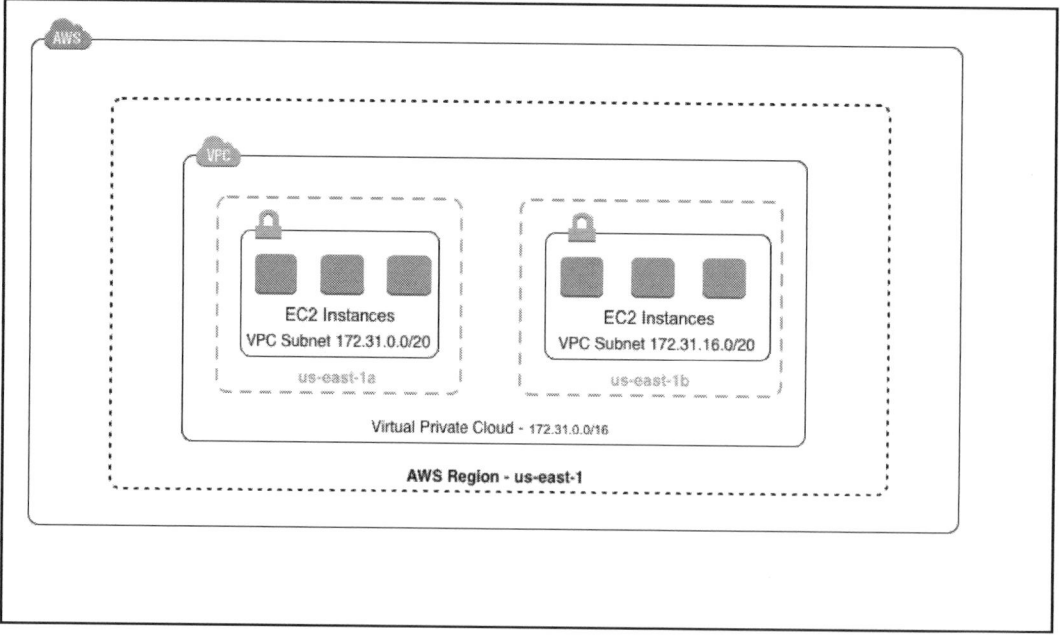

To identify our VPC ID, we can run the following command:

```
$ aws ec2 describe-vpcs
{
    "Vpcs": [
        {
            "VpcId": "vpc-f7dc4093",
            "InstanceTenancy": "default",
            "State": "available",
            "DhcpOptionsId": "dopt-0be0426e",
            "CidrBlock": "172.31.0.0/16",
            "IsDefault": true
        }
    ]
}
```

2. Now that we know the VPC ID (yours will be different), we can <create our new security group, as follows:

```
$ aws ec2 create-security-group \
    --group-name HelloWorld \
    --description "Hello World Demo" \
    --vpc-id vpc-f7dc4093
{
    "GroupId": "sg-11d4fe68"
}
```

3. By default, security groups allow all outbound traffic from the instance; we just need to open up ssh (tcp/22) and tcp/3000 for inbound traffic, as follows:

```
$ aws ec2 authorize-security-group-ingress \
    --group-name HelloWorld \
    --protocol tcp \
    --port 22 \
    --cidr 0.0.0.0/0

$ aws ec2 authorize-security-group-ingress \
    --group-name HelloWorld \
    --protocol tcp \
    --port 3000 \
    --cidr 0.0.0.0/0
```

4. We can now verify the change, using the following code, as the previous commands aren't verbose:

```
$ aws ec2 describe-security-groups \
      --group-names HelloWorld \
      --output text
SECURITYGROUPS  Hello World Demo  sg-11d4fe68 HelloWorld
511912822959    vpc-f7dc4093
IPPERMISSIONS   22 tcp    22
IPRANGES 0.0.0.0/0
IPPERMISSIONS   3000  tcp    3000
IPRANGES 0.0.0.0/0
IPPERMISSIONSEGRESS   -1
IPRANGES 0.0.0.0/0
```

As expected, we opened up the traffic to the proper ports. If you know how to find out your public IP, you can improve the `ssh` rule by replacing `0.0.0.0/0` with `your-ip/32` so that only you can try to `ssh` into that ec2-instance.

Using the `aws cli --ouput` **option**

By default, most of the command will return a JSON output. Structured logs like JSON are ideal for machine processing but sometimes hard to parse for humans. AWS has a certain number of options globally available. You can see them used a bit in this chapter. The first option is `--output` [json | text | table]:

```
$ aws ec2 describe-subnets --output table
----------------------------------------------------------------------------------------------------------
|                                            DescribeSubnets                                              |
+--------------------------------------------------------------------------------------------------------+
||                                             Subnets                                                  ||
|+----------------+------------------------+-------------+-------------+-----------------+--------+-------+|
|| AvailabilityZone | AvailableIpAddressCount |  CidrBlock  | DefaultForAz | MapPublicIpOnLaunch | State |  SubnetId | VpcId ||
|+----------------+------------------------+-------------+-------------+-----------------+--------+-------+|
|| us-east-1c   | 4091    | 172.31.48.0/20 | True | True | available | subnet-4decfe66 | vpc-f7dc4093 ||
|| us-east-1d   | 4091    | 172.31.0.0/20  | True | True | available | subnet-3e905944 | vpc-f7dc4093 ||
|| us-east-1e   | 4091    | 172.31.32.0/20 | True | True | available | subnet-82ba3fbf | vpc-f7dc4093 ||
|| us-east-1a   | 4090    | 172.31.16.0/20 | True | True | available | subnet-4f3bdb17 | vpc-f7dc4093 ||
|+----------------+------------------------+-------------+-------------+-----------------+--------+-------+|
$
```

Generating your ssh keys

By default, Amazon EC2 uses ssh key pairs to give you ssh access to your EC2 instances. You can either generate a key pair in EC2 and download the private key or generate a key yourself using a third-party tool such as OpenSSL and import the public key in EC2. We will use the first method:

```
$ aws ec2 create-key-pair --key-name EffectiveDevOpsAWS
{
   "KeyMaterial": "-----BEGIN RSA PRIVATE KEY-----
   \nMIIEogIBAAKCAQEAo6vZQ0BxnqdfZOSdcI66KRvypX0NwH5IEi6GUw06+
   [...]
sj4FAZVLp4OpaIeg+DxHaXUMx\njVHiSRmxmXv2NJAaiJr/q4wMq+eUq3WLn/DKbIPWkfB5lqnG
F2T/biie7igSvder3xE=\n-----END RSA PRIVATE KEY-----",
   "KeyName": "EffectiveDevOpsAWS",
   "KeyFingerprint":
"d2:ec:b5:07:af:83:74:4c:9c:5f:d1:3c:37:86:1b:f0:9c:1b:c1:cf"
}
```

The key is located in the KeyMaterial section of the JSON output. Save this output in a file. I recommend copying the output and using echo <paste> > file as this will interpret the \n characters:

```
$ echo "-----BEGIN RSA PRIVATE KEY-----
\nMIIEogIBAAKCAQEAo6vZQ0BxnqdfZOSdcI66KRvypX0NwH5IEi6GUw06+
[...]
sj4FAZVLp4OpaIeg+DxHaXUMx\njVHiSRmxmXv2NJAaiJr/q4wMq+eUq3WLn/DKbIPWkfB5lqnG
F2T/biie7igSvder3xE=\n-----END RSA PRIVATE KEY-----" >
~/.ssh/EffectiveDevOpsAWS.pem
$ chmod 600 ~/.ssh/EffectiveDevOpsAWS.pem
```

Launching an EC2 instance

We now have all the information required to launch our instance; let's finally launch it as follows:

```
$ aws ec2 run-instances \
      --instance-type t2.micro \
      --key-name EffectiveDevOpsAWS \
      --security-group-ids sg-11d4fe68 \
      --image-id ami-a4c7edb2
{
   "OwnerId": "511912822958",
   "ReservationId": "r-6d7c15c1",
   "Groups": [],
```

```
"Instances": [
    {
        "Monitoring": {
            "State": "disabled"
        },
        "PublicDnsName": "",
        "RootDeviceType": "ebs",
        "State": {
            "Code": 0,
            "Name": "pending"
        },
        "EbsOptimized": false,
        "LaunchTime": "2017-07-31T08:39:12.000Z",
        "PrivateIpAddress": "172.31.27.66",
        "ProductCodes": [],
        "VpcId": "vpc-f7dc4093",
        "StateTransitionReason": "",
        "InstanceId": "i-97000624",
        "ImageId": "ami-a4c7edb2",
        "PrivateDnsName": "ip-172-31-27-66.ec2.internal",
        "KeyName": "EffectiveDevOpsAWS",
        "SecurityGroups": [
            {
                "GroupName": "HelloWorld",
                "GroupId": "sg-11d4fe68"
            }
        ],
        "ClientToken": "",
        "SubnetId": "subnet-4f3bdb17",
        "InstanceType": "t2.micro",
        "NetworkInterfaces": [
            {
                "Status": "in-use",
                "MacAddress": "0e:fd:f8:18:bb:0f",
                "SourceDestCheck": true,
                "VpcId": "vpc-f7dc4093",
                "Description": "",
                "NetworkInterfaceId": "eni-1d23a243",
                "PrivateIpAddresses": [
                    {
                        "PrivateDnsName": "ip-172-31-
                        2766.ec2.internal",
                        "Primary": true,
                        "PrivateIpAddress": "172.31.27.66"
                    }
                ],
                "PrivateDnsName": "ip-172-31-27-66.ec2.internal",
                "Attachment": {
```

```json
                        "Status": "attaching",
                        "DeviceIndex": 0,
                        "DeleteOnTermination": true,
                        "AttachmentId": "eni-attach-6398c28f",
                        "AttachTime": "2017-07-31T08:39:12.000Z"
                    },
                    "Groups": [
                        {
                            "GroupName": "HelloWorld",
                            "GroupId": "sg-11d4fe68"
                        }
                    ],
                    "SubnetId": "subnet-4f3bdb17",
                    "OwnerId": "511912822958",
                    "PrivateIpAddress": "172.31.27.66"
                }
            ],
            "SourceDestCheck": true,
            "Placement": {
                "Tenancy": "default",
                "GroupName": "",
                "AvailabilityZone": "us-east-1a"
            },
            "Hypervisor": "xen",
            "BlockDeviceMappings": [],
            "Architecture": "x86_64",
            "StateReason": {
                "Message": "pending",
                "Code": "pending"
            },
            "RootDeviceName": "/dev/xvda",
            "VirtualizationType": "hvm",
            "AmiLaunchIndex": 0
        }
    ]
}
```

You can track the progress of the instance creation. To do that, get instance ID provided in the output of the `aws ec2 run-instances` command and run the following command:

```
$ aws ec2 describe-instance-status --instance-ids i-97000624
{
    "InstanceStatuses": [
        {
            "InstanceId": "i-97000624",
            "InstanceState": {
                "Code": 16,
                "Name": "running"
```

```
        },
        "AvailabilityZone": "us-east-1a",
        "SystemStatus": {
            "Status": "initializing",
            "Details": [
                {
                    "Status": "initializing",
                    "Name": "reachability"
                }
            ]
        },
        "InstanceStatus": {
            "Status": "initializing",
            "Details": [
                {
                    "Status": "initializing",
                    "Name": "reachability"
                }
            ]
        }
    }
  ]
}
```

The instance will be ready once the `Status` under `SystemStatus` changes from `initializing` to `ok`.

Connecting to the EC2 instance using ssh

The main goal of this chapter is to create a simple Hello World web application. Since we are starting off a vanilla OS, we need to connect to the host to make the necessary changes to turn our standard server into a web server. In order to `ssh` our instance, we need to find the DNS name of our running instance, as follows:

```
$ aws ec2 describe-instances \
  --instance-ids i-97000624 \
  --query "Reservations[*].Instances[*].PublicDnsName"
[
  [
    "ec2-54-88-134-38.compute-1.amazonaws.com"
  ]
]
```

We now have the public DNS name of our instance and the private key to `ssh` into our instance. The last thing to know is that in Amazon Linux for the OS that we selected when we chose our AMI, the default user account is called `ec2-user`:

```
$ ssh -i ~/.ssh/EffectiveDevOpsAWS.pem ec2-
user@ec2-54-88-134-38.compute-1.amazonaws.com
       __|  __|_  )
       _|  (     /    Amazon Linux AMI
      ___|\___|___|
[ec2-user@ip-172-31-22-234 ~]$
```

If you experience any sort of issue, add the `-vvv` option in your `ssh` command to troubleshoot it.

Creating a simple Hello World web application

Now that we are connected to our EC2 instance, we are ready to start playing around with it. In this book, we will focus on the most common use case for using AWS in tech companies: hosting an application. In terms of languages, we will use JavaScript which in the last few years has become the most popular language on GitHub. That said, this application is more there to give support to demonstrate how to best use AWS using the DevOps principles. Having any kind of knowledge about JavaScript isn't required to understand this book:

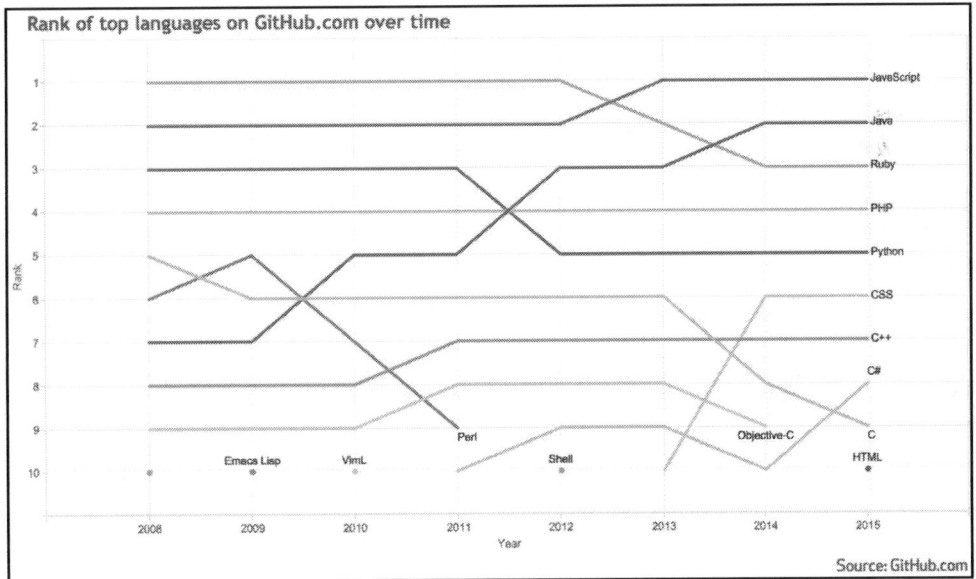

Some of the main advantages that JavaScript offers with regards to this book are that it:

- Is fairly easy to write and read, even for beginners
- Doesn't require to be compiled
- Can be run server side thanks to node.js (https://nodejs.org)
- Is officially supported by AWS and therefore the AWS SDK for JavaScript is a "first class citizen"

For the rest of the chapter, all the commands and code are to be run on our instance via ssh.

Installing node.js

The first thing we need to do is install node.js. Amazon Linux is based on **Red Hat Enterprise Linux** (RHEL) and uses the Yum utility to manage and install packages. The OS comes with **Extra Packages for Enterprise Linux** (EPEL) pre-configured in it. As we would expect, node.js is present in EPEL:

```
[ec2-user@ip-172-31-22-234 ~]$ sudo yum install --enablerepo=epel -y nodejs
[ec2-user@ip-172-31-22-234 ~]$ node -v
v0.10.48
```

This is definitely an old version of the node but it's going to be good enough for what we need.

Running a node.js Hello World.

Now that node is installed, we can create a simple Hello World application. Here is the code for creating this:

```
var http = require("http")

http.createServer(function (request, response) {

    // Send the HTTP header
    // HTTP Status: 200 : OK
    // Content Type: text/plain
    response.writeHead(200, {'Content-Type': 'text/plain'})
```

```
    // Send the response body as "Hello World"
    response.end('Hello World\n')
}).listen(3000)

// Console will print the message
console.log('Server running')
```

Feel free to copy this into a file, or if you want to save time, download this from GitHub:

```
[ec2-user@ip-172-31-22-234 ~]$ wget http://bit.ly/2vESNuc -O /home/ec2-
user/helloworld.js
--2017-01-31 23:58:20--  http://bit.ly/2vESNuc
Resolving bit.ly (bit.ly)... 69.58.188.39, 69.58.188.40
Connecting to bit.ly (bit.ly)|69.58.188.39|:80... connected.
HTTP request sent, awaiting response... 301 Moved Permanently
Location:
https://raw.githubusercontent.com/EffectiveDevOpsWithAWS/code-snippets/mast
er/helloworld.js [following]
--2017-01-31 23:58:21--
https://raw.githubusercontent.com/EffectiveDevOpsWithAWS/code-snippets/mast
er/helloworld.js
Resolving raw.githubusercontent.com (raw.githubusercontent.com)...
199.27.76.133
Connecting to raw.githubusercontent.com
(raw.githubusercontent.com)|199.27.76.133|:443... connected.
HTTP request sent, awaiting response... 200 OK
Length: 389 [text/plain]
Saving to: '/home/ec2-user/helloworld.js'
/home/ec2-user/helloworld.js
100%[===========================================================>]
389  --.-KB/s   in 0s
2017-01-31 23:58:21 (100 MB/s) - '/home/ec2-user/helloworld.js' saved
[389/389]
[ec2-user@ip-172-31-22-234 ~]$
```

And now, in order to run the `Hello World` application, we are simply going to run the following code:

```
[ec2-user@ip-172-31-22-234 ~]$ node helloworld.js
Server running
```

If everything goes well, you can now open this in your browser
`http://your-public-dns-name:3000`, in my case,
`http://ec2-54-88-134-38.compute-1.amazonaws.com:3000`, and see the result, as
follows:

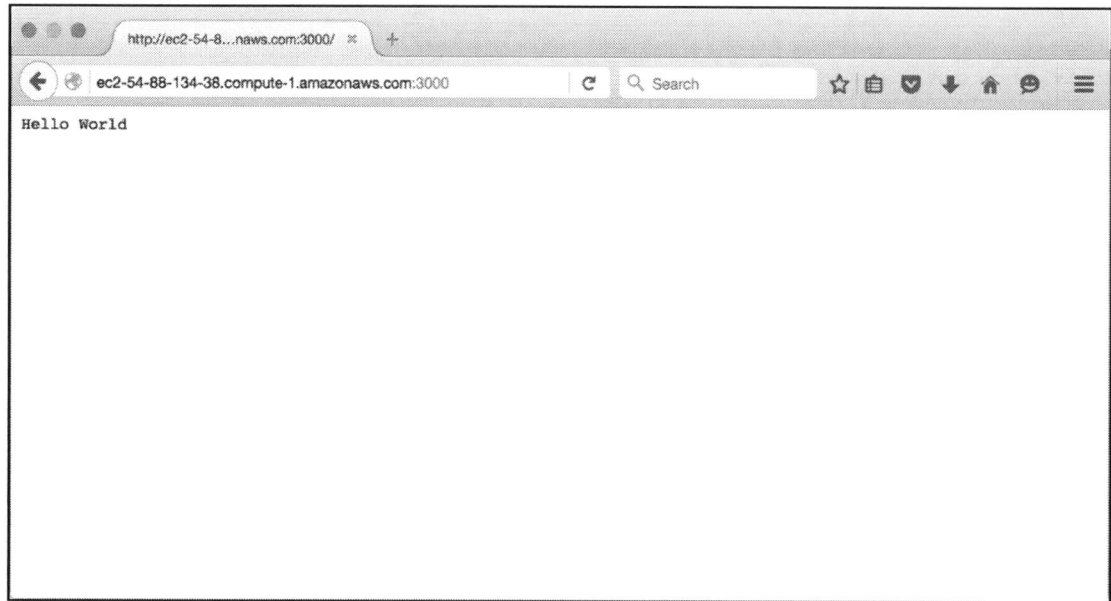

We will now stop the execution of the `helloworld` web application with Ctrl + C in your
terminal window.

Turning our simple code into a service using upstart

Since we started the node application manually in the terminal, closing the `ssh` connection
or hitting *Ctrl + C* on the keyboard will stop the node process, and therefore our `Hello`
`World` application will not work anymore.

Amazon Linux, unlike standard Red Hat-based distribution, comes with a system called upstart.

It is fairly easy to use and provides a couple of extra features that traditional System-V bootup scripts don't have, such as the ability to respawn a process that died unexpectedly. To add an upstart configuration, you need to create a file inside /etc/init on the EC2 instance.

Here is the code to insert in /etc/init/helloworld.conf:

```
description "Hello world Deamon"

# Start when the system is ready to do networking.
start on started elastic-network-interfaces

# Stop when the system is on its way down.
stop on shutdown

respawn
script
    exec su --session-command="/usr/bin/node /home/ec2-user/helloworld.js"
ec2-user
end script
```

why started on elastic-network-interfaces
If you are familiar with upstart outside of AWS, you might have used start on runlevel [345]. The problem with that in AWS is that your network comes from **Elastic Network Interface (ENI)**, and if your application starts before this service, it might not be able to connect to the network correctly.

```
[ec2-user@ip-172-31-22-234 ~]$ sudo wget http://bit.ly/2vVvT18 -O
/etc/init/helloworld.conf
--2017-02-01 00:20:03--  http://bit.ly/2vVvT18
Resolving bit.ly (bit.ly)... 69.58.188.39, 69.58.188.40
Connecting to bit.ly (bit.ly)|69.58.188.39|:80... connected.
HTTP request sent, awaiting response... 301 Moved Permanently
Location:
https://raw.githubusercontent.com/EffectiveDevOpsWithAWS/code-snippets/mast
er/helloworld.conf [following]
--2017-02-01 00:20:03--
https://raw.githubusercontent.com/EffectiveDevOpsWithAWS/code-snippets/mast
er/helloworld.conf
Resolving raw.githubusercontent.com (raw.githubusercontent.com)...
199.27.76.133
Connecting to raw.githubusercontent.com
(raw.githubusercontent.com)|199.27.76.133|:443... connected.
HTTP request sent, awaiting response... 200 OK
```

```
Length: 286 [text/plain]
Saving to: '/etc/init/helloworld.conf'
/etc/init/helloworld.conf
100%[==========================================================>]
286    --.-KB/s    in 0s
2017-02-01 00:20:03 (67.4 MB/s) - '/etc/init/helloworld.conf' saved
[286/286]
[ec2-user@ip-172-31-22-234 ~]$
```

We can now simply start our application, as follows:

```
[ec2-user@ip-172-31-22-234 ~]$ sudo start helloworld
helloworld start/running, process 23090
[ec2-user@ip-172-31-22-234 ~]$
```

As expected, `http://your-public-dns-name:3000` still works, and this time, we can safely close our `ssh` connection.

Terminating our EC2 instance

As with most `helloworld` exercises, once the **Hello World** message is displayed, the goal is reached. It is now time to think about shutting down our server. Since in AWS we only pay for what we consume, freeing up unnecessary resources such as this server is a good strategy to make AWS very cost effective.

We can do a clean shutdown of the Hello World service using the `stop` command, exit the virtual server and terminate our instance, as follows:

```
[ec2-user@ip-172-31-22-234 ~]$ sudo stop helloworld
helloworld stop/waiting
[ec2-user@ip-172-31-22-234 ~]$ ec2-metadata --instance-id
instance-id: i-d10e0e62
[ec2-user@ip-172-31-22-234 ~]$ exit
logout
$ aws ec2 terminate-instances --instance-ids i-d10e0e62
{
  "TerminatingInstances": [
    {
      "InstanceId": "i-d10e0e62",
      "CurrentState": {
        "Code": 32,
        "Name": "shutting-down"
      },
      "PreviousState": {
        "Code": 16,
        "Name": "running"
```

```
            }
         }
      ]
   }
```

Summary

This chapter was a quick and simple introduction to AWS and its most notorious service EC2. After signing up for AWS, we configured our environment in such a way that we could create a virtual server using the command-line interface. Leading to this, we selected our first AMI, created our first security group and generated our ssh keys which we will reuse throughout the book. After launching an EC2 instance we manually deployed a simple node.js application to display **Hello World**.

While the process wasn't very fastidious thanks to the AWS CLI, it still required going through numerous steps which aren't very repeatable. We also deployed the application without any automation or validation. Furthermore, the only way we can check if the application is running is by manually checking the endpoint. In the remainder of the book, we will revisit the process of creating and managing web applications and infrastructure but this time, we will follow the DevOps principles and incorporate its best practices.

Chapter 3, *Treating Your Infrastructure As Code*, will address one of the first issues we encountered: managing our infrastructure with automation. To do that, we write code to manage our infrastructure.

3
Treating Your Infrastructure As Code

In Chapter 2, *Deploying Your First Web Application*, we familiarized ourselves with AWS. We also created an EC2 instance and deployed a HelloWorld web application onto it but to get there, we had to go through a number of steps to configure the instance and its security groups. Because we did that in a very manual fashion using the command line interface those steps we went through will not be reusable or auditable, as you may recall from the first chapter when implementing DevOps best practices. Two key concepts are that you should source-control everything and should rely on automation as often as possible. In this chapter, we will see how to apply those principles to our infrastructure.

In a cloud environment where almost everything is abstracted and served through the intermediary of virtual resources, it is easy to imagine that code can describe the topology of a network and the configuration of a system. To go through that transformation, we will learn about two key concepts in an effective DevOps organization. The first one is commonly called **Infrastructure as Code (IAC)** and it is the process of describing all your virtual resources such as virtual servers or load balancers and the network layer after that. The second concept while very close to IAC focuses further on systems configuration and is called **Configuration Management**. Through configuration management systems, developers and system administrators have the ability to automate operating system configuration, package installation, and even application deployment.

Going through that transformation is a crucial step for any DevOps-focused organization. By having code to describe the different resources and their configurations, we will be able to use the same tools and processes as we do when doing application development. We will be able to use source control and make smaller changes in individual branches, submit pull requests and go through standard review processes, and finally, test changes before they are applied to our production environment. This will give us better clarity, accountability, and audit-ability for infrastructure changes. Because of that, we will also be able to manage a much bigger fleet of resources without necessarily needing more engineers or without spending a lot more time operating all the resources. This will also open up the door to more automation, as we will see with continuous deployment in Chapter 4, *Adding Continuous Integration and Continuous Deployment*.

In this chapter, we will look at two different applications. The first one is called **CloudFormation** and it is an AWS service that will let us create and configure any AWS resources through JSON configuration files. After that, we will look at **Ansible**, a configuration management tool. This will allow us to make more granular changes at the operating system level:

- Managing your infrastructure with CloudFormation
- Adding a configuration management system

Managing your infrastructure with CloudFormation

CloudFormation introduces a new way to manage services and their configurations. Through the creation of JSON or YAML files, CloudFormation lets you describe exactly the AWS architecture you would look like to build. Once your files are created, you can simply upload your files to CloudFormation, which will execute them and automatically create or update your AWS resources.

Most AWS managed tools and services are supported. You can get the full list at http://amzn.to/1Odslix. In this chapter, we will only look at the infrastructure we built so far but we will add more resources in the next chapters.

After a brief overview of how CloudFormation is structured, we will create a minimalist stack to recreate the Hello World web application from Chapter 2, *Deploying Your First Web Application*. After that, we will see two more options to create CloudFormation templates: the designer, which;lets you visually edit your template in a Web GUI, and CloudFormer, a tool to generate templates from existing infrastructure.

Getting started with CloudFormation

As you would expect, you can access CloudFormation via the AWS console (https://console.aws.amazon.com/cloudformation) or by using the command-line:

```
$ aws cloudformation help # for the list of options
```

The service is organized around the concept of stacks. Each stack typically describes a set of AWS resources and their configuration in order to start an application. When working with CloudFormation, most of your time is spent editing those templates.

There are different ways to get started with the actual editing of the templates. One of the easiest ways is to edit existing templates. AWS has a number of well-written examples available at http://amzn.to/27cHmrb.

At the highest level templates are structured as follows:

```
{
    "AWSTemplateFormatVersion" : "version date",
    "Description" : "Description string",
    "Resources" : { },
    "Parameters" : { },
    "Mappings" : { },
    "Conditions" : { },
    "Metadata" : { },
    "Outputs" : { }
}
```

`AWSTemplateFormatVersion` is currently always 2010-09-09 and represents the version of the template language used. The `Description` is for you to summarize what the template does. The `Resources` section describes which AWS services will be instantiated and what their configurations are. When you launch a template, you have the ability to provide some extra information to CloudFormation such as which `ssh` keypair to use, for example, if you want to give SSH access to your EC2 instances. This kind of information goes into the `Parameters` section. The `Mappings` section is useful when you try to create a more generic template.

You can, for example, define which AMI to use for a given region so that the same template can be used to start an application in any AWS region. The `Conditions` section allows you to add conditional logic to your other sections (if statements, logical operators, and so on). The `Metadata` section lets you add more arbitrary information to your resources. Finally, the `Outputs` section lets you extract and print out useful information based on the execution of your template such as the IP address of the EC2 server created, for example.

In addition to those examples, AWS also provides a couple of tools and services around CloudFormation template creation.

The first tool you can use to create your templates is called CloudFormationdesigner.

AWS CloudFormation designer

AWS CloudFormation designer is a tool that lets you create and edit CloudFormation templates using a graphic user interface. Designer hides a lot of the complexity of editing a CloudFormation template using a standard text editor. You can access it directly at `https://console.aws.amazon.com/cloudformation/designer` or in the CloudFormation dashboard after you click on **Create Stack**:

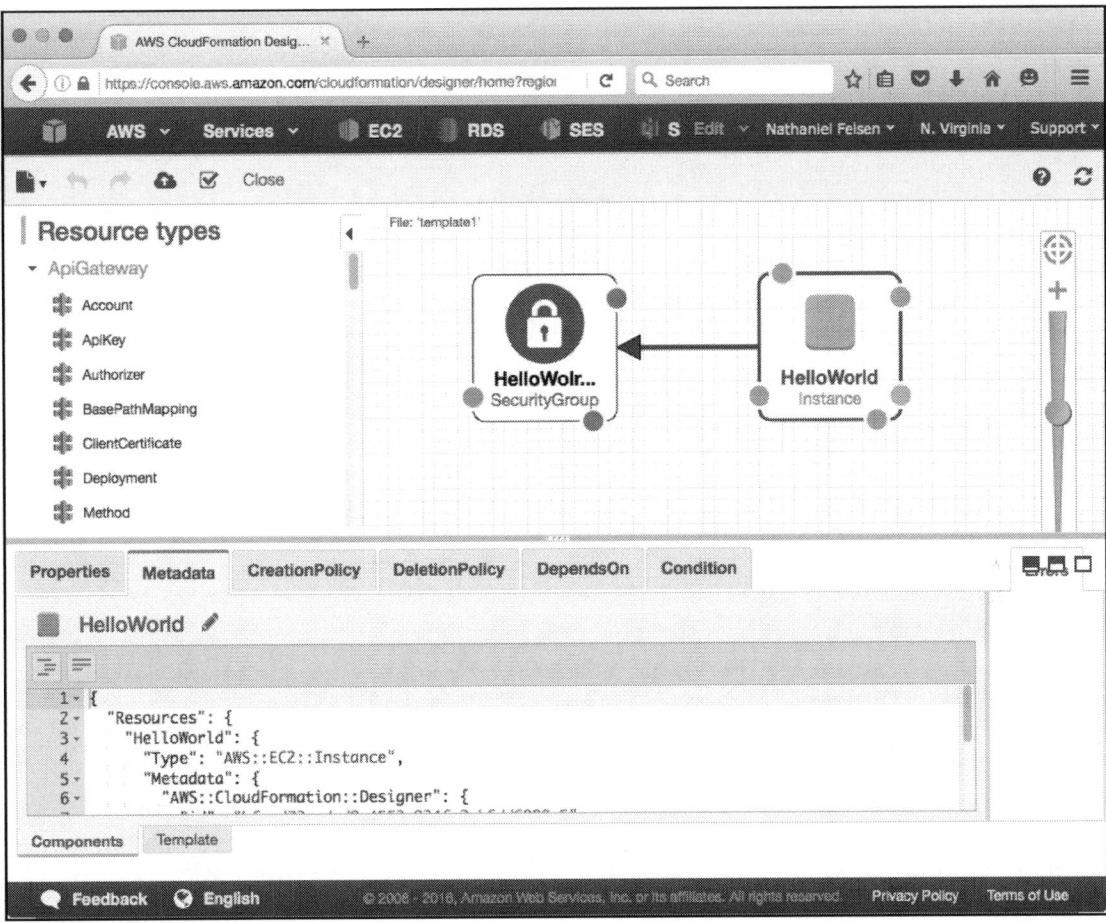

The workflow is fairly simple. You simply drag and drop resources from the left-hand side menu into a canvas. Once your resources are added, you can then connect them to other resources using the small dots surrounding each resource icon. In the preceding example, we are connecting an EC2 instance to its security group. There are a number of hidden gems that can help you when designing your template.

You can use right-click on resources and directly access the documentation for the CloudFormation resource, as follows:

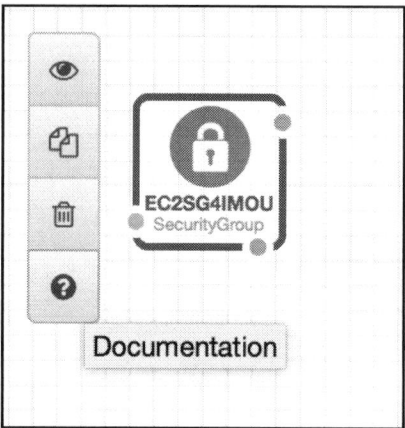

When dragging a dot to connect two resources together, designer will highlight resources compatible with that connection:

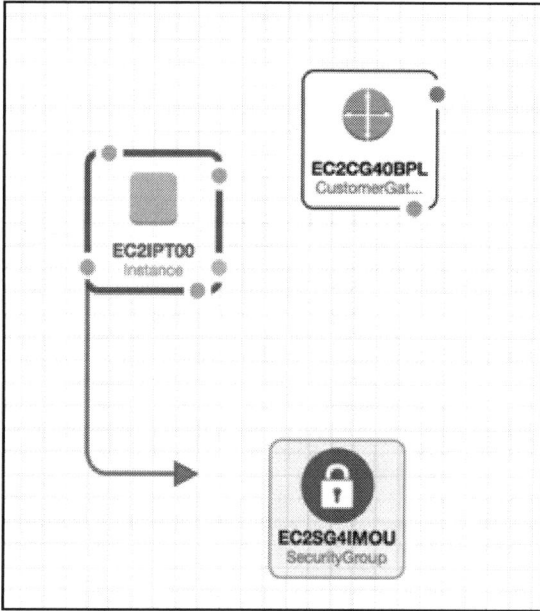

The editor on the bottom section of the designer supports auto completion using *Ctrl +* space:

Once your template is complete, you can simply click on a button and go from designing your stack to launching it.

The next tool we will look at is called **CloudFormer**.

CloudFormer

CloudFormer is a tool that lets you create CloudFormation templates looking at pre-existing resources. If you have a set of resources that you have already created on an ad-hoc basis like we have done so far in the book, you can use CloudFormer to group them under a new CloudFormation template. You can then later customize the template that CloudFormer generates using a text editor or even CloudFormation designer and make it fit your needs.

Unlike most AWS tools and services, CloudFormer isn't completely managed by AWS; it's a self-hosted tool that you can instantiate on demand using CloudFormation. To do so, follow the given steps:

1. Open `https://console.aws.amazon.com/cloudformation` in your browser.
2. Select the AWS region where the resources you are trying to templatize are.
3. In the **Select a sample template** drop-down menu, choose **CloudFormer** and click on **Next**
4. On that screen, at the top, you can provide a stack name (feel free to keep the default name `AWSCloudFormer`) and in the bottom part, you are asked to provide two extra parameters, a username, and a password. Those will be used later to log in to CloudFormer. Pick a username and a password, and click on **Next**.
5. On the next screen, you can provide extra tags and more advanced options, but we will simply continue by clicking on **Next**.

6. This brings us to the review page where we will check the checkbox to acknowledge that this will cause AWS CloudFormation to create IAM resources. Click on **Create**.

7. This will bring us back on the main screen of the CloudFormation console where we can see our AWS CloudFormer stack being created. Once the **Status** goes from **CREATE_IN_PROGRESS** to **CREATE_COMPLETE**, select it and click on the **Output** tab at the bottom.

At that point, you have created the resources needed to use CloudFomer. In order to create a stack with it, do the following:

In the **Outputs** tab (which illustrates the outputs section of CloudFormation), click on the website URL link. This will open up the CloudFormer tool. Log in using the username and password provided in the fourth step of the previous set of instructions. The following screen will appear:

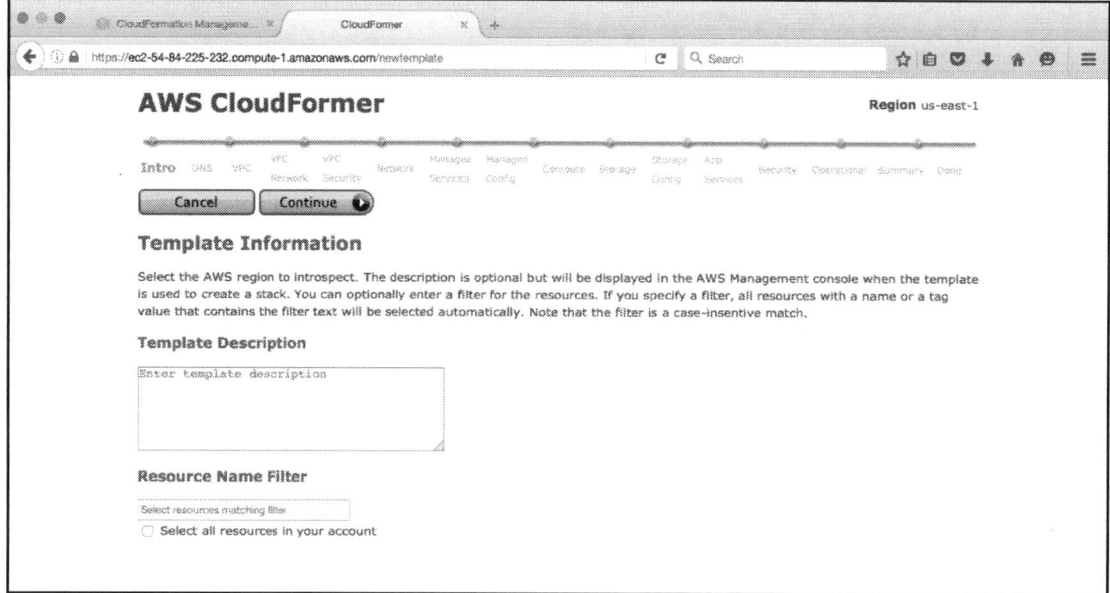

8. Follow the workflow proposed by the tool to select the different resources you want for your CloudFormation template as far as the last step.

9. In the end, you will be able to download the generated template or save it directly in S3.

The CloudFormation template generated by CloudFormer will usually need a bit of editing as you will often want to create a more flexible stack with input parameters and an outputs section.

Recreating our helloworld example with CloudFormation

Designer and CloudFormer are two very useful tools when you are in the process of architecting your infrastructure and are trying to add source control to your design.

That said, whenever you wear your DevOps hat, it's a different story. Using those tools markedly reduces the added value that CloudFormation provides by using the JSON format. If you got a chance to read some of the templates available or tried to use CloudFormer on your existing infrastructure, you probably noticed that raw CloudFormation templates tend to be fairly long and not **Don't Repeat Yourself (DRY)**.

From a DevOps perspective, one of the most powerful aspects of CloudFormation is the ability to write code to dynamically generate those templates. To illustrate that point, we are going to turn to Python and a library called troposphere to generate our Hello World CloudFormation template.

 There are also a number of more advanced tools to assist with the creation of CloudFormation templates. If you plan on using other third-party services in addition to just the AWS, you can take a look at Terraform from Hashicorp https://www.terraform.io, for example, which handles a number of other cloud providers and services in addition to CloudFormation.

Using troposphere to create a Python script for our template

We will first install the troposphere library:

```
$ pip install troposphere
```

Once the installation is done, you can then create a new file called helloworld-cf-template.py.

We will start our file by importing a number of definitions from the troposphere module:

```
"""Generating CloudFormation template."""

from troposphere import (
    Base64,
    ec2,
    GetAtt,
    Join,
    Output,
    Parameter,
    Ref,
    Template,
)
```

We are also going to define a first variable that will make editing the code easier for the remaining of the book as we will create new scripts building off this initial template:

```
ApplicationPort = "3000"
```

From a code standpoint, the first thing we will do is initialize a Template variable. By the end of our script, the template will contain the entire description of our infrastructure and we will be able to simply print its output to get our CloudFromation template:

```
t = Template()
```

Throughout this book, we will create and run concurrently several CloudFormation templates. To help us identify what's in a given stack, we have the ability to provide a description. After the creation of the template, add the description as follow:

```
t.add_description("Effective DevOps in AWS: HelloWorld web application")
```

When we launched EC2 instances using the web command line interface, we selected which key pair to use in order to gain SSH access to the host. In order to not lose this ability, the first thing our template will have is a parameter to offer the CloudFormation user the ability to select which key pair to use when launching the EC2 instance. To do that, we are going to create a `Parameter` object, and initialize it by providing an identifier, a description, a parameter type, a description and a constraint description to help to make the right decision when we launch the stack. In order for this parameter to exist in our final template, we will also use the `add_paramter()` function defined in the template class:

```
t.add_parameter(Parameter(
    "KeyPair",
    Description="Name of an existing EC2 KeyPair to SSH",
    Type="AWS::EC2::KeyPair::KeyName",
    ConstraintDescription="must be the name of an existing EC2 KeyPair.",
))
```

The next thing we will look at is the security group. We will proceed exactly as we did for our `KeyPair` parameter. We want to open up SSH and `tcp/3000` to the world. Port 3000 was defined in the variable `ApplicationPort` declared earlier; in addition, this time, the information defined isn't a parameter like before, but a resource. Therefore, we will add that new resource using the `add_resource()` function:

```
t.add_resource(ec2.SecurityGroup(
    "SecurityGroup",
    GroupDescription="Allow SSH and TCP/{} access".format(ApplicationPort),
    SecurityGroupIngress=[
        ec2.SecurityGroupRule(
            IpProtocol="tcp",
            FromPort="22",
            ToPort="22",
            CidrIp="0.0.0.0/0",
        ),
        ec2.SecurityGroupRule(
            IpProtocol="tcp",
            FromPort=ApplicationPort,
            ToPort=ApplicationPort,
            CidrIp="0.0.0.0/0",
        ),
    ],
))
```

In our next section, we will replace the need to log on to our EC2 instance and install by hand the `helloworld.js` file and its init scripts. To do so, we will take advantage of the UserData feature that EC2 offers. When you create an EC2 instance, you have the ability through the UserData optional parameter to provide a set of commands to run once the virtual machine has spawned up. You can read more on that topic at `http://amzn.to/1VU5b3s`. One of the constraints of UserData is that the script must be base64-encoded to be added to our API call. We are going to create a small script to reproduce the steps we went through in Chapter 2, *Deploying Your First Web Application,* encode it in base 64 and store it in a variable called `ud`. Note that installing the application in the home directory of the `ec2-user` isn't very clean. For now, we are currently trying to stay consistent with what we did in Chapter 2, *Deploying Your First Web Application.* We will fix that in Chapter 4, *Adding Continuous Integration and Continuous Deployment,* as we improve our deployment system:

```
ud = Base64(Join('\n', [
    "#!/bin/bash",
    "sudo yum install --enablerepo=epel -y nodejs",
    "wget http://bit.ly/2vESNuc -O /home/ec2-user/helloworld.js",
    "wget http://bit.ly/2vVvT18 -O /etc/init/helloworld.conf",
    "start helloworld"
]))
```

We will now focus on the main resource of our template, our EC2 instance. The creation of the instance requires providing a name for identifying the resource, an image ID, an instance type, a security group, the keypair to use for the SSH access, and the user data. In order to keep things simple, we will hard code the AMI ID (`ami-a4c7edb2`) and instance type (`t2.micro`). The remaining information needed to create our EC2 instances is the security group information and the `keypair` name, which we collected previously by defining a parameter and a resource. In CloudFormation, you can reference pre-existing subsections of your template by using the keyword `Ref`. In Troposphere, this is done by calling the `Ref()` function. As before, we will add the resulting output to our template with the help of the `add_resource` function:

```
t.add_resource(ec2.Instance(
    "instance",
    ImageId="ami-a4c7edb2",
    InstanceType="t2.micro",
    SecurityGroups=[Ref("SecurityGroup")],
    KeyName=Ref("KeyPair"),
    UserData=ud,
))
```

In the last section of our script, we will focus on producing the Outputs section of the template that gets populated when CloudFormation creates a stack. This selection allows you to print out useful information that was computed during the launch of the stack. In our case, there are two useful pieces information, the URL to access our web application and the public IP address of the instance so that we can SSH into it if we want to. In order to retrieve such information, CloudFormation uses the function `Fn::GetAtt`. In troposphere this is translated into using the `GetAttr()` function:

```
t.add_output(Output(
    "InstancePublicIp",
    Description="Public IP of our instance.",
    Value=GetAtt(instance, "PublicIp"),
))

t.add_output(Output(
    "WebUrl",
    Description="Application endpoint",
    Value=Join("", [
        "http://", GetAtt(instance, "PublicDnsName"),
        ":", ApplicationPort
    ]),
))
```

At that point, we can make our script output the final result of the template we generated:

```
print t.to_json()
```

The script is complete; we can save it and quit our editor. The file created should look like the file at http://bit.ly/2vXM5Py

We can now run our script giving it the proper permissions and generate the CloudFormation template by saving the output of our script in a file:

```
$ python helloworld-cf-template.py > helloworld-cf.template
```

CloudInit

CloudInit is a set of Python scripts compatible with most Linux distributions and cloud providers. It complements the UserData field by moving most standard operations, such as installing packages, creating files, and running commands, into different sections of the template. This book doesn't cover that tool, but if your CloudFormation templates heavily rely on the UserData field, take a look at it. You can get its documentation at `http://bit.ly/1W6s96M`.

Creating the stack in the CloudFormation console

At this point we can launch our template using the following steps:

1. Open the CloudFormation web console in your browser
   `https://console.aws.amazon.com/cloudformation`.
2. Click on **Create Stack**.
3. On the next screen, we will upload our newly generated template `helloworld-cf.template` by selecting **Upload a template to Amazon S3** and then browsing to select our `helloworld-cf.template` file.
4. We will then pick a stack name such as `HelloWorld`.
5. After the stack name, we can see the **Parameters** section of our template in action. CloudFormation lets us pick which SSH keypair to use. Select your Keypair using the drop-down menu.
6. On the next screen, we have to ability the add optional tags to our resources; in the advanced section we can see how we can potentially integrate CloudFormation and SNS, make decisions on what to do when a failure or a timeout occurs, and even add a stack policy that lets you control who can edit the stack, for example. For now, we will simply click on **Next**.
7. This leads us to the review screen where we can verify the information selected and even estimate how much it will cost to run that stack. Click on **Create**.
8. This will bring us to the main CloudFormation console. On that screen, we are able to see how our resources are created in the **Events** tab.
9. When the creation of the template is complete, click on the **Outputs** tabs, which will reveal information we generated through the Outputs section of our template:

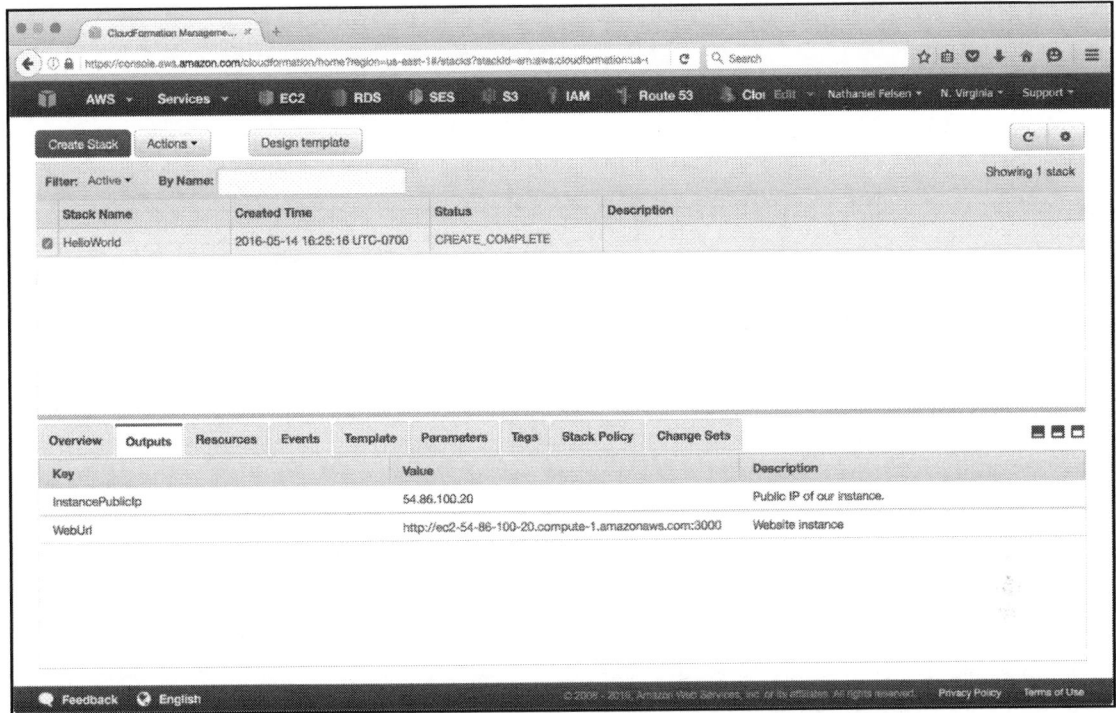

10. Click on the link in the value of the **WebUrl** key, which will open up our **HelloWorld** page.

Adding our template to a source control system

Now that we have tested our template and know it's working, we are going> to commit it to our source control system. This will allow us to keep track of changes and gives the ability to treat our infrastructure code up to the same standard as our application code (more on that in Chapter 4, *Adding Continuous Integration and Continuous Deployment*).

To do that, we will rely on Git. AWS has a service called AWS CodeCommit (http://amzn.to/2tKUj0n), which lets you easily manage Git repositories; however, because this service is a lot less popular than GitHub (https://github.com), we will instead use the latter. If you don't have an account for GitHub yet, start by signing up for the service (it's completely free.)

Once logged in to GitHub, create a new repository for the CloudFormation template:

1. In your browser, open `https://github.com/new`.
2. Call the new repository `EffectiveDevOpsTemplates`.
3. Check the checkbox **Initialize this repository with a README**.
4. Finally, click the button **Create repository**:

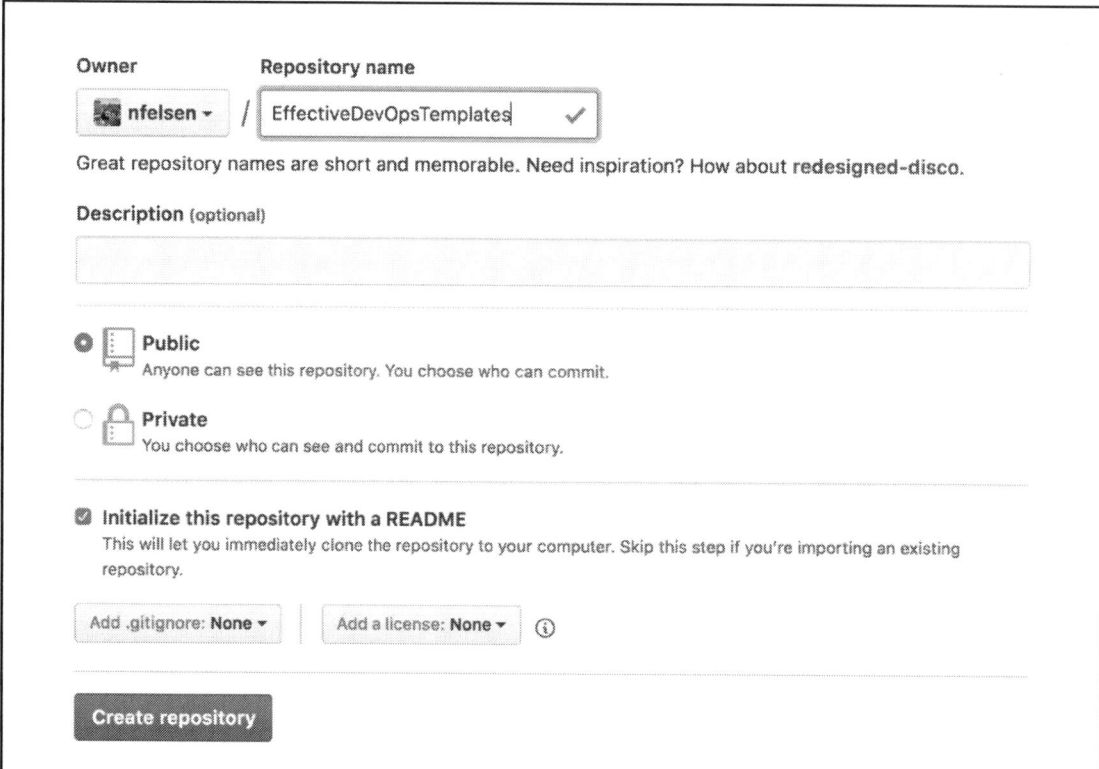

5. Once your repository is created, you will want to clone it into your computer. For that you need to have Git installed (search on Google for instructions on how to install Git for your operating system if you don't have it yet):

```
$ git clone
https://github.com/<your_github_username>/EffectiveDevOpsTempla
tes
```

6. Now that the repository is cloned, we will go into the repository and copy the template previously created in the new GitHub repository:

```
$ cd EffectiveDevOpsTemplates
$ cp <path_to_helloworld_template>/helloworld-cf-template.py .
```

7. Finally, we will add and commit that new file to our project and push it to GitHub:

```
$ git add helloworld-cf-template.py
$ git commit -m "Adding helloworld Troposphere template"
$ git push
```

Mono repos versus multi repos

When managing your code there are two common approaches to organizing your code repositories. You can create one repository for each project you have or decide to put your entire organization code under a single repository. We will choose the simplest option for this book, which is one repository per project but with the recent releases of several open source project such as Bazel from Google Buck from Facebook or Pants from Twitter, using a mono repo becomes a very compiling option as it avoids juggling between multiple repositories when making big changes in your infrastructure and services at the same time.

Updating our CloudFormation stack

One of the biggest benefits of using the CloudFormation template to manage our resources is that the resources created from CloudFormation are tightly coupled to our stack. If we want to make a change to our stack, we can update the template and apply the change to our existing CloudFormation stack. Let's see how that works.

Updating our Python script

Our `helloworld-cf-template.py` script is fairly basic. At this point, we are only taking advantage of Python to use the troposphere library to easily generate JSON output in a more pleasant way than if we had to write the JSON by hand. Of course, you might already realize that we are barely scratching the surface of what we can do when we have the ability to write scripts to create and manage infrastructures. Here is a simple example that will let us write a couple more lines of Python and illustrate the concept of updating a CloudFormation stack while taking advantage of more services and external resources.

The security groups we created in our previous example open up two ports to the world: 22 (SSH) and 3000 (the web application port). We could try to harden a bit of our security by only allowing our own IP to use SSH. This means changing the **Classless Inter-Domain Routing IP (CidrIp)** information in our Python script on the security group that handles the port 22 traffic. There are a number of free services online that will let us know what our public IP is. We are going to use one of them available at `https://api.ipify.org`.

We can see it in action with a simple curl command:

```
$ curl https://api.ipify.org
208.90.213.202%
```

We are going to take advantage of that service in our script. One of the reasons for using this particular service is that it has been packaged into a `python` library. You can read more on this at `https://github.com/rdegges/python-ipify`.

You can first install that library as follows:

```
$ pip install ipify
```

Our script requires a CIDR; in order to convert our IP address in CIDR, we will also install another library called `ipaddress`. The main advantage is that by combining those libraries is that we won't have to worry about handling IPv4 versus IPv6:

```
$ pip install ipaddress
```

Once those libraries are installed, reopen `helloworld-cf-template.py` in your editor. At the top of our script, we are going to import the libraries, then after the `ApplicationPort` variable definition, we will define a new variable called `PublicCidrIp` and combining the two libraries mentioned previously extract our CIDR as follows:

```
from ipaddress import ip_network

from ipify import get_ip

from troposphere import (...)

ApplicationPort = "3000"
PublicCidrIp = str(ip_network(get_ip()))
```

Lastly, we can change the `CidrIp` declaration for the SSH group rule:

```
SecurityGroupIngress=[
    ec2.SecurityGroupRule(
        IpProtocol="tcp",
        FromPort="22",
        ToPort="22",
        CidrIp=PublicCidrIp,
    ),
```

We can save the changes. The file created should look like the file at `http://bit.ly/2uvdnP 4`.

We can now generate a new CloudFormation template and run the `diff` command to visually verify the change:

```
$ python helloworld-cf-template.py > helloworld-cf-template-v2.template
$ diff helloworld-cf-v2.template helloworld-cf.template
44c44
<                         "CidrIp": "50.254.136.236/32",
---
>                         "CidrIp": "0.0.0.0/0",
$
```

As we can see, our `CirdIP` is now correctly restricting the connection to our IP. We can now apply that change.

Updating our stack

Having generated the new JSON CloudFormation template, we can get in the CloudFormation console and update the stack as follows:

1. Open the CloudFormation web console in your browser
   `https://console.aws.amazon.com/cloudformation`.
2. Select the `HelloWorld` stack that we previously created.
3. Click on **Action** then **Update Stack**.
4. Chose the `helloworld-cf-v2.template` file by clicking on the **Browse** button selecting the file, and then clicking on **Next**.
5. This brings us to the next screen that lets us update the details of our stack. In our case, nothing has changed in the parameters so we can continue by clicking on **Next**.

6. In the next screen as well, since we simply want to see the effect of our IP change, we can click on **Next**.

7. This brings us to the **Review** page where after a couple of seconds we can see CloudFormation giving a **Preview** of our change:

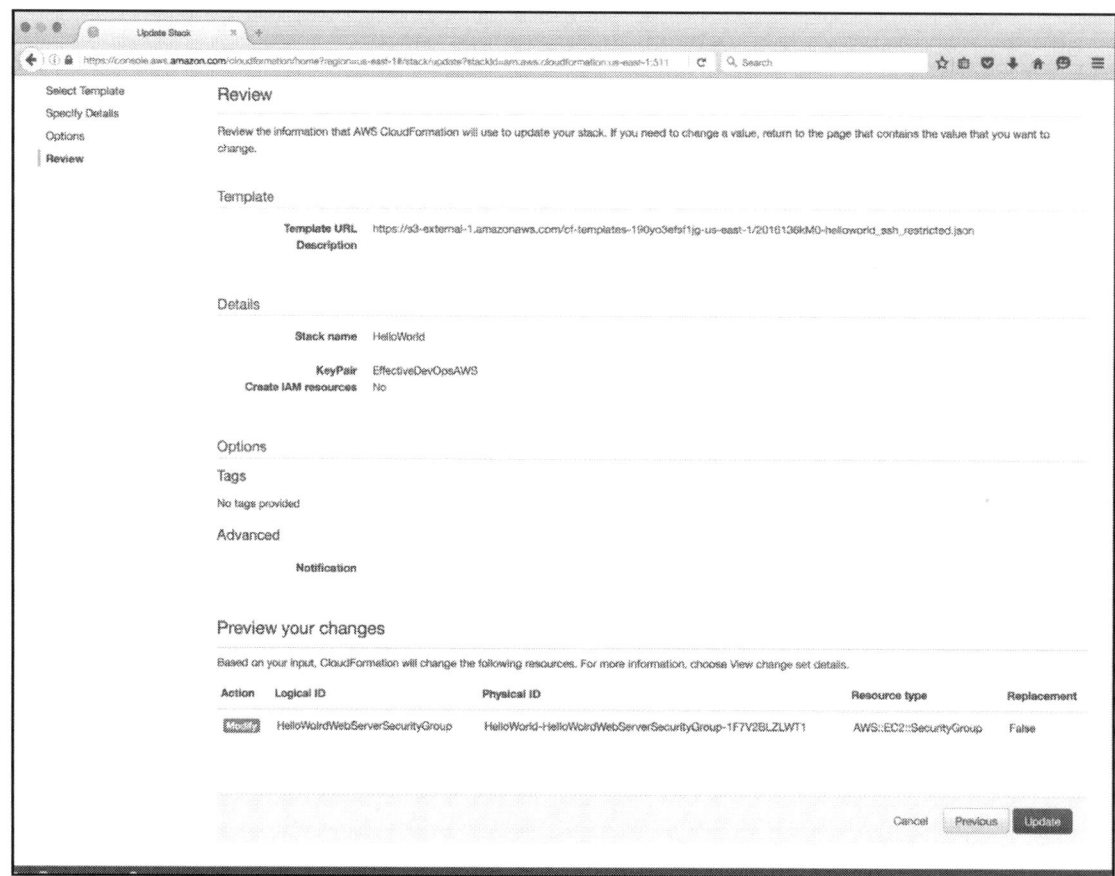

As you can see the only change will be an update on the Security group. Click on **Update**.

8. This will bring us back to the CloudFormation template where we will see the change being applied.

In this particular example, AWS is able to simply update the security group to take our change into account.

We can verify the change by extracting the physical ID from either the **Review** page or back in the console in the **Resources** tab:

```
$ aws ec2 describe-security-groups \
        --group-names HelloWorld-
HelloWolrdWebServerSecurityGroup-1F7V2BLZLWT1
```

Change sets

Our template only includes a web server and a security group that makes updating CloudFormation a fairly harmless operation. Furthermore, our change was fairly trivial as AWS could simply update the existing security group as opposed to having to replace it. As you can imagine, as the architecture becomes more and more complex so does the CloudFormation template. Depending on the update you want to perform, you might encounter unexpected changes when you review the change set in the final step of updating a template.

AWS offers an alternate and safer way to update templates. The feature is called change sets and is accessible from the CloudFormation console:

1. Open the CloudFormation web console in your browser
   https://console.aws.amazon.com/cloudformation.
2. Select the **HelloWorld** stack that we previously created.
3. Click on **Action** and then **Create Change Set**.

From there you can follow the same steps you took to create a simple Update. The main difference happens on the last screen:

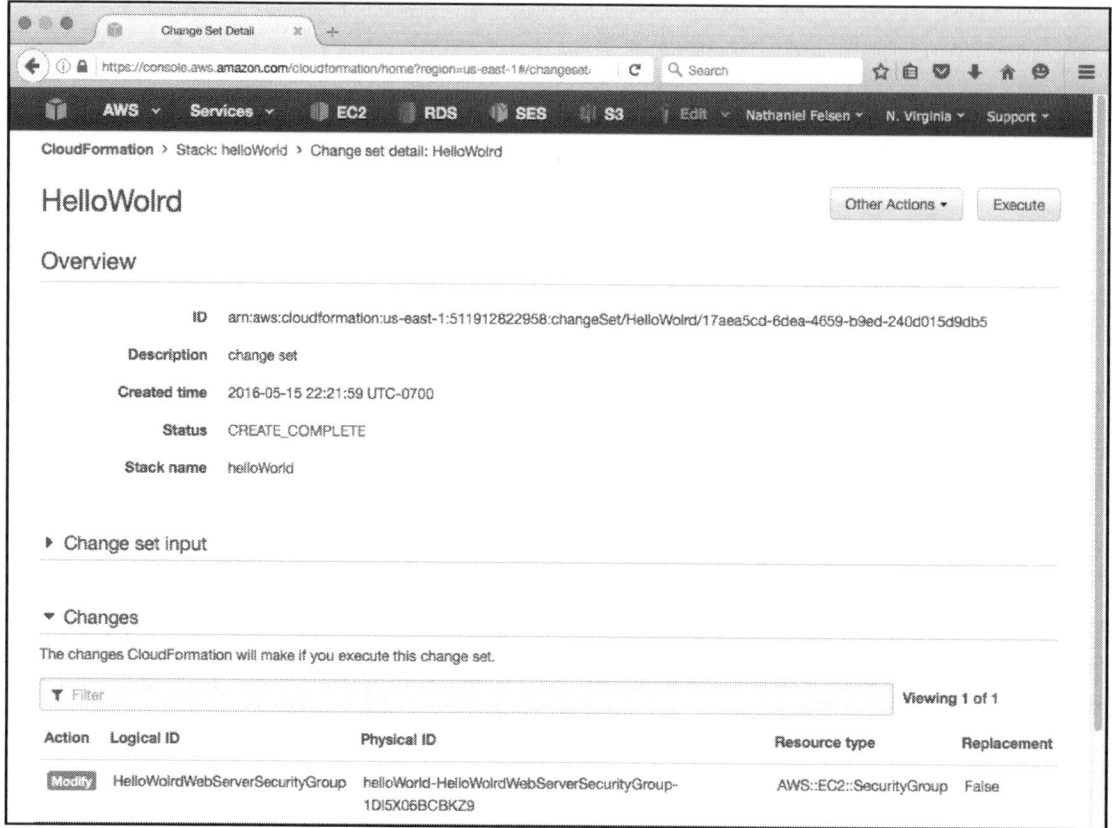

Unlike the regular stack updates, **Change Sets** have a strong emphasis on giving you the ability to review a change before applying it. If you are satisfied with the changes displayed, you have the ability to execute the update.

Lastly, when using a **Change Set** to update your stack, you can easily audit recent changes using the **Change Set** tab of your stack in the CloudFormation console.

Finally, we will commit the changes to the troposphere script with the following command:

```
$ git commit -am "Only allow ssh from our local IP"
$ git push
```

Deleting our CloudFormation stack

We saw in the last section how CloudFormation was able to update resources as we update our template. The same goes when you want to remove a CloudFormation stack and its resources. In a couple of clicks, you can delete your template and the various resources that got created at launch time. From a best practice standpoint, it is highly recommended to always use CloudFormation to make changes to your resources previously initialized with CloudFormation, including when you don't need your stack anymore.

Deleting a stack is very simple; you should proceed as follows:

1. Open the CloudFormation web console in your browser
   `https://console.aws.amazon.com/cloudformation`.
2. Select the `HelloWorld` stack that we previously created.
3. Click on **Action**, and then **Delete Stack**.

As always, you will be able to track completion in the **Events** tab:

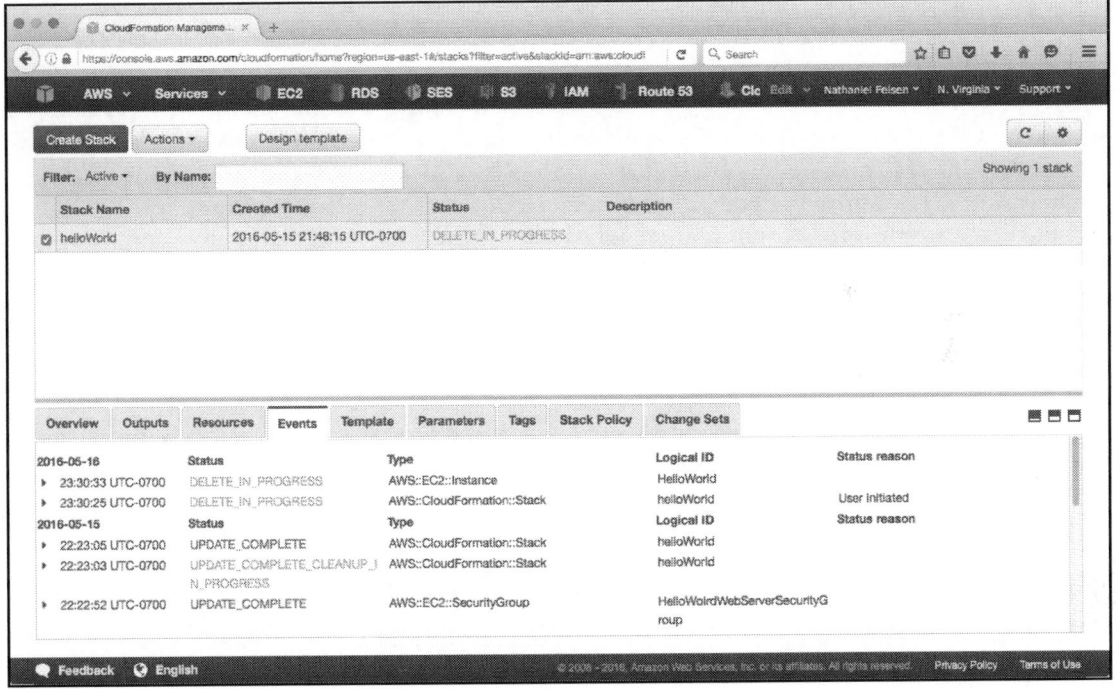

CloudFormation has a unique place in the AWS ecosystem. Most architectures as complex as they are can be described and managed through CloudFormation, allowing you to keep tight control over your AWS resources creation. While CloudFormation does a great job at managing the creation of resources, it doesn't always make things easy especially when you want to make simple changes on services such as EC2. Because CloudFormation doesn't keep track of the state of the resources once they are launched, the only reliable way to update an EC2 instance, for example, is to recreate a new instance and swap it with the existing instance once the new instance is ready. This creates somewhat of an immutable design (assuming that you don't run any extra commands once the instance is created). This may be an attractive architecture choice and in some cases, it may get you a long way, but you may wish to have the ability to have long-running instances where you can quickly and reliably make changes through a controlled pipeline like we did with CloudFormation. This is what configuration management systems excel at.

Adding a configuration management system

Configuration management systems are probably the most well-known components of a classic DevOps driven organization. Present in most companies including in the enterprise market, configuration management systems are quickly replacing home grown Shell, Python, and Perl scripts. There are many reasons why configuration management systems should be part of your environment. They offer domain-specific languages, which improves the readability of the code, and are tailored to the specific needs that organizations have when trying to configure systems. This means a lot of useful built-in features, and finally, the most common configuration management tools, have a big and active user community, which often means that you will be able to find existing code for the system you are trying to automatize.

Some of the most popular configuration management tools include Puppet, Chef, SaltStack, and Ansible. While all those options are fairly good, this book will focus on Ansible, the newest of those four tools mentioned. There are a number of key characteristics that make Ansible a very popular and easy to use solution. Unlike other configuration management systems, Ansible is built to work without a server, a daemon, or a database. You can simply keep your code in source control and download it on the host whenever you need to run it or use a push mechanism via SSH. The automation code you write is in YAML static files, which makes the learning curve a lot less steep than some of the other alternatives that use Ruby or specific DSL. In order to store our configuration files, we will instead rely on our file version control system, in our case GitHub.

AWS OpsWorks and its Chef integration
While Amazon hasn't really released a service dedicated to configuration management, it supports Chef within the OpsWorks service. Unlike the services we explored so far in the book, OpsWorks aims at being a *"complete application life cycle, including resource provisioning, configuration management, application deployment, software updates, monitoring, and access control."* If you are willing to trade some flexibility and control, OpsWorks might be able to handle what you need to run a simple web application. You can learn more about it at `http://amzn.to/108dTsn`.

Getting started with Ansible

We will first install Ansible on our computer; next, we will create an EC2 instance that will let us illustrate the basic usage of Ansible. After that, we will work on recreating the `Hello World Nodejs` application by creating and executing what Ansible calls a playbook. We will then look at how Ansible can run in pull mode, which offers a new approach to deploying changes. Finally, we will look at replacing the UserData block in our CloudFormation template with Ansible to combine the benefits of both CloudFormation and our configuration management system.

Ansible is fairly easy to use and well documented throughout the web. This book will cover enough to get you started and up-to-speed on simple configurations such as the one we need in our examples, but you might be interested in spending a bit more time learning about Ansible to be really efficient with it.

Installing Ansible on your computer

As mentioned before, Ansible is a really simple application <with very few dependencies. You can install Ansible on your computer using your operating system package manager or through `pip` (Ansible is written in Python):

```
$ sudo pip install ansible
```

This will install some binaries, libraries, and Ansible modules. Note that no daemon or database is installed as Ansible by default simply relies on static files and SSH to run.

At that point, we are ready to use Ansible.

Creating our Ansible playground

To illustrate the basic functionalities of Ansible, we are going to start by re-launching our `helloworld` application.

In the previous section, we saw how to create a stack using the web interface. As you would expect, it is also possible to launch a stack using the command line interface.

Go into your `EffectiveDevOpsTemplates` directory where you previously generated the `helloworld-cf-template-v2.template` file and run the following command:

```
$ aws cloudformation create-stack \
     --capabilities CAPABILITY_IAM \
     --stack-name ansible \
     --template-body file://helloworld-cf-template-v2.template  \
     --parameters ParameterKey=KeyPair,ParameterValue=EffectiveDevOpsAWS
{
    "StackId": "arn:aws:cloudformation:us-
east-1:511912822958:stack/ansible/6c52ef30-32b6-11e6-a0f4-500c524294d2"
}
```

Our instance will soon be ready. We can now bootstrap our environment by creating a workspace.

Creating our Ansible repository

Our first goal with Ansible is to be able to run commands on remote hosts. In order to do that efficiently, we can configure our local environment. Because we don't want to have to redo those steps time and time again and because ultimately we want to source-control everything, we will create a new Git repository. To do that, we will repeat the same steps as when we created our `EffectiveDevOpsTemplate` repository.

Once logged in to GitHub, create a new repository for the CloudFormation template:

1. In your browser, open `https://github.com/new`.
2. Call the new repository Ansible.
3. Check the checkbox **Initialize this repository with a README**
4. Finally, click the button **Create repository**.

5. Once your repository is created, clone it into your computer:

```
$ git clone https://github.com/<your_github_username>/ansible
```

6. Now that the repository is cloned, we will go into the repository and copy the template previously created in the new GitHub repository:

$ cd ansible

At its base, Ansible is a tool that can run commands remotely on the hosts in your inventory. The inventory can be managed manually, by creating an INI-like file where you list all your hosts and IPs, or dynamically if it can query an API. As you can imagine, Ansible is perfectly capable of taking advantage of the AWS API to fetch our inventory. To do so, we will download a Python script from the official Ansible Git repository and give the execution permissions:

```
$ curl -Lo ec2.py http://bit.ly/2v4SwE5
$ chmod +x ec2.py
```

Before we can start testing this Python script, we also need to provide a configuration for it.

Create a new file in the same directory and call it ec2.ini.

In it, we will put the following configuration:

```
[ec2]
regions = all
regions_exclude = us-gov-west-1,cn-north-1
destination_variable = public_dns_name
vpc_destination_variable = ip_address
route53 = False
cache_path = ~/.ansible/tmp
cache_max_age = 300
rds = False
```

Once this is done, you can finally validate that the inventory is in a working state by executing the ec2.py script:

$ ./ec2.py

This command should return a big nested JSON of the different resources found on your AWS account. Among those is the public IP address of the EC2 instance we created in the previous section.

The last step in our bootstrapping is to configure Ansible itself such that it knows how to get the inventory of our infrastructure, which user to use when it tries to SSH into our instances, how to become root, and so on.

We will create a new file in the same location and call it `ansible.cfg`.

Its content should be as follows:

```
[defaults]
inventory       = ./ec2.py
remote_user     = ec2-user
become          = True
become_method   = sudo
become_user     = root
nocows          = 1
```

At that point, we are ready to start running Ansible commands.

Ansible has a few commands and some simple concepts. We will first look at the `ansible` command and the concept of modules.

Executing modules

The `Ansible` command is the main command that drives the execution of the different modules on the remote hosts.

Modules are libraries that can be executed directly on remote hosts. Ansible comes with a number of modules as listed here `http://bit.ly/24rU0yk`. In addition to the standard modules, you can also create your own modules using Python. There are modules for most common use cases and technologies. The first module we will see is a simple module called ping that tries to connect to a host and returns pong if the host is usable.

Module documentation can also be accessed using the ansible-doc command, that is,

`$ ansible-doc ping.`

In the creating our Ansible playground section, we created a new EC2 instance using CloudFormation. So far we haven't looked up its IP address. Using `Ansible` and the `ping` command can discover that information. As mentioned before, we need to be in the `ansible` directory to run the `ansible` command. The command is:

```
$ ansible--private-key ~/.ssh/EffectiveDevOpsAWS.pem ec2 -m ping
54.175.86.38 | success >> {
    "changed": false,
    "ping": "pong"
}
```

As we can see, Ansible was able to find our EC2 instance querying the AWS EC2 API and the instance is ready to be used.

Configuring SSH

As Ansible relies heavily on SSH, it is worth spending a bit of time on configuring SSH via the `$HOME/.ssh/config` file. For instance, you use the following options to avoid having to specify `--private-key` and `-u` in the preceding example:

```
IdentityFile ~/.ssh/EffectiveDevOpsAWS.pem
User ec2-user
StrictHostKeyChecking no
PasswordAuthentication no
ForwardAgent yes
```

Once configured, you won't need to provide the `--private-key` option to Ansible.

Running arbitrary commands

The `Ansible` command can also be used to run arbitrary commands on remote servers. In the following example, we will run the `df` command only on all hosts matching `54.175.86.*` for their public Ip address (you will need to adapt this command to match you instance public IP as returned in the `ping` command of the previous example):

```
$ ansible --private-key ~/.ssh/EffectiveDevOpsAWS.pem '54.175.86.*' \
     -a 'df -h'
54.175.86.38 | success | rc=0 >>
Filesystem      Size  Used Avail Use% Mounted on
/dev/xvda1      7.8G  1.3G  6.5G  16% /
```

```
devtmpfs        490M    56K    490M    1% /dev
tmpfs           498M      0    498M    0% /dev/shm
```

Now that we have a basic understanding of how Ansible works, we can start combining calls to different Ansible modules to put in place our automation. This is called creating a playbook.

Ansible playbooks

Playbooks are the files containing Ansible's configuration, deployment, and orchestration language. By creating those files, you sequentially define the state of your systems from the OS configuration down to application deployment and monitoring. Ansible uses YAML, which is fairly easy to read. For that reason, similarly to what we did with CloudFormation, an easy way to get started with Ansible is to look at some examples inside the official Ansible GitHub repository: `https://github.com/ansible/ansible-examples`.

Creating a playbook

Ansible provides a number of best practices on their website at `http://bit.ly/1ZqdcLH`.

One emphasis in their documentation is on using roles.

"One thing you will definitely want to do though is using the "roles" organization feature, which is documented as part of the main playbooks page. See Playbook Roles and Include Statements. You absolutely should be using roles. Roles are great. Use roles. Roles! Did we say that enough? Roles are great."

Creating roles is a key component in making Ansible modular enough so that you can reuse your code across services and playbooks. To demonstrate a proper structure, we are going to create a role that our playbook will then call.

Creating roles to deploy and start our web application

We are going to use roles to recreate the `HellowWorld` stack we previously made using the UserDatablock of CloudFormation. If you recall, the UserData looked roughly like this:

```
yum install --enablerepo=epel -y nodejs
wget http://bit.ly/2vESNuc -O /home/ec2-user/helloworld.js
wget http://bit.ly/2vVvT18 -O /etc/init/helloworld.conf
start helloworld
```

You will notice three different types of operation in the preceding script. We are first preparing the system to run our application. To do that, in our example, we are simply installing node.js. Next, we copy the different resources needed to run the application, in our case, the JavaScript code and the upstart configuration. Finally, we start the service.

As always when programming, it is important to keep the code DRY. If deploying and starting our application is very unique to our HelloWorld project, installing node.js likely isn't. In order to make the installation of node.js a reusable piece of code, we are going to create two roles. One to install node.js and one to deploy and start the HelloWorld application.

By default, Ansible expects to see roles inside a roles directory at the root of the Ansible repository. The first thing we need to do is to create this directory and cd into it:

```
$ mkdir roles
$ cd roles
```

We can now create our roles.

Ansible has an ansible-galaxy command, which can be used to initialize the creation of a role. The first role we will look into is the role that will install node.js:

```
$ ansible-galaxy init nodejs
- nodejs was created successfully
```

> As briefly mentioned, Ansible like most other configuration management systems has a strong community support who share roles online via https ://galaxy.ansible.com/. In addition to using the ansible-galaxy command to create the skeleton for new roles, you can also use ansible-galaxy to import and install community supported roles.

This creates a directory nodejs and a number of sub directories that will let us structure the different sections of our role. We are going to go in that directory:

```
$ cd nodejs
```

The most important directory inside that nodejs directory is the one called tasks. When Ansible executes a playbook, it runs the code present in the file tasks/main.yml.

Open the file with your favorite text editor.

When you first open `main.yml`, you will see the following:

```
---
# tasks file for nodejs
```

The goal of the `nodejs` role is to install node.js and `npm`. To do so, we will proceed similarly to what we did in the UserData script and use yum to perform those tasks.

When writing a task in Ansible, you sequence a number of calls to various Ansible modules. The first module we are going to look at is a wrapper around the `yum` command. The documentation on it is available at `http://bit.ly/28joDLe`. This will let us install our packages. We are also going to introduce the concept of loops. Since we have two pages to install, we will want to call the yum module twice. We use the operator `with_items`.

After the initial three dashes and comments, we are going to call the yum module in order to install our packages:

```
---
# tasks file for nodejs

- name: Installing node and npm
  yum:
    name: "{{ item }}"
    enablerepo: epel
    state: installed
  with_items:
    - nodejs
    - npm
```

Whenever Ansible runs that playbook, it will look at packages installed on the system and if it doesn't find the `nodejs` or `npm` package it will install them.

This first role is complete. For the purpose of this book, we are keeping the role very simple, but you can imagine, in a more production-type environment, having a role that will install specific versions of node.js and npm, fetching the binaries directly from `https://nodejs.org/en/`, and maybe even installing specific dependencies.

Our next role will be dedicated to deploying and starting the `HelloWorld` application we previously built. We are going to go one directory up back into the roles directory and call `ansible-galaxy` one more time:

```
$ cd ..
$ ansible-galaxy init helloworld
- helloworld was created successfully
```

Like before, we will now go inside the newly created `helloworld` directory:

    $ cd helloworld

This time, we will explore some of the other directories present. One of the sub-directory that was created when we ran the `ansible-galaxy` command is the directory called files. Adding files to that directories will give us the ability to copy files on the remote hosts.

To do so, we are first going to download our two files in this directory:

    $ wget http://bit.ly/2vESNuc -O files/helloworld.js
    $ wget http://bit.ly/2vVvT18 -O files/helloworld.conf

We can now use task files to perform the copy on the remote system. Open the file `tasks/main.yml` and, after the initial three dashes and comment, add the following:

    - name: Copying the application file
      copy:
        src: helloworld.js
        dest: /home/ec2-user/
        owner: ec2-user
        group: ec2-user
        mode: 0644
      notify: restart helloworld

We are taking advantage of the copy module documented at http://bit.ly/1WBv08Eto copy our application file in the home directory of the `ec2-user`. On the last line of that call, we add at the end a notify option (note how the notify statement is aligned with the call to the copy module). Notify actions are triggers that can be added at the end of each block of tasks in a playbook. In this example, we are telling Ansible to call the restart hello world directive if the file `helloworld.js` changed (we will define how to do a restart of the `helloworld` application a bit later in a different file). One of the big differences between CloudFormation and Ansible is that Ansible is expected to run multiple times throughout the lifetime of your systems. A lot of the functionalities built into Ansible are optimized for long-running instances. As such, the notify option makes it easy to trigger events when a system changes state. Similarly, Ansible will know to stop the execution when an error in encountered preventing outages as far as possible.

Now that we have copied our application file, we can add our second file, the upstart script. After the previous call to copy the `helloword.js` file we are going to add the following call:

```
- name: Copying the upstart file
  copy:
    src: helloworld.conf
    dest: /etc/init/helloworld.conf
    owner: root
    group: root
    mode: 0644
```

The last task we need to perform is to start our service. We will use the service module for that. The module documentation is available at `http://bit.ly/22I7QNH`:

```
- name: Starting the HelloWorld node service
  service:
    name: helloworld
    state: started
```

Our task file is now completed. You should end up with something resembling the following: `http://bit.ly/2uPlJTk`. Having finished our task file, we are going to move on to the next file, which will give Ansible knowledge of how to restart `helloworld` as called out in the notify parameter of our task.

These types of interaction are defined in the handler section of the role. We are going to edit the file `handlers/main.yml`. Here too, we are going to use the service module. The following is a comment:

```
---
# handlers file for helloworld
```

Add the following:

```
- name: restart helloworld
  service:
    name: helloworld
    state: restarted
```

No surprises here; we are using the same module we previously used to manage the service. We need one more step in our role. In order for that role to work, the system needs to have node.js installed. Ansible supports the concept of role dependencies. We can explicitly tell that our `helloworld` role depends on the nodejs role we previously created such that, if the `helloworld` role is executed, it will first call the nodejs role and install the necessary requirements to run the app.

Open the file `meta/main.yml`.

This file has two sections. The first one under `galaxy_info` lets you fill in information on the role you are building. If you desire, you can ultimately publish your role on GitHub and link to it back into `ansible-galaxy` to share your creation with the Ansible community. The second section at the bottom of the file is called **dependencies** and it is the one we want to edit to make sure that nodejs is present on the system prior to starting our application.

Remove the square brackets (`[]`) and add an entry to call `nodejs` as follows:

```
dependencies:
  - nodejs
```

Your file should look like this `http://bit.ly/2uOUyry`.

This concludes the creation of the code for the role. From a documentation standpoint, it is good practice to also edit `README.md`.

Once done, we can move on to creating a playbook file that will reference our newly created role.

Creating the playbook file

At the top level of our Ansible repository (two directories up from the `helloworld` role), we are going to create a new file called `helloworld.yml`. In it, we are going to add the following:

```
---
- hosts: "{{ target | default('localhost') }}"
  become: yes
  roles:
    - helloworld
```

This basically tells Ansible to execute the role `HelloWorld` on to the hosts listed in the variable target or localhost if the target isn't defined. The become option will tell Ansible to execute the role with elevated privileges (in our case `sudo`). At this point, your Ansible repository should look like this: `http://bit.ly/2uPkROD`. We are ready to test our playbook.

Note that in practice, on a bigger scale, the roles sections could include more than a single role. If you deploy multiple applications or services to a target, you will often see playbook looking like this. We will see in later chapters more examples of this:

```
---
- hosts: webservers
  roles:
      - foo
      - bar
      - baz
```

Executing a playbook

Execution of playbooks is done using the dedicated `ansible-playbook` command. The command relies on the same Ansible configuration file as we used previously and therefore we want to run the command from the root of our Ansible repository.

The syntax of the command is:

```
ansible-playbook <playbook.yml> [options]
```

We will first run the following command (adapt the value of the private `key` option):

```
$ ansible-playbook helloworld.yml \
    --private-key ~/.ssh/EffectiveDevOpsAWS.pem \
    -e target=ec2 \
    --list-hosts
```

The option `-e` (or `--extra-vars`) allows us to pass extra options for execution. In our case, we are defining the variable target (which we declared in the hosts file of our playbook) to be equal to `ec2`. This first `ansible-playbook` command will tell Ansible to target all EC2 instances. The option `--list-hosts` will make Ansible return a list of hosts that match the hosts criteria. It won't actually run anything against those hosts.

The output of the command will be something like:

playbook: helloworld.yml

play #1 (ec2): host count=1

54.175.86.38

The list-hosts option is a good way to verify your inventory and, on more complex playbooks with more specific hosts values, to verify which hosts would run actual playbooks, allowing you to verify that they are targeting the hosts you expect.

We now know which hosts will be impacted if we were to use this value for the target. The next thing we want to check is what will happen if we run our playbook. The ansible-playbook command has an option -C (or --check) that will try to predict the change a given playbook will make:

```
$ ansible-playbook helloworld.yml \
    --private-key ~/.ssh/EffectiveDevOpsAWS.pem \
    -e target=54.175.86.38 \
    --check
```

PLAY [54.175.86.38]
****

GATHERING FACTS
****

ok: [54.175.86.38]

TASK: [HelloWorld | Installing node]
****

changed: [54.175.86.38]

TASK: [HelloWorld | Copying the application file]
****

changed: [54.175.86.38]

TASK: [HelloWorld | Copying the upstart file]
****

changed: [54.175.86.38]

TASK: [HelloWorld | Starting the HelloWorld node service]
****

failed: [54.175.86.38] => {"failed": true}

msg: no service or tool found for: helloworld

FATAL: all hosts have already failed -- aborting

```
PLAY RECAP
* * * * * * * * * * * * * * * * * * * * * * * * * * * * * * * * * * * * * * * * * * * * * * * * * * * * * * * * * * * * * * * * * *

to retry, use: --limit @/Users/nathanielfelsen/helloworld.retry

54.175.86.38 : ok=4 changed=3 unreachable=0 failed=1
```

Running that command will execute our playbook in dry-run mode. Through that mode, we can ensure that the proper tasks will be executed. Because we are in dry-run mode, some of the modules don't really find everything they need to simulate how they would run and that's why we see that error at the end of the service module.

Having verified the hosts and code, we can finally run `ansible-playbook` and execute our changes:

```
$ ansible-playbook helloworld.yml \
    --private-key ~/.ssh/EffectiveDevOpsAWS.pem \
    -e target=54.175.86.38
```

The output is very similar to the check command except that this time the execution finished properly. Our application is now installed and configured. We can verify that it is correctly running:

```
$ curl 54.175.86.38:3000
Hello World
```

We were able to reproduce what we previously did with CloudFormation using Ansible.

Now that we have tested our first playbook, we can commit our changes. We will do that in 2 commits to break down the initialization of the repository and the creation of the role:

From the root of your Ansible repository, run the following commands:

```
$ git add ansible.cfg ec2.ini ec2.py
$ git commit -m "Configuring ansible to work with EC2"
$ git add roles helloworld.yml
$ git commit -m "Adding role for nodejs and helloworld"
$ git push
```

Canary-testing changes

One of the great benefits of using Ansible to manage services is that you can easily make changes to your code and quickly push the change. In some situations where you have a big fleet of services managed by Ansible, you may wish to push out a change just to a single host to make sure things are how you expect them to be. This is often called canary testing.

With Ansible doing that is really easy. To illustrate that, we are going open the file `roles/helloworld/files/helloworld.js` and then simply change the response on line 11 from `Hello World` to `Hello New World`:

```
     // Send the response body as "Hello World"
     response.end('Hello New World\n');
}).listen(3000);
```

Save the file. Then run `ansible-playbook` again, first with the `--check` option:

```
$ ansible-playbook helloworld.yml \
       --private-key ~/.ssh/EffectiveDevOpsAWS.pem \
       -e target=54.175.86.38 \
       --check
```

This time Ansible detects only 2 changes. The first one overwrites the application file and the second one executes the notify statement, which means restarting the application. Seeing that it is what we expect, we can run our playbook without the `--check` options:

```
$ ansible-playbook helloworld.yml \
       --private-key ~/.ssh/EffectiveDevOpsAWS.pem \
       -e target=54.175.86.38
```

This produces the same output as in our previous command but this time the change is in effect:

```
$ curl 54.175.86.38:3000
Hello New World
```

Our change was very simple but if we had done that same change through updating our CloudFormation template, CloudFormation would have had to create a new EC2 instance to make it happen. Here we simply updated the code of the application and pushed it through Ansible on the target host.

We will now revert this change locally in Git:

```
$ git checkout roles/helloworld/files/helloworld.js
```

We will remove it from the EC2 instance as we illustrate a new concept, running Ansible asynchronously.

The sooner, the better
Being able to push changes in seconds instead of minutes may seem like a small win but it isn't. Speed matters, It is what sets apart successful start-ups and technologies. The ability to deploy new servers in minutes instead of days is a big factor in Cloud adoption. Similarly, the recent success of containers as we will see later in the book is also likely driven by the fact that it only takes seconds to run a new container while it still takes minutes to start a virtual server.

Running Ansible in pull mode

Having the ability to instantly make a change like we just did is a very valuable feature. We could easily and synchronously push the new code out and verify that the Ansible execution was successful. At a bigger scale, while being able to change anything across a fleet of servers remains as valuable as in our example, it is also sometimes a bit trickier. The risk of making changes that way is that you have to be very disciplined about not pushing changes just to a subset of hosts and forgetting other hosts that are also sharing the role that just got updated. Otherwise, very quickly, the increasing number of changes between the Ansible configuration repository and the running servers makes running Ansible a riskier operation. For those situations, it is usually preferable to use a pull mechanism that will automatically pull in the changes. Of course, you don't have to choose one or the other: it is easy to configure both push and pull mechanisms to deploy changes. Ansible provide a command called `ansible-pull`, which, as its name suggests, makes it easy to run Ansible in pull mode. The `ansible-pull` command works very much like `ansible-playbook` except that it starts by pulling your code from your GitHub repository.

Installing Git and Ansible on our EC2 instance

Since we need to be able to run Ansible and Git remotely, we first need to install those packages on our EC2 instance. For now, we will do that by manually installing those two packages. We will implement a reusable solution later in this chapter.

Since Ansible is a perfect tool to run remote commands and has a module to manage most common needs such as installing packages, instead of logging in on the host through ssh and running some commands, we are going to use Ansible to push out those changes. We will install Git from the Epel yum repository and Ansible using pip. This will require running commands as root, which you can do with the help of the become option. Adapting the IP address of your EC2 instance, run the following commands:

```
$ ansible '54.175.86.38' \
    --private-key ~/.ssh/EffectiveDevOpsAWS.pem \
    --become \
    -m yum -a 'name=git enablerepo=epel state=installed'
$ ansible '54.175.86.38' \
    --private-key ~/.ssh/EffectiveDevOpsAWS.pem \
    --become \
    -m pip -a 'name=ansible state=present'
```

With ansible-pull, our goal is for Ansible to apply the change locally; we can make a change to our Ansible repository to optimize this operation.

Configuring Ansible to run on localhost

Since ansible-pull relies on Git to clone locally the repository and execute it, we don't need the execution to happen over SSH. Go to the root directory of your Ansible repository to create a new file.

The file should be called localhost and contain the following:

```
[localhost]
localhost ansible_connection=local
```

Essentially, what we are doing is creating a static inventory and asking ansible to run commands in local (as opposed to using SSH) when the target host is localhost.

We can save the changes and commit the new file to GitHub:

```
$ git add localhost
$ git commit -m "Adding localhost inventory"
$ git push
```

Adding a cronjob to our EC2 instance

We are now going to create a crontab entry to periodically call `ansible-pull`. Here too, we will rely on Ansible create our cronjob remotely. Run the following command adapting the IP address:

```
$ ansible '54.175.86.38' \
      --private-key ~/.ssh/EffectiveDevOpsAWS.pem \
      -m cron -a 'name=ansible-pull minute="*/10"
job="/usr/local/bin/ansible-pull -U
https://github.com/<your_username>/ansible helloworld.yml -i localhost --
sleep 60"'
```

In the preceding command, we are telling Ansible to use the cron module targeting our `ec2` instance. We are providing a name that Ansible will use to track the cronjob over time, telling cron to run the job every 10 minutes, and finally the command to execute and its parameters. The parameters we are giving to `ansible-pull` are the GitHub URL of our branch, the inventory file we just added to our repository, and a sleep that will make the command start at a random time between 1 and 60 seconds after the call started.

This will help spread out the load on the network and prevent all node services from restarting at the same time if we have more than one server. After waiting for a bit, we can verify that our change is effective:

```
$ curl 54.175.86.38:3000
Hello World
```

After manually integrating Ansible to the EC2 instance we created using CloudFormation, we can now formalize the procedure.

Integrating Ansible with CloudFormation

While there are different strategies to integrate Ansible to CloudFormation, in our situation there is an obvious path. We are going to take advantage of the UserData field, and do the initialization of Ansible through the `ansible-pull` command.

We are going to start off the troposphere script we created earlier in this chapter. We will duplicate it and call the new script `ansiblebase-cf-template.py`.

Go to your `template` repository and duplicate the previous template as follow:

```
$ cd EffectiveDevOpsTemplates
$ cp helloworld-cf-template.py ansiblebase-cf-template.py
```

Then open the `ansiblebase-cf-template.py` script with your editor.

To keep the script readable, we will first define several variables.

Before the declaration of the application port, we will define an application name:

```
ApplicationName = "helloworld"
ApplicationPort = "3000"
```

We will also set a number of constants around the GitHub information. Replace the value of `GithubAccount` with your GitHub username or GitHub organization name:

```
ApplicationPort = "3000"

GithubAccount = "EffectiveDevOpsWithAWS"
GithubAnsibleURL = "https://github.com/{}/ansible".format(GithubAccount)
```

After the definition of `GithubAnsibleURL`, we are going to create one more variable that will contain the command line we want to execute to configure the host through Ansible. We will call `ansible-pull` and use the variables `GithubAnsibleURL` and `ApplicationName` that we just defined. This is what this looks like:

```
AnsiblePullCmd = \
    "/usr/local/bin/ansible-pull -U {} {}.yml -i localhost".format(
        GithubAnsibleURL,
        ApplicationName
    )
```

We are now going to update the `userdata` block. Instead of installing nodejs, downloading our application files and starting the service, we will change this block to install `git` and `ansible`, execute the command contained in the `AnsiblePullCmd` variable, and finally create a cronjob to re-execute that command every 10 minutes.

Delete the previous `ud` variable definition and replace it with the following:

```
ud = Base64(Join('\n', [
    "#!/bin/bash",
    "yum install --enablerepo=epel -y git",
    "pip install ansible",
    AnsiblePullCmd,
    "echo '*/10 * * * * {}' > /etc/cron.d/ansible-
pull".format(AnsiblePullCmd)
]))
```

We can now save our file and use it to create our JSON template and test it. Your new script should look like this: `http://bit.ly/2vZtvGD`

```
$ python ansiblebase-cf-template.py > ansiblebase.template
$ aws cloudformation update-stack \
      --stack-name HelloWorld \
      --template-body file://ansiblebase.template \
      --parameters  ParameterKey=KeyPair,ParameterValue=EffectiveDevOpsAWS
{
    "StackId": "arn:aws:cloudformation:us-
east-1:511912822958:stack/HelloWorld/ef2c3250-6428-11e7-a67b-50d501eed2b3"
}
```

We can now wait until the execution is complete:

```
$ aws cloudformation wait stack-create-complete \
      --stack-name HelloWorld
```

Now that the stack creation is complete, we can query CloudFormation to get the output of the stack and more particularly its public IP address:

```
$ aws cloudformation describe-stacks \
      --stack-name HelloWorld \
      --query 'Stacks[0].Outputs[0]'
{
    "Description": "Public IP of our instance.",
    "OutputKey": "InstancePublicIp",
    "OutputValue": "54.234.241.247"
}
```

And finally, we can verify that our server is up-and-running:

```
$ curl 54.234.241.247:3000
Hello World
```

We can now commit our newly created troposphere script to our `EffectiveDevOpsTemplates` repository:

```
$ git add ansiblebase-cf-template.py
$ git commit -m "Adding a Troposphere script to create a stack that relies
on Ansible to manage our application"
$ git push
```

We now have a complete solution to efficiently manage our infrastructure using code. We demonstrated it on a very simple example but, as you can imagine, everything is applicable to bigger infrastructure with a greater number of services.

This chapter is almost over, we can now delete our stack to free up the resources that we are currently consuming. In the earlier part the chapter, we did that using the web interface. As you can imagine, this can also be done easily using the command line interface as follow:

```
$ aws cloudformation delete-stack --stack-name HelloWorld
```

Monitoring

As you probably know by now, monitoring and measuring everything is an important aspect of a DevOps-driven organization. You will find on the internet a number of well-written blog posts and examples on how to efficiently monitor CloudFormation and Ansible. When working on monitoring CloudFormation, you will want to subscribe to an SNS topic your stack creation to receive all the events relating to your stack life cycle. It is important to look for CloudFormation stack creation failure. Ansible has a system of callback that will also give you a way to create some automation around the Ansible execution. Similarly to CloudFormation, getting notifications when Ansible fails to run to is important (it's even more important when Ansible is configured to run in pull mode) as your Ansible configuration won't reflect reality.

Summary

In this chapter, we learned how to efficiently manage infrastructure by using code. We first learned about CloudFormation, a service from AWS that lets you create templates for your different services to describe each AWS component used and it's configuration. In order to simplify the creation of those templates, we looked at a couple of options ranging from CloudFormation designer, a tool with a graphic user interface, to Troposphere, a Python library. After that, we looked at configuration management, one of the most well-known aspects of the DevOps philosophy. To illustrate this topic, we looked at Ansible, one of the most popular configuration management solutions. We first looked at the different ways to use `Ansible` commands and ran simple commands against our infrastructure. We then looked at how to create playbooks, which allowed us to orchestrate the different steps to deploy our web server. Finally, we looked at how Ansible can be used in pull mode, which usually makes more sense when managing sizable infrastructure.

We now have a good production environment ready to host any application. We have seen how to architect it and monitor our servers. In `Chapter 4`, *Adding Continuous Integration and Continuous Deployment*, we will continue to use CloudFormation and Ansible, but in the context of software delivery as we will learn how to put in place continuous integration testing and continuous deployment.

4
Adding Continuous Integration and Continuous Deployment

In the previous chapters, we focused on improving the creation and management of infrastructure, but a DevOps culture doesn't stop there. As you might recall from `Chapter 1`, *The Cloud and the DevOps Revolution*, some of the key characteristics of a DevOps culture also include having a very efficient process to test and deploy code. In 2009, at the Velocity conference, John Allspaw and Paul Hammond did a very inspirational talk on how Flickr was doing over 10 deployments a day (`http://bit.ly/292ASlW`). The presentation is often mentioned as a pivotal moment that contributed to the creation of the DevOps movement. In their presentation, John and Paul talk about the developers versus operations conflicts but also outline a number of best practices that allowed Flickr to deploy new code to production multiple times a day. With innovations like the Cloud, creating new startups has never been so easy. Because of that, the biggest problem companies are now facing is being able to stand apart from their competitors. Having the ability to iterate faster than most competitors can become a detrimental step for a company's success. Effective DevOps organization uses a number of tools and strategies to increase the velocity at which engineering organizations release new code to production. This is what we will focus on in this chapter.

We will first look at creating a **Continuous Integration (CI) pipeline**. A CI pipeline will allow us to automatically and continuously run our tests against proposed code changes. This will free up some of the developers and QAs time who won't have to do as much manual testing and make the integration work a lot easier. To implement our pipeline, we will use GitHub and one of the most widely used integration tools, Jenkins.

We will then look at creating a **Continuous Deployment (CD) pipeline**. Once the code has gone through the CI pipeline, we will use this continuous deployment pipeline to automatically deploy the new code. We will rely on two AWS services, AWS CodeDeploy, and AWS CodePipeline to implement this pipeline. The first service, CodeDeploy, will let us define how the new code needs to be deployed on our EC2 instances while AWS CodePipeline will let us orchestrate the full life cycle of our application.

In order to deploy our code to production, we will add an extra step that an operator can trigger with the push of a button to deploy the latest build present in staging to production. This ability to deploy code to production on-demand is called **Continuous Delivery**. Its main advantage is that it provides the ability for the deployment operator to validate a build in a staging environment before it gets deployed to production. At the end of the chapter, we will see a couple of techniques and strategies that effective engineering organizations use to convert their continuous delivery pipelines into continuous deployment pipelines so that the entire process of deploying code up to production can happen without any human intervention:

- Building a continuous integration pipeline
- Building a continuous deployment pipeline

Building a continuous integration pipeline

Originally, working in a CI environment meant that developers had to commit their code in a common branch as frequently as possible (as opposed to working off a separate branch or not committing changes for weeks). This allowed for better visibility of the ongoing work and encouraged communication to avoid integration problems commonly known as **Integration Hell**. As the different tooling around source control and build and release management matured, so did the vision of how code integration should look in an ideal world.

Nowadays, most effective engineering organizations will continue down the path of integrating early and often, but with a more modern development process where developers are required to edit the code and, at the same time, add or edit the different relevant tests to validate the change, this change drastically increases the overall productivity as it is now easier to find new bugs as the amount of code change between merges is fairly small.

To adopt such a workflow, using Git for example, you can proceed as such:

1. When as a developer, you want to make changes, you first start by creating a new Git branch branching off of the HEAD of the master branch.

2. Edit the code and, at the same time, add or edit the different relevant tests to validate the change.

3. Test the code locally.

4. When the code is ready, rebase the branch to integrate new eventual changes from other developers. If needed, resolve conflicts and test the code again.

5. If everything went well, the next step consists of creating a `pull request`. In this process, you tell other developers that your code is ready to be reviewed.

6. Once the pull request is created, an automated testing system such as the one we will build in this chapter will pick up the change and run the entire test suit available to make sure nothing is failing.

7. In addition, other interested parties will review the code and the different tests that were added into the branch. If they are satisfied with the proposed change, they will approve it, giving the developers the green light to merge their change.

8. In the last step, the developers will merge their pull requests, which will translate into merging their new code and tests into the master branch. Other developers will now integrate this change when they rebase or create new branches.

In the following section, we will create a continuous integration server using Jenkins running on top of an EC2 instance and GitHub.

 As projects get bigger, so does the number of tests and the time it takes to run them. While certain advanced build systems such as **Bazel** (`bazel.io`) have the ability to run only the tests relevant to a particular change, it is usually easier to start simple and create a CI system that runs all the tests available every time a new pull request is proposed. Having an external test infrastructure with the elasticity of AWS becomes a huge time saver for the developers who don't have to wait minutes or even sometimes hours to see all the tests being executed. This book focuses on web application development, but you may face a more challenging environment where you need to build software for a specific hardware and operating system. Having a dedicated CI system will allow you to run your tests on the hardware and software you are ultimately targeting.

Creating a Jenkins server using Ansible and CloudFormation

As mentioned before, we are going to use Jenkins as our central system to run our continuous integration pipeline. With over 10 years of development, Jenkins has been the leading open source solution to practice continuous integration for a long time. Famous for its rich plugin ecosystem, Jenkins has recently gone through a major new release (Jenkins 2.0), which has put the spotlight on a number of very DevOps centric features including the ability to create natively delivery pipelines that can be checked in and version-controlled and better integration with source control system such as GitHub, which we are using in this book.

We are going to continue using Ansible and CloudFormation the same way we did in `Chapter 3`, *Treating Your Infrastructure As Code*, to manage our Jenkins server.

Creating the Ansible playbook for Jenkins

We are going to start by navigating to our `ansible roles` directory:

```
$ cd ansible/roles
```

We should have in this directory the `helloworld` and `nodejs` directories containing the configurations we created previously in `Chapter 3`, *Treating Your Infrastructure As Code*. We are now going to create our Jenkins role with the `ansible-galaxy` command:

```
$ ansible-galaxy init jenkins
```

We are now going to edit the task definition for this new role by editing the file `jenkins/tasks/main.yml`.

Open up the file with your favorite text editor.

The goal of our task is to install and start Jenkins. In order to do so, since we are on a Redhat-based operating system, we are going to install an RPM package through yum. Jenkins maintain a `yum` repository so the first step will consist of importing the GPG key of that repository. Ansible has a module to manage these kinds of keys.

Below the initial comment of the tasks file, add the following:

```
- name: Import Jenkins GPG key
  rpm_key:
    state: present
    key: http://pkg.jenkins-ci.org/redhat/jenkins-ci.org.key
```

The next step will be to import the `yum` repository to our yum repository configuration (basically an entry in `/etc/yum.repos.d`):

```
- name: Add Jenkins repository
  yum_repository:
    name: jenkins
    description: jenkins repository
    baseurl: http://pkg.jenkins.io/redhat
    enabled: no
    gpgcheck: yes
```

By default, we are disabling the repository. This is a common practice put in place to prevent third-party repositories such as this one from upgrading any important system library that we would rather see being managed by the Amazon `yum` repository.

We have reached the point where we can now use yum to install Jenkins. We will do that with the following call:

```
- name: Install Jenkins
  yum:
    name: jenkins
    enablerepo: jenkins
    state: present
```

Since the `jenkins` repository is disabled by default, we are enabling it through the `enablerepo flag` for the execution of this `yum` command.

At this point, Jenkins will be installed. As a best practice, we will specify which version of Jenkins we want to install (in our case the current version is 2.45). We also want to start the service and have it enabled at the `chkconfig` level so that if the EC2 instance where `jenkins` is installed restarts, Jenkins will start automatically. We can do that using the service module. Add the following after the previous call:

```
- name: Start Jenkins
  service:
    name: jenkins-2.45
    enabled: yes
    state: started
```

For a simple Jenkins role, that's all we need.

 As you gain more experience with Jenkins and Ansible, explore the web or the Ansible galaxy, you will find more advanced roles allowing you to configure Jenkins in more detail, generate jobs, and select the plugins to install. It is an important step to go through that this book won't cover, but ideally, you want your entire system to be described by code. In addition, in this chapter, we are using Jenkins over HTTP. It is strongly encouraged to use it over an encrypted protocol like HTTPS or, as we will see in Chapter 8, *Hardening the Security of Your AWS Environment,* in a private subnet with a VPN connection.

We built a role that will allow us to install `jenkins`. We will want to create a new EC2 instance and install Jenkins on it with the end goal of testing our `nodejs` code on the instance. In order to be able to do that, the Jenkins host will need to also have node and npm installed.

We have two options. We can either add our `nodejs` role as a dependency of the Jenkins role like we did for the `helloworld` role or list the `nodejs` role in the list of roles for our playbook. Since ultimately Jenkins doesn't really require node to run, we will opt for the second approach. In the root directory of our `ansible` repository, create the playbook file. The filename is `jenkins.yml` and it should look like this:

```
---
- hosts: "{{ target | default('localhost') }}"
  become: yes
  roles:
    - jenkins
    - nodejs
```

Our role is now complete, so we can commit our new role and push it to GitHub.

Following the best practices described previously, we will start by creating a new branch:

```
$ git checkout -b jenkins
```

Add our files:

```
$ git add jenkins.yml roles/jenkins
```

Commit and finally push the changes:

```
$ git commit -m "Adding a Jenkins playbook and role"
$ git push
```

From there, submit a pull request inside GitHub and merge the branch back to master, and get back to the master branch:

```
$ git checkout master
```

In a real life situation, you likely also want to periodically run:

```
$ git pull
```

to retrieve other developers changes.

We can now create our CloudFormation template in order to call that role.

Creating the CloudFormation template

In order to keep our code fairly similar to what we saw in Chapter 3, *Treating Your Infrastructure As Code*, we are going to start off the `helloworld` troposphere code that we created in Chapter 3, *Treating Your Infrastructure As Code*. We are first going to duplicate the Python script. Go to your EffectiveDevOpsTemplates directory where you have your troposphere templates and then clone the `ansiblebase-cf-template.py`file:

```
$ cp ansiblebase-cf-template.py jenkins-cf-template.py
```

The Jenkins host will need to interact with AWS. For that, we will create an instance profile (more on that later) taking advantage of another library developed by the same authors as Troposphere. We will install it as follow:

```
$ pip install awacs
```

We are now going to edit `jenkins-cf-template.py`.

The first two changes we will do are the application name and port. Jenkins runs by default on `TCP/8080`:

```
ApplicationName = "jenkins"
ApplicationPort = "8080"
```

We also want to add an instance IAM profile to better control how our EC2 instance can interact with AWS services such as EC2. We previously used the IAM service in Chapter 2, *Deploying Your First Web Application*, when we created our user. You may recall that in addition to creating the user, we also assigned it the administrator policy which gives the user full access to all AWS services. On top of that, we generated an access key and secret access key which we are currently using to authenticate ourself as that administrator user and interact with services such as CloudFormation and EC2.

When you are using EC2 instances, the **instance profile** feature provided lets you specify an IAM role to your instance. In other words, we can assign IAM permissions directly to EC2 instances without having to use access keys and secret access keys.

Having an instance profile will be very useful in the later part of this chapter when we work on the continuous integration pipeline and integrate our Jenkins instance with AWS managed services. To do so, we will first import some extra libraries. Below the first `from troposphere import()` section, add the following:

```
from troposphere.iam import (
    InstanceProfile,
    PolicyType as IAMPolicy,
    Role,
)

from awacs.aws import (
    Action,
    Allow,
    Policy,
    Principal,
    Statement,
)

from awacs.sts import AssumeRole
```

Then, in between the instantiation of the variables `ud` and the creation of the instance, we are going to create and add our role resource to the template as such:

```
t.add_resource(Role(
    "Role",
    AssumeRolePolicyDocument=Policy(
        Statement=[
            Statement(
                Effect=Allow,
                Action=[AssumeRole],
                Principal=Principal("Service", ["ec2.amazonaws.com"])
            )
        ]
    )
))
```

Proceeding similarly to what we just did for the role, we can now create our instance profile and reference the role. Below the creation of our role, add the following:

```
t.add_resource(InstanceProfile(
    "InstanceProfile",
    Path="/",
```

```
    Roles=[Ref("Role")]
))
```

Finally, we can reference our new instance profile by updating the declaration of our instance. We will add a period after `UserData=ud` and on the line after initializing the `IamInstanceProfile` as such:

```
t.add_resource(ec2.Instance(
    "instance",
    ImageId="ami-a4c7edb2",
    InstanceType="t2.micro",
    SecurityGroups=[Ref("SecurityGroup")],
    KeyName=Ref("KeyPair"),
    UserData=ud,
    IamInstanceProfile=Ref("InstanceProfile"),
))
```

The file should now look like this `http://bit.ly/2uDvyRi`. You can save the changes, commit to GitHub the new script and generate the CloudFormation template:

```
$ git add jenkins-cf-template.py
$ git commit -m "Adding troposphere script to generate a Jenkins instance"
$ git push
$ python jenkins-cf-template.py > jenkins-cf.template
```

Launching the stack and configuring Jenkins

In order to create our EC2 instance with `Jenkins` running on it, we will proceed like in `Chapter 3`, *Treating Your Infrastructure As Code*, using either the web interface or the command-line interface as such:

```
$ aws cloudformation create-stack \
    --capabilities CAPABILITY_IAM \
    --stack-name jenkins \
    --template-body file://jenkins-cf.template \
    --parameters  ParameterKey=KeyPair,ParameterValue=EffectiveDevOpsAWS
```

As before, we can then wait until the execution is complete:

```
$ aws cloudformation wait stack-create-complete \
    --stack-name jenkins
```

And extract the host public IP:

```
$ aws cloudformation describe-stacks \
    --stack-name jenkins \
    --query 'Stacks[0].Outputs[0]'
  {
      "Description": "Public IP of our instance.",
      "OutputKey": "InstancePublicIp",
      "OutputValue": "54.175.97.69"
  }
```

Because we kept the **ansible Jenkins** role fairly simple, in order to complete the installation of Jenkins, we need to complete its configuration:

1. Open the port `8080` of the instance public IP in your browser (that is, in my case `http://54.175.97.69:8080`).

2. Using the following `ssh` command (adapt the IP address) and its ability to run commands remotely, we can extract the admin password, and provide it to that first configuration screen with the following command:

```
$ ssh -i ~/.ssh/EffectiveDevOpsAWS.pem ec2-user@54.175.97.69 \
    sudo cat /var/lib/jenkins/secrets/initialAdminPassword
```

3. On the next screen, choose to install the **suggested plugins**.
4. Create your first admin user on the next screen and click on **Save and Finish**.
5. Finally, click on **Start using Jenkins**.

Our Jenkins instance is now ready to be used.

Preparing our CI environment

We are going to use our Jenkins instance in conjunction with GitHub to recreate our `helloworld` application using a proper CI pipeline. To get there, we are going to go through a number of preliminary steps starting with the creation of a new GitHub repository.

Creating a new GitHub repository

We are now going to create a new repository dedicated to hosting our `helloworld` node application. We will create the repository using the same steps as in `Chapter 3`, *Treating Your Infrastructure As Code*:

1. Open `https://github.com/new` in your browser.
2. Call your repository `helloworld`.
3. Check the checkbox **Initialize this repository with a README**.
4. Click on **Create Repository**.

This will create the repository, a master branch, and a `README.md` file.

A proper CI pipeline works silently in the background. In order to achieve that, when the code is hosted on GitHub, Jenkins needs to get notifications from GitHub that the code has changed so that it can trigger a build automatically. This is something we can easily implement thanks to a plugin called `github-organization-plugin`. The plugin is part of the plugins that got installed when we selected to install the suggested plugins in Jenkins. In order to use it, we first need to create a personal access token in GitHub.

Creating a GitHub personal access token

Creating a personal access token will give the plugins the ability to access the code pushed to GitHub and create the necessary hooks to get notifications when new commits and pull requests occur. In order to create the token, use the following steps:

1. Open `https://github.com/settings/tokens` in your browser.
2. Click on **Generate new token**.
3. Give it a descriptive name like `Effective DevOps with AWS Jenkins`.
4. Select the scopes **repo, admin:repo_hook** and **admin:org_hook**.
5. Click on **Generate token**.
6. This brings you back to the main token page. Save the token generated. We will need it in a couple of steps.

Adding the access token to the credentials in Jenkins

We can now add the token to Jenkins as follows:

1. Open Jenkins, in my case `http://54.175.97.69:8080`.
2. Click on **credentials** in the left-hand side menu, then click on **System** just below, and then click on **Global credentials**.
3. On the next screen click on **Add credentials**.
4. The credentials we are going to create are of the type **Username with password**.
5. The scope should be **Global**.
6. Use your **GitHub username** (or your GitHub organization) as a username.
7. Use the **token generated** in the last **section** as your password.
8. The **Id** can be something like GitHub.
9. Optionally, give a **Description** and click **OK**.

The last step of our initialization process consists of creating the Jenkins job.

Creating the Jenkins job to automatically run the builds

As mentioned before, Jenkins has a plugin to help with the GitHub integration. We can easily take advantage of it by creating a GitHub organization job. To do so go through the following steps:

1. Open in your browser your Jenkins home page and click on **create new jobs**.
2. Below **Enter an Item name**, give it your GitHub username or (organization name), click on **Github Organization**, and then **OK**.
3. This will bring you to a new page where we will be able to configure the project where we will configure the Projects section:
   1. In the **credentials** drop-down menu, select your newly created credential.
   2. **Validate** that the owner is your username or organization name. This will be used by Jenkins to scan your all your repositories.
   3. Since we already know we are only interested only in the one called helloworld, Click on the **Add** button a the bottom of the **Behaviors** section and select the first option which should be **Filter by Name (with regular expression)**.

4. In the newly populated field, **Regular expression**, replace .* with
   `helloworld`.

4. Click on **Save**.

The job will be created and will scan the project to find any branch. It will find the master branch with the README file in it, but because we don't have any code yet we will not do anything. In the following section, we are going to remediate to that lack of code and implement our `helloworld` application.

Implementing the helloworld application using our CI environment

We will once again look at our simple `helloworld` web application that we created in Chapter 2, *Deploying Your First Web Application*. The goal here is more to illustrate the use of our CI pipeline than building a complex web application.

Initializing the project

We are going to use our computer as a development environment. Therefore, we need to have `nodejs` and `npm` installed on our computer. If you haven't done it yet, please refer to the instructions in Chapter 2, *Deploying Your First Web Application*.

Our first step will be to clone the `helloworld` GitHub repository that we created in the preceding section:

```
$ git clone https://github.com/<your_github_account>/helloworld.git
$ cd helloworld
```

We can now create a new branch:

```
$ git checkout -b initial-branch
```

And create an empty file called `helloworld.js`:

```
$ touch helloworld.js
```

One of the best ways to write tests for these types of projects is to have a **Test Driven Development (TDD)** approach. In that process, developers first create the tests, then run them to make sure they are failing, write the code, and test again. At that point, the tests should pass. We can create a pull request and once reviewed and approved, merge it.

Creating a functional test using mocha

In order to illustrate the process of writing tests for our TDD approach, we will use a tool called **Mocha** (https://mochajs.org/), a very common and easy to use JavaScript test framework and create a test.

We will install it locally on our system using the following **npm**, the node.js package manager.command:

We will first initialize npm with the following command:

```
$ npm init --yes
```

This will create a new file called package.json. Next, we will install mocha and add it to our list of develpment dependencies as follow:

```
$ npm install mocha@2.5.3 --save-dev
```

This will create a directory called node_modules and install mocha in it.

In addition to mocha, we will use a headless browser testing module to render our helloworld application. The one we will use is called **Zombie**. We can install it with the same command as such:

```
$ npm install zombie@3.0.15 --save-dev
```

In order to separate the tests from the rest of the project, we are now going to create a directory called test in the root location of our helloworld project. By default, mocha will look for tests in that directory:

```
$ mkdir test
```

The last boiling plate will be to configure npm to use mocha to run our tests. With your editor, open the **package.json** file and replace the test scripts with the following command:

```
"scripts": {
  "test": "node_modules/mocha/bin/mocha"
},
```

Inside the test directory, create and edit the file helloworld_test.js.

The first step consists of loading two modules that we are going to use and need in our test. The first one is zombie, our headline browser and the second one is the assert module, which the standard module uses to create unit testing in node.js applications:

```
var Browser = require('zombie')
var assert = require('assert')
```

Next, we need to load our application. This is done by calling the same require() function, but this time we will ask it to load the helloworld.js file that we will soon implement (for now it's an empty file):

```
var app = require('../helloworld')
```

We can now start creating the test. Mocha basic syntax tries to mimic what specification document could require. Below the three required statements, add the following:

```
describe('main page', function() {
  it('should say hello world')
})
```

We now need to add hooks into that test to interact with our web application.

The first step will be to point the test to our application endpoint. As you might remember from the previous chapters, the application is running on http://localhost:3000. We will use the hook called before() to set up a precondition. Above the call to it(), add the following to point our headless browser to the proper server:

```
describe('main page', function() {
  before(function() {
    this.browser = new Browser({ site: 'http://localhost:3000' })
  })

  it('should say hello world')
})
```

At that point, our headless browser will connect to our application, but it won't request any page. Let's add that in another `before()` hook as follows:

```
describe('main page', function() {
  before(function() {
    this.browser = new Browser({ site: 'http://localhost:3000' })
  })

  before(function(done) {
    this.browser.visit('/', done)
  })

  it('should say hello world')
})
```

At that point, the homepage is loaded, we now need to implement the code in the `it()` function to validate our assertion. We will edit the line with the `it()` call to add a callback function as follows:

```
describe('main page', function() {
  before(function() {
    this.browser = new Browser({ site: 'http://localhost:3000' })
  })

  before(function(done) {
    this.browser.visit('/', done)
  })

  it('should say hello world', function() {
    assert.ok(this.browser.success)
    assert.equal(this.browser.text(), "Hello World")
  })
})
```

Our test is ready. If everything went well, your code should look like this `http://bit.ly/2uYNYP6`.

We can test it in our Terminal, by simply calling the mocha command as follows:

```
$ npm test

./node_modules/mocha/bin/mocha
  main page
    1) "before all" hook
  0 passing (48ms)
  1 failing
  1) main page "before all" hook:
```

```
TypeError: connect ECONNREFUSED 127.0.0.1:3000
```

Our test is failing. It can't connect to the web application. This is of course excepted since we haven't implemented the application code yet.

Developing the remaining of the application

At this point, we are ready to develop our application. Since we already went through creating that exact code in Chapter 2, *Deploying Your First Web Application*, we are simply going to copy it again or download it directly as such:

```
$ curl -L http://bit.ly/2vESNuc > helloworld.js
```

We can now test the code again using the npm command:

```
$ npm test
Server running
  main page
      should say hello world
  1 passing (78ms)
```

Our test is now passing.

We are almost there. We satisfied one of our first goal, which was to have test coverage for our code. Of course, a real application with more complexity will have many more tests but what we want to focus on at this point is automation.

We validated how to test our code manually, we now want Jenkins to do that for us.

Creating the CI pipeline in Jenkins

As we saw earlier, Jenkins works by creating and executing jobs. Historically, one way to create the pipeline would be to open Jenkins in our browser, navigate to the job we previously created, and edit it to outline the different steps involved in testing our code. The problem with that solution is that there isn't a good review process involved and it's hard to track every change done over time. In addition, it's very hard for developers to make changes in a project that involves adding new build steps as the code of the project and the job building the project aren't synced together. Jenkins 2 made the concept of describing the build process into a local file a standard feature. We are going to use it. Here is how.

We are going to create and edit a new file in the project called Jenkinsfile (Capital J, no file extension). The file will be written in groovy (http://www.groovy-lang.org).

On the first line of the file, we are going to put the following:

```
#!groovy
```

This is a best practice mostly useful to the different IDEs and GitHub as they will understand the nature of the file. The first step of our script will consist of asking Jenkins to assign the job to a node as such:

```
node { }
```

Our Jenkins installation is fairly simple. We only have one server and therefore one node. If we had more nodes, we could add parameters to the call to target a node with a specific architecture or even drive the parallel execution.

Our CI testing can be logically broken up into a few steps:

1. Get the code from GitHub.
2. Install the different decencies by calling `npm install`.
3. Run our run with the command `mocha`.
4. Clean up.

Those steps have an equivalent concept in Jenkins called **stages**. We are going to add them inside the node routing. Here is what the first stage will look like:

```
node {
    stage 'Checkout'
        checkout scm
}
```

This will tell Jenkins to get the code from source control. We previously stated when we created the job that it was a GitHub organization job, so Jenkins will know how to interpret that correctly.

In our second stage, we need to call `npm install`. Groovy doesn't understand natively language specific feature such as calling `npm`. In order to implement that, we will use the `sh` command, which will allow us to spawn a shell and run a command. Here is what our second stage looks like:

```
    stage 'Checkout'
        checkout scm

    stage 'Setup'
        sh 'npm install'
```

In our next stage, we are going to run mocha. Below the `Setup` stage add the following:

```
stage 'Mocha test'
      sh './node_modules/mocha/bin/mocha'
```

Finally, we can proceed to clean up the repository with the following stage:

```
stage 'Cleanup'
      echo 'prune and cleanup'
      sh 'npm prune'
      sh 'rm node_modules -rf'
```

The Jenkins file is now ready, it should look like this: `http://bit.ly/2uDzkKm`.

We can now commit our code and test it:

```
$ git add Jenkinsfile helloworld.js package.json test
$ git commit -m "Helloworld application"
$ git push
```

This will create a remote branch called initial-branch. As the branch gets created, Jenkins will get a notification from GitHub about the change and will run the CI pipeline. In a matter of seconds, our test will run on Jenkins, which in turn will send the result back to GitHub. We observe it that way:

1. Open GitHub in your browser and navigate to the `helloworld` project you created.
2. Click on **Branch** and select the **initial-branch.**
3. From that screen, click on **New pull request**, provide a title and a good description of the change you are doing and, if possible, @mention other developers to get a thorough review of the change you are proposing.
4. Click on **Create pull request** and follow the steps to create a pull request. Once the pull request is created, you will be able to see how GitHub highlights that the pull requests passed all checks:

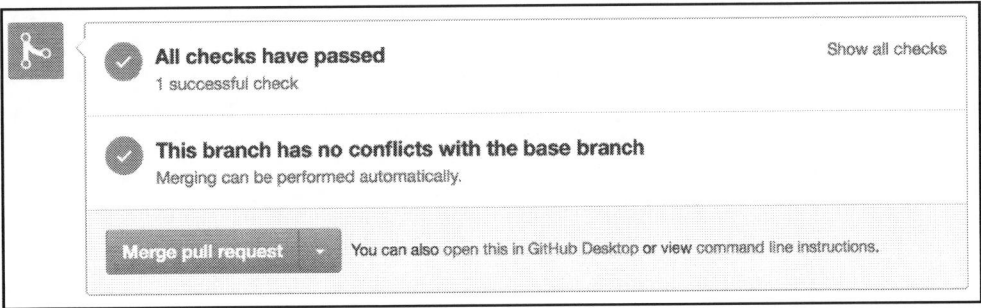

5. Optionally, you can click on the **detail** button, which will bring us back to the Jenkins job, where you can observe in more details the execution of the job and its pipeline:

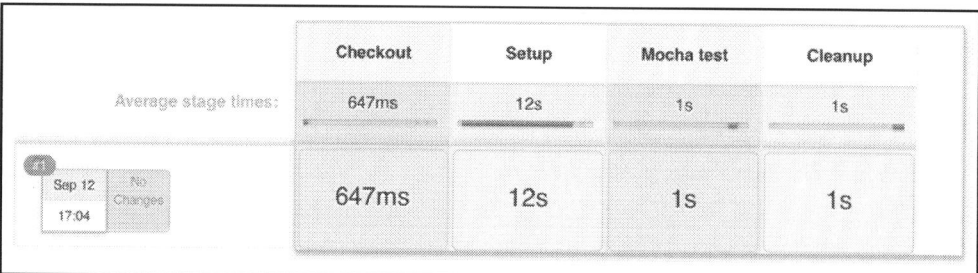

6. At that point, if you @mentioned other developers, they should get a notification and should look at the content of the pull request. Once reviewed and approved, the pull request can be merged. From that point on, when developers pull the master branch or rebase their branch, they will see your code.

Depending on the size of the team working off a repository, it is common to have to rebase a branch. The two most important times to do that are before creating the pull request (step 2) and before merging it (step 6).

Productionizing the CI pipeline

We put in place a basic, yet functional CI pipeline. While it is a good starting point, you will typically want to perfect certain details of this system.

As previously mentioned, our Ansible recipe for Jenkins can be improved to include the configuration of the jobs such as the `helloworld` job we manually created.

We only created a single functional test to illustrate using a test driven development approach and integrating a testing step in our pipeline. The success of a continuous integration pipeline depends highly on the quality and quantity of the tests produced. Tests will typically be broken up into functional and non-functional tests. In order to best take advantage of your pipeline, you will want to catch possible errors as early as possible. This means focusing on the functional tests and in particular the **unit tests,** which are used to validate small units of code such as a method in a class.

After this, you can focus on the **integration testing,** which covers a bit more ground and usually interacts with data stores and other functions in the code. Finally, you will want to add some **acceptance testing** to verify that all the requirements for your stories are complete:

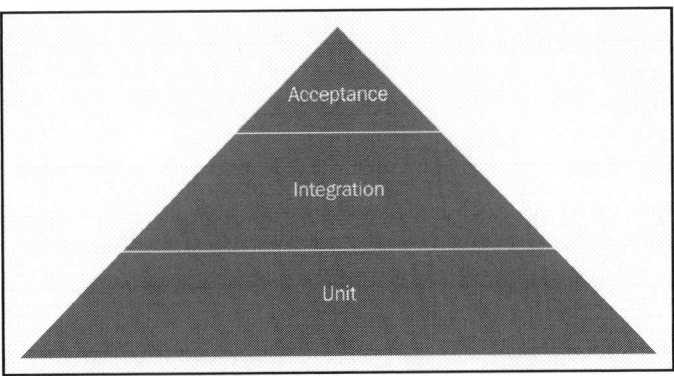

In terms of non-functional testing, you will usually want to look at **performance, security, usability,** and **compatibility** testing.

Finally, you can complement your own tests with code analyzer tools to get a sense of the code coverage (how many lines of code are executed by your automated tests).

As always with DevOps, it is important to collect metrics. In a CI pipeline, you will typically want to monitor the number of builds that go through the CI pipeline and the quality of the pull requests.

Like any other system, you will need to spend a bit of time to set up backups and monitoring. You may decide to back up the Jenkins home directory if you haven't moved to a model where your jobs and the Jenkins configuration are managed by your configuration management system (Ansible). In terms of metrics, keeping an eye on the system performance, its availability, and health are paramount. A build pipeline breakage should be considered a critical issue as it impacts all the developers and operator's productivity.

Finally, it is expected to have to scale up your CI infrastructure over time. As code and tests get added, it will take longer and longer to run the tests. You can decide to add more Jenkins slaves, which will allow you to run tests in parallel or/and use bigger instances. In the current format, Jenkins will run the `helloworld` pipeline every time a change is pushed to a branch. You may also decide to only run the pipeline once the pull requests are created.

In this initial section of the chapter, we adopted a new workflow where developers commit code and tests to individual branches and send frequent pull requests to share the proposed changes with the rest of the engineering organization. In addition, we made sure that the new code is fully tested by creating a continuous integration pipeline. To do so, we created a Jenkins server and hooked it to GitHub. Thanks to that system, all the tests committed with the project get automatically executed and the results are sent back to GitHub. We are now in an ideal situation to take our workflow to the next level and build some automation around deployment.

Are the QA teams gone with DevOps?
Yes, and No. In an effective DevOps organization, non technical QA jobs are usually gone. If everything is fully automated and the developers wrote enough tests to cover all aspects of the code, the organization doesn't need to task anyone to write and execute test plans. Instead of that, DevOps focused organizations will have engineers sometimes called QA engineers focusing on quality but with automation in mind. This means working on tooling and processes to improve the ability to automatically test code.

Building a continuous deployment pipeline

By creating a CI pipeline, we made a first step towards being an effective **engineering** organization. Thanks to the workflow of working in individual branches and merging them back to the master branch after going through automated testing and human reviews, we can assume that the code present in the master branch is of high quality and safe to deploy. Knowing that we will focus on the next challenge, releasing code automatically as new code gets merged into the master branch.

By continuously releasing new code, you drastically accelerate the feedback loop process that DevOps provides. Releasing new code to production at high-velocity lets you collect real customer metrics, which often leads to exposing new and often unexpected issues. For many companies, deploying new code to production is a challenge. It is easy to get anxious about that exercise if releasing code means thousands of new commits all going out to production at the same time in a process that is occurring only a few times a year. Those companies are often the ones who schedule their maintenances late at night and often during weekends. Adopting a more modern approach such as the one we will go through in the remainder of the chapters will have tremendous positive impact on the work life balance of the engineering team.

 Most of the highly admired tech companies such as Google don't deploy code on Fridays. The goal is to avoid pushing bugs out just before the weekend, which otherwise could lead to unexpected pages on Saturdays or Sundays. In addition, because they don't fear to deploy code, a lot of those changes will go out to production at pick hours so that they can quickly catch any issues related to load.

In order to implement our continuous deployment pipeline, we are going to look at two new AWS services called CodeDeploy and CodePipeline.

CodePipeline will let us create our deployment pipeline. We will tell it to take our code from GitHub, similarly to what we did before and send it to Jenkins to run our CI testing on it, but instead of simply returning the result to GitHub, we will then take the code and deploy to our EC2 instance with the help of AWS CodeDeploy.

CodeDeploy is a service that will let us properly deploy code to your EC2 instances. By adding a certain number of configuration files and script, we will be able to rely on CodeDeploy to reliably deploy and test our code. Thanks to CodeDeploy, we won't have to worry about any kind of complicated logic when it comes to sequencing our deployment. CodeDeploy is tightly integrated with EC2 and knows how to perform rolling updates across multiple instances and, if needed, perform a rollback.

In `Chapter 3`, *Treating Your Infrastructure As Code*, we looked at how to configure servers and deploy the helloworld application using Ansible. While this solution allowed us to illustrate how to use configuration management, this solution is as good as what we could hope for a more critical service. There isn't any notion of sequencing, no good feedback mechanism on how the deploy went, and we didn't implement any validation steps. Having a dedicated service geared towards doing deployment in AWS will make deploying applications a lot better as we will see.

In order to best demonstrate these services, we will first build new generic node.js web servers using Ansible.

Creating new web servers for continuous deployment

In order to use CodeDeploy, the EC2 instances need to be running the CodeDeploy agent. This is normally done by downloading an executable from an S3 bucket that varies depending on the region your instances are in and running it. Conveniently, AWS also released a custom Ansible library, which will automate those steps. Because that library isn't part of the standard Ansible library, we first need to add it to our `ansible` repository.

Importing a custom library to Ansible for AWS CodeDeploy

By default, Ansible expects to find the custom libraries in the `/usr/share/ansible` directory. As previously when we looked at the inventory script in Chapter 3, *Treating Your Infrastructure As Code*, we can change this default behavior by editing the `ansible.cfg` file. We will make the necessary changes so that the library is being downloaded onto the host with the rest of the Ansible files. The simplest way to accomplish that is to create a new directory at the root of our `ansible` repository and put the library in it.

On your computer, open a Terminal and go to your `ansible` directory:

In the root directory of our `ansible` repository where the `ansible.cfg` lives, we are going to add the new directory `library` to store the AWS CodeDeploy ansible library:

```
$ mkdir library
```

Once the folder is created, we can download the `ansible` library in it:

```
$ curl -L http://bit.ly/2cRAtYo > library/aws_codedeploy
```

Lastly, we are going to edit the `ansible.cfg` file present in the root directory of the `ansible` repository to specify the location of that `library` folder as follow:

```
# update ansible.cfg
[defaults]
inventory       = ./ec2.py
remote_user     = ec2-user
become          = True
become_method   = sudo
become_user     = root
nocows          = 1
library         = library
```

We are now ready to start using the library. CodeDeploy is a service that we are likely to reuse over time as new services get added to our system. In order to keep our `ansible` repository code DRY we are going to create an Ansible role dedicated to CodeDeploy.

Creating a CodeDeploy Ansible role

We are first going to go into the role directory that is present at the root location of our `ansible` repository:

```
$ cd roles
```

As before, we will rely on `ansible-galaxy` to put in place the scaffolding needed to create our role:

```
$ ansible-galaxy init codedeploy
```

Our role will be very simple; we are going to edit the file `codedeploy/tasks/main.yml` and make a call to the new module that the `aws_codedeploy` library brings as follows:

```
---
# tasks file for codedeploy
- name: Installs and starts the AWS CodeDeploy Agent
  aws_codedeploy:
    enabled: yes
```

At this point, we can create our new playbook for generic `nodejs` web servers.

We are going to go back in the root directory of the `ansible` repository:

```
$ cd ..
```

And create a new file called `nodeserver.yml`:

```
$ touch nodeserver.yml
```

We will take the same approach we did previously with our other playbooks. The goal of our servers will be to run node.js applications and run the CodeDeploy daemon.

Edit the `nodeserver.yml` file and add the following in it:

```
---
- hosts: "{{ target | default('localhost') }}"
  become: yes
  roles:
    - nodejs
    - codedeploy
```

 When using CodeDeploy in a config management system such as Ansible or CloudFormation, in order to avoid a race condition, it is important to always install all the dependencies for your application before starting the CodeDeploy.

We can now commit our changes to `git`.

We will first create a new branch and then add new files and directories that we created:

```
$ git checkout -b code-deploy
$ git add library roles/codedeploy nodeserver.yml ansible.cfg
```

And finally `commit` and `push` the changes:

```
$ git commit -m "adding aws_codedeploy library, role and a nodeserver
playbook"
$ git push
```

Like before, you can now create a pull request and once the pull request is reviewed and approved, merge it back to master.

In the end, your `ansible` repository should look like this `http://bit.ly/2uZ62bF`.

Creating the web server CloudFormation template

We now have our Ansible playbook ready, we are now going to create our CloudFormation template using troposphere.

We are going to start by duplicating the troposphere script we created for Jenkins earlier in the chapter:

```
$ cd EffectiveDevOpsTemplates
$ cp jenkins-cf-template.py nodeserver-cf-template.py
```

We are going to edit the file `nodeserver-cf-template.py` and make the following changes:

We will first change the Application name and port by updating the variables as follows:

```
ApplicationName = "nodeserver"
ApplicationPort = "3000"
```

In addition, our instances will need to download files from S3. In order to allow for that to happen, we will replace the policy that allowed CodePipeline on our Jenkins instance with a policy to allow S3. Edit the policy called `AllowCodePipeline` and update its name and action as follows.

Above the instantiation of our instance, add a new IAM policy resource as follow:

```
t.add_resource(IAMPolicy(
    "Policy",
    PolicyName="AllowS3",
    PolicyDocument=Policy(
        Statement=[
            Statement(
                Effect=Allow,
                Action=[Action("s3", "*")],
                Resource=["*"])
        ]
    ),
    Roles=[Ref("Role")]
))
```

This new script should look like this `http://bit.ly/2uDtR6g`.

The new script is ready; we can save it and generate the CloudFormation template as follows:

```
$ git add nodeserver-cf-template.py
$ git commit -m "Adding node server troposhere script"
$ git push
$ python nodeserver-cf-template.py > nodeserver-cf.template
```

Launching our web server

As before, we are going to launch our instance using CloudFormation. Note that we are calling this first stack `helloworld-staging`. We will first look at CodeDeploy as a way to deploy our code to a staging environment. We will use this name in CodeDeploy as a way to target the deployments to that specific stack:

```
$ aws cloudformation create-stack \
        --capabilities CAPABILITY_IAM \
        --stack-name helloworld-staging \
        --template-body file://nodeserver-cf.template \
        --parameters
ParameterKey=KeyPair,ParameterValue=EffectiveDevOpsAWS
```

In a few minutes, our instance will be ready.

We are at an important point in our DevOps transformation. Now that we created a very generic `nodejs` web servers with the ability to easily deploy code onto them, we are really close to a realistic environment that effective companies traditionally use to deploy and run their services. The fact that we are able to very simply create those environments on demand is key to success.

 When architecting services, always make sure that the infrastructure can easily be recreated. Being able to troubleshoot an issue is great, but being able to quickly rebuild a service host and stop the user impact is often even more desirable.

Integrating our helloworld application with CodeDeploy

Our servers are initiated and the CodeDeploy agent is running. We can start using them. To do this, we are going to go through a few steps. First we will create an IAM service role for CodeDeploy, we will then add an entry in the CodeDeploy service to define our application, and then, finally, we will add to the `helloworld` application our application specification file and a few scripts to help with deploying and running our service.

Creating the IAM service role for CodeDeploy

CodeDeploy permissions work with IAM at the individual application level. In order to provide sufficient permissions, we will create a new IAM service role with the following policy:

```
{
    "Version": "2012-10-17",
    "Statement": [
        {
            "Sid": "",
            "Effect": "Allow",
            "Principal": {
                "Service": [
                    "codedeploy.amazonaws.com"
                ]
            },
            "Action": "sts:AssumeRole"
        }
    ]
}
```

We will create our new role that will be called `CodeDeployServiceRole` using the command-line interface using the following command:

```
$ aws iam create-role \
    --role-name CodeDeployServiceRole \
    --assume-role-policy-document \
    http://bit.ly/2uCWY9V
```

We now need to attach the role policy to provide the proper permissions to the service role:

```
$ aws iam attach-role-policy \
    --role-name CodeDeployServiceRole \
    --policy-arn \
      arn:aws:iam::aws:policy/service-role/AWSCodeDeployRole
```

Our IAM service role is now ready, we can finally start interacting with CodeDeploy web interface.

Creating the CodeDeploy application

Now that we launched EC2 instances with the CodeDeploy service running on them and have defined our IAM service role, we have all the requirements needed to create a CodeDeploy application. As always, there are many ways to use AWS services, but we will demonstrate here the basics with the web interface:

1. Open `https://console.aws.amazon.com/codedeploy` in your browser.
2. If prompted, click on **Get Started Now**.
3. This leads us to a welcome screen with two options, **Sample Deployment** or **Custom Deployment**. Choose **Custom Deployment** and click on **Skip Walkthrough**. This brings us to a form called **Create New Application**.
4. In that form, under **Application Name**, give our application the name `helloworld`.
5. The deployment groups can be viewed as the environment in which the application will live. We will first create a staging environment, therefore, under **Deployment Group Name**, provide the name `staging`.

6. We now need to add instances to our application. Our goal is to target the EC2 instance we previously created with CloudFormation. As you might recall, we called our stack `helloworld-staging`. In the section **Add Instances Under the Search by Tags**, keep the **Amazon EC2 tag** type selected and type `helloworld-staging` in the **Value** field. Optionally, you can also provide the **Key** `aws:cloudformation:stack-name`, which will make sure that CodeDeploy only selects the instance we intend to use for our application. AWS CodeDeploy should confirm that it matched one instance:

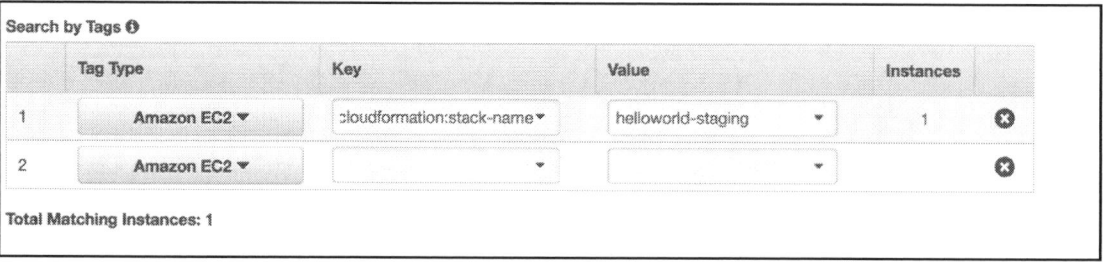

7. The next section is called deployment configuration. One of the strengths of CodeDeploy is its ability to understand how to deploy code to a cluster of servers. Thanks to that feature, avoiding outages during deployment is easy. By default, the service comes with three deployment options, one at a time, all at once, and half at a time. It is possible to create custom deployment configurations, but in our case, since we have only one instance, we can leave the default option **CodeDeployDefault.OneAtATime**.

8. The next two sections are called triggers and alarms. We aren't going to cover it in the book, but those triggers are key when it comes to collecting metrics around deployment and monitoring. By creating triggers to push notifications in SNS and creating CloudWatch metrics, you can easily collect metrics around deployments and answer questions like how many deployments are happening, how many fail, how many deploys lead to rollback, and so on.

9. Our application is somewhat stateless, therefore enabling rollback upon failure is a very safe operation. Select the option **Roll back when a deployment fails**.

10. Lastly, we need to select the service role we created in the previous steps. Under **Service Role ARN**, select the role that ends with **CodeDeployServiceRole**.

11. Finally, click on **Create Application**.

This brings us back to the CodeDeploy application page for our newly created `helloworld` application.

Creating the application in CodeDeploy allows us to define where our newly created application will be deployed. We will now look at how to deploy our code.

Adding the CodeDeploy configuration and scripts to our repository

When we worked on creating a Jenkins pipeline earlier in this chapter, we created a `Jenkinsfile` file inside the `helloworld` GitHub repository. The reason for this was that we could change the code and the way the code is tested in the same change set. For the very same reason, it is very practical to put the logic behind how to deploy our code with the code itself.

Our `helloworld` repository currently has the application and its tests. We are going to add the information CodeDeploy needs to execute a deploy of our service.

CodeDeploy relies on a file called `appspec.yml` (application specification file) to manage the deployment. We are first going to create it.

Go to the directory where the `helloworld` GitHub project is cloned and create a new branch off of master:

```
$ cd helloworld
$ git checkout master
$ git pull
$ git checkout -b helloworld-codedeploy
```

We are now going to create and edit the file `appspec.yml`:

```
$ touch appspec.yml
```

On the first line of the file, we are going to define the version of the AppSpec file. Currently, the only version supported is `0.0`:

```
version: 0.0
```

On the next line, we are going to specify the operating system on which we wish to deploy, in our case Linux:

```
os: linux
```

We are now going to describe which file goes where. To do that, we are going to create a section called files and put each file we want to deploy using a format source destination as such. Note that the file is written in YAML and therefore the spacing and alignment is important:

```
version: 0.0
os: linux
files:
  - source: helloworld.js
    destination: /usr/local/helloworld/
```

Thanks to that section, CodeDeploy now knows to copy the helloworld.js in the target destination /usr/local/helloworld. Our helloworld directory will be automatically created by CodeDeploy. In order to start the application, we will also need our upstart script that isn't currently in the repository.

Back into our Terminal in the root directory of the helloworld project, we are going to create a subdirectory called scripts and add the upstart script to it:

```
$ mkdir scripts
$ wget http://bit.ly/2uDrMam -O scripts/helloworld.conf
```

We can now add that new file to our appspsec.yml by adding another block with the source and destination of the upstart script as follows:

```
files:
  - source: helloworld.js
    destination: /usr/local/helloworld/
  - source: scripts/helloworld.conf
    destination: /etc/init/
```

The two files we need in order to run our application as a service will now be present in the appropriate locations, but in order to deploy our application, we need more. We need CodeDeploy to start and stop the service. Previously, we started the application using Ansible, but this time around we aren't using Ansible to manage our service. CodeDeploy has a much more elegant solution for that. When a deploy starts, the CodeDeploy agent running on the EC2 instance will go through the following sequence of events:

The archive containing our application will be downloaded on the system during the DownloadBundle event, and the install section will be used to copy the files defined in our template in their destinations.

CodeDeploy has a concept of hooks. In the `appspec.yml` file we can create a number of hooks to execute custom scripts during each of the stages described previously. We are going to create three scripts: A script to start our application, a script to stop it, and finally a script to check if the deployment was successful.

We will put those three scripts in the scripts directory we previously created. Let's create the first file `start.sh` and start editing it:

```
$ touch scripts/start.sh
```

The script is very straightforward. We are simply going to call upstart to start the service:

```
#!/bin/sh
start helloworld
```

That's all we need; we are now going to create our stop script file:

```
$ touch scripts/stop.sh
```

And like before, edit it:

```
#!/bin/sh
[[ -e /etc/init/helloworld.conf ]] \
  && status helloworld | \
    grep -q '^helloworld start/running, process' \
  && [[ $? -eq 0 ]] \
  && stop helloworld || echo "Application not started"
```

The stop script is slightly more complicated than the start script as it will be executed during the `BeforeInstall` step. The basic logic is the same, we are going to call stop helloworld. The reason why we have some extra calls before is that we need to handle the case of the first deployment where the application hasn't been installed and started before.

The last script we will create is called `validate.sh`:

```
$ touch scripts/validate.sh
```

Once again the code is very simple:

```
#!/bin/sh
curl -I localhost:3000
```

For the purposes of the book, we are making the most basic validation possible, doing a HEAD request on the only route our application has. In a more realistic application, we would test more routes and everything that could potentially go wrong when new code is pushed out.

Our scripts need to be executable to avoid any unnecessary warnings in CodeDeploy:

```
$ chmod a+x scripts/{start,stop,validate}.sh
```

We can now add our hooks in our `appspec.yml` file.

Open the file again and below the files section, create a hooks section:

```
version: 0.0
os: linux
files:
[...]
hooks:
```

We will first declare the stop script that we want to run at the `BeforeInstall` stage. In the hooks section, add the following:

```
hooks:
  BeforeInstall:
    - location: scripts/stop.sh
      timeout: 30
```

We are allowing 30 seconds for the execution of the stop command to complete.

We are going to repeat a similar operation to add our start and validate scripts as follows:

```
hooks:
  BeforeInstall:
    - location: scripts/stop.sh
      timeout: 30
  ApplicationStart:
    - location: scripts/start.sh
      timeout: 30
  ValidateService:
    - location: scripts/validate.sh
```

At the point when our deploy pipeline will run, it will try to do the following:

1. Download our application package and decompress it in a temporary directory.
2. Run the stop script.
3. Copy the application and upstart script.
4. Run the start script.
5. Run the validate script to make sure everything is working as expected.

We can add all our new files to `git`, commit and push the changes, and send a pull request:

```
$ git add scripts appspec.yml
$ git commit -m "Adding CodeDeploy support to the application"
$ git push
```

The branch will go through Jenkins and be tested. A peer can then review the code change and once approved, you can merge your pull request.

In order to perform a deployment, we essentially need to answer three questions: What to deploy? Where to deploy it? How to deploy it? We answered the where to deploy question when we created the job in CodeDeploy and just answered the how to deploy question with our `appspec` file and its helper scripts. We now need to look into the what to deploy question. This is where we are going to use AWS CodePipeline.

Building our deployment pipeline with AWS CodePipeline

AWS CodePipeline is a service dedicated to creating delivery pipelines. Picture the Jenkins pipelines feature with an AWS twist. The service is very integrated with the rest of the AWS ecosystem, which translates into a number of great features and advantages that using this service has over Jenkins. Because it's a fully managed service you don't have to worry about its uptime the way we need to with our single Jenkins instance. It integrates out of the box with CodeDeploy, which will be very handy for us. While we won't cover much of it, the service is fully integrated with the IAM service, which means that you have a very granular level of control over who can do what with the service preventing unauthorized users from performing deployments for example. But also, thanks to its API, a number of services can be integrated into your pipelines including Jenkins and GitHub.

We will first look into creating a basic pipeline with two stages. The first stage will get the code from GitHub, package it, and store the package on S3. The second stage will take that package and deploy it to our staging instance using CodeDeploy.

After that, we will go through a more advanced scenario. We will see how we can use our Jenkins instance to run our tests before deploying our code to staging. We will also create a production environment and add an on demand production deployment process. This is called doing a continuous delivery pipeline. In the end, we will see a couple of strategies that will allow us to build confidence in the code we push through our pipeline such that we will be able to remove that on demand production deployment step and turn it into a fully automated pipeline.

Creating a continuous deployment pipeline for staging

To create our first deployment pipeline with `CodePipeline`, we are going to use the AWS console which offers a very intuitive web interface:

1. Open the following link in your browser `https://console.aws.amazon.com/codepipeline`.

2. If prompted click on **Get started**.

3. On the next screen, give your pipeline the name `helloworld` and click on **Next Step**.

4. On the next step, for the **Source location**, select `Github` as a **Source provider** and click on **Connect to Github**. If requested, sign into your GitHub account.

5. This will bring you back to the AWS CodePipeline screen; we can now select a **Repository** and **Branch**. We will select the `helloworld` project and `master` branch. Click on **Next step.**

6. This brings us to stage three of our pipeline where we can select our **Build provider**. Our application is being written in `nodejs`; we don't need to build anything. Select **No build** and click on **Next step.**

7. The next step is called **Beta;** this is essentially our staging deployment step. Under **Deployment provider**, select **AWS CodeDeploy**, under Application name, select **helloworld**, and finally, select **staging** for the **deployment group**. Click on **Next step.**

8. This brings us to the step where we have to choose our **Role Name**. Conveniently, AWS also added a **Create Role** button. Click on it.

9. On the next screen, select **Create a new IAM Role** and give it the name `AWS-CodePipeline-Service`. Use the policy proposed and click on **Allow**.

10. Back on the CodePipeline step, make sure that **Role name** says **AWS-CodePipeline-Service** and click on **Next step.**

11. On that last screen, the review screen, make sure everything is correct. Finally, click on **Create Pipeline**:

> Because we are using the web interface, Amazon is automatically creating an S3 bucket on your behalf to store the artifacts produced when the pipeline runs.

Review your pipeline
We will create your pipeline with the following resources.
Source Stage
Source provider GitHub
Repository EffectiveDevOpsWithAWS/helloworld
Branch master
Build Stage
Build provider No Build
Beta Stage
Deployment provider AWS CodeDeploy
Application name helloworld
Deployment group staging
Pipeline settings
Pipeline name helloworld
Artifact location s3://codepipeline-us-east-1-805752931929/
AWS CodePipeline will use this existing S3 bucket to store artifacts for this pipeline. Depending on the size of your artifacts, you might be charged for storage costs. For more information, see Amazon S3 storage pricing.
Role name AWS-CodePipeline-Service

The pipeline will be created in a matter of seconds and run for the first time.

 For the purposes of illustrating the basic functions of CodeDeploy and CodePipeline, we used the web and command line interface. This process is very manual and doesn't go through any kind of review process. CloudFormation supports these two services. For a real production system, instead of making changes by hand it is best to use something like Troposphere to programmatically generate the templates to manage those services.

Once both steps have run, you can verify that the code has been deployed by opening in your browser `http://<instanceip>:3000`. The instance IP can be found in the CloudFormation template, in the EC2 console, or you can even verify the success with the following one liner:

```
$ aws cloudformation describe-stacks \
    --stack-name helloworld-staging \
    --query 'Stacks[0].Outputs[0].OutputValue' \
    | xargs -I {} curl {}:3000
Hello World
```

We have finished our basic pipeline. By taking advantage of CodePipeline, CodeDeploy, GitHub, and S3, we built a very elegant solution to handle deploying our web application. Every time a pull request is merged to master, our pipeline will pick up the change, automatically create a new package with our new code, store it on S3, and then deploy it to staging. Thanks to CodeDeploy we can have a basic test in place to verify that the version is working, but if needed, we can rollback to any revisions previously built.

Our pipeline doesn't have to be limited to staging; we can actually do a lot more with our solution. As previously mentioned, CodePipeline can integrate with Jenkins. We can use it to build artifacts, but also to run some extra series of tests. Let's add it to our pipeline before deploying to staging.

Integrating Jenkins to our CodePipeline pipeline

One of the features that makes Jenkins so popular is its plugin capability. AWS released a number of plugins to integrate different services to Jenkins. We are going to use the one created for CodePipeline. This will first require us to change the IAM profile role of the instance so that the instance can interact with CodePipeline. We will then install the CodePipeline plugin in Jenkins and create a job to run our test and finally edit our pipeline to integrate that new stage.

Updating the IAM profile through CloudFormation

In order to add the new privileges to the instance profile, we are going to edit the template we created earlier in the chapter.

Edit the file `jenkins-cf-template.py` we created earlier. We are going to add a policy to grant permissions to the Jenkins instance to communicate with CodePipeline. This step is very similar to the change we did to grant S3 access to our web server.

Above the instance variable instantiation, add the following:

```
t.add_resource(IAMPolicy("Policy",
    PolicyName="AllowCodePipeline",
    PolicyDocument=Policy(
        Statement=[
            Statement(Effect=Allow,
                Action=[Action("codepipeline", "*")],
                Resource=["*"])
        ]
    ),
    Roles=[Ref("Role")]
))
```

Then, save the changes and regenerate the template. The new template should look like this `http://bit.ly/2djBqbb`:

```
$ git add jenkins-cf-template.py
$ git commit -m "Allowing Jenkins to interact with CodePipeline"
$ git push
$ python jenkins-cf-template.py > jenkins-cf.template
```

And using the web interface, update the stack:

1. Open `https://console.aws.amazon.com/cloudformation`.
2. Check the checkbox next to the Jenkins stack and in the **Actions** menu, select **Update Stack**.
3. Browse to the newly generated `jenkins-cf.template` and click on **Next** until you get to the review screen:

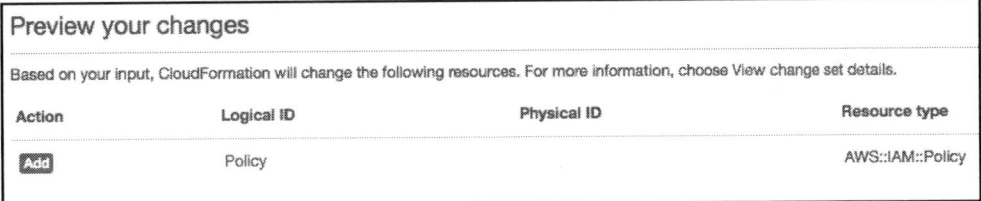

Preview your changes			
Based on your input, CloudFormation will change the following resources. For more information, choose View change set details.			
Action	Logical ID	Physical ID	Resource type
Add	Policy		AWS::IAM::Policy

4. As shown in the preceding screenshot, because we created our instance with an instance profile, only the IAM policy is being added. Our EC2 instance will stay untouched, making that change very safe. Click on **Update** to confirm the change.

The instance policy will get updated giving our Jenkins enough permissions to interact with CodePipeline. We can now install the Jenkins plugin for CodePipeline.

Installing and using the CodePipeline Jenkins plugin

Installing a plugin in Jenkins is very simple:

1. Open your Jenkins instance in your browser (in my case `http://54.175.97.69:8080`).
2. If needed, log in and then click on **Manage Jenkins**.
3. In the **Manage Jenkins** page, select **Manage Plugins**.
4. Search for the plugin called **AWS CodePipeline Plugin**, select it and install it.

   We can now start using the plugin:

5. Go back to the homepage of your Jenkins server.
6. Click on **New Item** in the left-hand side menu.
7. Give the new item the name `HelloworldTest`, select **Freestyle project,** and click on the **OK** button at the bottom of the page.
8. On the next screen, under the **Source Code Management**, select **AWS CodePipeline**. Because we configured the permissions at the instance profile level, the only options we need to configure are the **AWS Region** and **Category**, which are for us respectively **US_EAST_1** and **Test**.
9. Under **Build Triggers**, select **Poll SCM** and then type * * * * * to tell Jenkins to check with CodePipeline every minute for possible code test requests.
10. Under the **Build** section, click on **Add build step and** then **Execute shell**.
11. We are going to once again run the tests we created at the beginning of the chapter. In the **Command** section type the following:

```
npm install
./node_modules/mocha/bin/mocha
```

12. Add a **post-build action** and select the action called **AWS CodePipline Publisher**.

13. In the newly generated **AWS CodePipeline Publisher**, click on **Add**, and leave the **Location** blank.

14. You can optionally configure the rest of the job to your liking and then click on **Save** to create the new job.

Our test job in Jenkins is ready to be used. We can update our pipeline to take advantage of it.

Adding a test stage to our pipeline

We are going to use the web interface to make that change:

1. Open `https://console.aws.amazon.com/codepipeline` in your browser.

2. Select the **helloworld** pipeline we previously created.

3. On the helloworld pipeline page, click on the **Edit** button at the top of the pipeline.

4. We are now going to add a stage by clicking on the icon **+ Stage** button located between the **Source** and **Beta** stages.

5. Call that stage **Test** and click on **Action**.

6. In the right-hand side menu, in the **Action category** choose the action called **Test**.

7. Call your action `Jenkins` and for the **Test provider**, select **Add Jenkins**.

8. In the **Add Jenkins** menu, leave **Provider Name** set to **Jenkins**, provide your Jenkins URL, in my case `http://54.175.97.69:8080`. The project name needs to match the name of the job on Jenkins, in our case `HelloworldTest`. Once set, click on **Add action**.

9. Apply your change by clicking on **Save pipeline changes** at the top of the pipeline.

10. Run the pipeline again by clicking on **Release change**. After a few minutes, you should be able to see the Jenkins step being executed and, if everything went well, becoming green.

Our pipeline is starting to look very interesting now. We demonstrated the Jenkins integration in its most rudimentary function, but you can easily imagine more realistic scenarios where you would add a step after deploying your code to staging to do better validation with better integration, load, and even penetration testing.

The goal of AWS CodePipeline is to help you take services from source control all the way up to production. As you first start working on a service, you might not have the test coverage needed to build the confidence needed to continuously deploy to production so you might opt for a 1 click production deployment instead. We are going to take advantage of the automation we built so far in this chapter and build a continuous delivery pipeline for production.

Building a continuous delivery pipeline for production

In order to build our continuous delivery pipeline, we are going to first create a CloudFormation stack for a production environment. We will then add a new deployment group in CodeDeploy, which will provide us the ability to deploy code to that new CloudFormation stack. Finally, we will upgrade the pipeline to include an approval process to deploy our code to production and the production deployment stage itself.

Creating the new CloudFormation stack for production

We are going to reuse the exact same template we used for staging. In your Terminal, go to the location you used to generate the `nodeserver` template and then run the same command as before, but this time with the stack name `helloworld-production`:

```
$ aws cloudformation create-stack \
    --capabilities CAPABILITY_IAM \
    --stack-name helloworld-production \
    --template-body file://nodeserver.template \
    --parameters ParameterKey=KeyPair,ParameterValue=EffectiveDevOpsAWS
```

We can then run the following command to wait for the stack to be ready:

```
$ aws cloudformation wait stack-create-complete \
    --stack-name helloworld-production
```

> You might realize the weakness of our production stack with only one EC2 instance in it. We will address that concern in Chapter 5, *Scaling Your Infrastructure* when we talk about scaling strategies.

Creating a CodeDeploy group to deploy to production

We previously created a CodeDeploy application and a first deployment group that allowed us to deploy our code to staging. Using the command-line interface, we are now going to add a new deployment group to deploy our code to our newly created production environment.

One of the parameters needed to add new deployment groups is the `arn` of the policy we created initially. We can easily extract it from the staging deployment group we previously created. We will store the result in a variable called `arn`:

```
$ arn=$(aws deploy get-deployment-group \
    --application-name helloworld \
    --deployment-group-name staging \
    --query 'deploymentGroupInfo.serviceRoleArn')
```

We can now run the following command to create the new deployment group:

```
$ aws deploy create-deployment-group \
    --application-name helloworld \
    --ec2-tag-filters Key=aws:cloudformation:stack-
name,Type=KEY_AND_VALUE,Value=helloworld-production \
    --deployment-group-name production \
    --service-role-arn $arn
```

If everything went well, the new deployment group should be created. We can verify that by browsing to the application in the AWS CodeDeploy web page or using the command-line with the following command:

```
$ aws deploy list-deployment-groups \
    --application-name helloworld
{
    "applicationName": "helloworld",
    "deploymentGroups": [
        "staging",
        "production"
    ]
}
```

Adding a continuous delivery step to our pipeline

As we saw in this chapter, pipelines are composed of stages. In CodePipeline, stages are characterized by their categories. We have explored three categories so far, source, deploy and test. In order to add that confirmation step to deploy to production, we will use a new category called **approval**.

Approval actions offer a number of configuration options to get notifications when a job is pending approval. In order to best demonstrate it, we are going to create a new SNS topic and subscribe to it. SNS as you might remember from Chapter 3, *Treating Your Infrastructure As Code*, is the simple notification service that we used to create monitoring of our infrastructure.

We are going to use the command-line to create a new topic and subscribe to it:

```
$ aws sns create-topic --name production-deploy-appoval
{
    "TopicArn": "arn:aws:sns:us-east-1:511912822958:production-deploy-
    appoval"
}
```

We will use an email subscription, but SNS supports a number of other protocols such as SMS, HTTP, and SQS.

In order to subscribe, you need to know the TopicArn, which is in the output of the previous command:

```
$ aws sns subscribe --topic-arn \
    arn:aws:sns:us-east-1:511912822958:production-deploy-appoval \
    --protocol email \
    --notification-endpoint nfelsen@gmail.com
{
    "SubscriptionArn": "pending confirmation"
}
```

Go to your inbox to confirm the subscription.

We can now add our new stages, starting with the approval stage:

1. Open https://console.aws.amazon.com/codepipeline in your browser.
2. Select the **helloworld** application.
3. Click on **Edit** at the top of the pipeline.
4. Click on the **+ Stage** button at the bottom of the pipeline below the Beta stage.
5. Give it the name Approval.
6. Click on **+ Action.**
7. Select **Approval** in the **Action Category** menu.
8. Call the action Approval.
9. Select the approval type **Manual approval**.

10. Pick the **SNS topic** we just created. Typing production deploy should let you easily find the topic thanks to the autocomplete feature of the form.

11. Finally, click on **Add action**.

    We are now going to add the deployment to production steps below this approval.

12. Click on the **+ Stage** button below the newly created stage Approval.

13. Call this new stage `Production`.

14. Click on **+ Action**.

15. Select the **Deploy** category.

16. Call the action `Production`.

17. Select the **CodeDeploy** provider.

18. Pick **helloworld** as our application name.

19. Select the deployment group **production**.

20. Select the artifact **MyApp**.

21. Click on **Add action**.

22. Complete the creation of our new stages by clicking on **save pipeline changes** at the top of the pipeline.

We can once again click on **Release change** to test our updated pipeline.

The pipeline will go through the first three stages and then block on the approval stage. You can check your email inbox to find a link to provide your review or simply use the web interface and click on the review button in the approval stage:

After carefully reviewing the change on staging, approve or reject the change. If approved, the deployment will go to the last step of the pipeline and deploy the code to production.

We just completed automating our entire release process. Our `helloworld` application may not reflect what a real application might look like, but the pipeline we built around it is and what we built can be used as a blueprint for deploying more complex applications from environment to environment very safely in a well thought out process.

There is no question that your ability to move fast and get customers in front of your new features and services is paramount to your ability to fight off disruption. The last step of building a continuous deployment pipeline is to remove that manual approval process to release code to production and take out the last step involving humans in the release process. Over the years, different companies came up with a couple of strategies to make production deployments a safe process. Here are some solutions that you can implement.

Strategies to practice continuous deployments in production

As always, your first line of defense will always be to have enough test coverage and very sophisticated validation scripts that cover most sensitive routes and features in your product. In addition, there are some well-known strategies and techniques to make a continuous deployment pipeline safe for production. We will explore three common ones:

Fail fast

The pipeline we built is fairly fast and robust. Depending on the nature of your service, you may take an optimistic approach with regards to the quality of the code the team produces and always deploy code to production. With good monitoring around your logs and application metrics, you will be able to catch issues minutes after the code is deployed. You will then rely on CodeDeploy and its ability to deploy older releases fast to recover from that situation.

 If you take that approach and a problem is detected, simply roll back. You may know exactly what's wrong and know that it's an easy fix, but knowing that there is an ongoing issue impacting users usually produces enough anxiety to make more mistakes and make the situation worse.

Canary Deployment

Closely related to the previous strategy, you may try to optimistically deploy your code to production but for some time, only expose part of the traffic to the new code.

You can build a system where only a small percentage of the traffic will hit the new servers running the new code and compare the error rate and performance originating from each release for a short period. Usually, 10% of the traffic for 10 minutes is enough to collect enough signal about the quality of the new build. If after that time, everything looks good, move 100% of the traffic to the new version of the service. Bugs such as memory leak are usually slower to manifest themselves; once the deployment is completed, continue closely monitoring your different system and key metrics to make sure everything is good:

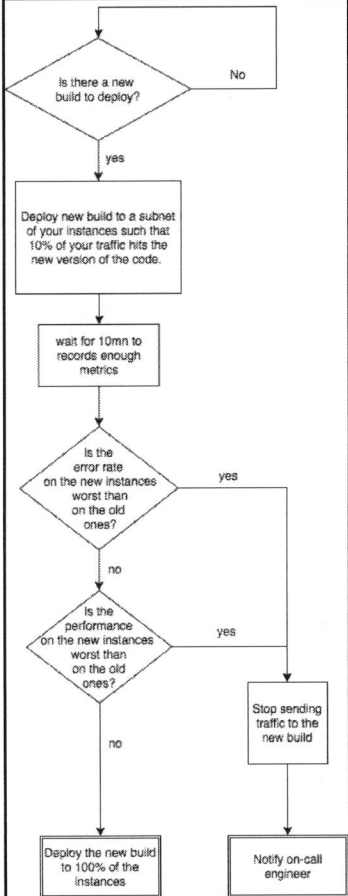

Feature flags

Also called dark launch, this last strategy is the hardest to implement but at the same time the most valuable of all. Most of the well-known tech companies use it. The idea is to have multiple smart switches on each of your features. When you first deploy the code for a new feature, you will want to do it with those switches turned off. You will then progressively turn them on for different subsets of users. You might start by only allowing employees of the company to experience the feature. Then you might decide to increase the number of persons exposed to that feature by adding a set of trusted users. You might then turn the feature on for 20% of your users, then 50%, and so on. In addition to allowing you to do a soft launch, these type of features can be used at the product level to do A/B testing, to do maintenance where you want to turn off a specific feature, or even to do load testing.

One of the best uses of dark launch is summarized in a blog post from Facebook. In 2008, Facebook launched their chat functionality. It was a very challenging feature as it was the first service Facebook developed in Erlang. In order to make sure the service would be able to handle the scale to which Facebook operates, they relied on a dark launch strategy. During the months leading up to the official launch, they simulated what the real traffic could look like by releasing the service without the UI. Real user's browsers would establish connections to the chat servers and invisibly send and receive messages to simulate the load. When it was time to launch, Facebook didn't push out new code, but simply turned the switch on to make the chat window visible in the UI:
`https://www.facebook.com/notes/facebook-engineering/facebook-chat/14218138919/`

Summary

In this chapter, we went through one of the most important aspects of the DevOps philosophy, changing the way code is released.

Our first objective was to improve the developers' productivity. To that effect, we built a continuous integration pipeline. Taking advantage of Jenkins and GitHub, we created a new workflow where developers commit their code in individual branches and submit pull requests. The branches are automatically tested with Jenkins and a final peer review ensures that the code committed is of high quality.

Thanks to that change, the code present in the master branch of our project is always good and worth being pushed to staging. To accomplish that, we built a continuous deployment pipeline. Thanks to AWS CodeDeploy and CodePipeline we were able to easily build a fully functional pipeline. The pipeline has all the desired features an operator could wish for. It automatically picks up changes from developers merging their pull requests, creates a package of the new version of the application, stores the package on S3, and then deploys it to staging. As the new code gets deployed to staging, validation steps ensure that the application isn't misbehaving and, if needed, the application can easily be rolled back.

Once our continuous deployment pipeline was done and allowed us to automatically deploy code to staging we extended it to build a continuous delivery capability so that we could do a production deployment on demand. We also added an extra stage to integrate testing through Jenkins within the pipeline itself.

In the end, we discussed different techniques and strategies to also have a continuous deployment pipeline for production that will allow for performing dozens of production deployments a day for any given service.

Since we started to take a more DevOps approach at managing our architecture and services, we didn't revisit the notions of high availability or load balancing. Even in this chapter, we only created one EC2 instance for our production environment. We will address that issue in Chapter 5, *Scaling Your Infrastructure*, as we look at tools and services to scale our infrastructure and handle massive amounts of traffic.

5
Scaling Your Infrastructure

In Chapter 4, *Adding Continuous Integration and Continuous Deployment*, in order to illustrate how deploying code works with CodeDeploy, we created a very rudimentary architecture to host our staging and production environments. Each of those environments is composed of only a single EC2 instance.

While this served us well to illustrate our CI/CD pipeline, this approach is of course not recommended when actually deploying an application in production. In this chapter, we will fix that design flow and also address most concerns an engineering organization could have with regards to scaling a typical web application.

We will look at scaling from the angle of performance where an application gets an increasing amount of traffic and also for redundancy purposes so that we can handle possible failures in our systems.

Scaling isn't necessarily a DevOps engineering philosophy. The cross-disciplinary nature that scaling an application requires coupled with the AWS offering in this area makes it a natural fit for an engineering team focusing on implementing DevOps principles using AWS.

Throughout this chapter, we will discover different tools and strategies to dynamically scale our application.

Typically, services are first implemented as a monolith, meaning that single application power the entire service. This approach is usually the most convenient to get an application "out of the door fast". In the first part of the chapter, we will see how to scale these types of architecture.

Next, we will see how to utilize some of the AWS managed services to improve performance and lower the costs of running our service.

In the end, we will see how to further break out an application and through a service-oriented architecture, handle even more traffic. So, in this chapter, we will cover the following topics:

- Scaling a monolithic application
- Improving performance and saving money
- Architecting your application to handle massive amounts of traffic

Scaling a monolithic application

While at a larger scale, most applications have a unique architecture, they usually start the same way as our `helloworld` with a simple monolith.

There are two common ways to scale a monolithic application:

- Scaling it vertically, meaning using bigger EC2 instances such that you get an instance with more CPU, more memory, and better network performance
- Scaling it horizontally, meaning adding more and more EC2 instances running the same code and load balance the traffic across them

Scaling vertically is, of course, the easiest approach when it comes down to handling more traffic, but because we are trying to solve both the performance and the redundancy issues, we need to include the horizontal scaling component to our scaling strategy. In addition, you may remember the "just-in-time infrastructure" concept explained in Chapter 1, *The Cloud and the DevOps Revolution*, that allows Amazon and many other start-ups to provision just enough servers to handle the traffic present on their site at any given time. This dynamic scaling concept can easily be implemented in AWS when using a horizontal scaling strategy thanks to a service called Auto Scaling Groups.

In the following section, we are going to revisit our stack. We will first add a load balancer and an Auto Scaling Group to our web servers. After that, we will update our CodeDeploy configuration to target that new set of instances.

Using Auto Scaling Groups to scale web servers

In the last chapter, we created our web server generic role using CloudFormation. When used, the template creates a single EC2 instance. We are going to do two things: replace the section that creates the EC2 instance in favor of creating an Auto Scaling Group and add a section to create an **Elastic Load Balancer (ELB)** that will serve as our new entry point to our application.

Combining ELB and Auto Scaling Groups creates a very robust architecture. While at the administrator level, an ELB instance looks like a single entity, under the hood, AWS will in fact provision multiple resources to handle possible failures and auto scale the resources to handle any surge in traffic. In addition, a number of managed services can be registered to an ELB. In this section, we will see how instead of interacting with EC2 instances, we will create an Auto Scaling Group and register it with an ELB such that instance added or removed from our Auto Scaling Group will also automatically appear and disappear from the load balancer instance pool. Lastly, both ELB and Auto Scaling Groups can work across multiple availability zones. This means that if an outage occurs on a subset of availability zones, the load balancer will be able to survive the outage and the Auto Scaling Group is able to re-provision hosts to get back to the desired instance count:

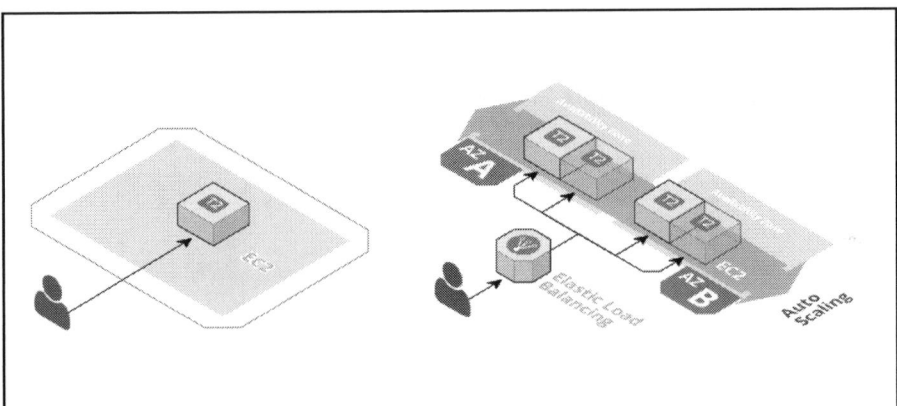

Updating our CloudFormation template

Our goal is to change our current template so that we go from connecting to a simple EC2 instance to a model where we connect to an ELB, which will be connected to an Auto Scaling Group allowing us to easily add and remove instances to scale up or down our cluster.

We will edit our troposphere script `nodeserver-cf-template.py` created in Chapter 4, *Adding Continuous Integration and Continuous Deployment*. Open the script in your editor. We will start by adding our ELB.

Before we start adding those resources to our template, we will first remove the instance creation blocks.

Removing the instance creation

When using an Auto Scaling Group, instance creation and termination is done by the service itself, therefore we can remove two blocks of code from our script.

The first one is the call to add the ec2 resource:

```
t.add_resource(ec2.Instance(...))
```

Now that the instance is gone, the second block that needs to be removed is the output that would previously list out the instance public IP and create the URL based on its public DNS name. At the bottom of the file, remove the two output sections:

```
t.add_output(Output(
    "InstancePublicIp",
    ...
))

t.add_output(Output(
    "WebUrl",
...
))
```

Now that we have removed what we won't need anymore, we start adding the new resources needed to implement our Auto Scaling Group, starting with the ELB.

Adding an ELB to our stack

We will go through the following changes. In the troposphere import section at the top of the script, we are going to import the sub-package `elasticloadbalancing` as follows:

```
from troposphere import (
    Base64,
    ec2,
    GetAtt,
    Join,
    Output,
    Parameter,
    Ref,
```

```
    Template,
    elasticloadbalancing as elb,
)
```

The creation of an ELB requires specifying the VPC in which to add the load balancer. We can easily select the proper VPC by adding a new parameter to our template. To do so, right after the key pair parameter section, add a new parameter as follows:

```
t.add_parameter(Parameter(
    "VpcId",
    Type="AWS::EC2::VPC::Id",
    Description="VPC"
))
```

In addition to selecting which VPC to use to create the ELB, we can also select which subnets to use in order to find instances. Below the VPC parameter selection, add a new block to pick our subnets with the following code:

```
t.add_parameter(Parameter(
    "PublicSubnet",
    Description="PublicSubnet",
    Type="List<AWS::EC2::Subnet::Id>",
    ConstraintDescription="PublicSubnet"
))
```

We now have all the parameters needed to build our ELB instance. We need one more piece of information, the security group. The security groups in ELB work roughly the same way as in EC2. The main differences with the EC2 security group is that in order to use ELB in a VPC, the security group needs to specify the ID of that VPC and, since it's a managed load balancer service, AWS doesn't provide an SSH access to those instances and therefore we don't need to open up port TCP/22.

After the previous subnet parameter section, we can create our ELB security group resource as follows:

```
t.add_resource(ec2.SecurityGroup(
    "LoadBalancerSecurityGroup",
    GroupDescription="Web load balancer security group.",
    VpcId=Ref("VpcId"),
    SecurityGroupIngress=[
        ec2.SecurityGroupRule(
            IpProtocol="tcp",
            FromPort="3000",
            ToPort="3000",
            CidrIp="0.0.0.0/0",
```

```
        ),
    ],
))
```

We can now create our ELB resource. After the creation of the load balancer security group, we will add a new resource for the load balancer. We are first going to create the resource and initialize it with the load balancer function. We will simply call that resource LoadBalancer:

```
t.add_resource(elb.LoadBalancer(
    "LoadBalancer",
```

ELBs can use for internal load balancing or at the edge of your network. In our case, we are trying to use it at our frontend endpoint and therefore we will want an Internet-facing scheme. On the next line, add the following:

```
Scheme="internet-facing",
```

We can now configure our listeners. This means defining which port to redirect to where and which protocol to use for that. In order to keep things simple, we can configure our load balancer to redirect all requests coming in port 3000 to port 3000 as follows:

```
Listeners=[
    elb.Listener(
        LoadBalancerPort="3000",
        InstancePort="3000",
        Protocol="HTTP",
        InstanceProtocol="HTTP"
    ),
],
```

In order to know whether a host is able to take on requests, the load balancer needs to verify that our application is running on the instances that the load balancer points to. This is done through a health check mechanism. Ours will verify that we are able to get the home page of our application, which is running on port 3000. We can do it as follows:

```
HealthCheck=elb.HealthCheck(
    Target="HTTP:3000/",
    HealthyThreshold="5",
    UnhealthyThreshold="2",
    Interval="20",
    Timeout="15",
),
```

Over time, EC2 instances will be added and removed from the load balancer; in order to make a smooth transition when hosts are removed, we want to allow enough time for any ongoing transaction to complete. We can put that in place through a draining policy. Ours will tell the load balancer to stop taking on new requests and wait 10 seconds such that previous connections can complete. Here is how:

```
ConnectionDrainingPolicy=elb.ConnectionDrainingPolicy(
    Enabled=True,
    Timeout=10,
),
```

We want our load balancer to distribute requests evenly across all instances in the pool regardless of the availability zone that the instances are in; this is done by setting the `CrossZone` option to `True`:

```
CrossZone=True,
```

Finally, we will reference the two resources we previously created to specify which subnets and security groups to use and close the opened parentheses:

```
Subnets=Ref("PublicSubnet"),
SecurityGroups=[Ref("LoadBalancerSecurityGroup")],
))
```

Our load balancer can now be created. It is going to be used as our endpoint for our application. In order to make it easy to find the new URL for our application, we are going to create a new output to reflect that architecture change. We will create an output similar to what we had in the previous chapter, but instead of pointing to the public IP of the instance that is now gone, we are going to expose the DNS name of our ELB as follows:

```
t.add_output(Output(
    "WebUrl",
    Description="Application endpoint",
    Value=Join("", [
        "http://", GetAtt("LoadBalancer", "DNSName"),
        ":", ApplicationPort
    ]),
))
```

We can now add our Auto Scaling Group.

Adding an auto scaling capability

We are now going to add the auto scaling capability to our application. This will be done in three major phases:

1. Create a launch configuration that the Auto Scaling Group uses to launch the EC2 instances.
2. Create the actual Auto Scaling Group.
3. Create the scaling policies that will enable us to have dynamic scaling capability by relying on CloudWatch metrics.

At the top of the script, in the import section, add the following:

```
from troposphere.autoscaling import (
    AutoScalingGroup,
    LaunchConfiguration,
    ScalingPolicy,
)
```

We will be able to reuse all the resources previously created when launching an EC2 instance. Most of them will stay untouched except for the security group. In the Auto Scaling Group, we need to specify which VPC ID to use. Find your security group and add the following to reference the VPC ID that we already configured for the load balancer:

```
t.add_resource(ec2.SecurityGroup(
    "SecurityGroup",
    GroupDescription="Allow SSH and TCP/{} access".format(ApplicationPort),
    SecurityGroupIngress=[...],
    VpcId=Ref("VpcId"),
))
```

We are going to make our CloudFormation template very flexible when it comes to creating the infrastructure to host our application. As mentioned before, we can scale vertically and horizontally, which, in other words, means what type of instance and how many of them. We can easily implement those two scaling strategies thanks to the parameter section of CloudFormation. We will first create a parameter to define how many instances to use at launch time. After the `PublicSubnet` parameter, add the following:

```
t.add_parameter(Parameter(
    "ScaleCapacity",
    Default="3",
    Type="String",
    Description="Number servers to run",
))
```

Below this parameter, we will add another one to allow for the selection of the instances using a drop-down menu as follows:

```
t.add_parameter(Parameter(
    'InstanceType',
    Type='String',
    Description='WebServer EC2 instance type',
    Default='t2.micro',
    AllowedValues=[
        't2.micro',
        't2.small',
        't2.medium',
        't2.large',
    ],
    ConstraintDescription='must be a valid EC2 T2 instance type.',
))
```

We are illustrating the vertical component with only the t2 class, but you can, of course, allow anything.

The next component of an Auto Scaling Group is the launch configuration. Every time the Auto Scaling Group decides to add an instance, it will refer to that configuration to know what type of instance to launch, which AMI to use, and all the configurations associated with it. This is essentially what replaces the ec2.Instance() call we removed at the top of this section and therefore it's no surprise that most parameters are parameters we defined in Chapter 4, *Adding Continuous Integration and Continuous Deployment* , when we were creating our initial EC2 instance. At the bottom of the file, just above the Ouput parameter, add the following

```
t.add_resource(LaunchConfiguration(
    "LaunchConfiguration",
    UserData=ud,
    ImageId="ami-a4c7edb2",
    KeyName=Ref("KeyPair"),
    SecurityGroups=[Ref("SecurityGroup")],
    InstanceType=Ref("InstanceType"),
    IamInstanceProfile=Ref("InstanceProfile"),
))
```

Finally, the last block of code needed is the actual Auto Scaling Group resource. We will create it like most other resources and start by referring to our resource and providing it with a name. Below the LaunchConfiguration, start creating your AutosScalingGroup as follow

```
t.add_resource(AutoScalingGroup(
    "AutoscalingGroup",
```

The next thing we will do is refer to the capacity parameter and launch the configuration resource that we just created:

```
DesiredCapacity=Ref("ScaleCapacity"),
LaunchConfigurationName=Ref("LaunchConfiguration"),
```

Auto Scaling Groups take min and max arguments to limit the number of EC2 instances a given Auto Scaling Group can manage; we are going to set our limits to 2 and 5 as follows:

```
MinSize=2,
MaxSize=5,
```

Auto Scaling Groups have the ability to be connected to ELBs. Through that connection, ELB and Auto Scaling Groups work hand in hand. Every time the Auto Scaling Group makes a decision to add or remove an instance, it will also add or remove it from the load balancer. This is done very simply by providing our load balancer reference as follows:

```
LoadBalancerNames=[Ref("LoadBalancer")],
```

Finally, we will specify which subnets to use and close the opened parentheses:

```
VPCZoneIdentifier=Ref("PublicSubnet"),
))
```

Our Auto Scaling Group is ready. We could launch our stack and benefit from our improved architecture with no single point of failure and the ability to scale up and down the number of instances with just a few clicks, but we can do even better. Our application is so basic that we can easily guess that the limiting factor is the CPU. By looking at how the CPU on our instance trends, we can automatize this process of scaling up or down the number of instances running our services. This is done by combining scaling policies and CloudWatch alarms. Here is how.

We will first add the necessary import at the top:

```
from troposphere.cloudwatch import (
    Alarm,
    MetricDimension,
)
```

Now, at the bottom of the script, after the creation of the Auto Scaling Group, we will create two scaling policies, one to scale down the number of instances and one to scale it up:

```
t.add_resource(ScalingPolicy(
    "ScaleDownPolicy",
    ScalingAdjustment="-1",
    AutoScalingGroupName=Ref("AutoscalingGroup"),
    AdjustmentType="ChangeInCapacity",
```

```
))

t.add_resource(ScalingPolicy(
    "ScaleUpPolicy",
    ScalingAdjustment="1",
    AutoScalingGroupName=Ref("AutoscalingGroup"),
    AdjustmentType="ChangeInCapacity",
))
```

As you can see, the policies are tied to the Auto Scaling Group through the `AutoScalingGroupName` parameter. We will now attach CloudWatch alarms to those policies, starting with the alarm to trigger a scale-down action.

Under the scaling policies, add the following:

```
t.add_resource(Alarm(
    "CPUTooLow",
    AlarmDescription="Alarm if CPU too low",
```

We will learn more about CloudWatch in `Chapter 7`, *Monitoring and Alerting*, but at a high level, CloudWatch breaks down metrics by service and metric type. We want to extract the metric called `CPUUtilization` for `EC2`. Here is how:

```
    Namespace="AWS/EC2",
    MetricName="CPUUtilization",
```

CloudWatch has a concept of key value pairs that can be associated with an alarm. It uses to further expands on the identity of a metric. In our case, we want the scaling decision to be made only on the instances present in our Auto Scaling Group. We will specify it as follows:

```
    Dimensions=[
        MetricDimension(
            Name="AutoScalingGroupName",
            Value=Ref("AutoscalingGroup")
        ),
    ],
```

We will now tell, that we want to look at the average value of the CPU utilization over a period of 1 minute and take the average value:

```
    Statistic="Average",
    Period="60",
    EvaluationPeriods="1",
```

We will set the threshold to 30, meaning that if the average usage of our CPU is more than 30 for a minute, we will scale down our cluster:

```
Threshold="30",
ComparisonOperator="LessThanThreshold",
```

And finally, we will tie that CloudWatch alarm to the scaling policy previously created through the `AlaramActions` parameter and close the parentheses as follows:

```
AlarmActions=[Ref("ScaleDownPolicy")],
))
```

We will do approximately the same work for scaling up our cluster. We will change the threshold to be higher than 60% for 1 minute and, in addition, also trigger the same event if we don't have any data, which could indicate that an instance is down. We can do that through the `InsufficientDataActions` parameter as follows:

```
t.add_resource(Alarm(
    "CPUTooHigh",
    AlarmDescription="Alarm if CPU too high",
    Namespace="AWS/EC2",
    MetricName="CPUUtilization",
    Dimensions=[
        MetricDimension(
            Name="AutoScalingGroupName",
            Value=Ref("AutoscalingGroup")
        ),
    ],
    Statistic="Average",
    Period="60",
    EvaluationPeriods="1",
    Threshold="60",
    ComparisonOperator="GreaterThanThreshold",
    AlarmActions=[Ref("ScaleUpPolicy"), ],
    InsufficientDataActions=[Ref("ScaleUpPolicy")],
))
```

Our newly updated template is ready to be tested. If everything went well, it should look like this:

```
http://bit.ly/2vahX7e
```

Launching our new stack

We will save those changes, generate our CloudFormation template and update our stack:

```
$ git add nodeserver-cf-template.py
$ git commit -m "Using autoscaling group instead of individual EC2
instances"
$ git push
$ python nodeserver-cf-template.py > nodeserver-cf.template
```

Then update (or recreate) the `helloworld` application with the following steps:

1. Open `https://console.aws.amazon.com/cloudformation` in your browser.
2. Select the `helloworld-production` stack and, in the **Action** menu, select **Update stack** (or go through the usual steps to create a CloudFormation stack).
3. Select the new template file `nodeserver-cf.template` and click **Next**. The new parameters page looks a lot more complete than previously:

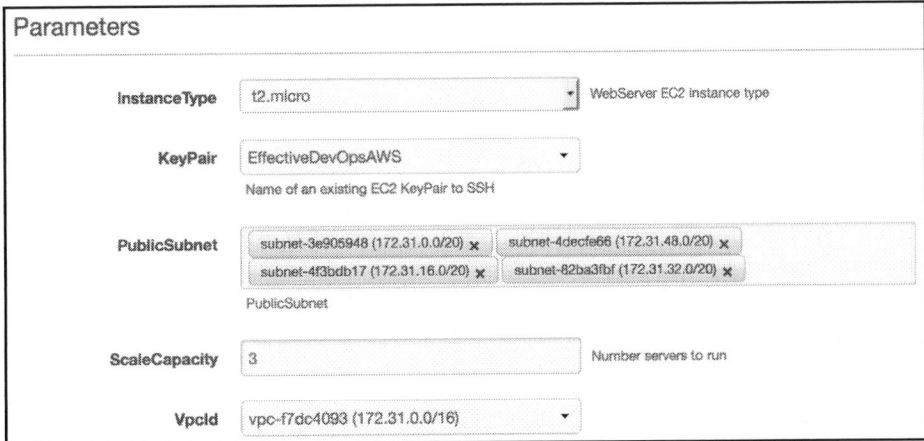

4. We can opt for scaling our stack vertically by select a different instance type than `t2.micro`. Note that only `t2.micro` is part of the free tier. For the purpose of the book, we can stick with `t2.micro`.
5. Keep or select your key pair.
6. On the next field, select all the public subnets available. There should be one per availability zone. If AWS was to have some issue with a particular availability zone, you could decide to update your stack and exclude the subnet targeting this particular AZ.

7. On the next option, we can select to start with anywhere between two and five instances. We will set this option set to our default, 3. Later, thanks to our auto scaling rules, AWS will automatically downscale our cluster to two hosts, which is the minimum required in order to keep our service highly available.

8. Finally, select the VPC ID- there should be only one and click **Next**.

9. On the next screen, click **Next** again. This will bring us to the review screen:

Preview your changes

Based on your input, CloudFormation will change the following resources. For more information, choose View change set details.

Action	Logical ID	Physical ID	Resource type	Replacement
Add	AutoscalingGroup		AWS::AutoScaling::AutoScalingGroup	
Add	CPUTooHigh		AWS::CloudWatch::Alarm	
Add	CPUTooLow		AWS::CloudWatch::Alarm	
Add	LaunchConfiguration		AWS::AutoScaling::LaunchConfiguration	
Add	LoadBalancer		AWS::ElasticLoadBalancing::LoadBalancer	
Add	LoadBalancerSecurityGroup		AWS::EC2::SecurityGroup	
Add	ScaleDownPolicy		AWS::AutoScaling::ScalingPolicy	
Add	ScaleUpPolicy		AWS::AutoScaling::ScalingPolicy	
Modify	SecurityGroup	helloWorld-SecurityGroup-63BGXIT1L6PV	AWS::EC2::SecurityGroup	True
Remove	instance	i-c18c64cf	AWS::EC2::Instance	

10. On that screen, we can confirm that the stack will do what we expect it to do, click on the checkbox to acknowledge the changes made to IAM resources, and click on **Update**.

This change is somewhat transformative and it highlights one of the reasons why using a cloud infrastructure is so powerful. Our production cluster is now able to dynamically scale with the traffic. As soon as we see a traffic spike, the auto scaler will add instances and once the spike of traffic is over, those extra instances will automatically be terminating, allowing us to only add more resources when needed. By relying on Auto Scaling Groups and CloudWatch, we were able to implement it in just a handful of steps. Without those tools, recreating the same system could take weeks if not longer.

We can track changes on how our cluster scales with the following command:

```
$ aws autoscaling describe-scaling-activities
```

Since our application doesn't get any traffic, after a few minutes, this command will show the termination of one of our three EC2 instances as the CPUTooLow alarm will have triggered.

In addition, our application has a new endpoint. We can extract it using the same command we used in Chapter 3, *Treating Your Infrastructure As Code*:

```
$ aws cloudformation describe-stacks \
      --stack-name helloworld-production \
      --query 'Stacks[0].Outputs[0]'
{
    "Description": "Application endpoint",
    "OutputKey": "WebUrl",
    "OutputValue":
"http://helloWorl-LoadBala-1ABKQHK92ZOJO-1157159557.us-east-1.elb.amazonaws
.com:3000"
}
```

But presently, nothing is running as we didn't deploy our application to the Auto Scaling Group yet. For that, we will need to update CodeDeploy.

Updating CodeDeploy

In Chapter 4, *Adding Continuous Integration and Continuous Deployment*, we saw CodeDeploy used while associated with an EC2 instance. In addition to being able to use it with EC2 instances, CodeDeploy can be used with Auto Scaling Groups. We can easily make the change using the web interface as follows:

1. Open CodeDeploy in your browser at https://console.aws.amazon.com/codedeploy.
2. Select the helloworld application.
3. In the **Application details**, select the deployment group called **production** and click on **Action** and then **Edit**.
4. In the **Tag Type** menu, switch from **Amazon EC2** to **Auto Scaling Group** and select the new Auto Scaling Group. Its name starts with **helloword-production**. Once selected, the instance count should reflect your new selection and have an instance count of 2 or 3.
5. Click **Save** at the bottom of the page to validate your change.

6. We now need to run the actual deployment. The easiest way to do it is to run it again on our pipeline. Head to the code pipeline interface at `https://console.aws.amazon.com/codepipeline/`.

7. Select the `helloworld` pipeline.

8. Click on **Release change** and confirm it in the next popup by clicking on **Release**. The pipeline will now run again and in the end, deploy our service to the Auto Scaling Group.

We can validate the change with `curl`:

```
$ curl -I
http://helloWorl-LoadBala-1ABKQHK92ZOJO-1157159557.us-east-1.elb.amazonaws.com:3000
hello world
```

 Here too, we made simple yet powerful changes. CodeDeploy, Auto Scaling Groups, and ELB synergies very well. When the traffic spikes up, new instances will be created thanks to the Auto Scaling Group. As Ansible does the initial run on our hosts, it will install the CodeDeploy daemon, which will then reach out to the backend services to know what to deploy and perform the deployment. This will make sure that all instances are running the same version of our application. Once the code is deployed, then finally the health check will start passing and the ELB will put the new host in service. If something was to happen to our instances as they get created and within a certain time window the service wasn't up and running, the system would be aware of the issue and it would automatically terminate the bad instance and create a new one.

Basics of scaling a traditional database

While our `helloworld` application doesn't have any data store such as a database, it is very likely that it won't be the case for most applications. There are many types of databases available on the market, but more often than not, the right thing to do will be to start with a traditional relational database such as MySQL or PostgreSQL. We will talk about NoSQL databases toward the end of this chapter, which at scale are a good supplement to relational databases, but in most cases starting with a different data store will be considered by most as a premature optimization.

In terms of architecture, it is best to break out our stack such that the databases are on their own layer. This is called building a three-tier architecture. The first tier is called the presentation tier and it will often be a browser of a mobile device, the second tier is the application tier, which is what we built so far in this book, our node service, and finally, the data tier will hold the different data stores used by our application including our databases. The data layer is often more critical and harder to manage than the application layer since it's a more stateful layer that contains data that isn't source controlled the same way our application or infrastructure code is controlled:

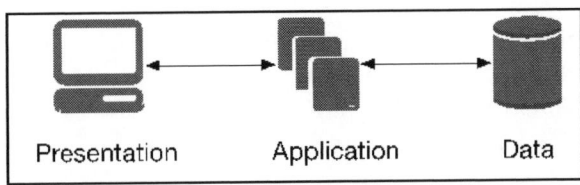

AWS offers the RDS service (http://amzn.to/2gOGi8s) which lets you create managed relational databases. The service offers a variety of flavors of relational databases, ranging from MySQL to Oracle. Using the RDS service is a really compelling option as Amazon will take all the administration burden off your plate. They will take care of some of the most critical tasks, including doing daily backups through snapshots and periodic maintenance to update the database code or the operating system.

One of the biggest concerns to have when adding a database to our system is its availability. You need to handle the following:

- The ability to survive the loss of the instance hosting your database in case of a hardware or network outage
- The ability to scale up your database to handle more read requests
- The ability to scale up your database to handle more write requests

Thanks to RDS, all those concerns are easily addressable. In order to sustain a major database failure, your database will need to not be a single point of failure. If you created a MySQL, PostgreSQL, or Oracle instance, you will want to use an option called Multi-AZ (http://amzn.to/2fLZANI). When enabled, this option will create a synchronized replica of your database in a different availability zone. In case the primary database was to suffer from an outage, the RDS service would perform an automatic failover to the standby instance and the web application would recover seamlessly from the outage.

With regards to scaling up the number of read requests, the RDS service provides the ability to create read replicas of your database (`http://amzn.to/2fuhFwA`). At the application level, this means using two different types of connections, one for write requests and one for read requests. For the read requests, you will likely want to connect to all your read replicas and round robin across them with your select statements.

Scaling the write requests is the hardest problem to address. Early on, the easiest way to handle that constraint is to scale vertically your RDS instances (meaning use more powerful instances).

In addition to the traditional MySQL, PostgreSQL, and Oracle databases, AWS offers its own relational database called Aurora. Aurora is fully compatible with MySQL and PostgreSQL (you select the type of the database upon creation). If you are developing against one of the two databases, then using Aurora will be a much better solution.

Aurora offers up to five times the performance of its standard counterpart. The data is more durable as each chunk of the database volume is replicated six ways across three availability zones. In addition, Aurora works with a concept of clusters. Instead of talking to the individual instances as described previously with read replica, Aurora exposes read and write endpoints for the cluster. Behind the scenes, AWS will automatically take care of adding the new instances when you scale up your cluster and even promote one of your replicas in the event that your master instance was to fail. Finally, Aurora will let you store up to 64 TB through an auto scaling storage feature, so you won't have to worry about running out of storage over time. You can read more about AWS Aurora at `http://amzn.to/2fjc9kj`.

At this point, assuming your application has a database, this is what your architecture could look like:

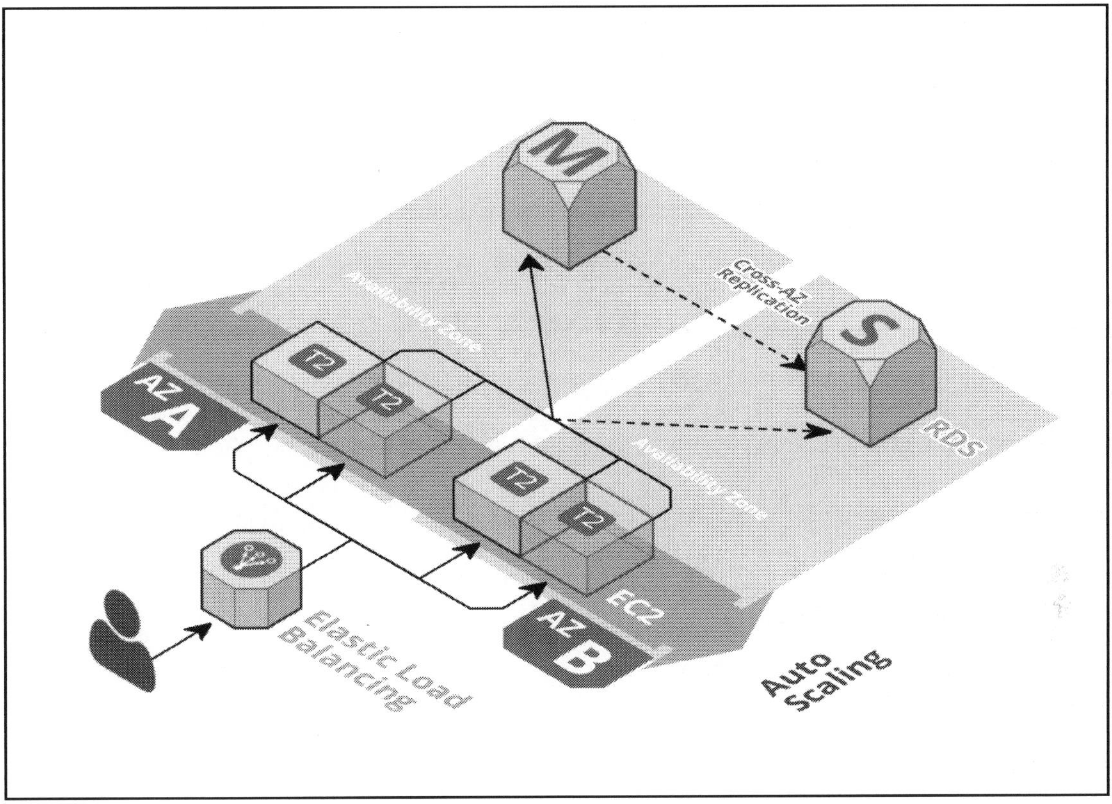

Depending on how big you expect your databases to become, it is also important to keep in mind that at a large scale, there are a number of functionalities that are best to avoid, such as the use of joins or transactions. You can read more on this topic by searching the web for database denormalization.

Our stack is now very scalable. AWS will auto scale the ELB service to handle any amount of traffic; on the other side of it, our application is managed through an Auto Scaling Group that will also automatically add more instances as needed and finally, we saw how to also scale up a data layer either vertically for writes or horizontally for reads. The next step in the evolution of our stack will be to optimize performance and cost by taking advantage of more managed services.

Improving performance and cost saving

That new architecture design will typically let you scale your service to hundreds of thousands of users. The next logical step will be to look at how to improve performance and lower costs.

As mentioned previously, one of the most compelling reasons to use AWS is the amount of managed services that can be used in conjunction with your application. A lot of those services are geared toward very specific needs. For instance, if you do a lot of image transcoding, you may look into Elastic Transcoder or if you need reliable systems to send emails, you could look at SES, but some other services are more ubiquitous. In the previous section, we talked about adding more computing resources to handle more traffic. With our current model, we add more EC2 instances as the average CPU utilization gets higher and uses bigger instance, or adds more read replicas to the data tier. This solution is easy to implement and works great at first, but over time, becomes somewhat expensive. There are a number of ways by which we can easily improve the situation and make our application work smarter by reusing previously computed data through a caching layer. AWS has a service called ElastiCache that can come in handy in those situations.

ElastiCache

ElastiCache is a managed service that lets you create in-memory key-value stores. At a very high level, you will create a cluster and then update your application to use it. The changes are fairly simple. Let's imagine a phonebook application. Whenever we want to retrieve the address of a business, we will need to access our database to retrieve that information. For popular businesses such as banks or post offices, for example, it is likely that the exact same query will be run very frequently. Instead of always reaching to our database, we can update our application logic to check the cache first and, if the information isn't cached, retrieve it from the database and then cache the result:

```
Sub get_address(name)
  address = cache.get(name, "address")
  If address Is Empty Then // cache miss
    address = db.query("SELECT address from businesses WHERE name = ?",
name)
    cache.set(name, "address", address)
  End If
  Return address
End Sub
```

With that system, the first time a business is being looked up, we will end up accessing our database, but after that, the data will be added to ElastiCache and the following calls will be quicker to execute and won't require accessing our database.

ElastiCache currently supports two of the most well-known open source projects in the category, Redis, and Memcached. In the most recent years, Redis started to become a more attractive option as it supports more data types, can be configured to be highly available and can store bigger keys than Memcached. In some specific scenarios, Memcached might still make sense as it has a more efficient internal memory management and is multithreaded.

By making very minimal changes to your application, you will be able to rely on ElastiCache to alleviate some pressure off of the database and lower the overall latency as accessing keys in ElastiCache is a lot faster than any well-known database. In addition to that speed benefit, using ElastiCache will allow us to scale down the number of RDS replicas we need, saving us a bit of money.

There are a number of ways to take advantage of this service. You can use it to store db query results like we saw in our example, but you can also decide to integrate it higher in your stack and store computed results, HTML snippets, images, or even counters.

You can read more about it at `http://amzn.to/2gKWCKe`.

That caching strategy works great for certain types of dynamic content as we just saw and it also really helps with static content. For completely static content, we can even do better than using ElastiCache by moving our caching layer closer to our users through a **content delivery network (CDN)** such as CloudFront.

CloudFront

Our application is currently hosted in the `us-east-1` region, which is physically located in Northern Virginia. Any visitor anywhere in the world needs to connect and retrieve data from the East of the United States to experience our application. As we all know, speed matters, Amazon published a few years ago that 100 milliseconds of latency on their e-commerce site can result in 1% of potential sales lost. If we consider users trying to open our application from Australia, just in order to establish a TCP connection and do a simple TCP handshake (SYN, SYN-ACK, ACK) this means connecting to an endpoint 10,000 miles (16,000 km) away and executing three round trips.

Even at the speed of light (186,000 mph), this adds overs 100 ms of latency and all that happens even before the first byte of data is being transferred. In order to improve the user experience, one of the solutions is to take advantage of CloudFront, the CDN from AWS. By essentially uploading all static assets such as HTML, CSS, images, and client side JavaScript to an S3 bucket and adding a CloudFront distribution in front of it, we accomplish two goals at once:

- We first make the application much faster to load for the users as they are now downloading assets from data centers near their physical location instead of Northern Virginia:

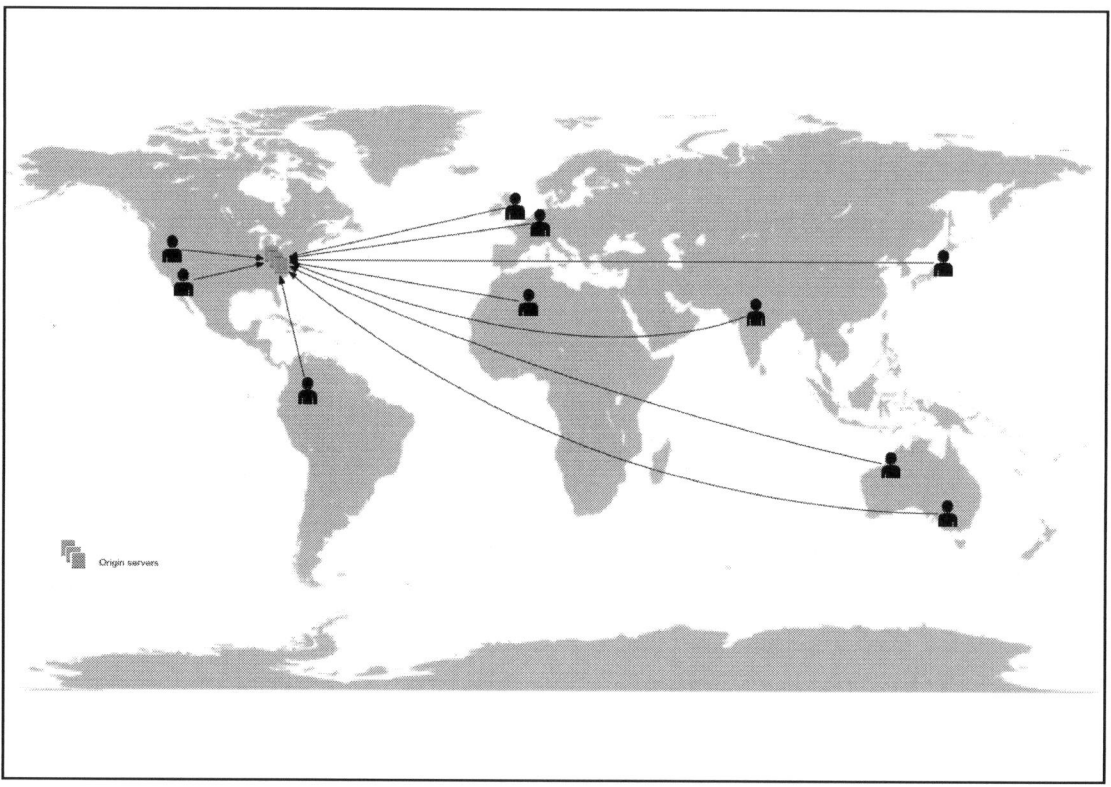

- Transferring data over HTTP is a very common and well understood need. Services such as CloudFront are much more suited to that task than our application. By making that change, we will see fewer requests hitting our applications taking some load off of our EC2 instances:

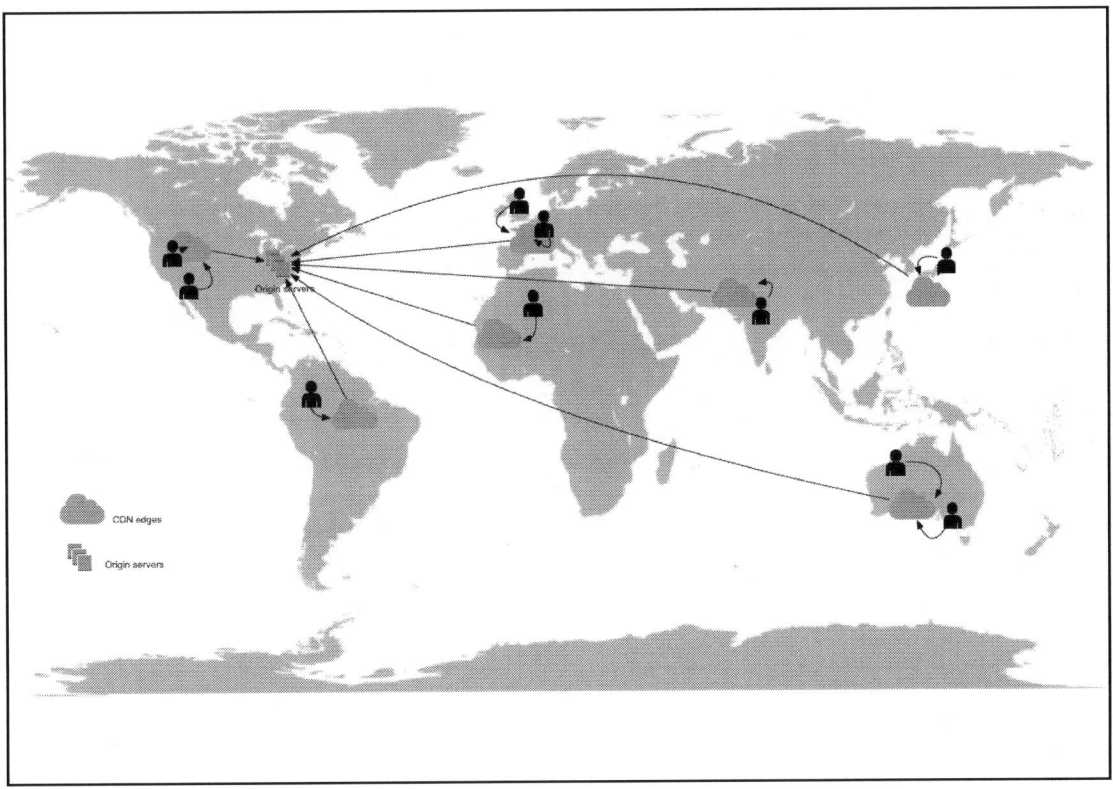

You can read more about CloudFront at `http://amzn.to/2gvlylO`.

After adding an ElastiCache and CloudFront to your application, your infrastructure may look like this:

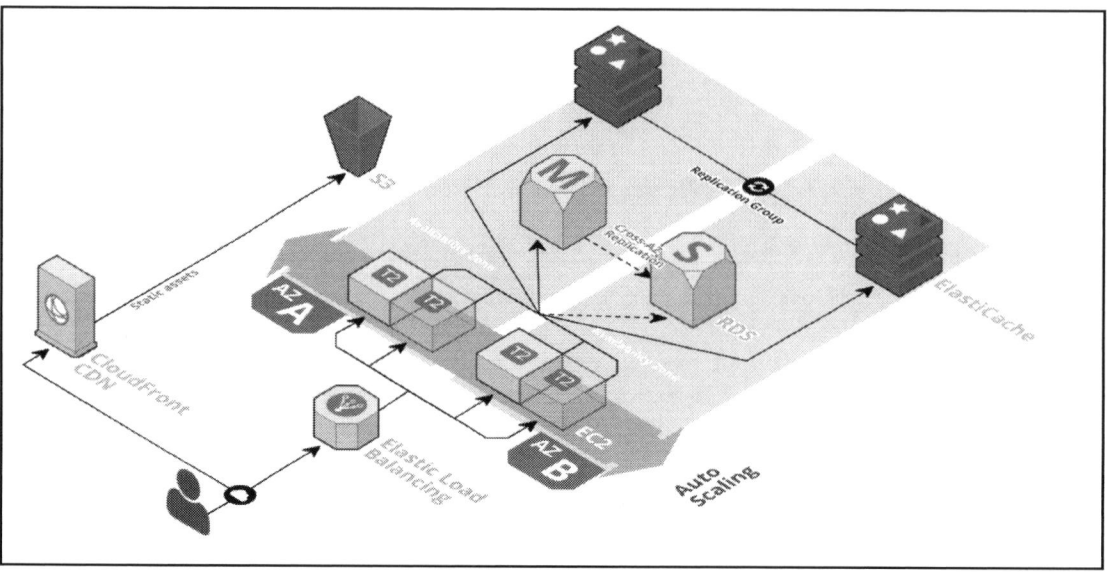

With that approach of relying on AWS managed services to complement our monolithic application, we can with very little changes in our application, scale even further our current stack, improve the user experience, and even save money in certain cases. The next steps into scaling our application will require changing the logic of certain aspects of our application.

Architecting your application to handle massive amounts of traffic

In the life time of an application, you sometimes get to a point where using a simple design architecture like the one we built isn't enough. As traffic keeps on increasing and you start seeing millions of users, you may need to start looking into changing parts of your architecture to make it more efficient. Ideally, you want to analyze your application and figure out which parts are hard to scale or hard develop against and carve off those pieces off of your monolith and create dedicated services. This is commonly called adopting a service oriented architecture. This is, of course, a very complex and disruptive exercise, but the benefits offset those inconveniences.

From an architecture/operations standpoint, breaking out services as such will allow for:

- Better reusability of the service as other applications will now be able to use that service
- Better reliability as the service will as standalone service and therefore won't depend on other issues in the code base
- Better scalability as you can scale each service independently making sure that you use an optimal amount of resources

For developers:

- Having multiple services makes the code base for each service smaller making it easy to navigate through the code and onboard new developers
- Each service can be rewritten in a language that's more suitable for the tasks
- Starting fresh will also help with developer productivity as you won't have as much legacy code to handle

As mentioned, the migration to a service oriented architecture is not easy, but thankfully, using AWS helps a lot as you can rely on a number of services to handle most of the pain points associated with using a service-oriented architecture.

Aside from the obvious things such as the fact that you will now have to manage and deploy a number of services, one of the difficulties associated with a service oriented architecture is that you now have to handle the service to service communication. In order to handle that, the first services you can turn to are the two load balancer services, ELB and **Application Load Balancer (ALB)**.

Load balancers

We used an ELB at the edge of our network to distribute the traffic across the instances in our Auto Scaling Group earlier in this chapter. This load balancer is called an internet facing load balancer. If you are trying to create a service to service communication between two services, you can use the same strategy and put a load balancer in front of your internal service. In that situation, if your services are in the same VPC, you can create an internal load balancer, which will differ from the internet facing load balancer only by the fact that they only have private IP addresses.

Elastic Load Balancer

From an implementation standpoint, using that strategy is fairly easy. You can simply duplicate the work done so far with the `helloworld` application. Each internal service would have:

- A set of Ansible configuration
- A CloudFormation template (generated with troposphere)
- A pipeline in CodePipeline and an application entry in CodeDeploy

Your edge service would then connect to the other service through their ELB as shown in the following figure and the communication would be done through a REST or RPC (remote procedure call) API:

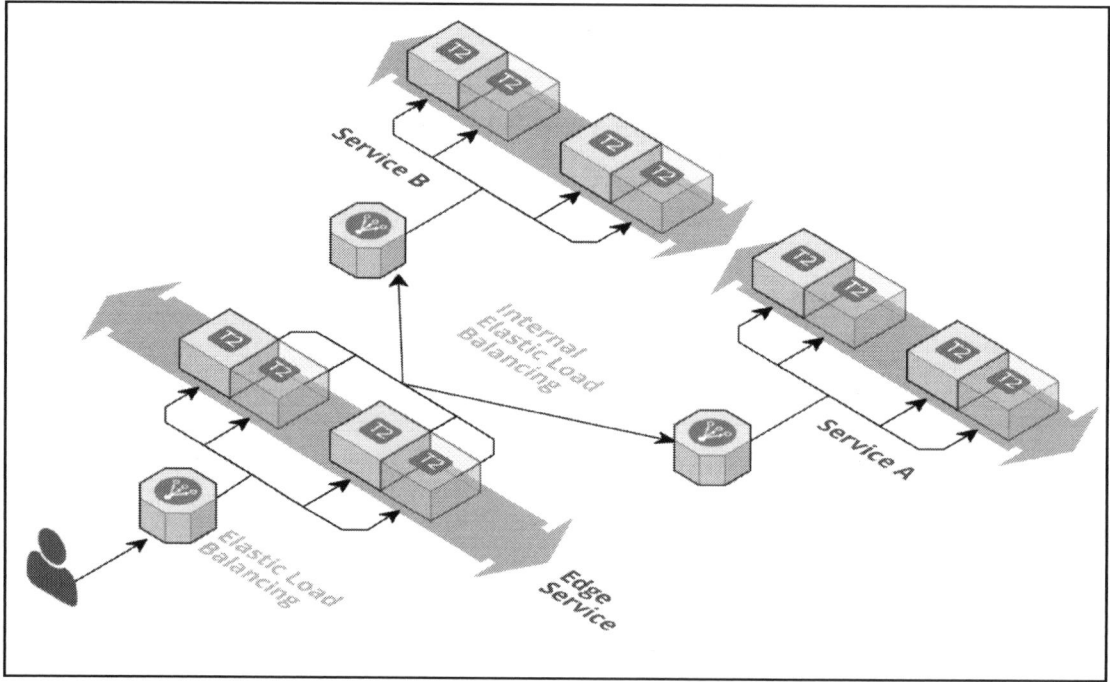

The second option is to use the ALB.

Application Load Balancer

While ELB and ALB are both load balancers, they function very differently. The main difference between the two services is that the ELB service works at the Layer 4 (transport) of the OSI model and the ALB is a Layer 7 (application) load balancer.

This means that the ELB service can only speak and understand up to the TCP/IP layer. When you configure an ELB you configure the load balancer port on one side and the instances addresses and ports on the other.

Because the ALB service is a layer 7 load balancer, in addition to what the ELB can do, it also understands application protocols such as HTTP.This allows for a more complex and granular configuration. A very common use case when using an ALB is to send requests to certain routes to a specific pool of hosts.

For example, you may decide to separate all API requests and put them in their own service while still keeping the access route to `https://domain.com/api/`. By implementing that logic in your ALB as shown in the following figure, your API requests will be able to directly hit your API service without having to go through the edge service:

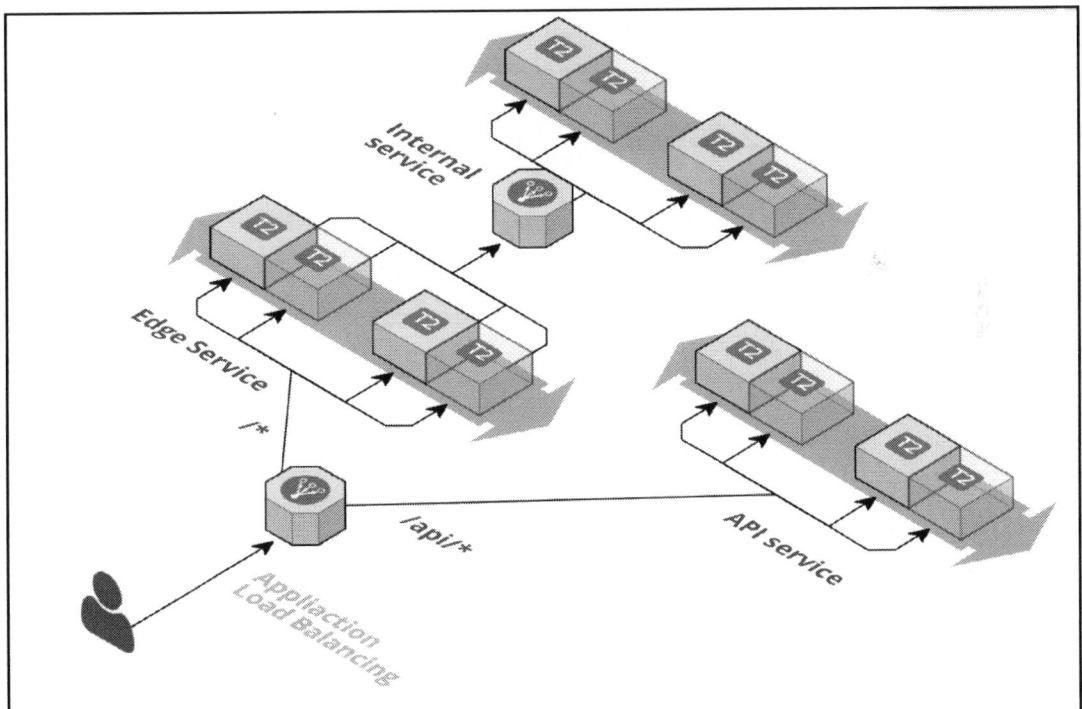

Up to this point, we saw a number of services that will help you with scaling while keeping the latency of your application low, but in some cases, latency doesn't matter as much. For those use cases, you can look into adding offline processing services.

Offline processing with SQS and Kinesis

Another fundamental change that you can easily implement with AWS is offline processing.

The idea behind offline processing is to change your application to execute in real time as little as possible and execute the rest asynchronously through other services. Implemented correctly, offline processing will make your application feel really responsive as most of the heavy lifting is done at a later time by non real-time services.

To explain this concept, we can take the extreme example of a traditional social network site such as Facebook. When you browse a feed and click on a **Like** button, it is very likely that the application will internally do a number of operations, including:

- Increasing the internal score of the post such that the same content may be promoted to more people
- Notifying the author to tell him that you liked his post
- Updating the feed of the people who follow you to mention that you liked a piece of content
- Updating your personal feed to include more content from the same author and more content of a similar type
- Changing the color of the link icon to give you the feedback that your click was taken into account:

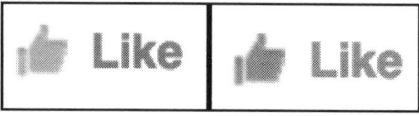

In terms of user experience, that very last operation is the only operation that needs to happen in real time. All the modifications to the different recommendations systems and notifications can happen later. From a code standpoint, the way this is implemented is by doing in real time the UI update and pushing a message to a queue as follows:

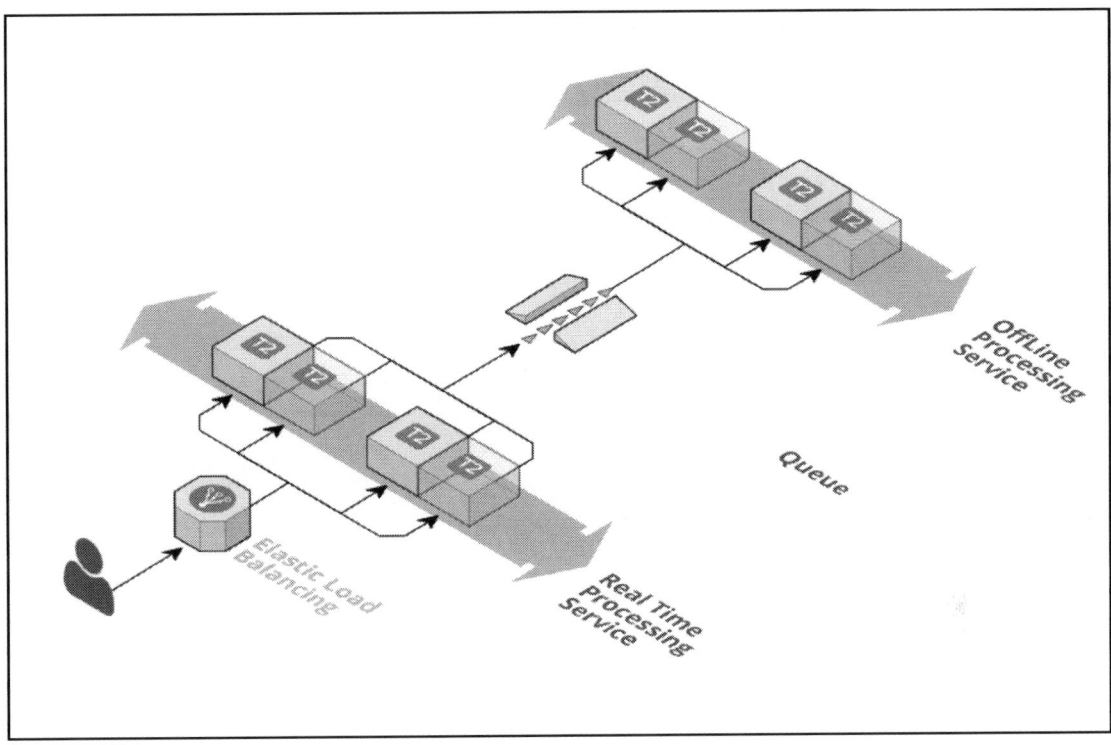

At a later time (think milliseconds to seconds), other systems will read from that queue and process the information indicating that you liked something in a given post.

Queues and offline processing are very common strategies found throughout the web to help with data processing. It makes scaling a lot easier as many processes can consume a single queue in parallel, it helps to control your server load as events will typically be consumed at a flat rate, which in turns helps to smooth spiky events behavior.

Here is a more visual example of write queries in a DynamoDB table. The write pattern is very spiky as we can see on the left-hand side, but by adding a queue in between the event wanting to write to the table and the actual table, we are able to smooth out the write pattern such that later as shown on the right side:

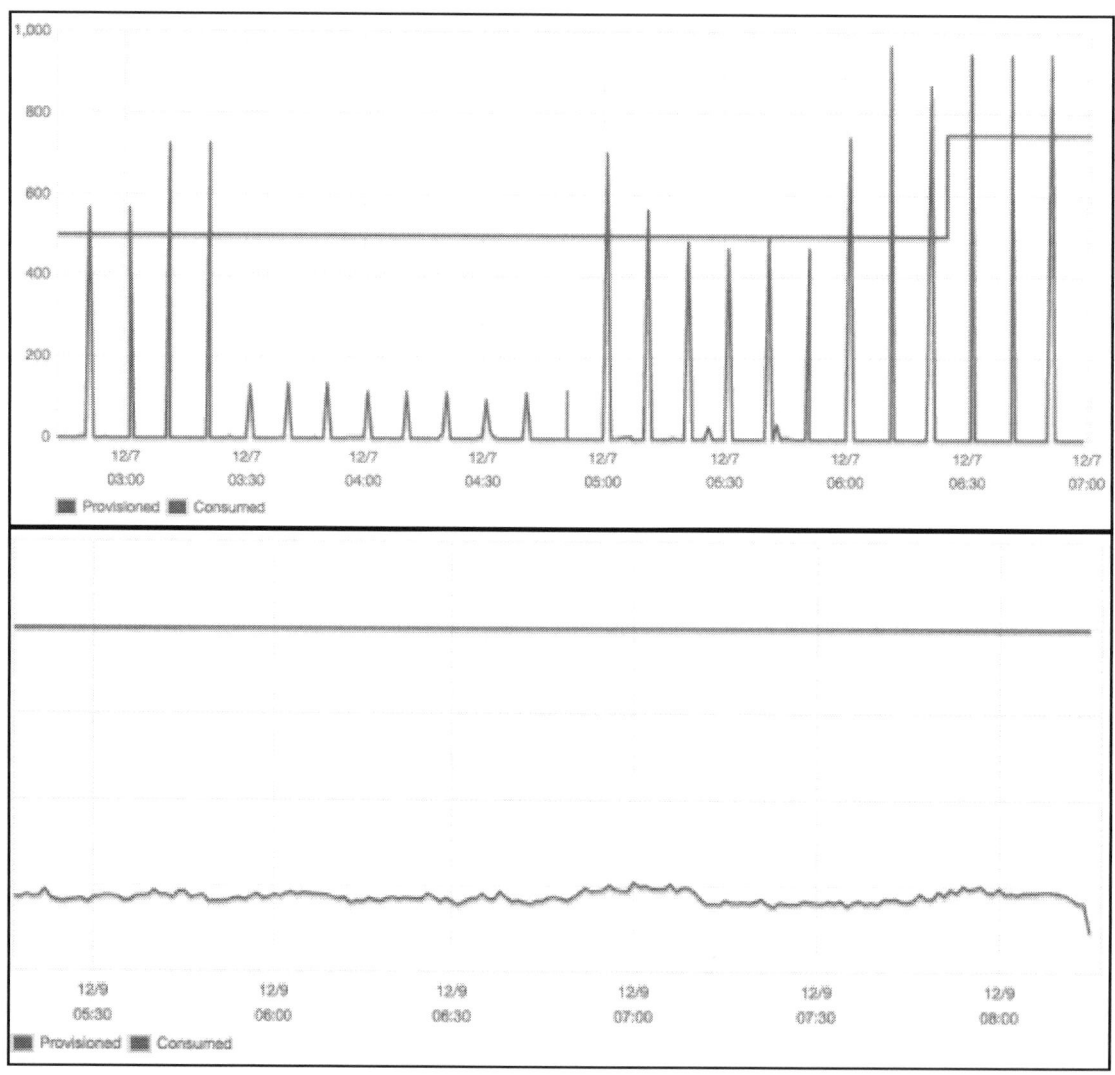

AWS has a number of options when it comes to adding queues to your infrastructure. The main ones are SQS, which is a more traditional message queue service, and Kinesis, which is more similar to Apache Kafka. Both services work very differently:

Kinesis	SQS
• Work following the concept of streams, multiple services can subscribe to a stream and consume the same events. • Messages expire after a certain number of hours (can be configured to up to seven days). • More appropriate for near real time processing. • Manual scaling through the number of shards configuration. • Ordering of the records guarantee.	• Messages are taken off the queues before being processed by at most one service. • Messages can stay in the queue for as long as you want before you consume them. • Can be configured to add delay to up to 15 min. • Native auto scaling features ready to handle virtually any load. • Choice between creating a regular queue that allows high throughput. but doesn't guarantee ordering or uniqueness and FIFO queue where the rate limit is 300 TPS.

You can refer to `http://amzn.to/2hagnrG` to read more about Kinesis and `http://amzn.to/2haiX0T` to learn more about SQS. You can also check out `http://amzn.to/2hahDe7` to read about different use cases on when to use SQS and Kinesis.

All the services we explored in this chapter have in common the fact that they are really easy to adopt and cheap to manage as AWS does most of the operating work required. You don't have to worry about installing the service, updating the operating system, dealing with hardware failure, running out of disk space, and so on. You may wish for similar properties to your application. That's what the idea behind building serverless architecture is.

Serverless architecture

Most services we explored such as databases, queues, caches, load balancers, or even CND are all very common pieces in technology in a standard web architecture. As a matter of fact, the 80/20 rule applies in this field. It's likely that 80% of what you need to run your application already exists and more often than not, AWS has a managed service that can be used to do this job. For the remaining 20% the facto way to handle it is to launch EC2 instances and run what you need on them, but in AWS, there is one more way to handle that and it's called building a serverless architecture.

If you take a closer look at your applications or services, even if the code is unique, there are still a number of common patterns that are likely to be found in other applications such as the programming language used to develop it or the way your service is triggered. For instance, a lot of web applications such as our `helloworld` will execute code based on an HTTP request.

For all those smaller services and in particular the ones that are event driven, you can turn to AWS Lambda to run your code.

AWS Lambda

Lambda is somewhat the next evolution in abstracting the hardware away from the application. Virtualization such as EC2 took the pain of dealing with hardware away from operation teams; Lambda does the same but to the operating system and scaling. The AWS Lambda lets you create custom code called Lambda functions are written in Node.js, Python, Java, and C# that will be triggered automatically in response to events. Those events can be emitted by your own application and a number of managed services. Among the services we previously explored are S3, CodePipeline, CodeCommit, Kinesis, and Aurora, but the list of services that integrate with Lambda is a lot longer than this. You can read more about the different services supported at `http://amzn.to/2hrCtYB`.

There are a number of ways to take advantage of AWS Lambda. You can use it to better scale some features in your applications. For instance, let's imagine a photo sharing service. As you do your initial development, you will likely add to your application a feature to upload photos. This feature will likely get the photos and store it on S3 and then generate a thumbnail for better preview. This feature will work well when executed by your main application, but you will have to pay attention to the number of photos that are being uploaded as you will sometimes run out of computing power if too many thumbnails are being generated at the same time. Instead, with AWS Lambda, you can create a function to generate the thumbnail and trigger it when new objects (in this case photos) are created in your S3 bucket. With that strategy, scaling the thumbnail generation will be a non-issue as each photo uploaded will trigger the execution of your function and AWS will make sure that the execution happens within milliseconds of the trigger.

You can also use AWS Lambda for more general engineering concepts. We saw earlier in the chapter how to easily add ElastiCache to our data layer to take some load off of our database. Checking if the data is already cached or caching new data is only half of the work needed when implementing a caching layer and, arguably, that's the easy half. The most difficult part is to handle the cache invalidation. Whenever we update a field in our database, we need to remove the entry from the cache such that the cache doesn't serve the old data whenever it is being queried. If we look back at our phonebook application example used in the ElastiCache section, if a business moves to a new location, the address will need to be updated in the database, but also, we will want to remove the current address of that business from ElastiCache.

In complexes architectures where multiple services interact with our database, it can be challenging to correctly handle the cache invalidation for each service that makes changes in our database. An easy way to implement the cache invalidation if you use Aurora is to create a Lambda function that will be invoked every time we run an update query is executed.

In order to get started with AWS Lambda, you can explore a number of blueprint including the exact function needed to generate photos thumbnails as mentioned in the previous example. To do so, open the Lambda service console at `https://console.aws.amazon.com/lambda`.

From a code standpoint, creating a Lambda function is fairly straightforward. You will simply need to implement a handler function as follows:

```
exports.handler = (event, context, callback) => {
    // TODO implement
    callback(null, 'Hello from Lambda');
};
```

The code can be implemented directly in the AWS console or uploaded as a ZIP file or imported from S3, but of course, those solutions aren't ideal when you are trying to make a complex application that may have multiple functions and staging and production environments. Instead of this, we are going to use an open source framework called Serverless. The Serverless framework (`https://serverless.com`) is a simple framework dedicated to managing serverless applications. By using this framework instead of simply CloudFormation, we can easily configure our application to handle many Lambda functions and easily connect them to some of the AWS services across multiple environments. In addition, the framework will make it easy to deploy and test our application.

To fully comprehend the framework, we will first start by installing it as follows:

```
$ npm install -g serverless
```

We can now start using it.

The framework supports developing applications in a number of languages including Python and Java, but in our case, we will use `nodejs` as this is the language we used previously to create our hello world application.

We first create a new `serverless` application using the following command:

```
$ serverless create --template aws-nodejs --path helloworld
```

The commands create a directory `helloworld` with two files in it, `serverless.yml`, the configuration file for our application, and `handler.js`, which will contain our code.

We are going to go in that directory and start editing the files:

```
$ cd helloworld
```

Open the file `handler.js` with your editor.

We find in it the definition of the `exports.handler` previously mentioned. By default, the application will return a JSON object. We are going to replace the body of the response to simply return the string `'Hello World'`. On line 6 of the file, you will find something like:

```
body: JSON.stringify({
  message: 'Go Serverless v1.0! Your function executed successfully!',
  input: event,
}),
```

Replace this block with:

```
body: 'Hello World'
```

And save the changes. For this example, we don't need to edit the `serverless.yml` file as by default, the values set for the service are what we need. The application is called `helloworld`, the provider is AWS, it will use `nodejs` at runtime, the stage is set to dev, and the region `us-east-1`.

We can now deploy the application using the following command:

```
$ serverless deploy
```

By running this command, the serverless framework will create a new CloudFormation stack called `helloworld-dev` (since our environment is dev), upload it to S3, then package the code and also upload it to S3 and, finally, run the deployment for us. In the end, the command will return something like:

```
Service Information

service: helloworld

stage: dev

region: us-east-1

api keys:

None

endpoints:

None

functions:

helloworld-dev-hello: arn:aws:lambda:us-
east-1:511912822958:function:helloworld-dev-hello
```

This gives us all the information we need. As we can see, our new function is called `helloworld-dev-hello`.

We can validate that everything worked by invoking our new function as follows:

```
$ serverless invoke --function hello
{
    "statusCode": 200,
    "body": "Hello World"
}
```

Other services are now able to take advantage of our function. Assuming generating "Hello World" string in our original helloworld application was a complicated task worth carving out of our monolith, we could decide to offload that operation to our Lambda function and change our architecture to look like this in order to get the response from the invocation of the Lambda function:

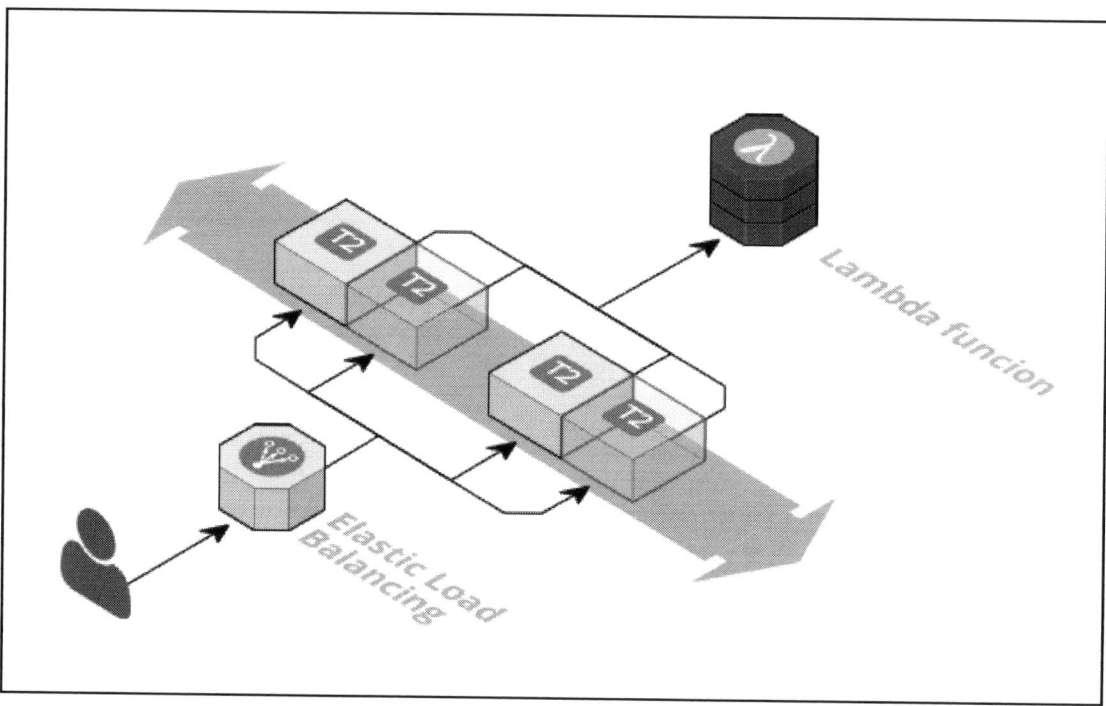

The code would then look something like this:

```
var aws = require('aws-sdk');
var http = require("http");
var lambda = new aws.Lambda({
  region: 'us-east-1'
});

http.createServer(function (request, response) {
  lambda.invoke({
    FunctionName: 'helloworld-dev-hello',
  }, function(err, data) {
    if (err) {
      console.log(err, err.stack);
    } else {
      response.writeHead(200, {'Content-Type': 'text/plain'});
```

```
        response.end(JSON.parse(data.Payload).body);
    }
  })
}).listen(3000)
console.log('Server running');
```

AWS StepFunctions

One of the difficulties you may face on more complex applications than our hello world demonstration is the need to invoke multiple Lambda functions either sequentially or in parallel. For those more complexes scenarios, AWS created a service called StepFunctions, which let you implement these sophisticated applications by creating a state machine approach. Everything can be created using a visual web interface inside the AWS console. You can read more about this service at
http://amzn.to/2hZjZ22.

We now saw how to incorporate some serverless components to our stack, but we can go even further in our serverless transformation and completely remove our EC2 and ELB instances with the help of the API Gateway service.

API Gateway

The API Gateway service, as its name suggests, is a service geared toward creating and managing APIs endpoint. From an architecture standpoint, the service can be seen a little bit like a load balancer such as the ALB or ELB that we saw earlier in the chapter. The ALB gives us the ability to do path-based routing and, for example, send all calls where the path starts with /api/ to the API service hosted on a specific Auto Scaling Group. In the case of the API gateway service, the configuration goes one step beyond and in addition to defining the path, we can also define a method (GET, POST, PUT, OPTIONS) and the integration type that can be almost anything (any AWS managed service, HTTP forwarding, or a static answer). This last specificity makes it a very compiling option when going for a serverless architecture as we can use it in conjunction with a Lambda function. By combining API Gateway and Lambda, we can replace the EC2 instance and load balancer from our stack and create complete web applications that can scale instantly to virtually any amount of traffic.

To implement this, we can use The API Gateway at the edge of your infrastructure, as shown in the following figure:

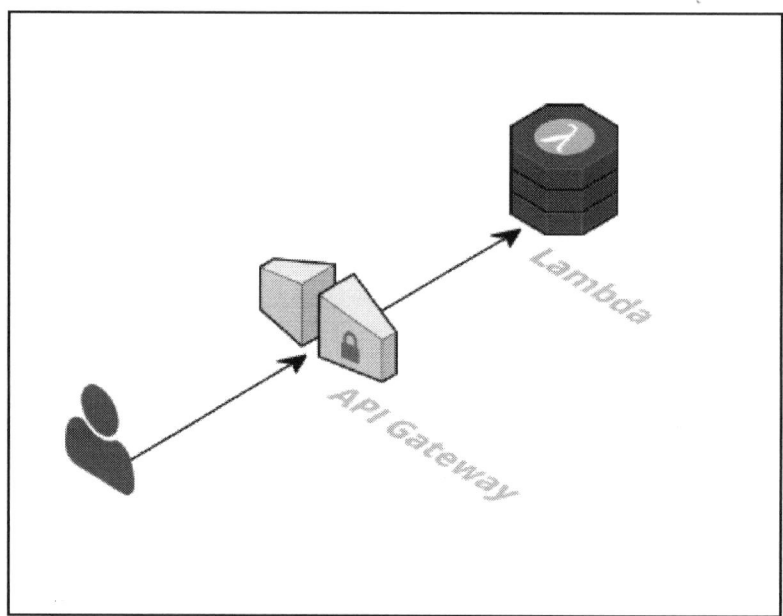

The service will accept inbound connections from browsers or mobile applications. It will then dispatch the different requests looking at the method and path to a number of Lambda functions, which in turn will execute the requests and, if needed, even interact with different data stores. This solution is particularly interesting cost wise to use for services or applications with a small to medium amount of traffic as you get billed on per execution basis.

You can read more about the API Gateway service at `http://amzn.to/2hRVQqW`.

We are going to update our serverless `helloworld` application to include an HTTP endpoint. Thanks to the framework we use, adding an API Gateway endpoint is very easy. The only change necessary is in the configuration of the service. With your editor, open the `serverless.yml` file.

Since Lambda is a service that is event based, we need to define an event to trigger our function. For that, we will go to line 56 of the file where our function is defined. In order to add an API Gateway endpoint and connect it to our function, we simply need to add the following:

```
functions:
  hello:
    handler: handler.hello
    events:
      - http: GET greet
```

We can now save the file and run the command deploy again:

```
$ serverless deploy
```

After a few seconds, the CloudFormation stack will get updated and we will now see a new endpoint appearing in the Service Information output:

```
Service Information

service: helloworld

stage: dev

region: us-east-1

api keys:

None

endpoints:

GET - https://j93ot13ktg.execute-api.us-east-1.amazonaws.com/dev/greet

functions:

helloworld-dev-hello: arn:aws:lambda:us-
east-1:511912822958:function:helloworld-dev-hello
```

We can now open that URL in our browser or use the `curl` command to validate the change:

```
$ curl https://j93ot13ktg.execute-api.us-east-1.amazonaws.com/dev/greet
Hello World
```

By combining Lambda and API Gateway we were able to create an application that can virtually absorb any amount of traffic.

Lambda at the Edge

We talked about how distance matters and that using CloudFront could speed up your application, especially for users far away from your infrastructure. Lambda has one more feature called Lambda at the edge, that lets you run your functions in the same edge location as CloudFront allowing you to quickly handle requests and responses that flow through your CloudFront distribution.

With this new set of options in our hands, we now have a number of ways to scale out the computing of our applications. At that point, it is likely that the next issue that will need to be tackled is scaling our data layer to also handle more than what we currently have.

Data stores at scale

Scaling the data layer is often the trickiest part about scaling an application. It's important to keep things in perspective and not try to over engineer a complex solution that will allow scaling high too prematurely, as it is often a complex and time-consuming effort, but at the same time, it is important to anticipate the upcoming growth to not have your back against the wall when it is time to rework that layer.

We can put things in perspective this way:

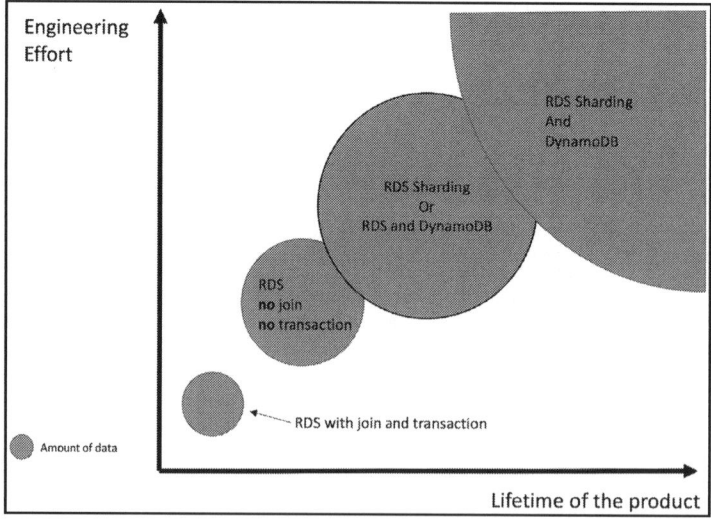

In this chapter, we saw so far that it is best to start with a well-known solution like a relational database such as AWS Aurora. In the project exploratory phase, it is best to not worry about scaling. Once things are getting more serious and you get ready to launch your application in production, it is best to avoid using join statement and transactions as it will make things harder for later. Instead, if you have a need for these features, you can implement similar concepts in your application layer. In addition, we saw that we can help scaling our read queries by adding read replica and by caching queries using ElastiCache, but with regards to scaling writes, we didn't engineer any solutions so far.

When you get to that next stage where handling the load or the amount of data becomes an issue, it is finally time to look into more complex solutions. This will typically require rewriting at least parts of the application data layer. The two most common approaches are to add a new data store to your infrastructure. In AWS, you probably would want to opt for a DynamoDB which is a hosted and very scalable database service or implementing a sharding strategy for your databases. The concept behind sharding a database is as follow:

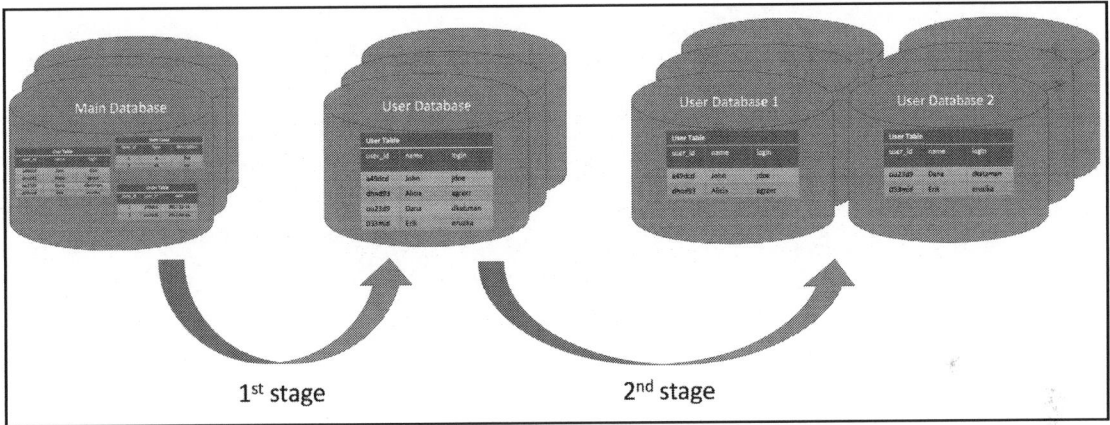

At first, the entire application is using a single database cluster. Because we are constraint to writing to only our primary instance and to a total of 10TB, it is likely that over time, we will have to break that pattern and start using separate database clusters for some of the most important tables. The problem is that even with a single table per cluster, performance or data size can still be an issue. Once that's the case, we get to the 2nd stage of sharding which consists in breaking out tables across multiple database clusters using a specific key. You may decide for example to break out your user database into two shards and have all login ranging from A to M be present in your 1st database while the user whose logins are ranging from N to Z would be present in the 2nd database.

Because there isn't a perfect solution that fits everyone needs, you need to look at your application requirements and decide which solution to adopt based on what you fear the most.

Brewer's (CAP) Theorem states that you can't have a distributed system optimized at the same time for Consistency (every one client will view the same data), Availability (you can always read or write), and Partition tolerance (the system will work well despite an arbitrary number of messages being dropped or delayed in between the database partitions). You basically need to pick two and chose the data store based on that. If you choose to optimize for availability and consistency, then it's likely that you will want to work on a sharding strategy for Aurora if you care the most about availability and partition tolerance, then DynamoDB will likely be a better pick.

Finally, here is a small comparison between those two data stores to help you understand some of their key differences:

	RDS Aurora	DynamoDB
Documentation	`http://amzn.to/2fjc9kj`	`http://amzn.to/2i3aA6v`
Model	Relational	Non-Relational
Data	Structured and stored in tables	Key / Value pairs Can store an infinite amount of items (each item can be up to 400KB)
Schema	Strict schema, making schema changes in a sharded cluster is complex	Schema-less
Availability / Consistency	Each chunk of data is replicated six ways across 3 AZ	Data stored in three geographically distributed replicas of each table
Scalability	At scale, requires a lot of work to implement a sharding strategy	Allows you to scale up and down your throughput on demand
Performance	High performance is achieved by scaling vertically the instance type used in your clusters	Low latency, can easily handle very high throughput as long as you picked a good partitioning key to avoid hot key issues

Of course, over time, when scaling your data layer becomes an even bigger issue, you will likely have to implement both a sharded Aurora clusters strategy and rely on a NoSQL database such as DynamoDB to keep up with your application growth.

We now have a number of options to handle multiple millions of users on our service. There is one last architecture change that we haven't talked about yet; it is having a service hosted on multiple regions.

Multi-region applications

Most of the big websites nowadays will be deployed in multiple physical locations. There are a number of obvious reasons for that. The first one, as we saw when we talked about CDN is physical locality. If your packets have less distance to travel, the application will perform better thanks to the lower latency. The second big win is availability. We hosted our application in the us-east-1 region and while our application is hosted on multiple AZ, it is still possible that an issue could affect the entire region. Internet backbone problems, fiber cut, or even natural disasters are things to expect over the years. As we all know from the first chapter of this book, AWS is available in multiple physical locations called regions so when the time is right, you can decide to make changes in your architecture and make your application available in multiple regions. In order to achieve this result, you will need to do a number of changes to the different services your application relies on.

The first set of changes will be around getting your application to be deployed in multiple regions. For that, you can easily edit your CloudFormation/troposphere scripts. AMIs are unique to a region, therefore; you will need to include a mapping function as follows:

```
def AddAMI(template):
    template.add_mapping("RegionMap", {
        "us-east-1": {"AMI": "ami-a4c7edb2"},
        "us-west-2": {"AMI": "ami-6df1e514"},
        "eu-west-1": {"AMI": "ami-327f5352"}
})
```

And change the section of the code that hard codes the AMI ID to be something like the following:

```
ImageId=FindInMap("RegionMap", Ref("AWS::Region"), "AMI"),
```

The next big issue you will need to tackle is replicating your data across different regions. Data replication could be the subject of a book of its own because of how complex it is to cover all aspects of those topics, but at a high level, here are the things you need to know.

There are two ways to architecture your different regions. The first approach, the easiest one, is to create what is called an active passive replication. You will have multiple regions and clients will be able to read from any regions, but the write operations are only happening in the active regions. Certain services including Aurora supports it natively `http://amzn.to/2i3gRiE`, some other services like DynamoDB have some open source tools (`http://bit.ly/2i3j911`) that will help you to implant the replication, some are natively global such as S3 (in the standard region), route 53, or CloudFormation, but for a lot of the other services, you will need to handle the replication on your own.

The second approach is called active and as you might guess, in that configuration, each region will accept both read and write operations. This is the most complex scenario as you now need to handle eventual consistency as similar write operations can happen at the same time in different regions, but conflict with one another (that is, what happens when two users sign up for your service at the same time in different AWS region but pick the same username).

The last set of change aspects to consider when implementing a multi- region replication is to decide how the traffic is being sent to a region or another. The easiest way to handle that is to implement the logic in route 53, the DNS service from AWS. Route 53 provides a number of routing types including latency and geolocation-based routing. In addition, those rules can be combined with health checks allowing you to automatically route the traffic away from unhealthy regions.

All those changes can easily be implemented using the command line interface and API as you would expect, but AWS also provides a nice GUI tool called **Traffic Flow** that lets you easily configure the rules you need. The GUI of the tool is shown as follows:

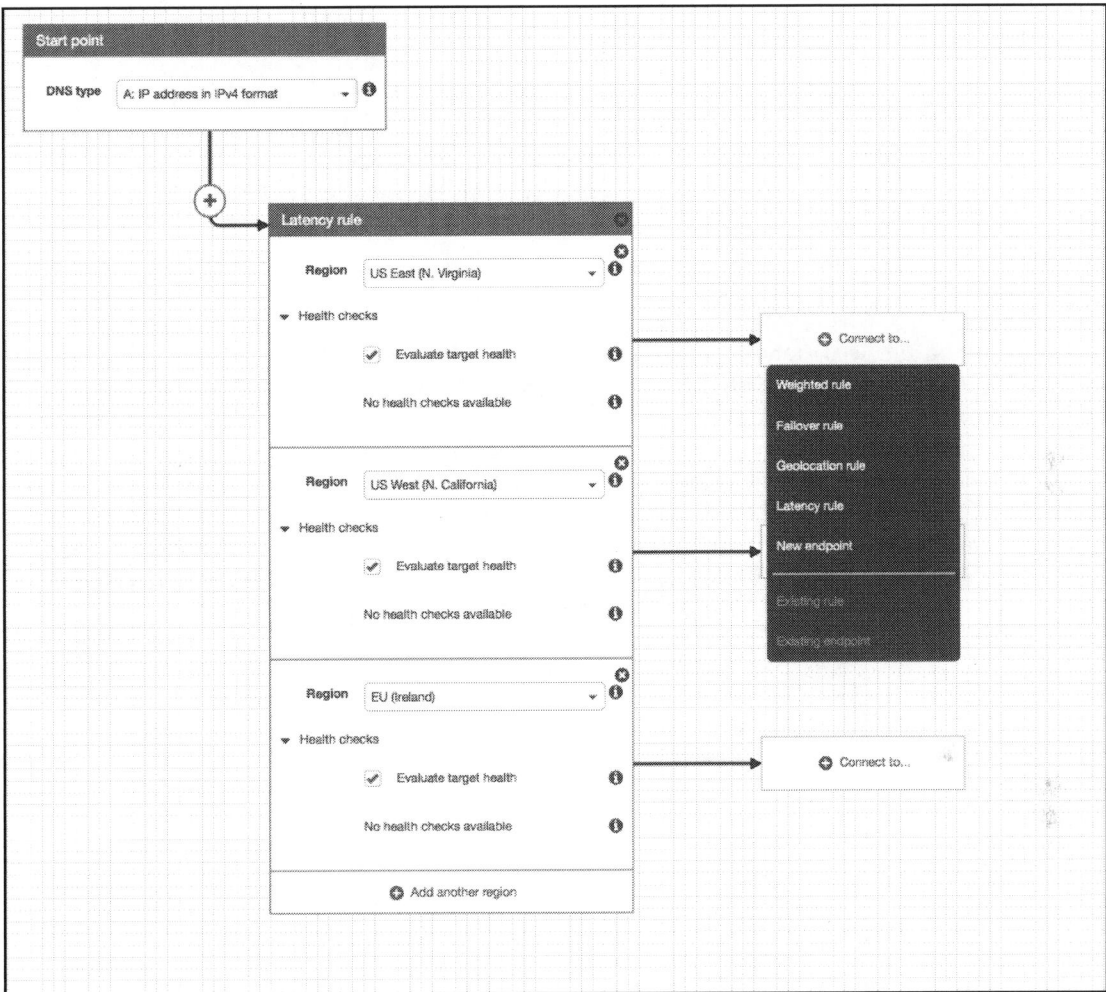

Summary

Throughout this chapter, we have explored a number of concepts and tools to scale a typical web application. We started off learning how to take advantage of the ELB and the Auto Scaling Group services to build a solid foundation that will handle almost any amount of traffic by automatically scaling up and down the number of instances used by our application. In addition, this solution will handle possible failures by replacing bad instances and it works great with our deployment pipeline created in Chapter 4, *Adding Continuous Integration and Continuous Deployment*. While that solution will almost always work, it can become very costly if we don't try to optimize for cost and performance, therefore, we looked at using ElastiCache and CloudFront to take some load off of our application and database.

In order to get to the next stage of scaling an application, we looked at breaking out our monolith into a service oriented architecture and explored other AWS managed services such as ALB, SQS, and Kinesis to better load balancing and better service to service communication.

We finally explored Lambda and API Gateway as an alternative to EC2 to execute code on our behalf. Under the hood, Lambda functions will rely on a container system to execute our code and while the Lambda API doesn't expose anything to manage those containers, AWS has a service of its own called **Elastic Container Service** (**ECS**) to run applications using Docker containers. This will be the subject of our Chapter 6, *Running Containers in AWS*.

6
Running Containers in AWS

Throughout Chapter 5, *Scaling Your Infrastructure*, our architecture changed quite a bit. We explored different ways to scale out applications in AWS. One of the major technologies that we left out is the concept of containers. Containers are at the heart of the **systems development life cycle (SDLC)** of many major technology companies.

So far in the book, we used our personal computer to develop our application. This works well for simple projects such as our helloworld application. On more complex projects with many dependencies, it's a different story. Ever heard of issues where a certain feature works on a developer's laptop but not for the rest of the organization or, even worse, not in production? A lot of those issues come from the differences between environments. When we built our staging and production environments we relied on CloudFormation and Ansible to keep those environments, consistent. Unfortunately, we can't replicate that to our local development environment with ease.

Containers bring a new concept that will address this issue. With them, we can package an application and include the operating system, the application code, and everything in between. Containers can also help at a later stage when it's time to break out monoliths.

In this chapter, we will look at Docker, the most popular container technology. After a brief explanation of what Docker is and how to use its basic functionalities, we will Dockerize our application. This will help us understand the value of using Docker as a developer.

To appreciate the value of Docker used in production, we will look into the **EC2 container service** (**ECS**) from AWS. Using CloudFormation, we will create new templates to run containers across our environments. This will also give us the opportunity to create ALB instances. Finally, in the last section of the chapter, we will create a new deployment pipeline. We will introduce a new service called CodeBuild which we will use to build new containers. We will then deploy our containers on top of ECS using CodePipeline. So, in this chapter, we will be looking at the following topics:

- Dockerizing our `helloworld` application
- Using the EC2 container service
- Updating our CI/CD pipeline to utilize ECS

> This book covers ECS but you have a few more options to use Docker in AWS. You can also take a look at CoreOS Tectonic (`https://tectonic.com/`), Mesosphere DC/OS (`https://mesosphere.com`) or Docker Datacenter (`https://www.docker.com/products/docker-datacenter`).

Dockerizing our helloworld application

Docker and containers in general are very powerful tools worth digging into. By combining resource isolation features, including union capable filesystems, Docker allows for the creation of packages called containers which include everything needed to run an application. Containers, like virtual machines, are self-contained but instead of virtualizing the hardware, they virtualize the operating system itself. In practice, this makes a huge difference. As you have probably noticed by now, starting a virtual machine such as an EC2 instance takes time. This comes from the fact that in order to start a virtual machine, the hypervisor (that's the name of the technology that creates and runs virtual machines) has to simulate all the motions involved in starting a physical server, loading an operating system, and finally going through the different run-levels. In addition, virtual machines have a much larger footprint on disk and in memory. With Docker, the added layer is hardly noticeable and the size of the containers can stay very small. In order to better illustrate that, we will first install Docker and explore its basic usage a bit.

Getting started with Docker

Before we start using Docker, it might be useful to understand better Docker's concept and architecture. We will first talk about Docker's fundamental changes with regards to the software life cycle development. Following that introduction, we will install Docker on our computers and see some of the most common commands needed to use Docker.

Docker fundamentals

The best way to understand how Docker works is to compare how using Docker differs from what we did so far:

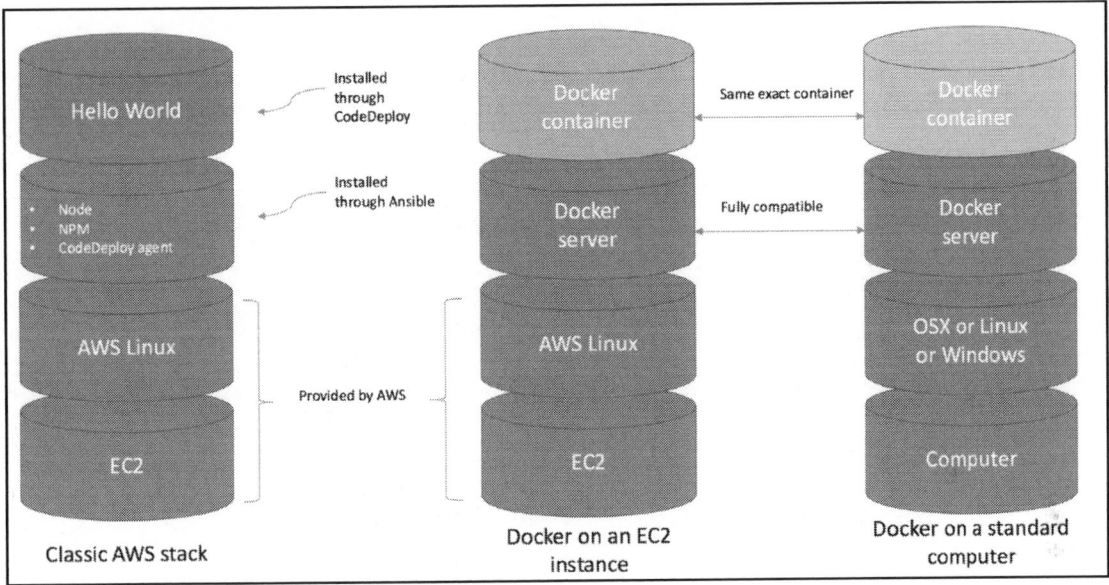

The first stack on the left is what we did so far: using the EC2 service, we picked an AMI providing AWS Linux and with the help of the user data field, installed Ansible to configure our system. When Ansible kicks in, it installs and configures the system so that, later, CodeDeploy can deploy our application and run it.

The middle stack represents what it means to use Docker on top of EC2. The process starts the same way with an AMI running AWS Linux but this time, instead of relying on Ansible and CodeDeploy, we will simply install the Docker server application. After that, we will deploy Docker containers, which will have everything that was previously provided by Ansible and CodeDeploy.

Finally, the big win of that architecture is what we see on the last stack on the right. No matter what the underlying technology is, as long as we can run a Docker server, we can run the exact same container. This means that we can easily test what we will deploy on EC2. Similarly, if an issue happens in a container running on an EC2 instance, we can pull the exact same container and run it locally to possibly troubleshoot the issue.

In order to make that happen, Docker relies on a couple of key concepts as shown in the following diagram:

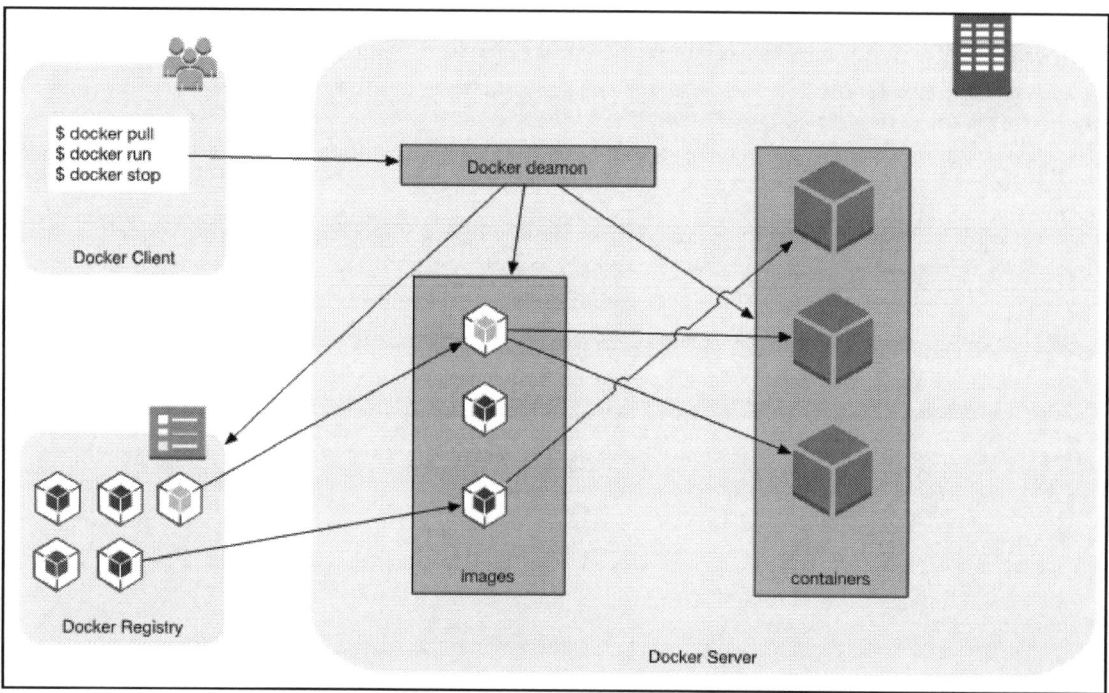

At its core, Docker runs a daemon that loads images (templates describing the stack of the application, including the operating system, application code, and everything in between) and run them in self-contained directories called containers. When working in Docker, as a developer, your work mostly consists of building new images by layering new commands on top of pre-existing images. Images are stored in external registries. Those registries can be public or private. Finally, all the interaction is done through a RESTful API, usually using the command-line interface.

Docker in action

To see Docker in action, we will start by installing it on our computer. The installation of Docker is very straightforward; you can follow the instructions using the link `http://dockr.ly/2iVx6yG` to install and start Docker on Mac, Linux, and Windows.

Once Docker is up and running, we can start using it:

1. The first thing we will do is pull an image from a registry. By default, Docker points to Docker Hub (`https://hub.docker.com`), the official Docker registry from the company Docker. In order to pull an image, we will run the following:

    ```
    $ docker pull alpine
    ```

2. Using default tag `latest`:

    ```
    latest: Pulling from library/alpine
    0a8490d0dfd3: Pull complete
    Digest:
    sha256:dfbd4a3a8ebca874ebd2474f044a0b33600d4523d03b0df76e5c5986
    cb02d7e8
    Status: Downloaded newer image for alpine:latest
    ```

3. In a matter of seconds, Docker will download the container called Alpine from the registry, which is a "minimal Docker image based on Alpine Linux with a complete package index and only 5 MB in size!".

    When working with Docker, the size of a container matters. Therefore, working with smaller base images such as Alpine Linux is highly recommended.

4. We can now run our container. We will start with a simple command:

    ```
    $ docker run alpine echo "Hello World"
    Hello World
    ```

5. On the surface, not a lot seemed to have happened and we end up with the same output as running echo `"Hello World"` without Docker. What really happened behind the scenes is a lot more interesting. Docker loaded the Alpine Linux image we previously pulled, loaded it, and then used that operating system echo command to print `"Hello World"`, then, finally, because the command echo completed, terminated the container.

6. Containers can also be used in a more interactive way. We can, for example, start a shell and interact with it using the following command:

```
$ docker run -it alpine /bin/sh
```

The option -i is for interactive; this will allow us to type commands in our container while the option -t allocates a pseudo-TTY to see what we are typing and the output of our commands.

7. Containers can also be run in the background using the -d option which will detach our container from the Terminal:

```
$ docker run -d alpine sleep 1000
9926beeb49e1ff4b53b855b4e7bbe25cf47477a3698b7a616a1c7876f904427
5
```

The command returns the ID of the container running the Alpine image and the command `sleep 1000`.

8. We can keep track of the different running containers using the following command:

```
$ docker ps
CONTAINER ID        IMAGE           COMMAND
CREATED             STATUS          PORTS
NAMES
9926beeb49e1        alpine          "sleep 1000"        34
seconds ago     Up 33 seconds
dreamy_euclid
```

Running containers can be stopped using the `stop` option followed by the container name or ID (adapt the ID and name based on the output of your `docker ps` command):

```
$ docker stop 9926beeb49e1
9926beeb49e1
```

You can also use the following:

```
$ docker stop dreamy_euclid
dreamy_euclid
```

They can be started again with the `start` option:

```
$ docker start dreamy_euclid
dreamy_euclid
```

9. Finally, containers can be removed using the the `rm` command:

```
$ docker rm 9926beeb49e1
9926beeb49e1
```

This brief overview should allow us to go through this chapter. We will discover a few more commands along the way but for the complete list of options, you can use the `docker help` command or consult the Docker CLI documentation at `http://dockr.ly/2jEF8hj`.

Running simple commands through containers is sometimes useful but, as we know, the real strength of Docker is its ability to handle any code, including our web application. In order to make that happen, we will use another key concept of Docker, a Dockerfile.

Creating our Dockerfile

Dockerfile are text files, usually collocated with applications that instruct Docker how build a new Docker image. Through the creation of those files, you have the ability to tell Docker which Docker image to start from, what to copy on the container filesystem, what network port to expose, and so on. You can find the full documentation of the Dockerfile at `http://dockr.ly/2jmoZMw`.

We are going to create a Dockerfile for our `helloworld` application at the root of the `helloworld` project:

```
$ cd helloworld
$ touch Dockerfile
```

The first instruction of a Dockerfile is always a from instruction. This tells Docker which Docker image to start from. We could use the Alpine image as we did but we can also save some time by using an image that has more than just an operating system.

Through Docker Hub, the official Docker registry, Docker provides a number of curated sets of Docker repositories called `official`. We know that in order to run our application, we need `node.js` and `npm`. We can use the CLI to look for an official node container. To do that, we will use the `docker search` command and filter only on official images:

```
$ docker search --filter=is-official=true node
NAME        DESCRIPTION                                      STARS
OFFICIAL    AUTOMATED
node        Node.js is a JavaScript-based platform for...    4260      [OK]
```

Alternatively, we can also search for it using our browser. We would end up with that same image `https://hub.docker.com/_/node/`.

We can see, using the preceding page, that this image comes in a variety of flavors:

Supported tags and respective **Dockerfile** links

- `7.4.0`, `7.4`, `7`, `latest` *(7.4/Dockerfile)*
- `7.4.0-alpine`, `7.4-alpine`, `7-alpine`, `alpine` *(7.4/alpine/Dockerfile)*
- `7.4.0-onbuild`, `7.4-onbuild`, `7-onbuild`, `onbuild` *(7.4/onbuild/Dockerfile)*
- `7.4.0-slim`, `7.4-slim`, `7-slim`, `slim` *(7.4/slim/Dockerfile)*
- `7.4.0-wheezy`, `7.4-wheezy`, `7-wheezy`, `wheezy` *(7.4/wheezy/Dockerfile)*
- `6.9.4`, `6.9`, `6`, `boron` *(6.9/Dockerfile)*
- `6.9.4-alpine`, `6.9-alpine`, `6-alpine`, `boron-alpine` *(6.9/alpine/Dockerfile)*
- `6.9.4-onbuild`, `6.9-onbuild`, `6-onbuild`, `boron-onbuild` *(6.9/onbuild/Dockerfile)*
- `6.9.4-slim`, `6.9-slim`, `6-slim`, `boron-slim` *(6.9/slim/Dockerfile)*
- `6.9.4-wheezy`, `6.9-wheezy`, `6-wheezy`, `boron-wheezy` *(6.9/wheezy/Dockerfile)*
- `4.7.2`, `4.7`, `4`, `argon` *(4.7/Dockerfile)*
- `4.7.2-alpine`, `4.7-alpine`, `4-alpine`, `argon-alpine` *(4.7/alpine/Dockerfile)*
- `4.7.2-onbuild`, `4.7-onbuild`, `4-onbuild`, `argon-onbuild` *(4.7/onbuild/Dockerfile)*
- `4.7.2-slim`, `4.7-slim`, `4-slim`, `argon-slim` *(4.7/slim/Dockerfile)*
- `4.7.2-wheezy`, `4.7-wheezy`, `4-wheezy`, `argon-wheezy` *(4.7/wheezy/Dockerfile)*

Docker images are always made up of a name and a tag, using the following syntax: `name:tag`. If the tag is omitted, Docker will default to `latest`. We can see in the `docker pull` preceding command how the output says **Using default tag: latest**. When creating a Dockerfile, it is best practice to use an explicit tag that doesn't change over time (unlike `latest`).

 If you are trying to migrate an application currently running on AWS Linux and make a certain number of assumptions based on that OS, you may want to look into using the official AWS Docker image. You can read more about it at `http://amzn.to/2jnmklF`.

On the first line of our file, we will add the following:

```
FROM node:argon
```

This will tell Docker that we want to use that specific version of the node image (argon is an LTS version of node). This means that we won't have to install `node` or `npm`.

Since we have the OS and runtime binaries needed by our application, we can start looking into adding our application to this image. We will first want to create a directory on top of the `node:argon` image's filesystem to hold our code. We can do that using the instruction `RUN`:

```
RUN mkdir -p /usr/local/helloworld/
```

We now want to copy our application files onto the image. We will use the `COPY` directive for that:

```
COPY helloworld.js package.json /usr/local/helloworld/
```

We will now use the `WORKDIR` instruction to set our new working directory to be that `helloworld` directory:

```
WORKDIR /usr/local/helloworld/
```

We can now run the `npm install` command to download and install our dependencies. Because we won't use that container to test our code, we can just install the npm packages needed for production:

```
RUN npm install --production
```

Our application uses port `3000`. We need to make this port accessible to our host. We will use the `EXPOSE` instruction for that:

```
EXPOSE 3000
```

Finally, we can start our application. For that, we will use the `ENTRYPOINT` instruction:

```
ENTRYPOINT [ "node", "helloworld.js" ]
```

We can save the file. It should look like this:

```
http://bit.ly/2vaWYRy
```

We can now build our new image.

Back in the Terminal, we will again use the `docker` command but this time with the argument `build`. We will also use the option `-t` to provide the name `helloworld` to our image:

```
$ docker build -t helloworld .
Sending build context to Docker daemon 96.77kB
Step 1/7 : FROM node:argon
argon: Pulling from library/node
ad74af05f5a2: Pull complete
2b032b8bbe8b: Pull complete
a9a5b35f6ead: Pull complete
3245b5a1c52c: Pull complete
afa075743392: Pull complete
9fb9f21641cd: Pull complete
ecc0815e8ade: Pull complete
f6ec10fc9751: Pull complete
Digest:
sha256:036ecc312ef9528f66d70c1bfa2f110bd4d67c1a0046eb2f5495c2e7ad45a82d
Status: Downloaded newer image for node:argon
 ---> bd1f9ee5b2ae
Step 2/7 : RUN mkdir -p /usr/local/helloworld/
 ---> Running in 3b492d59bf49
 ---> 137a7e793fe4
Removing intermediate container 3b492d59bf49
Step 3/7 : COPY helloworld.js package.json /usr/local/helloworld/
 ---> 13d400af5c43
Removing intermediate container 3db7e52c9b46
Step 4/7 : WORKDIR /usr/local/helloworld/
 ---> a32ed971f63b
Removing intermediate container e86fbe293ab6
Step 5/7 : RUN npm install --production
 ---> Running in 6bb8e44100d7
npm info it worked if it ends with ok
npm info using npm@2.15.11
npm info using node@v4.8.4
npm WARN package.json helloworld@1.0.0 No description
npm WARN package.json helloworld@1.0.0 No README data
npm info preinstall helloworld@1.0.0
npm info build /usr/local/helloworld
npm info linkStuff helloworld@1.0.0
npm info install helloworld@1.0.0
npm info postinstall helloworld@1.0.0
```

```
npm info ok
  ---> dd5d542838c0
Removing intermediate container 6bb8e44100d7
Step 6/7 : EXPOSE 3000
  ---> Running in 331073792dea
  ---> bbca00ed085d
Removing intermediate container 331073792dea
Step 7/7 : ENTRYPOINT node helloworld.js
  ---> Running in 9382c5b8fb60
  ---> 9d78e2a8ecff
Removing intermediate container f4921b7dd915
Successfully built 9d78e2a8ecff
Successfully tagged helloworld:latest
```

As you can see, each command produces a new intermediary container with the changes triggered by that step.

We can now run our newly created container with the following command:

```
$ docker run -p 3000:3000 -d helloworld
881d9d8dad59ea7fe82b55f9d6e72142471b0dac2adf1b0857d4f63758864314
```

Here, we are adding the -p option to our command to map the exposed port of our container to a port on our computer.

There are a few ways to validate that our container is working correctly. We can start by looking at the logs produced by our container (replace the container id with the output of the previous command) :

```
$ docker logs
881d9d8dad59ea7fe82b55f9d6e72142471b0dac2adf1b0857d4f63758864314
Server running
```

We can use the docker ps command to see the status of our container:

```
$ docker ps
CONTAINER ID        IMAGE               COMMAND                CREATED
STATUS              PORTS               NAMES
881d9d8dad59        e7deb47c0528        "node helloworld.js"   2 minutes
ago        Up 2 minutes        0.0.0.0:3000->3000/tcp   jovial_fermi
```

And of course, we can simply test the application with curl:

```
$ curl localhost:3000
Hello World
```

And finally, kill the container using the `docker kill` command and container Id:

```
$ docker kill 881d9d8dad59
881d9d8dad59
```

Since our image is correctly working, we can commit the code to GitHub:

```
$ git add Dockerfile
$ git commit -m "Adding Dockerfile"
$ git push
```

In addition, you can now create an account (for free) on Docker Hub and upload that new image. If you want to give it a try, you can follow the instructions at `http://dockr.ly/2ki6DQV`.

Having the ability to easily share containers makes a big difference when collaborating on projects. Instead of sharing code and asking people to compile or build packages, you can actually share a Docker image. For instance, by running the following:

```
docker pull effectivedevops/helloworld
```

You can experience the `helloworld` application, the exact way I see it, no matter what your underlying architecture is. This new way of running applications makes Docker a very strong solution to share work or collaborate on projects.

The strength of Docker doesn't stop at work collaboration. As we are about to see, using containers in production is also a very interesting option. In order to easily implement such a solution, AWS created the EC2 container service. We are going to use it to deploy our newly created `helloworld` image.

Using the EC2 container service

We just went over creating a Docker image for our application. We saw how easy and fast it is to start a container using Docker. This is a very transformative experience compared to using only virtual machine technologies such as EC2.

One possibility that we haven't explicitly mentioned so far is that you can start multiple containers with the same image.

We can, for example, start our `helloworld` container five times, binding five different ports using the following command (adapt the ID based on the image ID you built. If needed, run `docker images` to find its ID):

```
$ for p in {3001..3005}; do docker run -d -p ${p}:3000 e7deb47c0528; done
32631a70b37ab827de39d57fd1d415339202779cf8e16963791980dc9212680a
ad69359b9630446700cbf515c67bd8d5e9de461542de7f6f0614045f36be427f
fad5b94bb1d10a31304348b086a95e0bb82d2ee944b3f75ce64b06af0ccf2353
cd0819ce968c497f9002b47a503f315d8494cb615e88b31029504bf6bd4f2630
0b552a8707313f7294ddfe1b4de7b4320a8efb4885697d466491f426c9743b67
```

We can validate that everything is working using `ps` and `curl`:

```
$ docker ps
CONTAINER ID        IMAGE                    COMMAND                     CREATED
STATUS              PORTS                         NAMES
0b552a870731        e7deb47c0528             "node helloworld.js"     6 seconds
ago          Up 5 seconds          0.0.0.0:3005->3000/tcp     hungry_easley
cd0819ce968c        e7deb47c0528             "node helloworld.js"     7 seconds
ago          Up 6 seconds          0.0.0.0:3004->3000/tcp     nifty_meitner
fad5b94bb1d1        e7deb47c0528             "node helloworld.js"     8 seconds
ago          Up 7 seconds          0.0.0.0:3003->3000/tcp     agitated_khorana
ad69359b9630        e7deb47c0528             "node helloworld.js"     8 seconds
ago          Up 8 seconds          0.0.0.0:3002->3000/tcp     practical_poincare
32631a70b37a        e7deb47c0528             "node helloworld.js"     9 seconds
ago          Up 8 seconds          0.0.0.0:3001->3000/tcp     affectionate_pare
$ curl localhost:3005
Hello World
```

Cleaning up containers

We can clean up everything by stopping and removing all those containers with these two handy one-line commands:

```
$ docker stop $(docker ps -a -q)
$ docker system prune
```

This ability to start multiple containers on a single host with almost no overhead or latency makes Docker an ideal candidate for production.

In addition, more and more companies are deciding to take the service-oriented architecture approach to an all-new level by breaking out each business function into a separate service. This is often called using a microservices approach. Docker is a natural fit for micro services and for managing micro service architecture. It provides a platform that is language agnostic (you can start any type of application written in any language-inside your container), the ability to scale horizontally and vertically with ease, and a common story around deployment as we deploy containers instead of a variety of services.

We will implement our container architecture using the infrastructure as code best practices and use CloudFormation through the intermediary of Troposphere.

The first service we are going to look at is AWS's **EC2 Container Registry (ECR)**.

Creating an ECR repository to manage our Docker image

In the first part of the chapter, we used the Docker Hub public registry. AWS provides a similar service called ECR which will let you keep your images in a private registry called a **repository**. ECR is fully compatible with the Docker CLI but also integrates deeply with the rest of the ECS services. We are going to use it to store our `helloworld` images.

As mentioned, we will heavily rely on CloudFormation to make our changes. Unlike what we saw previously, because of its nature, the ECS infrastructure we are going to build needs to be very modular as in practice we will want to share some of those components with other services. Therefore, we will create a number of templates and link them to one another. One good way to do that is to rely on CloudFormation's export ability, which lets us do cross-stack referencing.

 One of the added bonuses that export provides is a fail-safe mechanism. You can't delete or edit a stack if another stack references an exported output.

We will create a new troposphere script to generate our template; Go to the EffectiveDevOpsTemplates repository and create a new script `ecr-repository-cf-template.py`.

We will start with the import of a number of modules, including the `Export` mentioned earlier and the `ecr` module to create our repository. We will also create our template variable `t` as we did in the previous chapters:

```
"""Generating CloudFormation template."""

from troposphere import (
    Export,
    Join,
    Output,
    Parameter,
    Ref,
    Template
```

```
)
from troposphere.ecr import Repository

t = Template()
```

Since we are going to create a number of CloudFormation templates in this chapter, we will add a description so that it's easier to understand which template does what when looking at them in the AWS console:

```
t.add_description("Effective DevOps in AWS: ECR Repository")
```

We will create a parameter for the name of the repository so that we will be able to reuse that CloudFormation template for every repository we create:

```
t.add_parameter(Parameter(
    "RepoName",
    Type="String",
    Description="Name of the ECR repository to create"
))
```

We can now create our repository:

```
t.add_resource(Repository(
    "Repository",
    RepositoryName=Ref("RepoName")
))
```

We are keeping the code very simple here and not enforcing any particular permissions. If you need to restrict who can access your repository and to see more complex configurations, you can refer to the AWS documentation and, in particular, http://amzn.to/2j7hA2P.

Lastly, we will output the name of the repository we created and export its value through a template variable:

```
t.add_output(Output(
    "Repository",
    Description="ECR repository",
    Value=Ref("RepoName"),
    Export=Export(Join("-", [Ref("RepoName"), "repo"])),
))

print(t.to_json())
```

We can save our script; it should look like this: http://bit.ly/2w2p2D5

We will now generate the CloudFormation template and create our stack as follows:

```
$ python ecr-repository-cf-template.py > ecr-repository-cf.template
$ aws cloudformation create-stack \
      --stack-name helloworld-ecr \
      --capabilities CAPABILITY_IAM \
      --template-body file://ecr-repository-cf.template \
      --parameters \
        ParameterKey=RepoName,ParameterValue=helloworld
```

After a few minutes, our stack will be created. We can validate that the repository was correctly created:

```
$ aws ecr describe-repositories
{
    "repositories": [
        {
            "registryId": "511912822958",
            "repositoryName": "helloworld",
            "repositoryArn": "arn:aws:ecr:us-
east-1:511912822958:repository/helloworld",
            "createdAt": 1484252219.0,
            "repositoryUri": "511912822958.dkr.ecr.us-
east-1.amazonaws.com/helloworld"
        }
    ]
}
```

We can see our exported output with the following command:

```
$ aws cloudformation list-exports
{
    "Exports": [
        {
            "ExportingStackId": "arn:aws:cloudformation:us-
east-1:511912822958:stack/helloworld-ecr/01473e10-
e1c2-11e6-8a73-500c219b8099",
            "Value": "helloworld",
            "Name": "helloworld-repo"
        }
    ]
}
```

Our repository can now be used to store our `helloworld` image. We will use the Docker CLI to do that. The first step of that process is to log in to the `ecr` service. You can do it with the following handy one-liner:

```
$ eval "$(aws ecr get-login --region us-east-1 --no-include-email )"
```

Back in our `helloworld` directory where the Dockerfile is, we will tag our image:

```
$ cd helloworld
```

It is a common practice to use the tag `latest` to designate the most recent version of an image. In addition, you need to adapt the following command based on the output of the `aws ecr describe-repositories` output (we assume here that you already built your image):

```
$ docker tag helloworld:latest 511912822958.dkr.ecr.us-
east-1.amazonaws.com/helloworld:latest
```

We can now push that image to our registry:

```
$ docker push 511912822958.dkr.ecr.us-
east-1.amazonaws.com/helloworld:latest
The push refers to a repository [511912822958.dkr.ecr.us-
east-1.amazonaws.com/helloworld]
105cbf48989e: Pushed
07063be54b8f: Pushed
91cb8cc7a37f: Pushed
520e3b31bf3e: Pushed
7cbcbac42c44: Pushed
latest: digest:
sha256:0e2ab02729d9f075abf79bb3a63dab90e2a4ce4f196a1ee8369edb95ba788e20
size: 1361
```

We can see how each layer of our image is pushed in parallel to our registry.

Once the operation completes, we can validate that the new image is present in our registry:

```
$ aws ecr describe-images --repository-name helloworld
{
    "imageDetails": [
        {
            "imageSizeInBytes": 13071647,
            "imageDigest":
"sha256:0e2ab02729d9f075abf79bb3a63dab90e2a4ce4f196a1ee8369edb95ba788e20",
            "imageTags": [
                "latest"
            ],
            "registryId": "511912822958",
            "repositoryName": "helloworld",
            "imagePushedAt": 1485551754.0
        }
    ]
}
```

At this point, our image is now available to the rest of our infrastructure. We are going to move on to the next step of our process, which is the creation of the ECS cluster.

Creating an ECS cluster

Creating an ECS cluster is very similar to what we did in Chapter 5, *Scaling Your Infrastructure*, when we created an Auto Scaling Group to run our helloworld application. The main difference is that there is one more level of abstraction. ECS will run a number of services called tasks.

Each of those tasks may exist multiple times in order to handle the traffic:

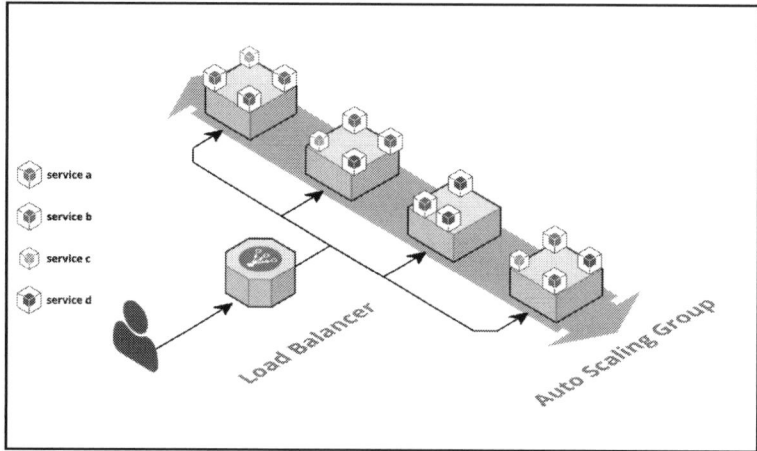

In order to do that, the ECS service provides an orchestration layer.

That orchestration layer is in charge of managing the life cycle of containers, including upgrading or downgrading and scaling up or down your containers. The orchestration layer also distributes all containers for every service across all instances of the cluster optimally. Finally, it also exposes a discovery mechanism that interacts with other services such as ALB and ELB to register and deregister containers.

Task placement strategies

While by default, the entire orchestration system is managed by AWS, you also have the ability to customize it through the creation of a task placement strategy. This will let you configure the orchestration to optimize for instance count, for load distribution or add constraints, and make sure that certain tasks are launched on the same instances. You can read more about task placement strategy at

http://amzn.to/2kn20X0. In addition, AWS is maintaining a collection of open source projects geared toward container management and orchestration. You can check those out at https://blox.github.io.

We will create a new script to generate our ECS cluster.

The filename will be ecs-cluster-cf-template.py.

This template starts almost exactly like the template we created in Chapter 5, *Scaling Your Infrastructure,* for the Auto Scaling Group:

```python
"""Generating CloudFormation template."""

from ipaddress import ip_network
from ipify import get_ip
from troposphere import (
    Base64,
    Export,
    Join,
    Output,
    Parameter,
    Ref,
    Sub,
    Template,
    ec2
)

from troposphere.autoscaling import (
    AutoScalingGroup,
    LaunchConfiguration,
    ScalingPolicy
)

from troposphere.cloudwatch import (
    Alarm,
    MetricDimension
)

from troposphere.ecs import Cluster

from troposphere.iam import (
    InstanceProfile,
    Role
)
```

The only new import is the `Cluster` one from the ECS module. Exactly like in Chapter 5, *Scaling Your Infrastructure,* we will extract our IP address in order to use it later for the SSH security group, create our template variable, and add a description to the stack:

```
PublicCidrIp = str(ip_network(get_ip()))

t = Template()

t.add_description("Effective DevOps in AWS: ECS Cluster")
```

We will now proceed with adding our parameters, which are the exact same parameters as in Chapter 5, *Scaling Your Infrastructure,* the `ssh keypair`, the `vpc id`, and its subnets:

```
t.add_parameter(Parameter(
    "KeyPair",
    Description="Name of an existing EC2 KeyPair to SSH",
    Type="AWS::EC2::KeyPair::KeyName",
    ConstraintDescription="must be the name of an existing EC2 KeyPair.",
))

t.add_parameter(Parameter(
    "VpcId",
    Type="AWS::EC2::VPC::Id",
    Description="VPC"
))

t.add_parameter(Parameter(
    "PublicSubnet",
    Description="PublicSubnet",
    Type="List<AWS::EC2::Subnet::Id>",
    ConstraintDescription="PublicSubnet"
))
```

Next, we will look at creating our security group resources:

```
t.add_resource(ec2.SecurityGroup(
    "SecurityGroup",
    GroupDescription="Allow SSH and private network access",
    SecurityGroupIngress=[
        ec2.SecurityGroupRule(
            IpProtocol="tcp",
            FromPort=0,
            ToPort=65535,
            CidrIp="172.16.0.0/12",
        ),
        ec2.SecurityGroupRule(
            IpProtocol="tcp",
            FromPort="22",
```

```
            ToPort="22",
            CidrIp=PublicCidrIp,
        ),
    ],
    VpcId=Ref("VpcId")
))
```

 There is one important difference here. In Chapter 5, *Scaling Your Infrastructure*, we opened up port 3000 since that's what our application is using. Here, we are opening every port to the CIDR 172.16.0.0/12, which is the private IP space of our internal network. This will give our ECS cluster the ability to run multiple helloworld containers on the same hosts, binding different ports.

We will now create our cluster resource; this can simply be done with the following call:

```
t.add_resource(Cluster(
    'ECSCluster',
))
```

Next, we will focus on configuring instances of the cluster starting with their IAM role. Overall, this is one of the more complex resources to create in ECS as the cluster will need to perform a number of interactions with other AWS services. We can create a complete custom policy for it or import the policies AWS created:

```
t.add_resource(Role(
    'EcsClusterRole',
    ManagedPolicyArns=[
        'arn:aws:iam::aws:policy/service-role/AmazonEC2RoleforSSM',
        'arn:aws:iam::aws:policy/AmazonEC2ContainerRegistryReadOnly',
        'arn:aws:iam::aws:policy/service-
role/AmazonEC2ContainerServiceforEC2Role',
        'arn:aws:iam::aws:policy/CloudWatchFullAccess'
    ],
    AssumeRolePolicyDocument={
        'Version': '2012-10-17',
        'Statement': [{
            'Action': 'sts:AssumeRole',
            'Principal': {'Service': 'ec2.amazonaws.com'},
            'Effect': 'Allow',
        }]
    }
))
```

We can now tie our role with the instance profile as follows:

```
t.add_resource(InstanceProfile(
    'EC2InstanceProfile',
    Roles=[Ref('EcsClusterRole')],
))
```

The next step is to create our launch configuration. This is what this looks like:

```
t.add_resource(LaunchConfiguration(
    'ContainerInstances',
    UserData=Base64(Join('', [
        "#!/bin/bash -xe\n",
        "echo ECS_CLUSTER=",
        Ref('ECSCluster'),
        " >> /etc/ecs/ecs.config\n",
        "yum install -y aws-cfn-bootstrap\n",
        "/opt/aws/bin/cfn-signal -e $? ",
        "        --stack ",
        Ref('AWS::StackName'),
        "        --resource ECSAutoScalingGroup ",
        "        --region ",
        Ref('AWS::Region'),
        "\n"])),
    ImageId='ami-04351e12',
    KeyName=Ref("KeyPair"),
    SecurityGroups=[Ref("SecurityGroup")],
    IamInstanceProfile=Ref('EC2InstanceProfile'),
    InstanceType='t2.micro',
    AssociatePublicIpAddress='true',
))
```

In this example, we don't install Ansible like we did before. Instead, we are using an ECS-optimized AMI (you can read more about it at `http://amzn.to/2jX0xVu`) and using the `UserData` field to configure the ECS service and start it.

Now that we have our launch configuration, we can create our Auto Scaling Group resources.

When working with ECS, scaling is needed at two levels:

- The containers level, as we will need to run more containers of a given service if the traffic spikes
- The underlying infrastructure level

Containers, through the intermediary of their task definitions, set a requirement for CPU and memory. They will require, for example, 1024 CPU units, which represents 1 core and 256 memory units, which means 256 MB of RAM. If the ECS instances are close to being filled up on one of those two constraints, the ECS Auto Scaling Group needs to add more instances:

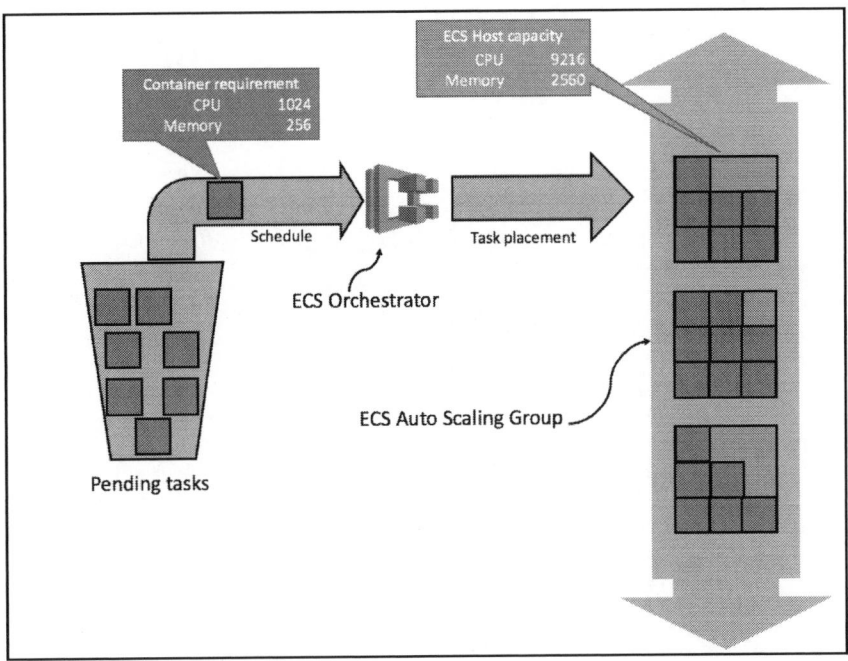

In terms of implementation, the process if very similar to what we did in Chapter 5, *Scaling Your Infrastructure*.

We first create the `AutosScalingGroup` resource:

```
t.add_resource(AutoScalingGroup(
    'ECSAutoScalingGroup',
    DesiredCapacity='1',
    MinSize='1',
    MaxSize='5',
    VPCZoneIdentifier=Ref("PublicSubnet"),
    LaunchConfigurationName=Ref('ContainerInstances'),
))
```

Next, we will create `ScalingPolicies` and `Alarms` to monitor the CPU and memory reservation metrics. In order to accomplish that, we will take advantage of Python to generate our stack and create for loops as follows:

```python
states = {
    "High": {
        "threshold": "75",
        "alarmPrefix": "ScaleUpPolicyFor",
        "operator": "GreaterThanThreshold",
        "adjustment": "1"
    },
    "Low": {
        "threshold": "30",
        "alarmPrefix": "ScaleDownPolicyFor",
        "operator": "LessThanThreshold",
        "adjustment": "-1"
    }
}


for reservation in {"CPU", "Memory"}:
    for state, value in states.iteritems():
        t.add_resource(Alarm(
            "{}ReservationToo{}".format(reservation, state),
            AlarmDescription="Alarm if {} reservation too {}".format(
                reservation,
                state),
            Namespace="AWS/ECS",
            MetricName="{}Reservation".format(reservation),
            Dimensions=[
                MetricDimension(
                    Name="ClusterName",
                    Value=Ref("ECSCluster")
                ),
            ],
            Statistic="Average",
            Period="60",
            EvaluationPeriods="1",
            Threshold=value['threshold'],
            ComparisonOperator=value['operator'],
            AlarmActions=[
                Ref("{}{}".format(value['alarmPrefix'], reservation))]
        ))
        t.add_resource(ScalingPolicy(
            "{}{}".format(value['alarmPrefix'], reservation),
            ScalingAdjustment=value['adjustment'],
            AutoScalingGroupName=Ref("ECSAutoScalingGroup"),
            AdjustmentType="ChangeInCapacity",
        ))
```

Finally, we will output a small amount of resource information, namely the stack ID, the VPC ID, and public subnets:

```
t.add_output(Output(
    "Cluster",
    Description="ECS Cluster Name",
    Value=Ref("ECSCluster"),
    Export=Export(Sub("${AWS::StackName}-id")),
))

t.add_output(Output(
    "VpcId",
    Description="VpcId",
    Value=Ref("VpcId"),
    Export=Export(Sub("${AWS::StackName}-vpc-id")),
))

t.add_output(Output(
    "PublicSubnet",
    Description="PublicSubnet",
    Value=Join(',', Ref("PublicSubnet")),
    Export=Export(Sub("${AWS::StackName}-public-subnets")),
))

print(t.to_json())
```

CloudFormation provides a number of pseudo-parameters such as AWS::StackName. Throughout the chapter, we will rely on it to make our template generic enough to be used across different environments and services. In the preceding code, we created an ECR repository for our helloworld container. The name was generated by the stack creation command. If needed, we could reuse that exact same template to create another repository for another container.

The script is complete; it should look like this: http://bit.ly/2vatFi9

As before, we can now commit our script and create our stack by first generating our template:

```
$ git add ecs-cluster-cf-template.py
$ git commit -m "Adding Troposphere script to generate an ECS cluster"
$ git push
$ python ecs-cluster-cf-template.py > ecs-cluster-cf.template
```

To create our stack, we need three parameters, the `keypair`, the `VPC id`, and the `subnets`. In the previous chapters, we used the web interface to create those stacks. Here, we will see how to get that information using the CLI.

To get the VPC ID and subnet IDs, we can use the following:

```
$ aws ec2 describe-vpcs --query 'Vpcs[].VpcId'
[
    "vpc-f7dc4093"
]
$ aws ec2 describe-subnets --query 'Subnets[].SubnetId'
[
    "subnet-4decfe66",
    "subnet-3e905948",
    "subnet-82ba3fbf",
    "subnet-4f3bdb17"
]
```

We can now create our stack by combining those outputs. Since ECS clusters can run a variety of containers and, through that, run a number of application and services, we will aim for one ECS cluster per environment, starting with staging. In order to differentiate each environment, we will rely on the stack name. Therefore, it is important to call your stack `staging-cluster` as shown here:

```
$ aws cloudformation create-stack \
      --stack-name staging-cluster \
      --capabilities CAPABILITY_IAM \
      --template-body file://ecs-cluster-cf.template \
      --parameters \
        ParameterKey=KeyPair,ParameterValue=EffectiveDevOpsAWS \
        ParameterKey=VpcId,ParameterValue=vpc-f7dc4093 \
ParameterKey=PublicSubnet,ParameterValue=subnet-3e905948\\,subnet-4decfe66\
\,subnet-4f3bdb17\\,subnet-82ba3fbf
{
    "StackId": "arn:aws:cloudformation:us-
east-1:511912822958:stack/staging/6b2a2510-e21a-11e6-a834-50d501eed2b3"
}
```

We are now going to add a load balancer. In the previous chapter, we used an ELB for our Auto Scaling Group. Later, we also mentioned the existence of the ALB service. This time, we will create ALB instance to proxy our application traffic.

Creating an ALB

As mentioned, ECS provides an orchestrator that takes care of allocating the containers across our Auto Scaling Group. It also keeps track of which port each container uses and integrates with ALB so that our load balancer can correctly route the incoming traffic to all containers running a given service.

ECS supports both the ELB and ALB services but the ALB gives more flexibility when working with containers. We will demonstrate how to create an ALB using CloudFormation through Troposphere.

We will start by creating a new file and calling it `helloworld-ecs-alb-cf-template.py`.

We will then put our usual `import`, and create our template variable and add a description:

```python
"""Generating CloudFormation template."""

from troposphere import elasticloadbalancingv2 as elb

from troposphere import (
    Export,
    GetAtt,
    ImportValue,
    Join,
    Output,
    Ref,
    Select,
    Split,
    Sub,
    Template,
    ec2
)

t = Template()

t.add_description("Effective DevOps in AWS: ALB for the ECS Cluster")
```

We are now going to create our security group. No surprise here, we are opening TCP/3000 to the world as we did in Chapter 5, *Scaling Your Infrastructure*, with the ELB:

```python
t.add_resource(ec2.SecurityGroup(
    "LoadBalancerSecurityGroup",
    GroupDescription="Web load balancer security group.",
    VpcId=ImportValue(
        Join(
            "-",
            [Select(0, Split("-", Ref("AWS::StackName"))),
```

```
                    "cluster-vpc-id"]
            )
        ),
        SecurityGroupIngress=[
            ec2.SecurityGroupRule(
                IpProtocol="tcp",
                FromPort="3000",
                ToPort="3000",
                CidrIp="0.0.0.0/0",
            ),
        ],
    ))
```

The main difference with what we did previously is that instead of starting with a parameter section and requesting, yet again, to provide the VPC ID and public subnets, we are taking advantage of the value we just exported before. When we launch this stack, we will call it `staging-alb`. The block of code inside the `ImportValue` does the following:

1. We first get the name of our stack. We will launch that stack under the name `staging-alb`.
2. The `split` function breaks the stack name on the character -, meaning that we end up with `['staging', 'alb']`.
3. The `select` function takes the first element of the list, `staging`.
4. The `join` function concatenates that element with the string `-cluster-vpc-id`. In the end, we get `Import("staging-cluster-vpc-id")`, which is the name of the key we defined to export the VPC ID when we created our ECS cluster.

We are now going to create our ALB. ALB, being more flexible and feature-rich than ELB, requires a bit more effort when it comes to configuration. ALB works through the intermediary of three different resources. The first one is the ALB resource which handles incoming connections. On the opposite side, we can find the target groups which are the resources used by the ECS clusters register to those ALB. Finally, in order to tie the two, we find the listener's resources:

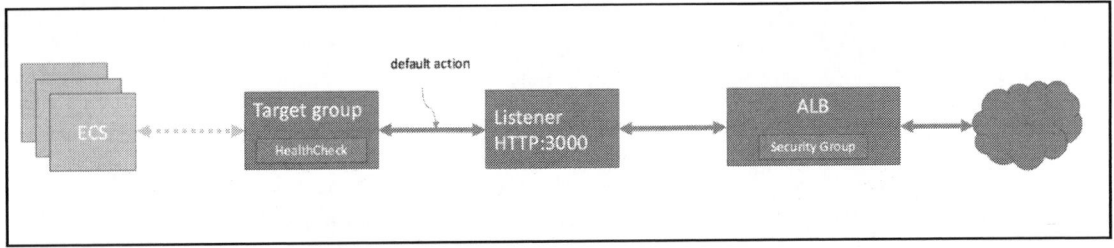

We will first define our load balancer resource:

```
t.add_resource(elb.LoadBalancer(
    "LoadBalancer",
    Scheme="internet-facing",
    Subnets=Split(
        ',',
        ImportValue(
            Join("-",
                [Select(0, Split("-", Ref("AWS::StackName"))),
                 "cluster-public-subnets"]
                )
            )
    ),
    SecurityGroups=[Ref("LoadBalancerSecurityGroup")],
))
```

We use a very similar series of calls to the function to import our subnet as we did just before for the VPC ID.

We are now going to create our target group and configure our health check:

```
t.add_resource(elb.TargetGroup(
    "TargetGroup",
    DependsOn='LoadBalancer',
    HealthCheckIntervalSeconds="20",
    HealthCheckProtocol="HTTP",
    HealthCheckTimeoutSeconds="15",
    HealthyThresholdCount="5",
    Matcher=elb.Matcher(
        HttpCode="200"),
    Port=3000,
    Protocol="HTTP",
    UnhealthyThresholdCount="3",
    VpcId=ImportValue(
        Join(
```

```
            "-",
        [Select(0, Split("-", Ref("AWS::StackName")))],
            "cluster-vpc-id"]
        )
    ),
))
```

Finally, we will add the listener to connect our target group to our load balancer:

```
t.add_resource(elb.Listener(
    "Listener",
    Port="3000",
    Protocol="HTTP",
    LoadBalancerArn=Ref("LoadBalancer"),
    DefaultActions=[elb.Action(
        Type="forward",
        TargetGroupArn=Ref("TargetGroup")
    )]
))
```

Lastly, we will want to create two outputs. The first output is the target group. We will export its value so that our application can register to the group. The second output is the DNS record of the ALB. This will be the entry point to our application:

```
t.add_output(Output(
    "TargetGroup",
    Description="TargetGroup",
    Value=Ref("TargetGroup"),
    Export=Export(Sub("${AWS::StackName}-target-group")),
))

t.add_output(Output(
    "URL",
    Description="Helloworld URL",
    Value=Join("", ["http://", GetAtt("LoadBalancer", "DNSName"), ":3000"])
))

print(t.to_json())
```

The file is ready and should look like this:

```
http://bit.ly/2vbhd1r
```

We can now generate our template and create our stack as follows:

```
$ git add helloworld-ecs-alb-cf-template.py
$ git commit -m "Adding a Load balancer template for our helloworld
application on ECS"
$ git push
$ python helloworld-ecs-alb-cf-template.py > helloworld-ecs-alb-cf.template
$ aws cloudformation create-stack \
      --stack-name staging-alb \
      --capabilities CAPABILITY_IAM \
      --template-body file://helloworld-ecs-alb-cf.template
```

As mentioned, it is important to call it `staging-alb` and that first word is used to import the VPC ID and subnets.

The last stack we need is the creation of our container service.

Creating our ECS hello world service

We have an ECS cluster and a load balancer ready to take on traffic on one side and an ECR repository containing the image of our application on the other side. We now need to tie the two together. This is done by creating an ECS service resource.

We will create a new file called `helloworld-ecs-service-cf-template.py` and start as usual with its imports, template variable creation, and template description:

```
"""Generating CloudFormation template."""

from troposphere.ecs import (
    TaskDefinition,
    ContainerDefinition
)
from troposphere import ecs

from awacs.aws import (
    Allow,
    Statement,
    Principal,
    Policy
)
from troposphere.iam import Role

from troposphere import (
    Parameter,
    Ref,
    Template,
```

```
        Join,
        ImportValue,
        Select,
        Split,
    )

    from awacs.sts import AssumeRole

    t = Template()

    t.add_description("Effective DevOps in AWS: ECS service - Helloworld")
```

Our template will take one argument: the tag of the image we want to deploy. Currently, our repository only has one image tagged as `latest` but in the next section, we will update our deployment pipeline and automatize the deployment of our service to ECS:

```
    t.add_parameter(Parameter(
        "Tag",
        Type="String",
        Default="latest",
        Description="Tag to deploy"
    ))
```

In ECS, applications are defined by their task definitions. This is where we declare which repository to use to get our image, how much CPU and memory the application needs, and all other system properties such as port mapping, environment variables, mount points, and so on. We will keep our task definition minimal; in order to select the proper image, we will utilize the `ImportValue` function (we previously exported the repository name) combined with a `Join` to craft the repository URL. We will require 32 MB of RAM and one-quarter of a core to run our application. Finally, we will specify that port 3000 needs to be mapped onto the system:

```
    t.add_resource(TaskDefinition(
        "task",
        ContainerDefinitions=[
            ContainerDefinition(
                Image=Join("", [
                    Ref("AWS::AccountId"),
                    ".dkr.ecr.",
                    Ref("AWS::Region"),
                    ".amazonaws.com",
                    "/",
                    ImportValue("helloworld-repo"),
                    ":",
                    Ref("Tag")]),
                Memory=32,
                Cpu=256,
```

```
                Name="helloworld",
                PortMappings=[ecs.PortMapping(
                    ContainerPort=3000)]
            )
        ],
    ))
```

As for most of the AWS managed services, the ECS service needs a certain set of permissions provided by the intermediary of a role. We will create that role and use the vanilla policy for the ECS service role:

```
t.add_resource(Role(
    "ServiceRole",
    AssumeRolePolicyDocument=Policy(
        Statement=[
            Statement(
                Effect=Allow,
                Action=[AssumeRole],
                Principal=Principal("Service", ["ecs.amazonaws.com"])
            )
        ]
    ),
    Path="/",
    ManagedPolicyArns=[
        'arn:aws:iam::aws:policy/service-
role/AmazonEC2ContainerServiceRole']
))
```

We will complete the creation of our template with the addition of the ECS service resource which ties the task definition, the ECS cluster, and the ALB together:

```
t.add_resource(ecs.Service(
    "service",
    Cluster=ImportValue(
        Join(
            "-",
            [Select(0, Split("-", Ref("AWS::StackName"))),
                "cluster-id"]
        )
    ),
    DesiredCount=1,
    TaskDefinition=Ref("task"),
    LoadBalancers=[ecs.LoadBalancer(
        ContainerName="helloworld",
        ContainerPort=3000,
        TargetGroupArn=ImportValue(
            Join(
                "-",
```

```
                    [Select(0, Split("-", Ref("AWS::StackName")))),
                        "alb-helloworld-target-group"]
                ),
            ),
        )],
        Role=Ref("ServiceRole")
    ))
```

Finally, as always, we will output the template generated by our code:

```
print(t.to_json())
```

The script is ready and should look like this:

```
http://bit.ly/2uB5wQn
```

We will now generate the template and create our stack:

```
$ git add helloworld-ecs-service-cf-template.py
$ git commit -m "Adding helloworld ECS service script"
$ git push
$ python helloworld-ecs-service-cf-template.py > helloworld-ecs-service-
cf.template
$ aws cloudformation create-stack \
      --stack-name staging-helloworld-service \
      --capabilities CAPABILITY_IAM \
      --template-body file://helloworld-ecs-service-cf.template \
      --parameters \
        ParameterKey=Tag,ParameterValue=latest
```

After a few minutes, the stack should be created. We can circle back to the output of the ALB stack to get the URL of our newly deployed application and test its output:

```
$ aws cloudformation describe-stacks \
      --stack-name staging-alb \
      --query 'Stacks[0].Outputs'
[
    {
        "Description": "TargetGroup",
        "OutputKey": "TargetGroup",
        "OutputValue": "arn:aws:elasticloadbalancing:us-
east-1:511912822958:targetgroup/stagi-Targe-1XEVVSL4W45ZU/318c23a83212c5bf"
    },
    {
        "Description": "Helloworld URL",
        "OutputKey": "URL",
        "OutputValue":
"http://stagi-LoadB-1C1GMX1ULESJZ-1294651738.us-east-1.elb.amazonaws.com:30
00"
```

```
        }
]
$ curl
http://stagi-LoadB-1C1GMX1ULESJZ-1294651738.us-east-1.elb.amazonaws.com:300
0
Hello World
```

We completed the creation of our staging ECS environment.

At this point, we can easily manually deploy new code to our staging as follows:

1. Make the changes in the `helloworld` code locally.
2. Log in to the `ecr` registry:

    ```
    $ eval "$(aws ecr get-login --region us-east-1 --no-include-
    email)"
    ```

3. Build your `docker` container:

    ```
    $ docker build -t helloworld
    ```

4. Pick a new unique tag and use it to tag your image, that is let say, your new tag is `foobar`:

    ```
    $ docker tag helloworld 511912822958.dkr.ecr.us-
    east-1.amazonaws.com/hello-repos-1llamst2oolbl:foobar
    ```

5. Push the image to the `ecr` repository:

    ```
    $ docker push 511912822958.dkr.ecr.us-
    east-1.amazonaws.com/hello-repos-1llamst2oolbl:foobar
    ```

6. Update the ECS service CloudFormation stack:

    ```
    $ aws cloudformation update-stack \
         --stack-name staging-helloworld-service \
         --capabilities CAPABILITY_IAM \
         --template-body file://helloworld-ecs-service-cf.template
    \
         --parameters \
           ParameterKey=Tag,ParameterValue=foobar
    ```

Using this sequence of events, we are going to automate the deployment process and create a new continuous integration/continuous deployment pipeline.

Creating a CI/CD pipeline to deploy to ECS

As we know, having the ability to continuously deploy code across our environments is a very powerful tool as it helps to break out those traditional Dev versus Ops silos and improve the velocity at which new code is being released. We created a pipeline that allows us to automatically deploy new changes from our `helloworld` application to our Auto Scaling Groups for staging and production. We will create a similar pipeline but, this time, it will deploy changes to ECS. Our ECS infrastructure will be as follows:

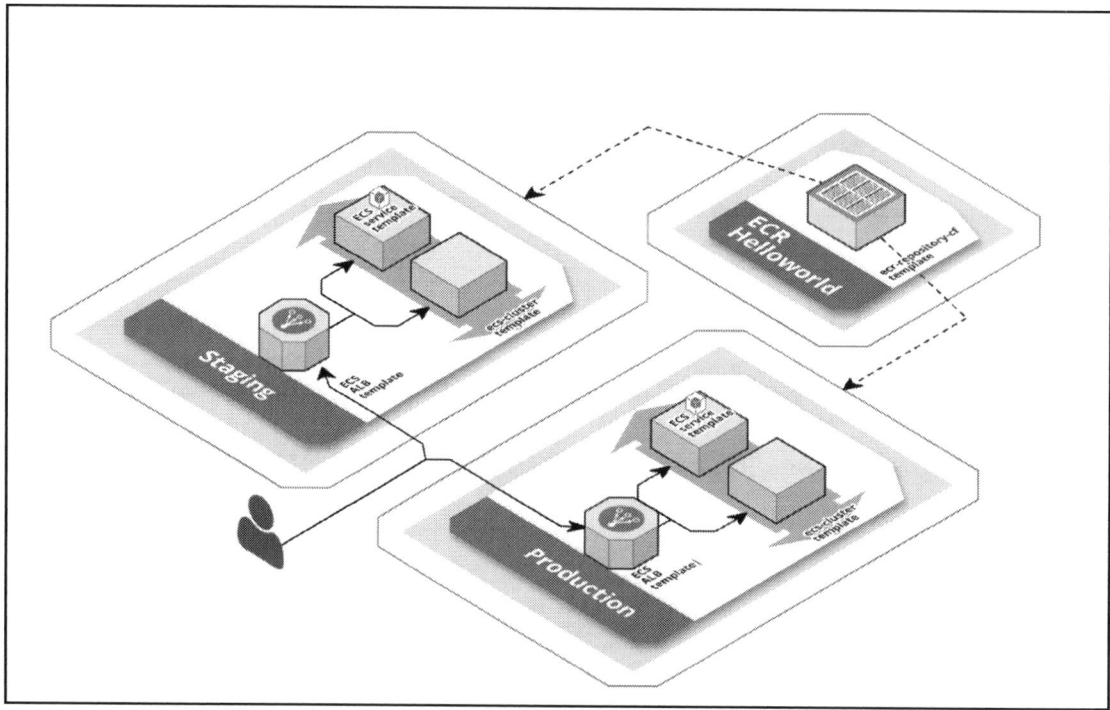

Reusing the CloudFormation templates produced in the previous section will create a production environment identical to the staging one. Note that the `ecr` repository is meant to be unique for a given application, therefore will share it across our environments.

In addition, we will follow the best practices learned in Chapter 3, *Treating Your Infrastructure As Code*, and create our pipeline through a CloudFormation stack.

Our first step will be to create an ECS cluster for production.

Creating our production ECS cluster

Thanks to the upfront work we did with our CloudFormation templates, adding a new environment will be trivial.

We will start by launching a production ECS cluster:

```
$ aws cloudformation create-stack \
      --stack-name production-cluster \
      --capabilities CAPABILITY_IAM \
      --template-body file://ecs-cluster-cf.template \
      --parameters \
        ParameterKey=KeyPair,ParameterValue=EffectiveDevOpsAWS \
        ParameterKey=VpcId,ParameterValue=vpc-f7dc4093 \
        ParameterKey=PublicSubnet,ParameterValue=subnet-3e905948\\,subnet-
        4decfe66\\,subnet-4f3bdb17\\,subnet-82ba3fbf{
    "StackId": "arn:aws:cloudformation:us-
east-1:511912822958:stack/production-
cluster/53833670-e519-11e6-aa35-50fae984a035"
    }
```

We need to wait for the creation of the stack to complete as we need to get some of the exported values from the cluster creation. We can run the following command to get our Terminal to hang until we can crate our next stack:

```
$ aws cloudformation wait stack-create-complete \
      --stack-name production-cluster
```

We move on to creating our ALB and waiting until completion:

```
$ aws cloudformation create-stack \
      --stack-name production-alb \
      --capabilities CAPABILITY_IAM \
      --template-body file://helloworld-ecs-alb-cf.template
{
    "StackId": "arn:aws:cloudformation:us-
east-1:511912822958:stack/production-alb/08592870-e51a-11e6-
ae6e-500c28b04cd1"
    }

$ aws cloudformation wait stack-create-complete --stack-name production-alb
```

Finally, we can create our service:

```
$ aws cloudformation create-stack \
      --stack-name production-helloworld-service \
      --capabilities CAPABILITY_IAM \
      --template-body file://helloworld-ecs-service-cf.template \
```

```
        --parameters \
          ParameterKey=Tag,ParameterValue=latest
{
    "StackId": "arn:aws:cloudformation:us-
east-1:511912822958:stack/production-helloworld-service/91a5ee60-e51a-11e6-
a0f4-500c221b72d1"
}

$ aws cloudformation wait stack-create-complete \
        --stack-name production-helloworld-service
```

At this point, our production environment should be working. We can get its URL by
looking at the output of the ALB stack creation and `curl` the endpoint to make sure the
application is up and running:

```
$ aws cloudformation describe-stacks \
        --stack-name production-alb \
        --query 'Stacks[0].Outputs'
[
    {
        "Description": "TargetGroup",
        "OutputKey": "TargetGroup",
        "OutputValue": "arn:aws:elasticloadbalancing:us-
east-1:511912822958:targetgroup/produ-Targe-1WL80TIPA6T8A/02cf0b93549c04a4"
    },
    {
        "Description": "Helloworld URL",
        "OutputKey": "URL",
        "OutputValue":
"http://produ-LoadB-1NDDH03862MMQ-1994089665.us-east-1.elb.amazonaws.com:30
00"
    }
]
$ curl
http://produ-LoadB-1NDDH03862MMQ-1994089665.us-east-1.elb.amazonaws.com:300
0
Hello World
```

Now that our production environment is ready, we will look into automating the creation
of containers. In order to accomplish that, we will rely on the CodeBuild service.

Automating the creation of containers with CodeBuild

AWS CodeBuild is a managed service geared toward compiling source code. It is comparable to Jenkins but since it's a managed service that conforms to AWS standards, it presents a different set of features and benefits. In our case, using CodeBuild over Jenkins will allow us to create containers without having to spin up and manage an extra EC2 instance. The service also integrates well with CodePipeline which, as before, will drive our process.

We will use CloudFormation through the intermediary of Troposphere to create our CodeBuild project.

We will create a new script and call it `helloworld-codebuild-cf-template.py`.

We will start with our usual import, template variable creation, and description:

```
"""Generating CloudFormation template."""

from awacs.aws import (
    Allow,
    Policy,
    Principal,
    Statement
)

from awacs.sts import AssumeRole

from troposphere import (
    Join,
    Ref,
    Template
)

from troposphere.codebuild import (
    Artifacts,
    Environment,
    Project,
    Source
)
from troposphere.iam import Role

t = Template()

t.add_description("Effective DevOps in AWS: CodeBuild - Helloworld
container")
```

We will now define a new role to grant the proper permissions to our CodeBuild project. The CodeBuild project will interact with a number of AWS services such as ECR, CodePipeline, S3, and CloudWatch logs. To speed up the process, we will rely on the AWS vanilla policies to configure the permissions. This gives us the following:

```
t.add_resource(Role(
    "ServiceRole",
    AssumeRolePolicyDocument=Policy(
        Statement=[
            Statement(
                Effect=Allow,
                Action=[AssumeRole],
                Principal=Principal("Service", ["codebuild.amazonaws.com"])
            )
        ]
    ),
    Path="/",
    ManagedPolicyArns=[
        'arn:aws:iam::aws:policy/AWSCodePipelineReadOnlyAccess',
        'arn:aws:iam::aws:policy/AWSCodeBuildDeveloperAccess',
        'arn:aws:iam::aws:policy/AmazonEC2ContainerRegistryPowerUser',
        'arn:aws:iam::aws:policy/AmazonS3FullAccess',
        'arn:aws:iam::aws:policy/CloudWatchLogsFullAccess'
    ]
))
```

CodeBuild projects require defining a number of elements. The first one we will define is the environment. This tells CodeBuild what type of hardware and OS we need to build our project, and what needs to be preinstalled. It will also let us define extra environment variables. We will use a Docker image that AWS provides, which will give us everything we need to get our work done. The Docker image comes with the AWS and Docker CLI preinstalled and configured. We will also define an environment variable to find our `ecr` repository endpoint:

```
environment = Environment(
    ComputeType='BUILD_GENERAL1_SMALL',
    Image='aws/codebuild/docker:1.12.1',
    Type='LINUX_CONTAINER',
    EnvironmentVariables=[
        {'Name': 'REPOSITORY_NAME', 'Value': 'helloworld'},
        {'Name': 'REPOSITORY_URI',
            'Value': Join("", [
                Ref("AWS::AccountId"),
                ".dkr.ecr.",
                Ref("AWS::Region"),
                ".amazonaws.com",
                "/",
```

```
            "helloworld"])},
    ],
)
```

In CodeBuild, most of the logic is defined in a resource called a `buildspec`. The `buildspec` defines the different phases of the build and what to run during those phases. It is very similar to the JenkinsFile we created in `Chapter 4`, *Adding Continuous Integration and Continuous Deployment*. The `buildspec` can be created as part of the CodeBuild project or added as a YAML file to the root directory of the projects that are being built. We will opt for the first option and define the `buildspec` inside our CloudFormation template. We will create a variable and store a YAML string into it. Since it's going to be a multiline variable, we will use the Python triple quote syntax.

The first key-pair we need to specify is the version of the template. The current version of CodeBuild templates is `0.1`:

```
buildspec = """version: 0.1
```

The goal of our build process is to generate a new container, tag it, and push it to the `ecr` repository. This will be done in three phases:

1. **The pre-build phase**: Will generate the container tag and log in to ECR.
2. **The build phase**: Will build the new container.
3. **The post-build phase**: Will push the new container to ECR and update the latest tag to point to the new container.

In order to easily understand what's in each container, we will tag them with the SHA of the most recent Git commit of the `helloworld` project. This will help in understanding what's in each container as we will be able to run commands such as `git checkout <container tag>` or `git log <container tag>`.

Because of how CodeBuild and CodePipeline are architected, getting this tag in CodeBuild requires a bit of work. We will need to run two complex commands:

- The first one will exact the execution Id of the current code pipeline execution. We perform that by combining the AWS CLI and the environment variables `CODEBUILD_BUILD_ID` and `CODEBUILD_INITIATOR`, which are defined by the CodeBuild service when a build starts.
- Next, we will use that execution Id to extract the artifact revision Id which happens to be the commit SHA we are looking for.

Those commands use some of the most advanced features of the query filter option (you can read more about it at `http://amzn.to/2k7SoLE`).

 In CodeBuild, each command runs in its own environment and therefore the easiest way to share data across steps is to use temporary files.

Right after the `buildspec` version definition, add the following to generate the first part of our pre-build phase and extract the tag:

```
phases:
  pre_build:
    commands:
      - aws codepipeline get-pipeline-state --name
"${CODEBUILD_INITIATOR##*/}" --query
stageStates[?actionStates[0].latestExecution.externalExecutionId==\`$CODEBU
ILD_BUILD_ID\`].latestExecution.pipelineExecutionId --output=text >
/tmp/execution_id.txt
      - aws codepipeline get-pipeline-execution --pipeline-name
"${CODEBUILD_INITIATOR##*/}" --pipeline-execution-id $(cat
/tmp/execution_id.txt) --query
'pipelineExecution.artifactRevisions[0].revisionId' --output=text >
/tmp/tag.txt
```

Our tag is now present in the `/tmp/tag.txt` file. We now need to generate two files. The first one will contain the argument for the Docker tag command (something like `<AWS::AccountId>.dkr.ecr.us-east-1.amazonaws.com/helloworld:<tag>`). To do that, we will take advantage of the environment variable defined earlier in our template. The second file will be a JSON file which will define a key-value pair with the tag. We will use that file a bit later when we work on deploying our new containers to ECS.

After the previous commands, add the following commands to generate those files:

```
      - printf "%s:%s" "$REPOSITORY_URI" "$(cat /tmp/tag.txt)" >
/tmp/build_tag.txt
      - printf '{"tag":"%s"}' "$(cat /tmp/tag.txt)" > /tmp/build.json
```

To conclude the `pre_build` section, we will log in to our `ecr` repository:

```
      - $(aws ecr get-login --no-include-email)
```

We will now define our build phase. Thanks to the `build_tag` file created earlier, the build phase will be straightforward. We will simply call the `docker build` command similarly to how we did in the first section of this chapter:

```
build:
  commands:
    - docker build -t "$(cat /tmp/build_tag.txt)" .
```

We will now add the `post_build` phase to complete the build. In this section, we will push the newly built container to our `ecr` repository:

```
post_build:
    commands:
        - docker push "$(cat /tmp/build_tag.txt)"
        - aws ecr batch-get-image --repository-name $REPOSITORY_NAME --image-
ids imageTag="$(cat /tmp/tag.txt)" --query 'images[].imageManifest' --
output text | tee /tmp/latest_manifest.json
        - aws ecr put-image --repository-name $REPOSITORY_NAME --image-tag
latest --image-manifest $(cat /tmp/latest_manifest.json)
```

In addition to the phases, one of the sections that is also defined in a `buildspec` is the `artifacts` section. This section is used to define what needs to be uploaded to S3 after the build succeeds and how to prepare it. We will export the `build.json` file and set the `discard-path` variable to `true` so we don't preserve the `/tmp/` directory information. In the end, we will close our triple quote string:

```
artifacts:
    files: /tmp/build.json
    discard-paths: yes
"""
```

Now that our `buildspec` variable is defined, we can add our CodeBuild project resource. Through the instantiation of the project, we will set a name for our project, set its environment by calling the variable previously defined, set the service role, and configure the source and artifact resources which define how to handle the build process and its output:

```
t.add_resource(Project(
    "CodeBuild",
    Name='HelloWorldContainer',
    Environment=environment,
    ServiceRole=Ref("ServiceRole"),
    Source=Source(
        Type="CODEPIPELINE",
        BuildSpec=buildspec
    ),
    Artifacts=Artifacts(
        Type="CODEPIPELINE",
        Name="output"
    ),
))
```

As always, we will conclude the creation of the script with the following `print` command:

```
print(t.to_json())
```

Our script is now complete. It should look like this:

```
http://bit.ly/2w3nDfk
```

We can save the file, add it to git, generate the CloudFormation template, and create our stack:

```
$ git add helloworld-codebuild-cf-template.py
$ git commit -m "Adding CodeBuild Template for our helloworld application"
$ git push
$ python helloworld-codebuild-cf-template.py > helloworld-codebuild-
cf.template
$ aws cloudformation create-stack \
        --stack-name helloworld-codebuild \
        --capabilities CAPABILITY_IAM \
        --template-body file://helloworld-codebuild-cf.template
```

In a matter of minutes, our stack will be created. We will now want to take advantage of it. To do so, we will turn to CodePipeline once again and create a brand new and container-aware pipeline.

Creating our deployment pipeline with CodePipeline

We will use AWS CodePipeline to build a pipeline very similar to the one we created in `Chapter 4`, *Adding Continuous Integration and Continuous Deployment*:

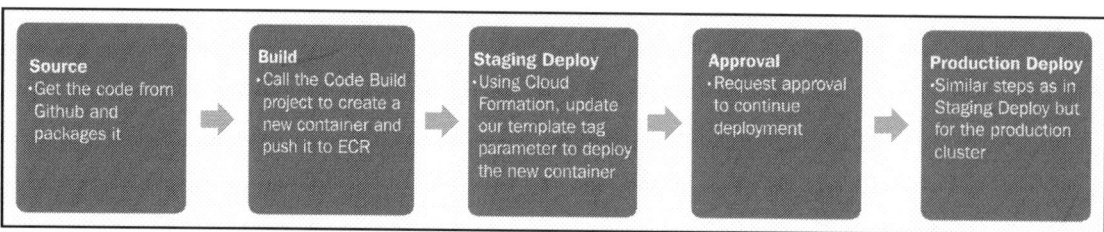

We will start with a **Source** step, where we will connect to GitHub and trigger new pipelines that run automatically when the code changes. Next, we will build a new container and push it to our `ecr` repository relying on the CodeBuild project we just created. We will then deploy the new container to staging. To do that, we will use the CloudFormation integration provided by CodePipeline combined with the `build.json` file produced in the `buildspec` section of our CodeBuild project. You may recall that our `helloworld` service templates take the tag to deploy as an argument. We will trigger a stack update action and override the default value for that parameter with what's defined in the `build.json` file. After that, we will add a manual approval step before triggering the same deployment again but this time for production.

Deploying and updating CloudFormation templates through CodePipeline will require specifying the location of the template within the inputs. In order to easily provide it, we will first start by adding the CloudFormation template to our source.

Adding the CloudFormation template to our code base

ECS changes are driven by the task definition present in our `helloworld-ecs-service-cf.template` file. So far we only stored in GitHub our python script. We will have to make a special case for that template and store the JSON output of it so that CodePipeline can interact with our stack. We will add this file to our Git repository in a new directory as follow:

```
$ cd helloworld
$ mkdir templates
$ curl -L http://bit.ly/2uB5wQn | python > templates/helloworld-ecs-
service-cf.template
$ git add templates
$ git commit -m "Adding CloudFormation template for the helloworld task"
$ git push
```

Now that our template is present in our source, we can create our CloudFormation template for our pipeline.

Creating a CloudFormation template for CodePipeline

We will start by creating a file and calling it `helloworld-codepipeline-cf-template.py`.

We will start the script with our boilerplates:

```
"""Generating CloudFormation template."""

from awacs.aws import (
    Allow,
    Policy,
    Principal,
    Statement,
)
from awacs.sts import AssumeRole
from troposphere import (
    Ref,
    GetAtt,
    Template,
)
from troposphere.codepipeline import (
    Actions,
    ActionTypeID,
    ArtifactStore,
    InputArtifacts,
    OutputArtifacts,
    Pipeline,
    Stages
)
from troposphere.iam import Role
from troposphere.iam import Policy as IAMPolicy

from troposphere.s3 import Bucket, VersioningConfiguration

t = Template()

t.add_description("Effective DevOps in AWS: Helloworld Pipeline")
```

The first resource we will create is the S3 bucket that the pipeline will use to store all the artifacts produced by each stage. We will also turn on versioning on that bucket:

```
t.add_resource(Bucket(
    "S3Bucket",
    VersioningConfiguration=VersioningConfiguration(
        Status="Enabled",
    )
))
```

We will now create the IAM roles needed:

   1. The first role we are going to define will be for the CodePipeline service:

```
t.add_resource(Role(
    "PipelineRole",
    AssumeRolePolicyDocument=Policy(
        Statement=[
            Statement(
                Effect=Allow,
                Action=[AssumeRole],
                Principal=Principal("Service",
["codepipeline.amazonaws.com"])
            )
        ]
    ),
    Path="/",
    Policies=[
        IAMPolicy(
            PolicyName="HelloworldCodePipeline",
            PolicyDocument={
                "Statement": [
                    {"Effect": "Allow", "Action":
"cloudformation:*", "Resource": "*"},
                    {"Effect": "Allow", "Action":
"codebuild:*", "Resource": "*"},
                    {"Effect": "Allow", "Action":
"codepipeline:*", "Resource": "*"},
                    {"Effect": "Allow", "Action": "ecr:*",
"Resource": "*"},
                    {"Effect": "Allow", "Action": "ecs:*",
"Resource": "*"},
                    {"Effect": "Allow", "Action": "iam:*",
"Resource": "*"},
                    {"Effect": "Allow", "Action": "s3:*",
"Resource": "*"},
                ],
            }
        ),
    ]
))
```

2. The second role will be used by the deploy stages to perform CloudFormation changes:

```
t.add_resource(Role(
    "CloudFormationHelloworldRole",
    RoleName="CloudFormationHelloworldRole",
    Path="/",
    AssumeRolePolicyDocument=Policy(
        Statement=[
            Statement(
```

```
                        Effect=Allow,
                        Action=[AssumeRole],
                        Principal=Principal(
                            "Service",
        ["cloudformation.amazonaws.com"])
                    ),
                ]
            ),
            Policies=[
                IAMPolicy(
                    PolicyName="HelloworldCloudFormation",
                    PolicyDocument={
                        "Statement": [
                            {"Effect": "Allow", "Action":
        "cloudformation:*", "Resource": "*"},
                            {"Effect": "Allow", "Action": "ecr:*",
        "Resource": "*"},
                            {"Effect": "Allow", "Action": "ecs:*",
        "Resource": "*"},
                            {"Effect": "Allow", "Action": "iam:*",
        "Resource": "*"},
                        ],
                    }
                ),
            ]
        ))
```

3. We can now create our pipeline resource. We will first configure its name and specify the role **Amazon Resource Name (ARN)** of the role we just created:

```
t.add_resource(Pipeline(
    "HelloWorldPipeline",
    RoleArn=GetAtt("PipelineRole", "Arn"),
```

4. After this, we will reference the S3 bucket created earlier so that we have a place to store the different artifacts produced through the pipeline execution:

```
ArtifactStore=ArtifactStore(
    Type="S3",
    Location=Ref("S3Bucket")
),
```

5. We will now define each stage of the pipeline. The CloudFormation structure reflects what we did previously using the web interface. Each stage has a unique name and is composed of actions. Each action is defined by a name, a category, a configuration, and, optionally, input and output artifacts.

Our first stage will be the GitHub stage:

```
Stages=[
    Stages(
        Name="Source",
        Actions=[
            Actions(
                Name="Source",
                ActionTypeId=ActionTypeID(
                    Category="Source",
                    Owner="ThirdParty",
                    Version="1",
                    Provider="GitHub"
                ),
                Configuration={
                    "Owner": "ToBeConfiguredLater",
                    "Repo": "ToBeConfiguredLater",
                    "Branch": "ToBeConfiguredLater",
                    "OAuthToken": "ToBeConfiguredLater"
                },
                OutputArtifacts=[
                    OutputArtifacts(
                        Name="App"
                    )
                ],
            )
        ]
    ),
```

6. We will create a first `artifact` called `App` with the content of the repository. In order to avoid hardcoding any `OAuthToken`, we will configure the GitHub integration after creating the CloudFormation stack.

Our next step will be to configure our build. As mentioned, we will simply call out to the CodeBuild stack we spawned up in the last section. Note we will store the output artifact under the name `BuildOutput`, meaning that we now have two artifacts, the `App` one and `BuildOutput`, which contains the `tag.json` file produced by CodeBuild:

```
    Stages(
        Name="Build",
        Actions=[
            Actions(
                Name="Container",
                ActionTypeId=ActionTypeID(
                    Category="Build",
                    Owner="AWS",
```

```
                        Version="1",
                        Provider="CodeBuild"
                    ),
                    Configuration={
                        "ProjectName": "HelloWorldContainer",
                    },
                    InputArtifacts=[
                        InputArtifacts(
                            Name="App"
                        )
                    ],
                    OutputArtifacts=[
                        OutputArtifacts(
                            Name="BuildOutput"
                        )
                    ],
                )
            ]
        ),
```

7. We will now create our staging deployment. Unlike before, we won't use CodeDeploy but directly update our CloudFormation template. In order to accomplish that, we will need to provide the location of the template to the configuration of our action. Since we added it to our `helloworld` GitHub repository, we can reference it with the help of the `App` artifact. Our template is present under `<directory root>/templates/helloworld-ecs-service-cf.template`, which in turns means for CodePipeline `App::templates/helloworld-ecs-service-cf.template`.

The next trick in configuring our CloudFormation action relies on the fact that we can override the parameters provided for the stack. CloudFormation provides a couple of functions to help with dynamic parameters. You can read more about those at `http://amzn.to/2kTgIUJ`. We will rely on a particular one, `Fn::GetParam`. This function returns a value from a key-value pair file present in an artifact. This is where we take advantage of the file we created in CodeBuild as it will contain a JSON string, like `{ "tag": "<latest git commit sha>" }`:

```
            Stages(
                Name="Staging",
                Actions=[
                    Actions(
                        Name="Deploy",
                        ActionTypeId=ActionTypeID(
                            Category="Deploy",
                            Owner="AWS",
```

```
                                Version="1",
                                Provider="CloudFormation"
                            ),
                            Configuration={
                                "ChangeSetName": "Deploy",
                                "ActionMode": "CREATE_UPDATE",
                                "StackName": "helloworld-ecs-staging-
        service",
                                "Capabilities": "CAPABILITY_NAMED_IAM",
                                "TemplatePath":
        "App::templates/helloworld-ecs-service-cf.template",
                                "RoleArn":
        GetAtt("CloudFormationHelloworldRole", "Arn"),
                                "ParameterOverrides": """{"Tag" : {
        "Fn::GetParam" : [ "BuildOutput", "build.json", "tag" ] } }"""
                            },
                            InputArtifacts=[
                                InputArtifacts(
                                    Name="App",
                                ),
                                InputArtifacts(
                                    Name="BuildOutput"
                                )
                            ],
                        )
                    ]
                ),
```

8. After the staging deployment completes, we will request a manual approval:

```
            Stages(
                Name="Approval",
                Actions=[
                    Actions(
                        Name="Approval",
                        ActionTypeId=ActionTypeID(
                            Category="Approval",
                            Owner="AWS",
                            Version="1",
                            Provider="Manual"
                        ),
                        Configuration={},
                        InputArtifacts=[],
                    )
                ]
            ),
```

9. Finally, we will create a last stage to run the production deployment. The code is exactly the same as for staging except for the name of the stage and the stack targeted by our configuration:

```
Stages(
    Name="Production",
    Actions=[
        Actions(
            Name="Deploy",
            ActionTypeId=ActionTypeID(
                Category="Deploy",
                Owner="AWS",
                Version="1",
                Provider="CloudFormation"
            ),
            Configuration={
                "ChangeSetName": "Deploy",
                "ActionMode": "CREATE_UPDATE",
                "StackName": "helloworld-ecs-
production-service",
                "Capabilities": "CAPABILITY_NAMED_IAM",
                "TemplatePath":
"App::templates/helloworld-ecs-service-cf.template",
                "RoleArn":
GetAtt("CloudFormationHelloworldRole", "Arn"),
                "ParameterOverrides": """{"Tag" : {
"Fn::GetParam" : [ "BuildOutput", "build.json", "tag" ] } }"""
            },
            InputArtifacts=[
                InputArtifacts(
                    Name="App",
                ),
                InputArtifacts(
                    Name="BuildOutput"
                )
            ],
        )
    ]
)
],
))
```

Our pipeline resource is now created; we can conclude the creation of our script by printing out our template:

```
print(t.to_json())
```

The script is ready to be used. It should look like this:

```
http://bit.ly/2w3oVHw
```

We can now create our pipeline.

Starting and configuring our CloudFormation stack

We will proceed as usual for the first part:

```
$ git add helloworld-codepipeline-cf-template.py
$ git commit -m "Adding Pipeline to deploy our helloworld application using
ECS"
$ git push
$ python helloworld-codepipeline-cf-template.py > helloworld-codepipeline-
cf.template
$ aws cloudformation create-stack \
      --stack-name helloworld-codepipeline \
      --capabilities CAPABILITY_NAMED_IAM \
      --template-body file://helloworld-codepipeline-cf.template
```

We are using the CAPABILITY_NAMED_IAM capability in this case, as we are defining custom names at the IAM level.

This will create our pipeline. There is a small gotcha to it which is that we didn't specify the GitHub credentials in the pipeline. The main reason for that is that we don't want to store it in clear text in GitHub. AWS offers a service within IAM to do encryption but we won't cover it in this book, therefore, we are simply going to edit the pipeline the first time around:

1. Open https://console.aws.amazon.com/codepipeline in your browser.
2. Select your newly created pipeline.
3. Click on **Edit** at the top.
4. Click on the pen icon on the GitHub action:

5. Click on **Connect to GitHub** on the right-hand-side menu and follow the steps to authorize Authorize AWS CodePipeline.

6. Select your `helloworld` project in the repository step and the `master` branch.

7. Click on **Update**, save pipeline changes, and finally, **Save and Continue**.

After a few seconds, your pipeline will trigger and you should see your first deployment going through. This concludes the creation of our CI/CD pipeline.

Summary

In this chapter, we explored the concept of containers using Docker and ECS. After exploring the basics of how Docker works, we created a container for our application. After running locally, we created a new set of resources to run Docker containers on AWS. We did that using the DevOps best practices. We used CloudFormation to generate our resources, treating our infrastructure as code. This allows us to keep those changes under source control. Resource-wise, we created an `ecr` repository to manage the different revisions of our containers, two ECS clusters with auto scaling capability for staging and production, two ALBs to proxy the traffic to our containers, a set of tasks, and an ECS service to configure and deploy our application.

In the end, we reimplemented a CI/CD pipeline. We did that by using CodeBuild, CodePipeline, and their integration with CloudFormation.

In `Chapter 7`, Monitoring and Alerting, we will continue improving our systems and implement one of the last key characteristics of DevOps: measuring everything. By taking advantage of a number of features present in the different services we use and by coupling that with other AWS services such as CloudWatch, we will be able to implement a monitoring strategy for our infrastructure and services.

7

Monitoring and Alerting

In previous chapters, we built a state of the art infrastructure and implemented a number of engineering best practices following the DevOps principles. One of the principle we haven't covered yet is the concept of measuring everything.

The core concept of measuring everything is the goal of collecting actionable feedback. We want to create the following feedback loop that will let us assess the impact of a change:

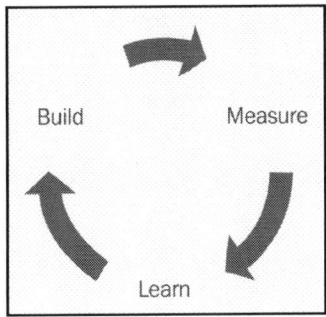

This idea isn't unique to DevOps. Most reputable companies will rely on similar systems to dynamically steer their teams in the right direction, as intuition and gut feeling isn't enough anymore when making most decisions and trying to stay competitive.

By applying this concept to our infrastructure and services, we can take them to the next level and implement a monitoring and alerting solution, which is, of course, a must-have for any production environment. In the first part of the chapter, we will make changes to our application to better expose how our application is behaving. Following this, we will do the same to our infrastructure. Thanks to our understanding of infrastructure as code, we will be able to add those crucial components by extending the different CloudFormation templates we created.

Finally, we will implement an alert functionality on some of the public key metrics indicators to help us improve the availability of our application. This chapter will contain the following sections:

- Instrumenting our application for monitoring
- Monitoring our infrastructure
- Creating alarms using CloudWatch and SNS

Instrumenting our application for monitoring

In this section, we are going to make a couple of changes to our application to provide insight into what our code is doing and how it's behaving.

Because monitoring isn't as trivial as it may sound, there is no shortage of monitoring solutions. Since this book is focused on AWS, we will want to utilize what AWS provides as much as possible, starting with CloudWatch.

Furthermore, because of the rudimentary nature of the application, most of what we will implement won't be very meaningful, aside from demonstrating your different options, as well as the ideas behind the process.

AWS CloudWatch

CloudWatch centralizes most essential functionalities for a monitoring solution. We used some of its functionalities previously when we created our Auto Scaling Groups and needed an alarm to trigger Auto Scaling Events, but CloudWatch can do a lot more.

In the world of infrastructure, data mostly comes in two types—metrics and logs. CloudWatch supports both data types. In addition, they also have a third type of data called events.

As with most services, you can access it using the web console, the command-line interface, and, of course, the API and various SDKs. We will first look at the different types of data.

Metrics

Metrics are often used to monitor things that can be quantified, such as system metrics (CPU utilization, free memory, network consumption), page views, or HTTP status (the current error rate in my application).

In CloudWatch, metrics are defined as tuples and contain the following:

- Resource ID
- Service name
- Metric name
- A metric value
- A timestamp

For example, a metric of i-e434d47f | EC2 | CPUUtilization | 13.4 | 2017-08-14T12:00:00.000Z shows that the CPU utilization of the EC2 instance ID i-e434d47f was at 13.4% on 2017-08-14T12:00:00.000Z.

Most AWS will integrate natively with CloudWatch. By going to https://console.aws.amazon.com/cloudwatch, you can start browsing the different metrics already generated by the different services we used using the metrics menu on the left-hand side or the **Browse Metrics** button on the **Metrics Summary** page.

We can display, for example, a metric representing how much data we have in our S3 bucket as follows:

1. From the CloudWatch dashboard, click on **Browse Metrics**.
2. Select the S3 service from the **Namespaces** section.
3. Select **Storage Metrics**.
4. Find the bucket used to store artifacts and pick the metric **BucketSizeBytes**:

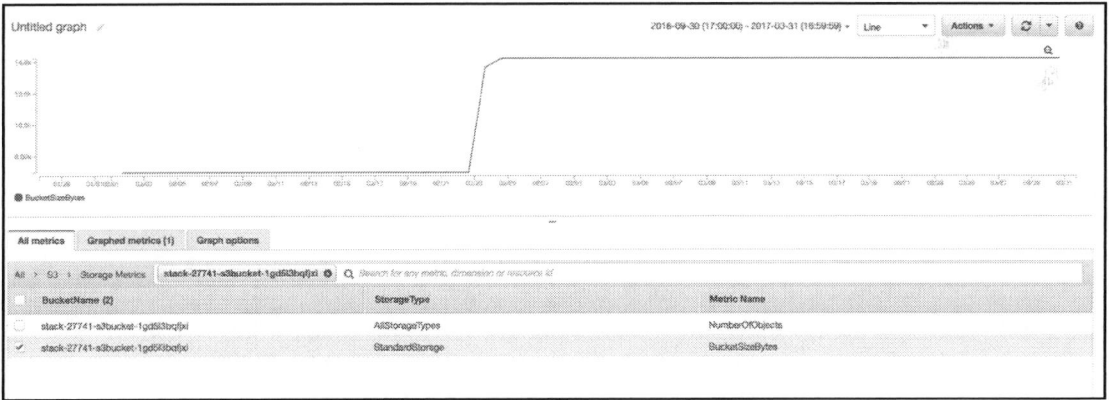

Logs

Log files are probably the most well-known way of monitoring systems. They are a great complement to metrics as they provide more flexibility. Because you aren't limited to a key-value pair system, like our metrics, you can use log files to provide very detailed information on events occurring in your application. For instance, you may capture, through your metric system, an increase in the error rate of your application, but to know what exactly is happening, you will want to access your application logs to see if there are exceptions, stack traces, or error messages that can help you troubleshoot that issue. The downside of logs is that they are much bigger than metrics. This means that they are more expensive to store, but also harder to index, search, and aggregate.

CloudWatch logs are organized around a few key concepts:

- Each log is called a log event and contains a raw message and a timestamp.
- The logs events produced by a unique source are grouped into a log stream.
- Log streams send their log event to log groups. Each log group has its own policy in terms of data retention (how many days you want to keep your log event for, who can access those logs, and so on).

As an example of that, we can retrieve the events produced by our CodeBuild execution logs:

1. In your browser, open the CloudWatch service at
   `https://console.aws.amazon.com/cloudwatch`.
2. Clock on **Logs in** the left-hand side menu.
3. From there, you can see the different log groups. Select one of the `/aws/codebuild/` groups to access the log streams.
4. Open one of the log streams to access the logs produced by CodeBuild.

Events

CloudWatch Events are a concept particular to AWS. You can see them as a hybrid of logs and metrics. Events have identifiers and context the same way metrics have a name and resources id, but can also carry a payload with custom information. AWS uses it extensively in their infrastructure and services. Every time resources in your environment change, AWS creates an event that goes into a stream that the CloudWatch events service can subscribe to. You can create rules to match events of interest and either send the information to a service, such as SQS or SNS, or directly execute code using some pre-program functionalities or Lambda.

Using CloudWatch to monitor our helloworld application

Now that we know a bit more about the different monitoring functionalities that CloudWatch offers, we will make changes in our `helloworld` application to better illustrate how to get the best out of CloudWatch. We will first look at producing better logs. Following this, we will add metrics and finally events. Once the changes are in place, we will then make some changes to our infrastructure and its permission to start collecting that data.

Adding logs to our application

When we initially created our application, we added a consoleconsole log to state that the application is running on the last line:

```
console.log('Server running')
```

As you might imagine, this is not enough. In order to improve this, we will create a new logger.

Creating a custom logger for our application

To be useful, the logs need to be put in a context. In an environment where things are quickly changing, you want to provide some extra information in your messages, including the type of log (info, warning, critical, and so on), which version of your application produced it, and an accurate timestamp of when the error was produced. If your logs are all aggregated in the same place, you may also want to include the name of the service and the server that produced it. We will change our code to include that information.

When we first created the application, we kept the code to a bare minimum and avoided the use of extra packages. This made it easy to initially deploy the service. Now that we have more tooling around it, adding extra libraries is a non-issue. To improve our logging, we will rely on a library called **winston** (`https://www.npmjs.com/package/winston`). Winston is one of the most common logging libraries in JavaScript. The library has many features and lets you manipulate your logs in several powerful ways, as we will see shortly.

On your computer, go to the root directory of the `helloworld` application:

```
$ cd helloworld
```

Then install the `winston` library, as follows:

```
$ npm install winston --save
```

Adding the `--save` option will make npm include the package definition in the `package.json` file.

With your text editor, open the `helloworld.js` file containing your application.

After the initialization of the `http` variable, we will initialize the `Winston` library as follows:

```
var http = require("http")
var winston = require("winston")
```

Next, we will create a new variable to specify the version of the code. One of the ways we can achieve this is by assuming that this information will be provided later through the use of environment variables. For now, we will simply import the values as follows:

```
var version = process.env.HELLOWORLD_VERSION
```

We will now create our custom logger. This will allow us to specify that we want a `timestamp` and provide the code to define that `timestamp`:

```
var logger = new winston.Logger({
  transports: [new winston.transports.Console({
    timestamp: function() {
      var d = new Date()
      return d.toISOString()
    },
  })]
})
```

To add the remaining context to all our logs, we will use a feature of the library called a rewriter, which allows us to modify the content of the meta.

Under the definition of the `var logger` variable definition, add the following:

```
logger.rewriters.push(function(level, msg, meta) {
  meta.version = version
  return meta
})
```

Lastly, we now need to use the logger we just created and configured. For that, we will select the following code fragment:

```
console.log("Server running")
```

We replace this code fragment with the following:

```
logger.info("Server running")
```

We can now test our application by running it locally:

```
$ node helloworld.js
```

As the application starts, it produces logs that look as follows:

```
2017-09-01T01:59:06.095Z - info: Server running version=undefined
```

Your `helloworld.js` file should look as shown at `http://bit.ly/2uHZ0p3`

The collection of logs on EC2 and ECS are typically different. We will show how to make both collections starting with EC2.

At this point, the console log isn't captured anywhere on EC2. We need to make some changes to our upstart script to save the console log and set the `HELLOWORLD_VERSION` environment variable.

Making changes to provide the version and save the console log

Our upstart configuration is locatedlocated in the subdirectory scripts. With your code editor, open the file `scripts/helloworld.conf`.

We will edit the script section of the file as follows:

```
script
    set -a
    . /usr/local/helloworld/version
    mkdir -p /var/log/helloworld/
    chown ec2-user:ec2-user /var/log/helloworld/
    exec su --session-command="/usr/bin/node
/usr/local/helloworld/helloworld.js >> /var/log/helloworld/helloworld.log
2>&1" ec2-user
end script
```

The first set of changes will allow us to define the `HELLOWORLD_VERSION` environment variable. To get there, we will add a call to `set -a` to force our variables to be exported and source a new file, `/usr/local/helloworld/version`, which we will create later. The second part of the changes will allow us to log the console output onto the filesystem. To do that, we need to create a directory in `/var/log` and change the command that starts the application to save `stdout` and `stderr` into that new directory.

We now have a log file containing our console log. Whenever you add new logs, you should always think about how to rotate those logs. We will do that using `logrotate`.

We will create a new folder and configuration file for it.

In the root of the `helloworld` directory, create a new folder `conf` and a new file called `logrotate`:

```
$ mkdir conf
$ touch conf/logrotate
```

We will now edit that file and put the following configuration in it:

```
/var/log/helloworld/*.log {
   rotate 3
   size=100M
   copytruncate
   nocompress
}
```

You may, of course, adjust it to your liking.

We will now address the creation of the `/usr/local/helloworld/version` file. Our goal is to generate a new version file every time new code is released with CodeDeploy. One of the functionalities that we didn't cover is that whenever CodeDeploy runs, it sets some environment variables of its own. We will use those to generate a version.

Create a new script in the script directory, call it `setversion.sh`, and set its permissions to be executable:

```
$ touch scripts/setversion.sh
$ chmod +x scripts/setversion.sh
```

Open the file and simply put the following:

```
#!/bin/sh
echo "HELLOWORLD_VERSION=${APPLICATION_NAME}-${DEPLOYMENT_GROUP_NAME}-
${DEPLOYMENT_GROUP_ID}-${DEPLOYMENT_ID}" > /usr/local/helloworld/version
```

We can now make changes to CodeDeploy to incorporate all our changes.

Making changes to CodeDeploy to better handle logging

We will first make CodeDeploy generate the version file. To do that, we will open the `appspec.yml` file at the root of the `helloworld` application directory.

At the bottom of the file, after the ValidateService hook, we will use a new hook to trigger our `setversion` script. This operation will need to happen after the `helloworld` application is installed. As such, we will want to add the following hook:

```
AfterInstall:
   - location: scripts/setversion.sh
     timeout: 180
```

We now need to handle our new files. The first one is the `logrotate` configuration. In the files section at the top of our `appsec` file, add the following:

```
   - source: conf/logrotate
     destination: /etc/logrotate.d/helloworld
```

Lastly, we need to handle the installation of our libraries now that we have some extra dependencies. There are a few ways to deal with dependencies. The most obvious one is to run `npm install` during the deployment. This allows you to keep your code base small and light. The downside is that you now rely on `https://www.npmjs.com/` to be working to get a deployment out, which can be risky. Imagine the scenario where you have to deploy a fix for a major bug, but can't because the installation of your dependencies is failing. To avoid this, it is best practice to also commit the `node_modules` directory with your code.

After the previous configuration to deploy the `logrotate` configuration, add the following:

```
   - source: node_modules
     destination: /usr/local/helloworld/node_modules
```

Your new `appsec` file should look like this `http://bit.ly/2uI4BvE`.

We can now commit all the changes:

```
$ git add helloworld.js node_modules package.json conf
scripts/setversion.sh appsec.yml scripts/helloworld.conf
$ git commit -m "Adding logging to helloworld"
$ git push
```

Thanks to our pipelines, those changes will be deployed to our EC2 instances, and in no time, we will start seeing logs populated on the hosts.

We will now add metrics and events to our application.

Adding metrics and events to our application

As you might expect, there are several ways to add metrics. You can either opt for a generic protocol, such as StatsD, which will let you reuse your metrics across a variety of products, both SaaS and open source or, if you want to get something working quickly, use the AWS native SDK. Both options have pros and cons, but we will focus on the AWS native SDK.

We will once again start off from the root directory of our `helloworld` application. We will first start by installing the AWS SDK for JavaScript as follows:

```
$ npm install aws-sdk --save
```

This will install into the `node_modules` directory the library and its dependencies and update the `package.json` file.

Once the library is installed, open the `helloworld.js` file with your editor.

We will first instantiate the library.

At the top of the file, after the initialization of the `winston` library, add the following:

```
var http = require("http")
var winston = require("winston")
var AWS = require("aws-sdk")
```

The AWS object will let us interact with all AWS services. Our infrastructure is located in `us-east-1`. We will configure our application to use this region to access the different services. After the definition of the AWS variable, add the following:

```
AWS.config.update({region:"us-east-1"})
```

Next, we will create a variable to access the CloudWatch metric and event service:

```
var cwevents = new AWS.CloudWatchEvents({apiVersion: "2015-10-07"})
var cw = new AWS.CloudWatch({apiVersion: "2010-08-01"})
```

In a more realistic world, an application will have different use case for events and metrics. You would add an event if you wish to run a Lambda function when a specific event happens, while you would add metrics extensively to measure everything that's happening in your application. Here, since our application is only doing one thing, we don't need that luxury, and we will create a metric and an event whenever someone accesses the application.

We will add an event inside the `http`. We will start by creating an event variable to define a simple event. We will join the content of the request header to that event:

```
http.createServer(function (request, response) {
  var event = {
    Entries: [{
      Detail: JSON.stringify(request.headers),
      DetailType: "hellworld application access request",
      Source: "helloworld.app"
    }]
  }
```

We will also create a metric. A lot of the time, you want your metrics to be associated with several dimensions. We will create a simple metric of `page_viewed`, but to illustrate the concept of dimensions better, we will associate the version of our application with the metric.

We can do that as follows:

```
var metric = {
  MetricData: [{
    MetricName: "page_viewwed",
    Dimensions: [{
      Name: "Version",
      Value: version
    }],
    Unit: "None",
    Value: 1.0
  }],
  Namespace: "Helloworld/traffic"
}
```

We will see the metrics used to monitor disk space on the root partition of our instances a bit later in this chapter. In that case, for example, the dimensions will be partitions, mount paths, and `instance-id`.

We will now emit those two events just after the `response.end("Hello World\n")` call, as follows:

```
response.end("Hello World\n")
cwevents.putEvents(event, function(err, data) {
  if (err) {
    logger.error("error", "an error occurred when creating an event",
{error: err})
  } else {
    logger.info("created event", {entries: data.Entries})
  }
```

```
  })
  cw.putMetricData(metric, function(err, data) {
    if (err) {
      logger.error("an error occurred when creating a metric", {error:
err});
    } else {
      logger.info("created metric", {data: JSON.stringify(data)});
    }
  })
```

Note how we are relying on the logging capability to catch possible issues with putting metrics or events into CloudWatch.

Log cardinality

If you look closely at the logs we just produced, you will notice that our logs are made of constant strings. The extra information, such as the detail of the error or the event ID, is provided in a separate meta.

Having structured logs makes querying and indexing a lot better. For example, thanks to that format, we will be able to extract all logs matching "an error occurred when creating a metric" and group the error message that follows. This will in turn allow us to state the reason why we fail to create a metric by count. We will see that in action a bit later when we send logs to ElasticSearch.

At this point, if we were to run this code on our EC2 instances, we would see some errors in our logs because we don't have the permissions to send logs and metrics to AWS. In addition, we are producing our logs, but we aren't sending them to the CloudWatch logs yet. We will address those issues in the next 2 sections.

Sending logs, events, and metrics to CloudWatch from EC2

Our application is now producing logs, metrics, and events. We are going to make changes to Ansible and CloudFormation to collectcollect all those elements. We will add a new service to collect the logs and grant sufficient permissions to our EC2 instance roles.

Creating an Ansible role for CloudWatch logs

To send our logs to CloudWatch, AWS provides a daemondaemon called `awslogs`. We are going to install and configure it through Ansible.

Go into your `ansible roles` directory:

```
$ cd ansible/roles
```

Create a new role called `awslogs`:

```
$ ansible-galaxy init awslogs
- awslogs was created successfully
```

We will first edit the task file `awslogs/tasks/main.yml`. Our first operation will be to install the package. For that, we will use the yum module:

```
---
# tasks file for awslogs

- name: install awslogs
  yum:
    name: awslogs
    state: present
```

We will want to configure the service dynamically with Ansible. For that, we will want to create a handler to restart `awslogs` when the configuration changes.

Edit the file `awslogs/handlers/main.yml` and add the following:

```
---
# handlers file for awslogs

- name: restart awslogs
  service:
    name: awslogs
    state: restarted
```

We can now configure the service. You can refer to `http://amzn.to/2qMhaEt` for the full documentation of the configuration of the service. In our case, we will keep it very simple. The service is configured through a set of INI files. The first one goes into `/etc/awslogs/awslogs.conf`. We will create the file using the file module from Ansible.

Create a new file in `awslogs/files/`, call it `awslogs.conf`, and put the following in it:

```
[general]
state_file = /var/lib/awslogs/agent-state
```

Now that the file is created, we are going to copy it to its target destination, `/etc/awslogs/awslogs.conf`. For that, we will use the copy module. Back in the `awslogs/tasks/main.yml` task file, we will add the following:

```
- name: copy global configuration
  copy:
    src: awslogs.conf
    dest: /etc/awslogs
  notify: restart awslogs
```

Thanks to the notify handler we created, if we were to change our configuration file, `awslogs` would automatically restart and, through that, load the new configuration.

We now want to use Ansible to configure which file needs to be collected. We will do that by creating new INI files inside the `/etc/awslogs/config` directory. To make it easy to operate, we will create one INI file per log file we want to collect. We will take advantage of the INI file module that Ansible provides to implement that. At the bottom of the task file, create a new command as follows:

```
- name: configure awslogs to collect {{ file }}
  ini_file:
```

We want our role to be generic and able to collect a variety of logs. As such, we will take advantage of the variable system that Ansible provides. The idea is that whenever we call this role, we will provide the information needed, such as the file to collect and its name.

The INI module requires us to provide the path of the INI file we want to configure. We will do that as follows:

```
    path: "/etc/awslogs/config/{{ name }}.conf"
```

Here as well, we are calling the variable name that will be provided when we instantiate the module. The section of the configuration file will be the filename we want to collect:

```
    section: "{{ file }}"
```

Now that the section is created, we are going to configure the different options. We will want to configure six different options. To keep the code dry, we will take advantage of the `with_items` keyword to iterate over the list of options and values:

```
    option: "{{ item.option }}"
    value: "{{ item.value }}"
```

Finally, we can list the different options and values as follows:

```
with_items:
  - { option: file, value: "{{ file }}" }
  - { option: log_group_name, value: "{{ file }}" }
  - { option: log_stream_name, value: "{instance_id}" }
  - { option: initial_position, value: "start_of_file" }
  - { option: buffer_duration, value: "5000" }
```

```
    - { option: datetime_format, value: "{{ datetime_format | default('%b
%d %H:%M:%S') }}" }
```

Here too, we rely heavily on the fact that most values will be provided later. Note how we are making the `datetime_format`field optional. If it's not provided, we will try to read our logs as if they were formatted by the syslog. You can refer to the Python `datetime.strptime()` documentation for the full list of format variables.

We will conclude this call with a `notify` to `restart awslogs` if the configuration changed:

```
    notify: restart awslogs
```

The last call of our task file will be to start the service and enable it so that `awslogs` starts right away, and upon reboot:

```
- name: start awslogs and enable it
  service:
    name: awslogs
    state: started
    enabled: yes
```

Our role is ready, we will use it inside our `nodeserver.yml` file. We will collect `/var/log/messages` and `/var/log/helloworld/helloworld.log`. Each entry will have a unique name (`messages` and `helloworld`) and their full path. In addition, we need to specify the logging format that our `helloworld` application is using:

```
---
- hosts: "{{ target | default('localhost') }}"
  become: yes
  roles:
    - nodejs
    - codedeploy
    - { role: awslogs, name: messages, file: /var/log/messages }
    - {
        role: awslogs,
        name: helloworld,
        file: /var/log/helloworld/helloworld.log,
        datetime_format: "%Y-%m-%dT%H:%M:%S.%f"
      }
```

Your code should be similar to `http://bit.ly/2v3bp9G`.

Before we commit those changes, we are going to update our CloudFormation template to add proper permissions.

Updating our CloudFormation template

The last time we worked on EC2 was in Chapter 5, *Scaling Your Infrastructure,* when we implemented the Auto Scaling Groups. We are going to edit the troposphere script we used for this and make the necessary changes.

Go to your template directory and with your text editor, open the file `nodeserver-cf-template.py`from our EffectiveDevOpsTemplates repository.

Previously, we created a policy to allow access to S3, which we needed for CodeDeploy. We will add a second policy and grant access to CloudWatch, CloudWatch logs, and CloudWatch events. After the creation of the IAM policy `AllowS3`, add the following resource:

```
t.add_resource(IAMPolicy(
    "MonitoringPolicy",
    PolicyName="AllowSendingDataForMonitoring",
    PolicyDocument=Policy(
        Statement=[
            Statement(
                Effect=Allow,
                Action=[
                    Action("cloudwatch", "Put*"),
                    Action("logs", "Create*"),
                    Action("logs", "Put*"),
                    Action("logs", "Describe*"),
                    Action("events", "Put*"),
                ],
                Resource=["*"])
        ]
    ),
    Roles=[Ref("Role")]
))
```

We can save our template and generate the new CloudFormation template:

```
$ git add nodeserver-cf-template.py
$ git commit -m "Adding permissions to interact with CloudWatch Logs,
Events"
$ git push
```

To update our existing stack, we are going to use the AWS CLI. In this particular instance, the main change is at the IAM level where we are creating the Monitoring Policy. The parameters we previously set when we initially created our stacks don't need to be changed. Instead of providing the same parameters again, we are going to use the **UsePreviousValue** option to update our helloworld stacks as follows:

```
$ python nodeserver-cf-template.py > nodeserver-cf.template
$ aws cloudformation update-stack \
      --capabilities CAPABILITY_IAM \
      --stack-name helloworld-staging \
      --template-body file://nodeserver-cf.template \
      --parameters \
          ParameterKey=InstanceType,UsePreviousValue=true \
          ParameterKey=KeyPair,,UsePreviousValue=true \
          ParameterKey=PublicSubnet,,UsePreviousValue=true \
          ParameterKey=ScaleCapacity,,UsePreviousValue=true \
          ParameterKey=VpcId,,UsePreviousValue=true

$ aws cloudformation update-stack \
      --capabilities CAPABILITY_IAM \
      --stack-name helloworld-production \
      --template-body file://nodeserver-cf.template \
      --parameters \
          ParameterKey=InstanceType,UsePreviousValue=true \
          ParameterKey=KeyPair,UsePreviousValue=true \
          ParameterKey=PublicSubnet,UsePreviousValue=true \
          ParameterKey=ScaleCapacity,UsePreviousValue=true \
          ParameterKey=VpcId,UsePreviousValue=true
```

Once the stack update is done, we can commit and merge our ansible changes. Your code should be similar to `http://bit.ly/2v3Nqr0`:

```
$ cd ansible
$ git add nodeserver.yml roles/awslogs
$ git commit —m "Adding awslogs role and permission to use CloudWatch"
$ git push
$ cd helloworld
$ git add .
$ git commit —m "Adding CloudWatch support to our application"
$ git push
```

Within a few minutes, you should be able to see your new log groups in CloudWatch under the **Logs** section, and inside them, the different log streams of our different hosts, and in the **Metrics** section, our helloworld traffic graph:

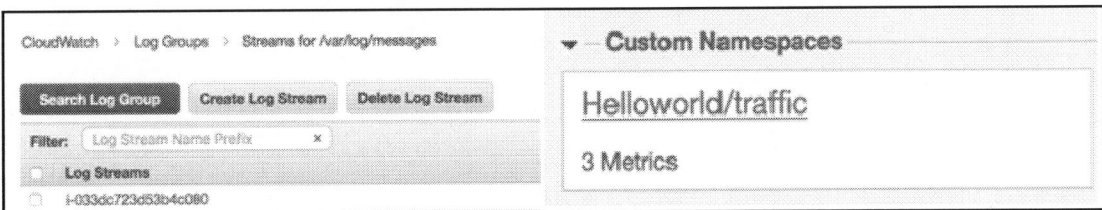

We now have an elegant solution to send logs from an EC2 instance into CloudWatch.

We won't cover this in the book, but CloudWatch has a dashboard feature that will let you create custom views to group some of the critical metrics. For example, if you are monitoring a web application, you may create a dashboard with your application error rate, latency, and **queries per second** (**QPS**).

Average, 95th, and 99th percentile
Averages can be misleading when looking at certain metrics. A classic example is latency. To monitor the latency of your application, you want to collect and graph the worst 95th and 99th percentiles as opposed to simply the mean or average. These two graphs will often tell you a different story of how some users are perceiving the latency on the site.

We now need to provide the same functionalities to ECS.

Handling logs, events, and metrics in ECS

In the previous section, we added an extra step in our deployment process to identify and export the version for our application. In the case of EC2 and CodeDeploy, we created a version string using the deployment execution information. As such, we can easily correlate the logs produced by the deployment execution. In the case of ECS, what matters the most is to be able to identify the container ID within the ECR registry, as we are working with immutable containers. Therefore, we will update our code to use the container tag information as our application version.

In addition, we collected logs on EC2 instances using the `awslogs` agent. In the case of ECS, while we could do something similar by mounting the `/var/log` volume onto the ECS host and running the same agent, there is a much better way to do that.

ECS has many settings that we didn't explore, among them, the ability to configure environment variables and change how logs are managed. We will edit the troposphere script `helloworld-ecs-service-cf` created in the last chapter to send the logs produced in the console directly to the CloudWatch logs.

With your text editor, open the file `helloworld-ecs-service-cf-template.py`.

We will first add a new `troposphere.ecs` import as follows:

```
from troposphere.ecs import (
    TaskDefinition,
    ContainerDefinition,
    LogConfiguration,
    Environment,
)
```

We will use these classes inside the `TaskDefinition` section. Locate the `TaskDefinition`, and after the port mapping definition, add the following to define our `HELLOWORLD_VERSION` variable and the logging configuration:

```
PortMappings=[ecs.PortMapping(
    ContainerPort=3000)],
Environment=[
    Environment(Name='HELLOWORLD_VERSION', Value=Ref("Tag"))
],
LogConfiguration=LogConfiguration(
    LogDriver="awslogs",
    Options={
        'awslogs-group': "/aws/ecs/helloworld",
        'awslogs-region': Ref("AWS::Region"),
    }
),
```

Once those changes are in place, we will create the volume group using the command-line interface:

```
$ aws logs create-log-group --log-group-name /aws/ecs/helloworld
```

In the last chapter, we created our cluster with all the permissions that we need to go through this chapter, therefore we won't need to do anything else to get our logs, events, and metrics sent to CloudWatch.

We can save the changes and commit them:

```
$ git commit -am "Configuring logging"
$ git push
```

You can then generate the new CloudFormation template and commit it to the template directory of our `helloworld` application:

```
$ cd helloworld
$ curl -L http://bit.ly/2v3fryS | python > templates/helloworld-ecs-
service-cf.template
```

```
$ git commit -am "Configuring logging"
$ git push
```

Thanks to our pipeline, a new version of the container will soon be deployed and you will be able to observe the logs and metrics produced by your container.

Our monitoring infrastructure is now looking good. We are collecting and indexing metrics, events, and logs. In most cases, this is enough to get started. We can improve our metrics by creating dashboards to display some of the key metrics and search in our logs for a particular event or timeframe. As applications get more complex, it is common for these types of monitoring architectures to reach their limits. Sometimes, you would like to be able to group logs to find out what type of errors are happening often, or do some complex queries. In addition, you may want to have a more hybrid approach to how you store your logs and keep them indexed for just a few days, but archive them on S3 for a much longer period. To do that, we will need a logging infrastructure made up of ElasticSearch, Kibana, and Kinesis Firehose.

Creating a health check endpoint
It is a good practice to create a route dedicated to monitoring in your application. This endpoint can then be used with your load balancers and ECS tasks to validate that the application is in a working state. The code behind that route will commonly check that the application can connect to your databases, storages, and other services that it depends on before returning an HTTP 200 (OK) to signal that the application is healthy.

Advanced logging infrastructure with ElasticSearch, Kibana, and Firehose

In the world of telemetry, one of the favorite sets of tools that engineers like to use to store their logs is called the ELK stack. The ELK stack consists of ElasticSearch, Logstash, and Kibana. Logs that are captured and filtered by Logstash, converted into JSON documents and sent to ElasticSearch, a distributed search and analytics engine. ElasticSearch is then queried via Kibana, which lets you visualize your data. You can look at this stack on https://www.elastic.co/.

AWS has a very similar system that you can use that also involves ElasticSearch and Kibana, but instead of Logstash, we will use Kinesis Firehose. That variation on the classic ELK stack is a very compelling option as you have even fewer services to manage, and potentially, the fact that Kinesis will retain information for up to five days makes it a better candidate than Logstash to transit your logs.

In addition, Kinesis will let us write our logs to both ElasticSearch and S3 such that if a log fails to be written to ElasticSearch, it will be saved to S3:

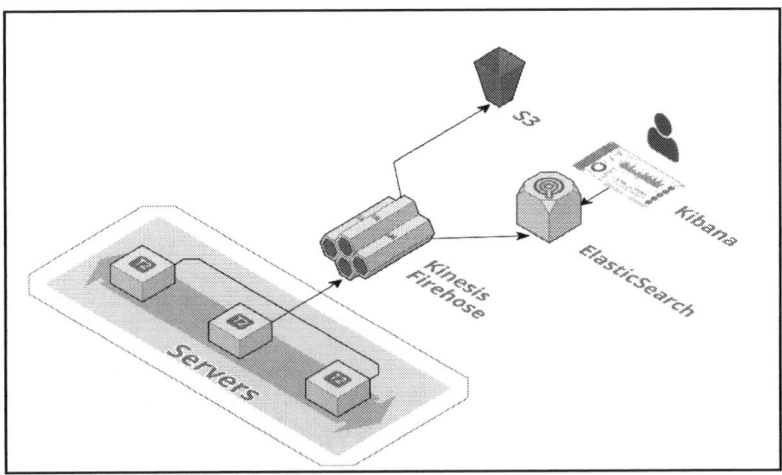

To create our stack, we will once again rely on CloudFormation templates and the troposphere. We will first create an ElasticSearch stack. AWS provides ElasticSearch as a service, and it comes with Kibana preinstalled and configured for your cluster.

Following this, we will create a KinesisThe reasoning for Firehose stack. The reasoning for this is that you may want to use multiple Firehose streams for your different services, but also centralize all your logs into a single ElasticSearch cluster.

Once the new stack is in place, we will change our application a bit to deliver our logs to the Kinesis stream.

Creating and launching an ElasticSearch cluster

As mentioned, AWS has a managed service for ElasticSearch. We will use it to create our cluster.

Create a new file and call it `elasticsearch-cf-template.py`. Our script will start almost like the `nodeserver-cf-template.py` file, but with a number of imports, including some for the `elasticsearch` service:

```
"""Generating CloudFormation template."""

from ipaddress import ip_network
```

```
from ipify import get_ip

from troposphere import (
    GetAtt,
    Join,
    Output,
    Export,
    Parameter,
    Ref,
    Template,
)

from troposphere.elasticsearch import (
    Domain,
    EBSOptions,
    ElasticsearchClusterConfig,
)
```

We will continue the script with the creation of the template and the extraction of the IP address. In the context of ElasticSearch, limiting who can access your cluster is very important, as there is no other authentication mechanism in place:

```
t = Template()

PublicCidrIp = str(ip_network(get_ip()))
```

We will now provide a brief description and collect the different parameters. The first parameter to select, the instance size. We will provide a few options here, but you can refer to http://amzn.to/2s32Vvb for the full list of available instance types:

```
t.add_description('Effective DevOps in AWS: Elasticsearch')

t.add_parameter(Parameter(
    "InstanceType",
    Type="String",
    Description="instance type",
    Default="t2.small.elasticsearch",
    AllowedValues=[
        "t2.small.elasticsearch",
        "t2.medium.elasticsearch",
        "m4.large.elasticsearch",
    ],
))
```

We will also provide the ability to set the number of instances present in our cluster. In the context of the book, we are assuming that the cluster will store just a few GB of logs. For bigger clusters, you may consider altering the template to also provide the ability to have dedicated master instances:

```
t.add_parameter(Parameter(
    "InstanceCount",
    Default="2",
    Type="String",
    Description="Number instances in the cluster",
))
```

The t2 and m4 instances don't come with any attached storage. We will use EBS volumes to store our logs. This next option will let us set the size of the EBS volumes:

```
t.add_parameter(Parameter(
    "VolumeSize",
    Default="10",
    Type="String",
    Description="Size in Gib of the EBS volumes",
))
```

The different parameters we wish to configure are now all present. We can proceed with the creation of our ElasticSearch cluster. ElasticSearch clusters are called domains. We will create a Domain resource and give it a name as follows:

```
t.add_resource(Domain(
    'ElasticsearchCluster',
    DomainName="logs",
```

We then configure which version of ElasticSearch to use. We will pick version 5.3 which is the most recent version of ElasticSearch released when this was published:

```
    ElasticsearchVersion="5.3",
```

Next, we will configure our cluster. As mentioned earlier, we are assuming that the cluster will stay fairly small, and, therefore, we won't need dedicated master instances. For the same reason, we will also opt out of the zone awareness feature, which creates node replicas on the different AZ of the region the cluster is created in. Finally, we will reference the desired instance count and instance type from the parameters of the template:

```
    ElasticsearchClusterConfig=ElasticsearchClusterConfig(
        DedicatedMasterEnabled=False,
        InstanceCount=Ref("InstanceCount"),
        ZoneAwarenessEnabled=False,
        InstanceType=Ref("InstanceType"),
    ),
```

We will also want to specify a few advanced options as follows:

```
AdvancedOptions={
    "indices.fielddata.cache.size": "",
    "rest.action.multi.allow_explicit_index": "true",
},
```

After configuring the cluster, we will configure the EBS volume for our instances. Here too, we will reference our parameters to get the volume size of our volumes:

```
EBSOptions=EBSOptions(EBSEnabled=True,
                      Iops=0,
                      VolumeSize=Ref("VolumeSize"),
                      VolumeType="gp2"),
```

We will conclude the creation of our domain with the configuration of the access policy:

```
AccessPolicies={
    'Version': '2012-10-17',
    'Statement': [
        {
            'Effect': 'Allow',
            'Principal': {
                'AWS': [Ref('AWS::AccountId')]
            },
            'Action': 'es:*',
            'Resource': '*',
        },
        {
            'Effect': 'Allow',
            'Principal': {
                'AWS': "*"
            },
            'Action': 'es:*',
            'Resource': '*',
            'Condition': {
                'IpAddress': {
                    'aws:SourceIp': PublicCidrIp
                }
            }
        }
    ]
},
))
```

Finally, we will conclude the creation of our template with two outputs and our final print statement. The output will be the Kibana URL and the `domainArn` of our ElasticSearch domain, which we will use in the next section. To do so, we are going to export it under the name `LogsDomainArn`:

```
t.add_output(Output(
    "DomainArn",
    Description="Domain Arn",
    Value=GetAtt("ElasticsearchCluster", "DomainArn"),
    Export=Export("LogsDomainArn"),
))

t.add_output(Output(
    "Kibana",
    Description="Kibana url",
    Value=Join("", [
        "https://",
        GetAtt("ElasticsearchCluster", "DomainEndpoint"),
        "/_plugin/kibana/"
    ])
))

print t.to_json()
```

Our template is now completed. Your script should be similar to `http://bit.ly/2v3DHRG`.

We can commit it, and create our ElasticSearch domain:

```
$ python elasticsearch-cf-template.py > elasticsearch-cf.template
$ git add elasticsearch-cf-template.py
$ git commit -m "Adding ElasticSearch template"
$ git push
$ aws cloudformation create-stack \
      --stack-name elasticsearch \
      --template-body file://elasticsearch-cf.template \
      --parameters \
          ParameterKey=InstanceType,ParameterValue=t2.small.elasticsearch \
          ParameterKey=InstanceCount,ParameterValue=2 \
          ParameterKey=VolumeSize,ParameterValue=10
```

Creating and launching a Kinesis Firehose stream

Within a few minutes, our ElasticSearch cluster should be up and running. We will now focus on the Kinesis Firehose component of our stack, which will let us feed data into ElasticSearch.

We will create a new script and call it `firehose-cf-template.py`.

The script starts as usual with several imports, the creation of a template variable, and a brief description:

```
"""Generating CloudFormation template."""

from troposphere import (
    GetAtt,
    Join,
    Ref,
    Template,
    ImportValue
)

from troposphere.firehose import (
    BufferingHints,
    CloudWatchLoggingOptions,
    DeliveryStream,
    S3Configuration,
    ElasticsearchDestinationConfiguration,
    RetryOptions,
)

from troposphere.iam import Role

from troposphere.s3 import Bucket

t = Template()

t.add_description('Effective DevOps in AWS: Kinesis Firehose Stream')
```

The first resource we will create is an S3 bucket:

```
t.add_resource(Bucket(
    "S3Bucket",
    DeletionPolicy="Retain"
))
```

Following this, we will create a new role to give the permissions to our Firehose stream to communicate with ElasticSearch and S3. To save a bit of time, we are going to use some of the managed policies that AWS provides. In a production environment, these policies might be too open for your liking, and you may instead opt for writing your own:

```
t.add_resource(Role(
    'FirehoseRole',
    ManagedPolicyArns=[
        'arn:aws:iam::aws:policy/AmazonS3FullAccess',
```

```
            'arn:aws:iam::aws:policy/AmazonESFullAccess',
    ],
    AssumeRolePolicyDocument={
        'Version': '2012-10-17',
        'Statement': [{
            'Action': 'sts:AssumeRole',
            'Principal': {'Service': 'firehose.amazonaws.com'},
            'Effect': 'Allow',
        }]
    }
))
```

Finally, we will create our Firehose stream. We will create a new resource of the type DeliveryStream and give it the name `FirehoseLogs`:

```
t.add_resource(DeliveryStream(
    'FirehoseLogs',
    DeliveryStreamName='FirehoseLogs',
```

DeliveryStreams can be used to deliver data to several services. In our case, we want it to deliver data to ElasticSearch. For that, we will create an `ElasticSearchDestinationConfiguration` parameter as follows:

```
ElasticsearchDestinationConfiguration=ElasticsearchDestinationConfiguration
(
```

The first piece of information we need to provide is the identifier of the ElasticSearch domain. We will do that by referencing the `LogsDomainArn` variable that we exported in the previous section:

```
DomainARN=ImportValue("LogsDomainArn"),
```

Next, we will reference the IAM role we just defined before the creation of our DeliveryStream:

```
RoleARN=GetAtt("FirehoseRole", "Arn"),
```

We will then specify the index name. You can picture that as the name of the database you want your logs to be in. We call our index logs to keep things simple:

```
IndexName="logs",
```

In addition, in ElasticSearch, indices contain documents of different types (each type has its own name and mapping). We will name ours `Logs`:

```
TypeName="Logs",
```

One of the common ways to shard data across an ElasticSearch cluster is to use temporal sharding. In our case, we will pick a daily rotation. For instance, an index containing the logs of March 24 2020 will be called `logs-2020.03.24`. To do that, we will configure the `IndexRotationPeriod` to rotate logs every day:

```
IndexRotationPeriod="OneDay",
```

Occasionally, ElasticSearch might get congested and won't reply right away. We will configure our stream to retry delivering data for 5 minutes:

```
RetryOptions=RetryOptions(
    DurationInSeconds="300"
),
```

Kinesis Firehose works by buffering data until you reach a certain duration or a certain size. We will set them to do the minimum which, is 1 minute and 1 MB:

```
BufferingHints=BufferingHints(
    IntervalInSeconds=60,
    SizeInMBs=1
),
```

At this point, Kinesis Firehose has all the information it needs to send data to ElasticSearch. We will now configure it to also store all those logs on S3. We will first configure the stream to back up all documents (the alternative is backing up only the ones that failed being inserted into ElasticSearch):

```
S3BackupMode="AllDocuments",
```

Following this, we will configure the S3. This will involve configuring the buffering like we did for ElasticSearch, referencing the bucket we created at the beginning of the template, stating whether we want to compress those logs, referencing the prefix for our files and, finally entering the role to use for these operations:

```
S3Configuration=S3Configuration(
    BufferingHints=BufferingHints(
        IntervalInSeconds=300,
        SizeInMBs=5
    ),
    BucketARN=Join("", [
        "arn:aws:s3:::", Ref("S3Bucket")
    ]),
    CompressionFormat='UNCOMPRESSED',
    Prefix='firehose-logs',
    RoleARN=GetAtt("FirehoseRole", "Arn"),
```

```
        ),
    )
))
```

We will conclude our script by printing the JSON output of our template:

```
print t.to_json()
```

Your script should look as follows http://bit.ly/2v2tFAo.

We can now commit the script, create the template and launch it

```
$ git add firehose-cf-template.py
$ git commit -m "Adding Firehose template"
$ git push
$ python firehose-cf-template.py > firehose-cf.template
$ aws cloudformation create-stack \
      --stack-name firehose \
      --template-body file://firehose-cf.template \
      --capabilities CAPABILITY_IAM
```

At this point, we have a working Firehose-to-ElasticSearch pipeline (also known as the **EKK stack**). We now need to circle back to our application and make some changes to deliver our logs to it.

Updating our application to send logs to the Firehose endpoint

Our options to send logs to Kinesis Firehose are very similar to CloudWatch logs. We could use the aws-kinesis-agent provided in the yum repo as a replacement for the awslogs agent, but instead, we will demonstrate another way to do that. We are going to make our application send its logs directly to Kinesis instead of writing them on disk first.

Before making those changes, we will adjust the permissions to allow our instances to interact with Firehose.

Adding permissions to EC2 to communicate with Firehose

We will once again edit our nodeserver-cf-template.py script. Open the file with your editor and in the MonitoringPolicy policy, add the following to allow our EC2 instance to communicate with Firehose and put a record into the stream:

```
t.add_resource(IAMPolicy(
    "MonitoringPolicy",
```

```
        PolicyName="AllowSendingDataForMonitoring",
        PolicyDocument=Policy(
            Statement=[
                Statement(
                    Effect=Allow,
                    Action=[
                        Action("cloudwatch", "Put*"),
                        Action("logs", "Create*"),
                        Action("logs", "Put*"),
                        Action("logs", "Describe*"),
                        Action("events", "Put*"),
                        Action("firehose", "Put*"),
                    ],
                    Resource=["*"])
            ]
        ),
        Roles=[Ref("Role")],
))
```

Save the new script, commit your changes, and, following the same step as before, deploy the new version of the template. Your new template should look like `http://bit.ly/2v3bK sY`:

```
$ git add nodeserver-cf-template.py
$ git commit -m "Allowing our application to send logs to Firehose"
$ git push
$ python nodeserver-cf-template.py > nodeserver-cf.template

$ aws cloudformation update-stack \
        --capabilities CAPABILITY_IAM \
        --stack-name helloworld-staging \
        --template-body file://nodeserver-cf.template \
        --parameters \
            ParameterKey=InstanceType,UsePreviousValue=true \
            ParameterKey=KeyPair,,UsePreviousValue=true \
            ParameterKey=PublicSubnet,,UsePreviousValue=true \
            ParameterKey=ScaleCapacity,,UsePreviousValue=true \
            ParameterKey=VpcId,,UsePreviousValue=true

$ aws cloudformation update-stack \
        --capabilities CAPABILITY_IAM \
        --stack-name helloworld-production \
        --template-body file://nodeserver-cf.template \
        --parameters \
            ParameterKey=InstanceType,UsePreviousValue=true \
            ParameterKey=KeyPair,UsePreviousValue=true \
```

```
ParameterKey=PublicSubnet,UsePreviousValue=true \
ParameterKey=ScaleCapacity,UsePreviousValue=true \
ParameterKey=VpcId,UsePreviousValue=true
```

In the case of ECS, we already added the proper permissions in the last chapter when we created our clusters.

Now that this is in place, we will make changes to our code.

Changing the logging transport to send logs to Firehose

Our logging library, winston, has a system to extend some of its functionalities, including its transport system. We will install a new transport system that can talk to Kinesis Firehose.

In your terminal, go to the root directory of your `helloworld` application and run the following command:

```
$ npm install winston-firehose@1.0.6 --save --save-exact
```

This will install specifically version `1.0.6` of the `winston-firehose` package and update the `package.json` accordingly. We need to enforce this version because our EC2 instance is running an old version of Node.js.

Then, open the `helloworld.js` file with your code editor.

After the declaration of our winston variable, we will define a new variable as follows:

```
var WFirehose = require('winston-firehose')
```

When we used the `awslogs` agent or the ECS logging driver, the service was able to specify the hostname or container ID that the logs were coming from. In addition, each logfile was in its own log group, which made it easy to identify what service and what instance of this service emitted a given log. The new architecture we are migrating to doesn't offer this. We will make some changes to our code to expose the service name and the host that produced the logs.

After the creation of the version variable, add the following:

```
var hostname = process.env.HOSTNAME
```

This will get the hostname of the server from our environment.

A bit below, we will edit the rewriter to include this extra information as follows:

```
logger.rewriters.push(function(level, msg, meta) {
  meta.version = version
  meta.hostname = hostname
  meta.appname = "helloworld"
  return meta
})
```

Lastly, we will replace the logger variable definition. Find the following code:

```
var logger = new winston.Logger({
  transports: [new winston.transports.Console({
    timestamp: function() {
        var d = new Date();
        return d.toISOString()
    },
  })]
})
```

Replace this code with the reference to our Firehose endpoint:

```
var logger = new (winston.Logger)({
  transports: [new WFirehose({
    'streamName': 'FirehoseLogs',
    'firehoseOptions': {
      'region': 'us-east-1'
    }
  })]
})
```

Once those changes are in place, we can add the new module to `git`, `commit`, and `push` the changes:

```
$ git add helloworld.js package.json node_modules
$ git commit -m "Sending logs to Firehose directly"
$ git push
```

Within a few minutes, CloudWatch logs should stop receiving logs, while your Firehose delivery service should start seeing traffic. You can open `https://console.aws.amazon.com/firehose/home?region=us-east-1#/details/Firehose Logs?edit=false` to verify that the last changes are working:

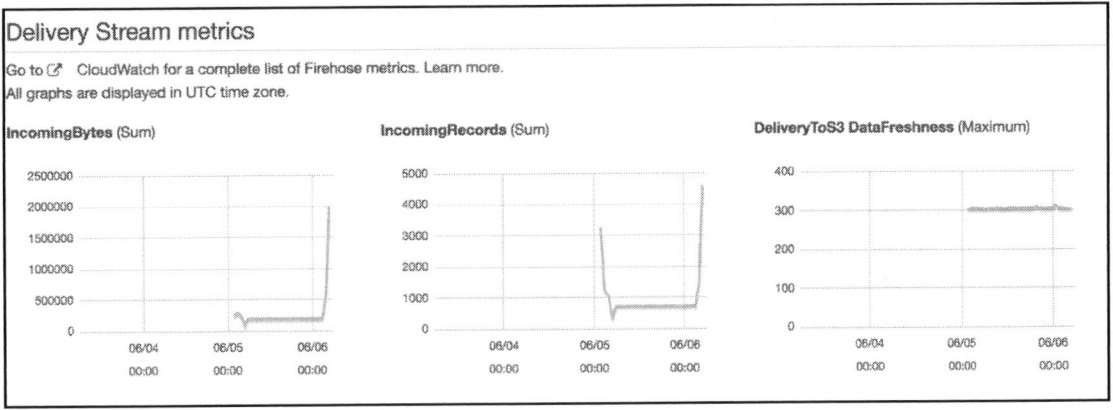

We can now look at our logs in Kibana.

Using Kibana to visualize logs

At this point, our application logs are going to ElasticSearch via Kinesis Firehose. One of the best ways to access our logs now is to use Kibana. You can find the URL of your Kibana instance by looking at the output of the ElasticSearch CloudFormation stack we launched earlier:

```
$ aws cloudformation describe-stacks \
    --stack-name es \
    --query 'Stacks[0].Outputs'
[
    {
        "Description": "Kibana url",
        "OutputKey": "Kibana",
        "OutputValue": "https://search-logs-
x7c2g5zqbrtpxotpv3b3jw2uk4.us-east-1.es.amazonaws.com/_plugin/kibana/"
    },
    {
        "Description": "Domain Arn",
        "OutputKey": "DomainArn",
        "OutputValue": "arn:aws:es:us-east-1:511912822958:domain/logs"
    }
]
```

Using your browser, open the Kibana URL:

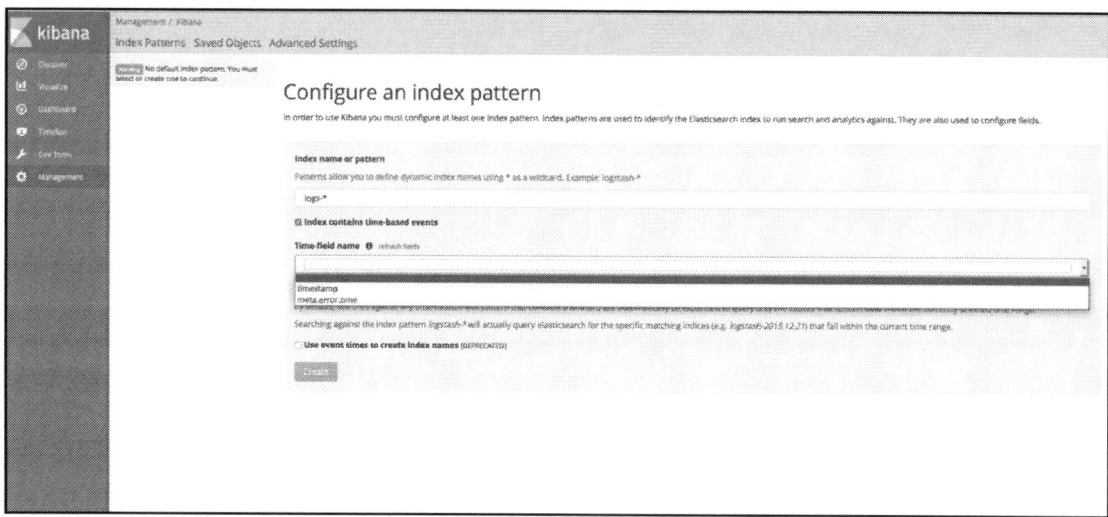

This brings you to a screen resembling the one shown in the preceding screenshot where you will have to do the initial configuration:

1. Set the value of the **Index name or pattern** field to `logs-*`.
2. Doing so will make Kibana analyze your logs to find out the possible time field names. We will select the one called **timestamp**.
3. Once you have selected the proper values, click on **Create**.

This will lead you to the management screen of the index pattern we just created. As you will see, each meta has been analyzed. At that point, you can click on **Discover** to see all your logs and explore the different visualization options to create dashboards for your logs.

You can Google Kibana to get some inspiration on what you can do and what to put in your dashboards:

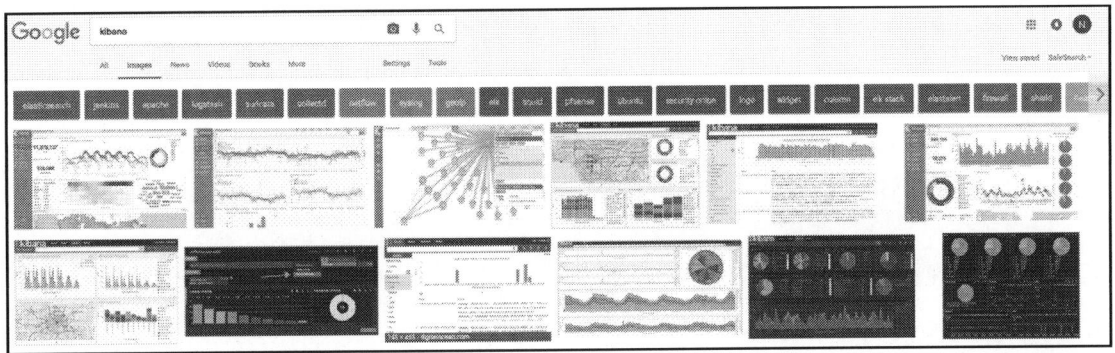

Deleting old logs using Curator

Unlike CloudWatch logs, the deletion of old logs isn't a built-in feature of this stack. To delete old logs, look at Elastic Curator at `http://bit.ly/2rFHzUT`. You can easily deploy it using a Lambda function that will run once a day, for example.

Over the course of the last few pages, we went over several concepts to improve logging. With the help of several AWS services, we were able to collect logs, events, and metrics from our application and send them to different services, including CloudWatch, S3, and ElasticSearch. Of course, logging doesn't stop here. The monitoring stack we explored can be reused to monitor virtually anything that would matter to you and your company. Among the other functionalities worth exploring is how to monitor the rest of our AWS infrastructure.

Monitoring our infrastructure

Monitoring is one of those tasks with no finish line. There is always something that you could add or improve. Because of that, it is important to prioritize the areas on which you will focus most of your efforts, especially at the beginning, or when new services are released. In addition, different services require different levels of attention. For instance, services such as Lambda, S3, or DynamoDB are considered serverless. AWS takes care of almost everything. You don't need to handle failures, security patches, scaling, high availability, and so on. At the opposite end of the spectrum, you have services such as EC2 where, aside from the hardware itself, you control every aspect of the instance, and therefore, you need to also invest time and effort in monitoring. Lucky for us, most services that AWS creates have a native integration with CloudWatch. Rather than going down the full list of services we used so far and seeing how monitoring is done, we will look at the different ways to add monitoring to our existing templates.

Monitoring EC2

EC2 instances are created on top of a hypervisor, which is controlled by AWS. Thanks to the hypervisor, AWS is able to extract several metrics and feed them into CloudWatch metrics. This includes CPU utilization, network utilization (NetworkIn and NetworkOut), and disk performance (DiskReadOps, DiskWriteOps, DiskReadBytes, DiskWriteBytes).

Those metrics are available in the EC2 console when you select your instances and also in the CloudWatch metrics menu:

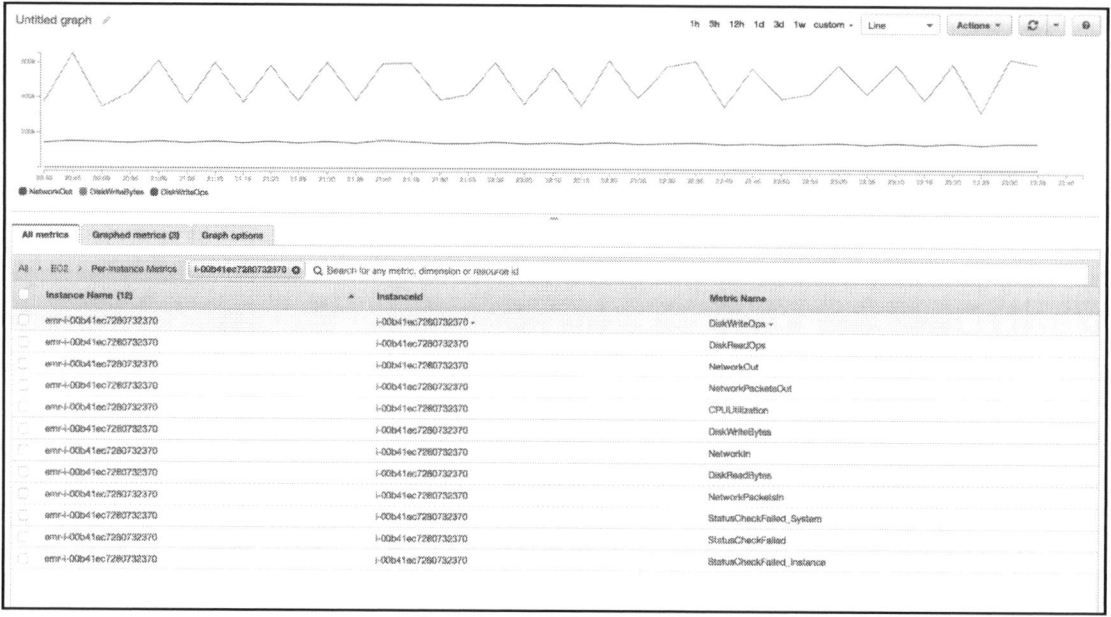

By default, the resolution of those metrics is 5 minutes. This means that new data points for your EC2 instances are collected every 5 minutes. If you have critical hosts where you wish to have a higher resolution, you can enable a feature called **detailed monitoring** on a per instance basis, which will increase the frequency of those metrics to a 1 minute resolution.

Unfortunately, only relying on the hypervisor metrics isn't enough. As you might have noticed, CloudWatch has information on how your disk performs, for example, but not on how much disk space you have left. That's because the hypervisor doesn't have visibility of the operating system. To supply that information, we will need to install an agent on our EC2 instances to collect those extra metrics.

Providing custom metrics to CloudWatch

We are going to complement the metrics we already have with OS-specific information. This will include more detailed information about the CPU, disk usage, and memory.

When browsing the EC2 metrics, you will notice that you can query those metrics by Auto Scaling Group:

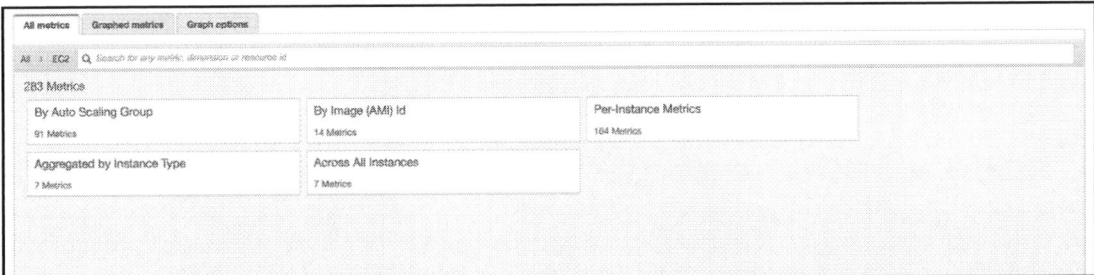

It is important to retain this ability to query a set of metrics by specific criteria, especially by Auto Scaling Groups. To provide the same capability to our custom metrics, we need to make a change in our CloudFormation template to allow our EC2 instances to get the Auto Scaling Group information.

Updating our CloudFormation template

Open the `nodeserver-cf-template.py` script

After that first IAM policy, add the following `MonitoringPolicy` IAM policy. Simply add the following action to the statement:

```
t.add_resource(IAMPolicy(
    "MonitoringPolicy",
    PolicyName="AllowSendingDataForMonitoring",
    PolicyDocument=Policy(
        Statement=[
            Statement(
                Effect=Allow,
                Action=[
                    Action("cloudwatch", "Put*"),
                    Action("logs", "Create*"),
                    Action("logs", "Put*"),
                    Action("logs", "Describe*"),
                    Action("events", "Put*"),
                    Action("firehose", "Put*"),
                    Action("autoscaling", "DescribeAutoScalingInstances"),
```

```
              ],
              Resource=["*"])
        ]
     ),
     Roles=[Ref("Role")]
))
```

Save the file. It should be similar to `http://bit.ly/2v3cdeM`.

Then, once again, update the stacks:

```
$ git add nodeserver-cf-template.py
$ git commit -m "Allowing the instance to describe the ASG instances"
$ git push
$ python nodeserver-cf-template.py > nodeserver-cf.template

$ aws cloudformation update-stack \
      --capabilities CAPABILITY_IAM \
      --stack-name helloworld-staging \
      --template-body file://nodeserver-cf.template \
      --parameters \
          ParameterKey=InstanceType,UsePreviousValue=true \
          ParameterKey=KeyPair,,UsePreviousValue=true \
          ParameterKey=PublicSubnet,,UsePreviousValue=true \
          ParameterKey=ScaleCapacity,,UsePreviousValue=true \
          ParameterKey=VpcId,,UsePreviousValue=true

$ aws cloudformation update-stack \
      --capabilities CAPABILITY_IAM \
      --stack-name helloworld-production \
      --template-body file://nodeserver-cf.template \
      --parameters \
          ParameterKey=InstanceType,UsePreviousValue=true \
          ParameterKey=KeyPair,UsePreviousValue=true \
          ParameterKey=PublicSubnet,UsePreviousValue=true \
          ParameterKey=ScaleCapacity,UsePreviousValue=true \
          ParameterKey=VpcId,UsePreviousValue=true
```

Next, we are going to create a new role in our Ansible repository to install and configure a tool to emit those metrics.

Creating a CloudWatch role in Ansible

We first need to go into the `roles` directory of our Ansible repository:

```
$ cd roles
```

We will use the `ansible-galaxy` command to generate our new role:

```
$ ansible-galaxy init cloudwatch
- cloudwatch was created successfully
```

We will create a minimal role that allows us to report some of those missing stats. With your text editor, open the file `cloudwatch/tasks/main.yml`.

We will use an open source tool called `cloudwatchmon`. You can access its code source and documentation on the GitHub page of the project at `http://bit.ly/2pYjhI9`. The tool is written in Python and is available through `pip`. To install `pip` packages, `ansible` provides a `pip` module. After the initial comment of the task, add the following:

```
---

# tasks file for cloudwatch

- name: Installing cloudwatchmon
  pip:
    name: cloudwatchmon
```

This tool works through the intermediary of `cronjob`. We will use the `cron` module of Ansible to create what we will call `cloudwatchmon`.

After the call to the `pip` module, call the `cron` module as follows:

```
- name: Execute cloudwatchmon every 5min
  cron:
    name: "cloudwatchmon"
    minute: "*/5"
    job: /usr/local/bin/mon-put-instance-stats.py --auto-scaling --loadavg-
percpu --mem-util --disk-space-util --disk-path=/ --from-cron"
```

In this case, we are configuring our job to trigger the `mon-put-instance-stats.py` every 5 minutes. We are also specifying the list of metrics we want to collect in the command. The `mem-util` option will provide the percentage of memory utilization while `disk-space-util` will do the same, but referring to the disk space on the / partition. You can refer to the documentation of the script to check the full list of options available.

Percentage versus raw values

There are two ways to report these resource usages. You can provide the utilization percentages (for example, "the partition is full at 23%") or look at the exact value (for example, "there are 2 GB free on that partition"). For our purposes, suffice it to say that monitoring infrastructures using percentages tends to speed up iteration time as you can create more generic alerts. This tends to change over time, as your different applications will often have different constraints requiring different types of hardware.

Before committing our change, we are going in go one directory up and edit the file `nodeserver.yml`:

```
$ cd ..
```

We need to include the new role we just created to our service. We can do that simply by adding a new entry to the roles section, as shown here:

```
---
- hosts: "{{ target | default('localhost') }}"
  become: yes
  roles:
    - nodejs
    - codedeploy
    - cloudwatch
    - { role: awslogs, name: messages, file: /var/log/messages }
    - {
        role: awslogs,
        name: helloworld,
        file: /var/log/helloworld/helloworld.log,
        datetime_format: "%Y-%m-%dT%H:%M:%S.%f"
    }
```

We can save all the changes and commit them:

```
$ git add roles/cloudwatch nodeserver.yml
$ git commit -m "Adding new role for CloudWatch monitoring"
$ git push
```

Since Ansible pulls changes every 10 minutes, within 15 minutes at most we should start seeing a new section in CloudWatch called **Linux System**, containing the new metrics of our hosts:

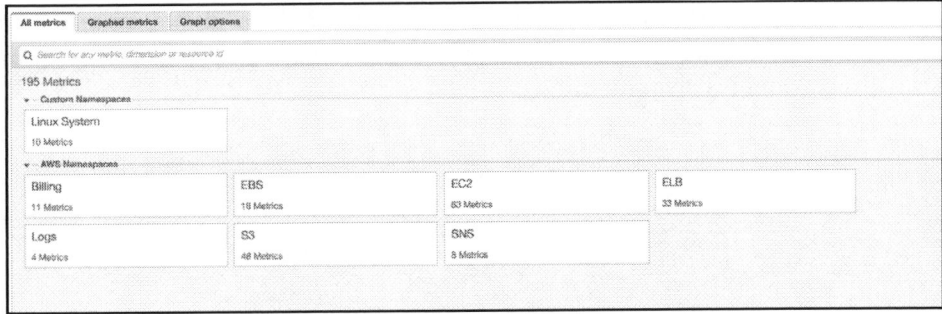

Now that we have all the visibility we need on our EC2 instances, we can put some alarms in place.

In many cases, especially with applications exposed to the internet, you tend to observe occasional strange behavior, but can't easily understand how the application gets in that state. One of the most useful pieces of information to have in those cases is the access logs of your load balancer.

Currently, our load balancer exposes several metrics in CloudWatch, but can't tell us the full story. What routes are causing a 5xx error? What is the latency? Where are the users coming from? How aggressively are they using your application? To gain access to those insights, we make a few changes to our ELB and ALB instances.

Monitoring ECS clusters

When it comes to monitoring, EC2 and ECS are very similar. We can slice ECS into three components: the ECS hosts, the ECS service, and the containers.

Monitoring ECS hosts

ECS runs on top of EC2. Therefore, everything that can be done for EC2 can and should be done for ECS, including disk space monitoring. The main difference is that you have more options on how to implement it:

1. Your first option consists of duplicating what we did with EC2 and have the cloudwatchmon run on every EC2 instance running ECS. To implement this, you can create a new Ansible role for the ECS host and add the installation and execution of Ansible to the UserData variable of the ecs-cluster-cf-template.py, the way we did it in nodeserver-cf-template.py.

2. Your second option also relies on the UserData field, but this time, you create a new container that runs `cloudwatchmon` and creates a task for it. The UserData file would end with something like:

```
$ aws ecs start-task \
      --cluster $cluster \
      --task-definition cloudwatchmon:1 \
      --container-instances $instance_arn \
      --region $region
```

3. Your last option is to take advantage of the task placement feature that ECS offers. This will let you run your containers using a spread strategy such that, by launching as many containers as you have ECS hosts, you will be able to collect the stats of each ECS server. You can read more about task placement at `http://amzn.to/2kn2OXO`.

Once you have that part under control, you can look at the ECS service itself.

Monitoring the ECS service

Often with managed services, AWS natively provides the metrics you need to care about. If you go into the console and look at the monitoring tabs, you will see two graphs. The first graph focuses on CPU allocation and the second one on memory utilization. Because we configured Auto Scaling Groups, the usage shown in these graphs should always stay within the thresholds we set:

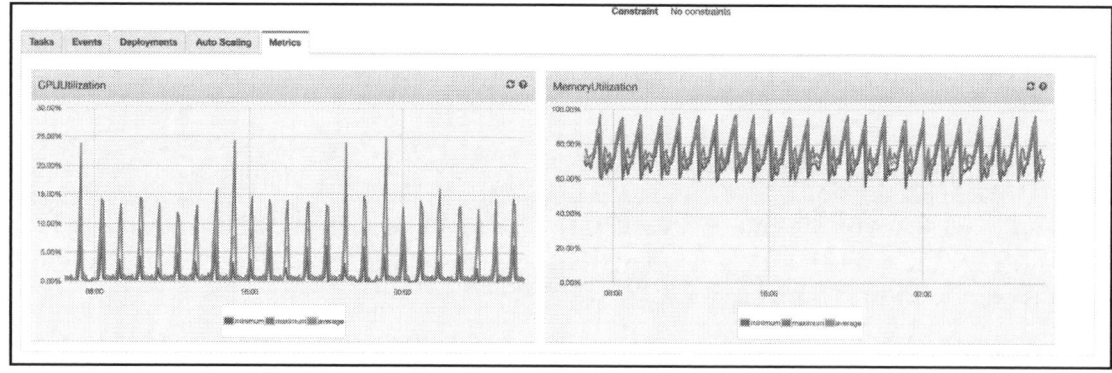

Lastly, you can monitor your tasks and containers.

Monitoring your containers

We containerized our applications, but, fundamentally, nothing about the application really changed. The best way to monitor your application is through the creation of metrics and logs, as we did in the earlier part of this chapter. That said, if you experience some issues with your containers, you may want to search for unhealthy events in the ECS clusters menu:

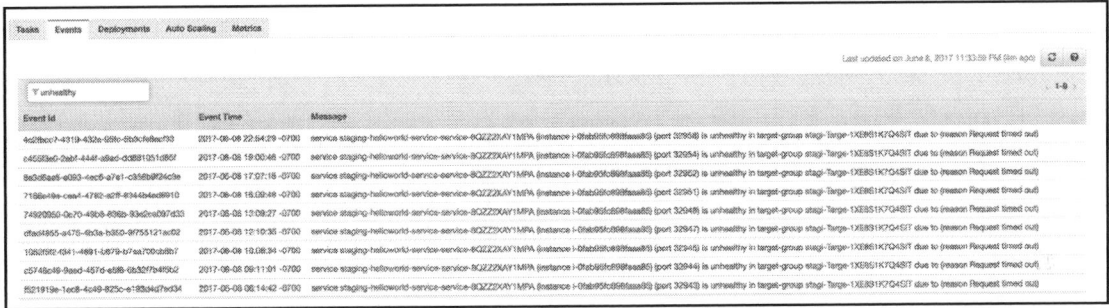

Those issues are often caused by misconfiguration of the tasks, when you don't provide enough CPU and memory reservation, or by bugs or bad user behavior. For those issues, it is often hard to diagnose them by solely looking at metrics. To help with the diagnosis of these issues, we can turn on logging on our load balancers.

Monitoring ALB and ELB instances

ALB and ELB both provide a fair amount of top-level metrics, giving you a sense of how your services are behaving, but sometimes, metrics aren't enough. You want to produce an access log and track the detail of each request hitting your services. Both ELB and ALB provide the ability to generate an access log and store it on S3. We will illustrate how to turn on this feature by making changes to our CloudFormation templates. We will take the example of our ALB template to turn on logging.

With your editor, open the file `helloworld-ecs-alb-cf-template.py`.located in the EffectiveDevOpsTemplates repository.

In order to create the access log, we will need to create an S3 bucket and provide it a special policy so that AWS can access our bucket. This will require including a few extra classes. In the import section, add the following:

```
from awacs.aws import Allow, Policy, Principal, Statement

from awacs.s3 import PutObject, ARN

from troposphere.s3 import (
    Bucket,
    BucketPolicy,
)
```

Next, we will create our S3 bucket. After the creation of the template variable and the addition of its description, add the following resource:

```
t.add_resource(Bucket(
    "S3Bucket",
    DeletionPolicy="Retain",
))
```

We are setting a deletion policy such that if we delete the CloudFormation template, the S3 bucket will remain and the logs will still be available. The next resource we are going to create is the special policy for that bucket. The policy will start by referencing the bucket we just created:

```
t.add_resource(BucketPolicy(
    'BucketPolicy',
    Bucket=Ref("S3Bucket"),
```

The next part is the creation of the policy. The policy contains a statement that tells the bucket that the AWS account `127311923021` is allowed to put object operations into the `/AWSLogs/511912822958/` prefix. The account `127311923021` is a special account that AWS operates. You can refer to `http://amzn.to/2r8AqPI` for the list of account ids in case your bucket isn't in `us-east-1`. In addition `511912822958` needs to be replaced with your own AWS account id:

```
PolicyDocument=Policy(
    Version='2012-10-17',
    Statement=[
        Statement(
            Action=[PutObject],
            Effect=Allow,
            Principal=Principal("AWS", ["127311923021"]),
            Resource=[Join('',
                        [ARN(''),
```

```
                              Ref("S3Bucket"),
                                "/AWSLogs/511912822958/*"])),
               )
          ]
     )
))
```

Now that the bucket is created and contains the specific policy, we can turn on the access log in our ALB resource as follows:

```
t.add_resource(elb.LoadBalancer(
    "LoadBalancer",
    Scheme="internet-facing",
    Subnets=Split(
        ',',
        ImportValue(
            Join("-",
                [Select(0, Split("-", Ref("AWS::StackName"))),
                 "cluster-public-subnets"]
                )
        )
    ),
    SecurityGroups=[Ref("LoadBalancerSecurityGroup")],
    LoadBalancerAttributes=[
        elb.LoadBalancerAttributes(
            Key="access_logs.s3.enabled",
            Value="true",
        ),
        elb.LoadBalancerAttributes(
            Key="access_logs.s3.bucket",
            Value=Ref("S3Bucket"),
        )
    ],
))
```

Once those changes are in place, you can save and commit your changes, generate the new template, and update your stack. The code should be similar to http://bit.ly/2v3bUAA

```
$ git add helloworld-ecs-alb-cf-template.py
$ git commit -m "Sending ALB logs to S3"
$ git push
$ python helloworld-ecs-alb-cf-template.py > helloworld-ecs-alb-cf.template
$ aws cloudformation update-stack \
      --stack-name staging-alb \
      --template-body file://helloworld-ecs-alb-cf.template
$ aws cloudformation update-stack \
      --stack-name production-alb \
      --template-body file://helloworld-ecs-alb-cf.template
```

Logs will now be automatically uploaded every 5 minutes to the S3 bucket.

Using AWS Athena to efficiently retrieve logs
Once your logs are in S3, you can either download them and analyze them locally or, if you are looking for specific information, you can use AWS Athena (`http://amzn.to/2rSsrn7`) to run SQL queries against your logs. For example, to get the list of the most active IP addresses, you can run the following query:

```
SELECT client_ip, COUNT(*) as count
FROM logs.alb
GROUP BY client_ip
ORDER BY COUNT(*) DESC LIMIT 100;
```

As you would expect, each service AWS releases comes with documentation that covers every aspect of its monitoring. You can refer to it to see what you need to expose and implement it with code using one of the strategies we showed in this section.

The last part of adding a monitoring solution is to create alarms to automatically notify engineers when something abnormal is happening. We will use CloudWatch in conjunction with SNS to create those alarms.

Creating alarms using CloudWatch and SNS

Up to this point, we have focused on exposing metrics to better understand what is happening around us. We can now access the data and create nice visualizations of it, but that is not enough. **Mean time to discover (MTD)** and **Mean time to recover (MTTR)** are two very common metrics used to see how the operations team, and by extension the DevOps team, is performing. To keep those two metrics as low as possible, automated alerts are essential. A good alerting system will often help to rapidly identify issues in your systems and help minimize service degradation and disruption. That said, creating the proper alarms isn't always as easy as it sounds.

What should we be alerted about? Measuring everything doesn't mean being alerted about everything. As a rule of thumb, aim at creating alerts about symptoms rather than causes, and be mindful of when to page someone versus sending a less distributive email or message (like slack) notification. You want to avoid alert fatigue as much as possible. This is when on-call engineers become numb to certain alerts that occur too often. In addition, you want to avoid flooding the on-call engineer with a sea of noisy alerts.

Alerts, and in particular the ones that create pages, should always be timely and actionable:

- Think about limiting the scope of what your alerts are covering to important resources, such as your production environment, only. Make sure that planned maintenances are also factored into your alerting policy. We won't show that in this book, but you might extend the work done in the AWS health section of this chapter to disable the alarms of the services impacted by some of the planned maintenance around EC2.
- As your infrastructure grows and the number of EC2 instances needed to run a service increases, you may want to avoid sending a page of information if only a small portion of your infrastructure is having issues. For instance, the architectures we used in this book put our EC2 instances behind load balancers. If one of your instances stops working, the user impact will be minimal and paging someone is likely not required.

To create our alerts, we will once again turn to CloudWatch. In addition to its capacity to log metrics, create logs, and trigger events, CloudWatch also features many functionalities to watch metrics. We already used some of its features in Chapter 6, *Running Containers in AWS*, when we configured the scaling component of our Auto Scaling Groups in EC2 and ECS. We will use it here in conjunction with SNS.

AWS Simple Notification Service (SNS)

SNS is a web service that enables applications, end users, and devices to send and receive notifications. We already briefly used it in our deployment pipeline to receive email notifications to approve production deployment. We will use SNS to notify us about important events.

The service is logically broken up into four parts: producers, topics, protocols, and subscriptions.

The message producers are the applications and services producing the messages, and those messages are organized around topics. Topics are like access points. As you create your SNS topics, AWS will associate them with an ARN that other services can subscribe to.

Once the topic is created, other systems or end users can subscribe (or be subscribed) to those topics via a number protocols, such as HTTP(S), email, Amazon SQS, Amazon Lambda, SMS, or the mobile endpoint (mobile application and devices):

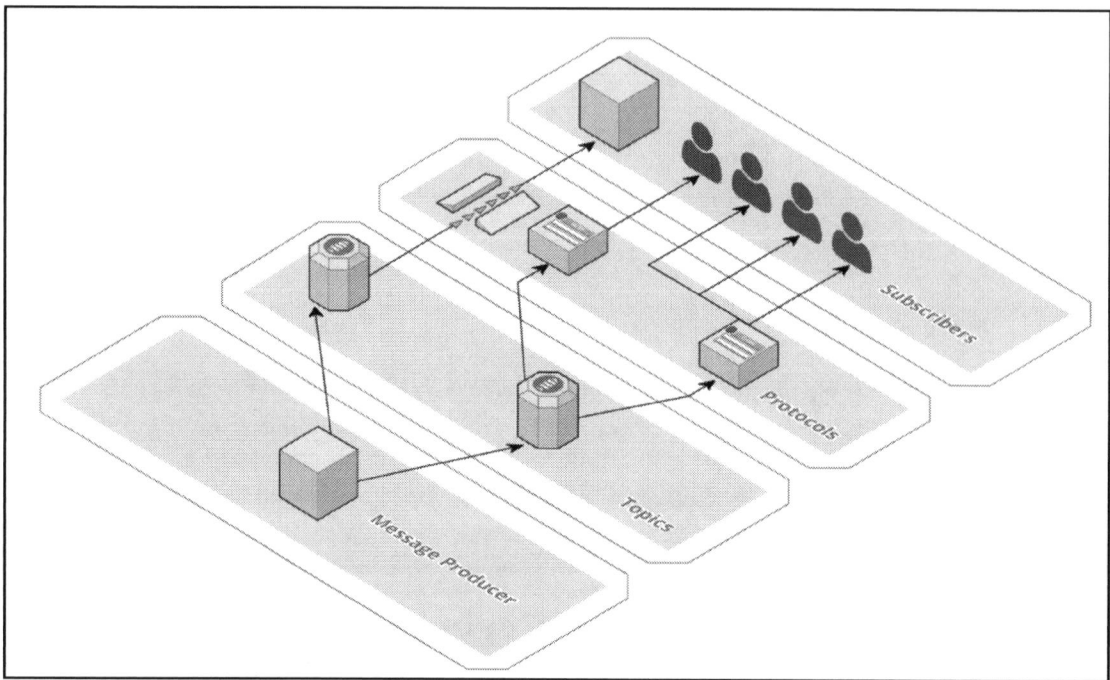

We will type of notifications, one for nonurgent issues. In this case, we will simply send emails. The second one will be used to notify us of critical and time-sensitive issues. For the latter, we will rely on SMS notifications.

We will use the AWS command-line interface to create them.

The first step will be to create the two topics as follows:

```
$ aws sns create-topic --name alert-email
{
    "TopicArn": "arn:aws:sns:us-east-1:511912822958:alert-email"
}
$ aws sns create-topic --name alert-sms
{
    "TopicArn": "arn:aws:sns:us-east-1:511912822958:alert-sms"
}
```

This part is straightforward: the only difference is the same for those topics. We will now put our protocols in place, starting with the email protocol. To do that, we will use the `sns subscribe` option and specify the following:

- The `topic-arn` returned by the previous command
- The protocol, in this case email
- The notification endpoint, which should be your email address

```
$ aws sns subscribe \
    --topic-arn arn:aws:sns:us-east-1:511912822958:alert-email \
    --protocol email \
    --notification-endpoint email@domain.com
{
    "SubscriptionArn": "pending confirmation"
}
```

At this point, you should check your inbox and confirm that you want to subscribe:

AWS Notifications <no-reply@sns.amazonaws.com>
to me ▾

You have chosen to subscribe to the topic:
arn:aws:sns:us-east-1:511912822958:alert-email

To confirm this subscription, click or visit the link below (If this was in error no action is necessary):
Confirm subscription

Please do not reply directly to this email. If you wish to remove yourself from receiving all future SNS subscription confirmation requests please send an email to sns-opt-out

---

The SMS subscription is very similar to the email subscription, with the addition of an extra step of setting a `DisplayName` attribute, which is required for the SMS protocol subscription:

```
$ aws sns set-topic-attributes \
    --topic-arn arn:aws:sns:us-east-1:511912822958:alert-sms2 \
    --attribute-name DisplayName \
    --attribute-value helloworld
```

The notification endpoint should be your cellphone number prefixed with the country code (for example, in the US, if your number is +1 (222) 333-4444, you will need to use `12223334444`):

```
$ aws sns subscribe \
    --topic-arn arn:aws:sns:us-east-1:511912822958:alert-sms2 \
    --protocol sms \
    --notification-endpoint 12223334444
```

At that point, the first time around, you will receive an SMS to confirm your subscription.

Integrating with PagerDuty, Opsgenie, or Victorops

We are showing in this book a minimum viable solution to send SMS notifications for important issues using only SNS. If you want to use a more feature-rich solution, such as PagerDuty, Opsgenie, or VictoOps, to name a few, you will simply need to change the type of subscription in the last command. Instead of using SMS, you will use the HTTPS protocol and provide the webhook url of your service provider.

Now that our notification system is in place, we can start feeding notifications to our topics. For that, we will turn to AWS CloudWatch.

Creating an alert of an elevated error rate in our application

As a reminder, our `helloworld` application has a very simple design:

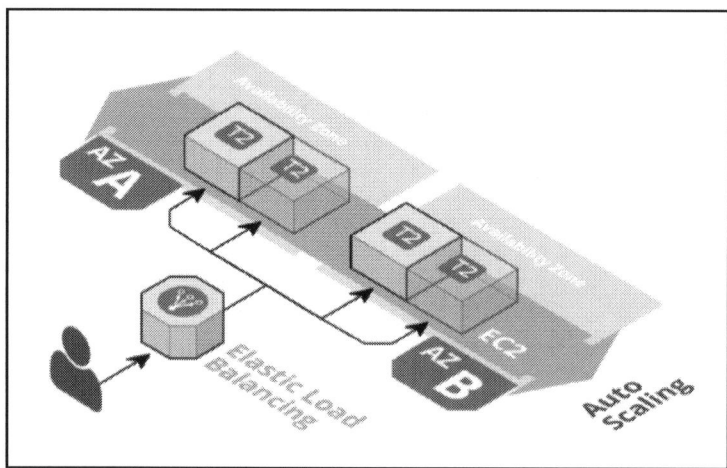

All user traffic is going through an ELB instance. Since we use the HTTP to communicate, we can easily identify when something unexpected is happening.

If you take a closer look at the monitoring tab of one of your load balancer instances (`http://amzn.to/2rsEaLY`), you will see some of the top-level metrics you should care about:

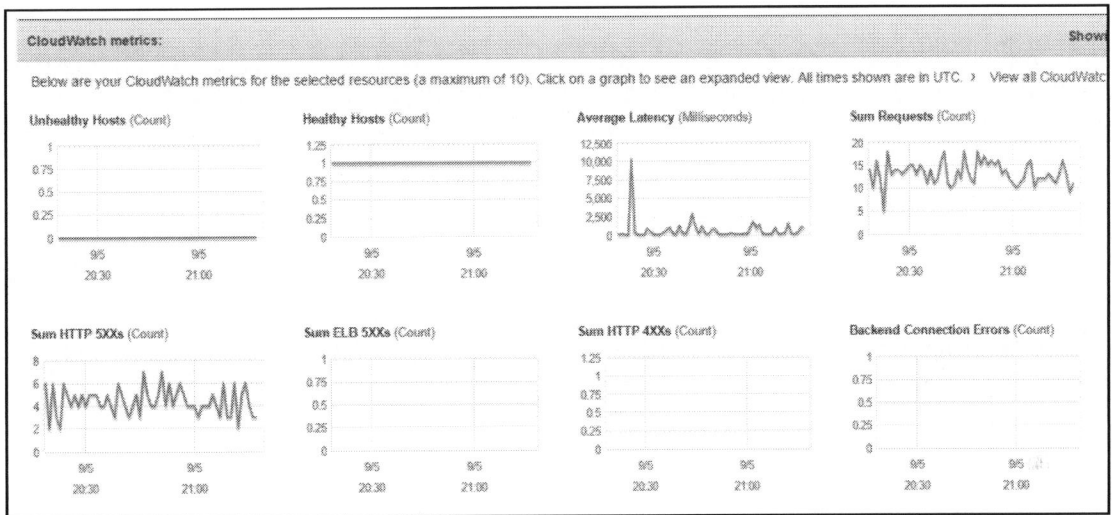

While each application has its own behavior, an increase in latency or HTTP **5XXs** is usually a good signal that someone needs to take a closer look at the service.

We will incorporate the monitoring of those two metrics in our template.

We will reopen our troposphere script `helloworld-ecs-alb-cf-template.py`

We will first add some new import as such:

```
from troposphere.cloudwatch import (
    Alarm,
    MetricDimension,
)
```

Then, we will go to the bottom of the file, where we already created the alarms `CPUTooLow` and `CPUTooHigh`.

Just before the last print statement, we will add a new `Alarm` resource as follows:

```
t.add_resource(Alarm(
    "ELBHTTP5xxs",
    AlarmDescription="Alarm if HTTP 5xxs too high",
```

We are giving it a reference and a description. To target the proper metric, we need to specify the namespace of the ELB service and the name of the metric, as shown here:

```
Namespace="AWS/ELB",
MetricName="HTTPCode_Backend_5XX",
```

We want our alert to target the load balancer instance created with that template. For that, we'll reference the load balancer resource in the metric dimension as follows:

```
Dimensions=[
    MetricDimension(
        Name="LoadBalancerName",
        Value=Ref("LoadBalancer")
    ),
],
```

We want the alert to trigger if the number of HTTP 5xx is, on average, greater than 30 for three consecutive periods of 1 minute. This is done using the following properties:

```
Statistic="Average",
Period="60",
EvaluationPeriods="3",
Threshold="30",
ComparisonOperator="GreaterThanOrEqualToThreshold",
```

The last part of the alert consists of selecting the action to perform when the alert triggers. In our case, we will want to send a message with the `alert-sms` SNS topic. In order to do that, we need to get this topic's ARN. We can do it using the following command:

```
$ aws sns list-topics
```

Once you have the information, you can specify the information in `AlarmActions` and `OKActions`. Additionally, we will leave the `InsufficientDataActions` action empty as this metric is what we call a sparse metric, meaning that if no 5xxs are emitted, the service will not produce any data points, as opposed to creating an entry with a value of 0. The `OKActions` is also somewhat optional and is more a question of taste. Configured as such, CloudWatch will emit another SMS when the alert resolves:

```
AlarmActions=["arn:aws:sns:us-east-1:511912822958:alert-sms"],
OKActions=["arn:aws:sns:us-east-1:511912822958:alert-sms"],
InsufficientDataActions=[],
```

This concludes the creation of that alarm. We can close our open parenthesis:

```
))
```

After that new alarm, we will create the alarm to target the latency. Almost everything is identical. We are going to create a new resource and give its identifier and description as follows:

```
t.add_resource(Alarm(
    "ELBHLatency",
    AlarmDescription="Alarm if Latency too high",
```

We will use the same namespace, but with a different metric name:

```
    Namespace="AWS/ELB",
    MetricName="Latency",
```

The dimensions are the same as before:

```
    Dimensions=[
        MetricDimension(
            Name="LoadBalancerName",
            Value=Ref("LoadBalancer")
        ),
    ],
```

For the case of latency, we are looking at five evaluations of 1 minute and a threshold of 500 ms to trigger the alarm:

```
    Statistic="Average",
    Period="60",
    EvaluationPeriods="5",
    Threshold="0.5",
    ComparisonOperator="GreaterThanOrEqualToThreshold",
    AlarmActions=["arn:aws:sns:us-east-1:511912822958:alert-sms"],
    OKActions=["arn:aws:sns:us-east-1:511912822958:alert-sms"],
    InsufficientDataActions=[],
))
```

This concludes the creation of our alarms. Your new template should look as follows http ://bit.ly/2v3s0dQ

You can commit the changes, generate the new CloudFormation template, and deploy it using the usual steps:

```
$ git add helloworld-ecs-alb-cf-template.py
$ git commit -m "Creating SNS alarms"
$ git push
$ python helloworld-ecs-alb-cf-template.py > helloworld-ecs-alb-cf.template
$ aws cloudformation update-stack \
    --stack-name staging-alb \
    --template-body file://helloworld-ecs-alb-cf.template
```

```
$ aws cloudformation update-stack \
      --stack-name production-alb \
      --template-body file://helloworld-ecs-alb-cf.template
```

Blameless post-mortems

To close our feedback loop, we need to talk about learning. When failures happen, one of the best approaches to building that learning component is to create post-mortem documents that describe the incident, the timeline, the root cause, and how it was resolved. John Allspaw, one of the "founding fathers" of the DevOps movement, did some extensive thinking in that area and created the concept of blameless post-mortems, which describe in more detail this approach that emphasizes learning over finger-pointing.

One of the restrictions that CloudWatch has is the notion of alarm dimensions. In our last example, the ELB represents only one resource, which made it easy to create our alert as we could reference the resource name. For more dynamic resources, such as our EC2 instances, we might want to monitor a resource that's not exposed at the load balancer level.

To accomplish such things, we need to look at CloudWatch events.

Using CloudWatch events and Lambda to create alerts on custom metrics

In the previous section, we added two alarms to our CloudFormation template. Whenever possible, keeping your monitoring information with the resources they are monitoring is good practice. Unfortunately, it isn't always easy to do. For instance, we are keeping track of the disk space usage of our EC2 instances. Those EC2 instances are created by our Auto Scaling Group. Because of that, adding alerts for that metric in our troposphere code is a lot more complicated as we don't have some of the critical information, such as the instance id. To get around that issue, we are going to see how to create alerts based on infrastructure changes.

As we saw earlier, whenever a change occurs in your AWS infrastructure, the event is emitted in real time to a CloudWatch event. This includes the creation of EC2 instances. We will create a rule to capture those events and send that information to a Lambda function that will create our alarms.

We will implement that using the serverless framework (https://serverless.com/) that we looked at in Chapter 5, *Scaling Your Infrastructure*.

We will first create a new serverless application. In Chapter 5, *Scaling Your Infrastructure,* we demonstrated how to create a `helloworld` application using Node.js. Lambda and Serverless are also both able to handle other languages, including Python. We will use Python and the Boto library to manage the creation of our alarms. To get started, we need to create a new application using the following command:

```
serverless create --template aws-python \
    --name disk-free-monitoring \
    --path disk-free-monitoring
```

This will create all the boilerplate we need inside a directory called `disk-free-monitoring`:

```
$ cd disk-free-monitoring
```

The directory contains two files, `handler.py` and `serverless.yml`. The handler file will contain the code of our Lambda function while `serverless.yml` will have the information about how to deploy and configure our function. We will start there.

With your text editor, open the `serverless.yml` file.

The file is broken up into different sections.

The first change we will do is to add IAM permissions to our function. We want our function to be able to create and delete alarms. For that, find the provider block in the configuration file and add the following:

```
provider:
  name: aws
  runtime: python2.7
  iamRoleStatements:
    - Effect: "Allow"
      Action:
        - "cloudwatch:PutMetricAlarm"
        - "cloudwatch:DeleteAlarms"
      Resource: "*"
```

Toward the middle of the file, a section defines the name of the handler:

```
functions:
  hello:
    handler: handler.hello
```

While ultimately we could create a function and call it `hello`, we can also come up with something more descriptive about the action. We will change the name to `alarm` as follows:

```
functions:
  alarm:
    handler: handler.alarm
```

Lastly, we need to define how our function will get triggered. After the handler definition, add the following (events and handler are aligned):

```
events:
  - cloudwatchEvent:
      event:
        source:
          - "aws.ec2"
        detail-type:
          - "EC2 Instance State-change Notification"
        detail:
          state:
            - running
            - stopping
            - shutting-down
            - stopped
            - terminated
```

We will now edit the `handler.py` file.

When you first open the file, it shows a basic `hello` function. We won't keep any of it. As a first step, delete everything in that file.

We will start our file with the import and initialization of the `boto3` library:

```
import boto3
client = boto3.client('cloudwatch')
```

We will now create a function and call it `alarm` in reference to the handler value defined in our last file (`handler.alarm`). The function takes two arguments, `event` and `context`:

```
def alarm(event, context):
```

The `event` will contain a JSON with the information that the EC2 instance state change received. You can see sample events by using the CloudWatch event web interface. With your browser, open
`https://console.aws.amazon.com/cloudwatch/home?region=us-east-1#rules:action=cr`
`eate` and then provide the new information of the event you want to match, as shown in this screenshot:

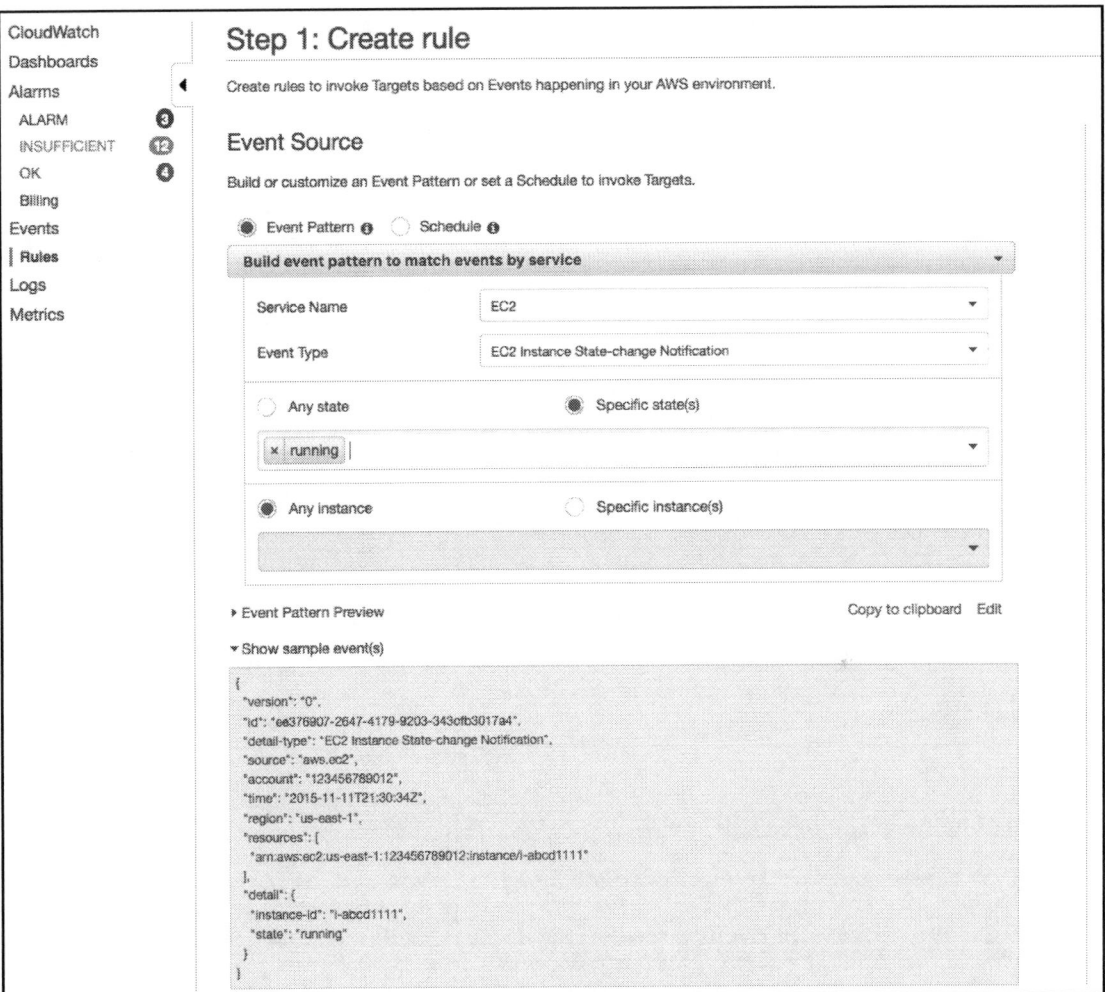

In our case, we want to extract two pieces of information, the `instance-id` and the `state`. We will do that as follows:

```
instance = event['detail']['instance-id']
state = event['detail']['state']
```

We want to create alarms when an instance is running and delete them when they are in one of the other states listed in the `serverless.yml` file (stopping, shutting-down, stopped, terminated). We will create two alarms: a warning email alert when the partition is filled to 60% and a page for when we reach 80%.

We will do that by creating two functions, `put_alarm` and `delete_alarms`. For now, we will simply call them as follows:

```
if state == "running":
    warning = put_alarm(instance, 60, 'alert-email')
    critical = put_alarm(instance, 80, 'alert-sms')
    return warning, critical
else:
    return delete_alarms(instance)
```

We can now define our two functions, starting with the `put_alarm` function:

```
def put_alarm(instance, threshold, sns):
```

The function takes three arguments, the instance id, the threshold of the alarm, and the topic information.

We will first define the `sns_prefix` information. We can get that value using the following command:

```
$ aws sns list-topics \
    sns_prefix = 'arn:aws:sns:us-east-1:511912822958:'
```

The next step will be to create the alarm. We will want to store the response so that we can return that to the Lambda execution:

```
response = client.put_metric_alarm(
```

We now need to provide all the information needed to create the alarm, starting with its name. The name of the alarm has to be unique to the AWS account. We will make sure this is the case by using the instance ID and `sns` suffix to generate the alarm name:

```
AlarmName='DiskSpaceUtilization-{}-{}'.format(instance, sns),
```

We now need to provide the details of the metric to monitor as follows. We will first provide the metric name and namespace followed by the dimensions. In the dimensions section, we are able to limit the monitoring to only our instance ID thanks to the information provided by CloudWatch through the `event` variable:

```
MetricName='DiskSpaceUtilization',
Namespace='System/Linux',
Dimensions=[
    {
        "Name": "InstanceId",
        "Value": instance
    },
    {
        "Name": "Filesystem",
        "Value": "/dev/xvda1"
    },
    {
        "Name": "MountPath",
        "Value": "/"
    }
],
```

We are going to define the threshold information as follows:

```
Statistic='Average',
Period=300,
Unit='Percent',
EvaluationPeriods=2,
Threshold=threshold,
ComparisonOperator='GreaterThanOrEqualToThreshold',
TreatMissingData='missing',
```

In this particular case, we want to have two consecutive executions of 5 minutes where the average disk usage is higher than 60 or 80% to trigger the alarms. Finally, we are going to specify the topics to send the message to when the alert triggers and recovers:

```
AlarmActions=[
    sns_prefix + sns,
],
OKActions=[
    sns_prefix + sns,
]
)
return response
```

The function finishes with the return of the response. We will now create the function that deletes them. For that, we will create the function and call it `delete_alarms`. The code to delete the alarm is a lot simpler. We simply need to call the `boto` function, `delete_alarms`, and provide it an array with the two names of the alert we created:

```
def delete_alarms(instance):
    names = [
        'DiskSpaceUtilization-{}-alert-email'.format(instance),
        'DiskSpaceUtilization-{}-alert-sms'.format(instance)
    ]
    return client.delete_alarms(AlarmNames=names)
```

The `handler.py` is done, but in order to make this code work, we need to create a few extra files. The first file we want to add is `requirements.txt`. This file defines the libraries required by our Python code to run. In our case, we need `boto`.

In the same directory as `handler.py` and `serverless.yml`, create a file and call it `requirements.txt`. In it, add the following:

```
boto3==1.4.4
```

`serverless` doesn't automatically handle those requirement files. In order to handle them, we need to create a `package.json` file in the same directory as the other files and put the following in it:

```
{
  "name": "disk-free-monitoring",
  "version": "1.0.0",
  "description": "create cloudwatch alarms for disk space",
  "repository": "tbd",
  "license": "ISC",
  "dependencies": {
    "serverless-python-requirements": "^2.3.3"
  }
}
```

We now can run the command `npm install`.

With those two extra files created, we are ready to deploy our application as follows:

```
$ serverless deploy
Serverless: Packaging service...
Serverless: Creating Stack...
Serverless: Checking Stack create progress...
.....
Serverless: Stack create finished...
Serverless: Uploading CloudFormation file to S3...
```

```
Serverless: Uploading artifacts...
Serverless: Uploading service .zip file to S3 (1.17 KB)...
Serverless: Updating Stack...
Serverless: Checking Stack update progress...
....................
Serverless: Stack update finished...
Service Information
service: disk-free-monitoring
stage: dev
region: us-east-1
api keys:
  None
endpoints:
  None
functions:
  alarm: disk-free-monitoring-dev-alarm
```

From that point on, any EC2 instance that gets created in `us-east-1` will automatically get two dedicated alarms while the instances are running:

| OK | DiskSpaceUtilization-i-01d531a579ddb3b09-alert-sms | DiskSpaceUtilization >= 80 for 10 minutes |
| OK | DiskSpaceUtilization-i-01d531a579ddb3b09-alert-email | DiskSpaceUtilization >= 60 for 10 minutes |

We won't show it in the book, but there are many things you can improve in this script, including looking at the EC2 tags of your instances to see if it's a production system or not.

Lastly, we will take a closer look at a service that AWS calls personal health.

Monitoring and alerting with AWS health

While AWS is mostly stable, and outages are rare, it is not exempt from occasional service degradation. To check on the general health of their service, you go to their main dashboard at `https://status.aws.amazon.com`.

Note that this dashboard also provides an RSS feed, which can be integrated with most communication services, such as slack:

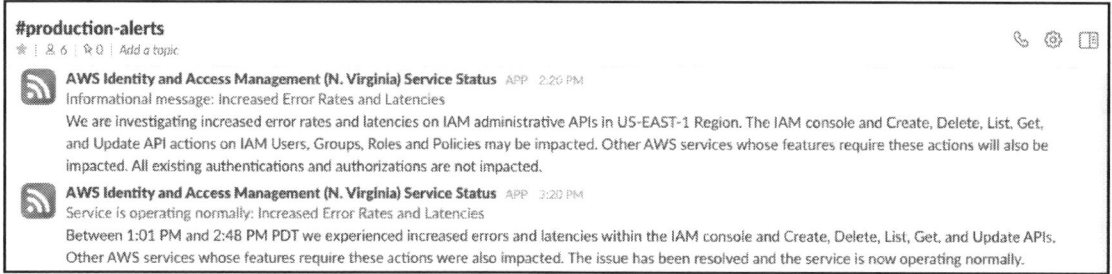

In addition to that global status page, you can also access a personalized health dashboard in the AWS console by clicking on the bell icon:

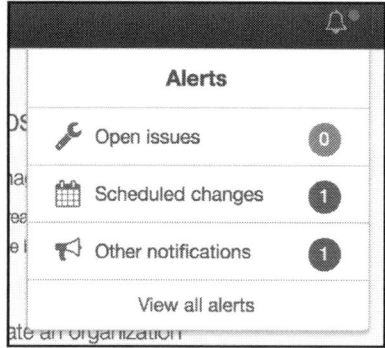

You can also access the dashboard directly by opening `https://phd.aws.amazon.com` in your browser. The personalized health dashboard will display information affecting all customers in the region and also notifications that are specific to your account, such as when one of your instances is scheduled for maintenance and reboot. The personalized health dashboard doesn't have an RSS feed, but instead is integrated into the CloudWatch event.

We are going to create a new rule in the CloudWatch event to send us email notifications of the different alerts.

We will do that using the command-line interface:

1. The first step will be to create a rule that matches all events coming from the endpoint `aws.health`. We will do that with the following command:

```
$ aws events put-rule \
      --name AWSHealth \
      --event-pattern '{"source":["aws.health"]}' \
      --state ENABLED
{
    "RuleArn": "arn:aws:events:us-
east-1:511912822958:rule/AWSHealth"
}
```

2. Next, we will get the information of our target. In our case, the target is the SNS topic created earlier in the chapter. We will need to get the `topicARN`, which you can get with the following command:

```
$ aws sns list-topics | grep alert-email
          "TopicArn": "arn:aws:sns:us-
east-1:511912822958:alert-email"
```

3. Finally, we can tie the two together. The target's command expects a JSON entry, which we provide here using the following shorthand syntax:

```
aws events put-targets \
      --rule AWSHealth\
      --targets Id=1,Arn=arn:aws:sns:us-
east-1:511912822958:alert-email
```

Throughout the course of this section, we explored how to create alerts and applied this method to a few of our key public indicators. If you wish, you can continue that exercise, reusing some of the techniques we explored to put in place more alarms to make sure you don't miss any important events.

Documentation
All the work done so far will only be useful if you create good documentation to go with it. At the very least, your documentation should cover the different failure scenarios and how to recover from them.

Summary

In this chapter, we explored several ways to add monitoring and alerting to our application and infrastructure. We could do it reasonably well by taking advantage of some of the services AWS provides, including CloudWatch, ElasticSearch, and SNS. You can now continue the work of measuring everything. Ultimately, measurement needs to become part of the company culture.

There are several areas to explore, including the following:

- At the infrastructure level, you can start tracking AWS costs and create budgets. You can also put monitoring around your backups to make sure that you aren't missing backup failures.
- At the service level, you can look at X-Ray, the distributed request tracking service, to monitor performance.
- At the build and release pipelines level, with a couple of changes to CloudFormation, CodeDeploy, and CodePipeline, you can start tracking the frequency of deployments and rollbacks. In addition, you can do the same to Ansible and create an alert when Ansible returns an error when it runs.
- Quality can also get this kind of treatment. You can start collecting test code coverage information to make sure you don't push new code without unit testing. It is also interesting to compare outage frequency and bugs/tickets. You can sometimes find a correlation between quality going down and outages going up.
- While it may not seem obvious at times, the DevOps movement is first and foremost about people. All those improvements in our process and the adoption of new technologies are means to that end. For that reason, you also want to find ways to track the impact all those changes have on the different people in the company.

In Chapter 8, *Hardening the Security of Your AWS Environment*, we will continue using some of the components we built in this chapter, but this time from the perspective of security.

8

Hardening the Security of Your AWS Environment

Our infrastructure is getting more and more advanced. One of the last area that deserves a lot more attention is the security.

Security teams used to live in a silo, the same way operations teams once did before the DevOps revolution. Now that applications are running in the cloud and the rate of iteration and deployment frequency has drastically increased, the role of security needs to be *moved to the left*. Security related issues need to be caught as early as possible. New movements such as DevSecOps and Rugged DevOps were created with the goal of bringing the same concepts that revolutionized the operations world to the security industry. These concepts include increasing the collaboration and communication between security teams and the rest of the engineering organization, treating your security as code, and adding security checks in your CI/CD pipeline. As an engineer implementing a DevOps philosophy, you are in an ideal position to also handle aspects of the security.

In this chapter, we will take a closer look at how to implement some of the most common security best practices. AWS provides several services and features to help with . At the application level, you take advantage of a certificate manager to get free SSL certificates for your load balancers and CloudFront distribution. You can take advantage of the encryption key feature within IAM to protect your data at rest or encrypt passwords and backups. What is even more interesting, and will be the focus of this chapter, is the number of tools and services we can rely on to improve the security of our infrastructure.

AWS and other cloud providers use a shared responsibility model. We will first see what this means. Following this, we look at several tools that will help us to audit our security. In the remaining part of the chapter, we will focus on improving the security of our systems. We will first look at better managing users, services, and their permissions.

We will then improve the security of our network and finally, we will learn how to protect against targeted attacks. Therefore, in this chapter we'll be covering the following points:

- Understanding where to focus your effort
- Improving the security of the IAM layer
- Strengthening the security at the network level
- Protecting against targeted attacks

Understanding where to focus your effort

Keeping your customers' data safe is the result of keeping multiple layers of the infrastructure and services secured. Because we are in a cloud environment, we don't have access to every layer of our infrastructure. For instance, we don't have physical access to the data centers where our EC2 instances are running. Therefore, keeping each layer secured is a responsibility shared between you and AWS.

The shared responsibility model

In this world of shared responsibility, AWS provides the security of the cloud and as an AWS user, you are responsible for providing the security in the cloud. In other words, AWS will take care of securing the datacenters, the physical infrastructure, the physical network, the virtualization layer, and the host's operating systems. In turn, as an AWS user, you are responsible for managing and operating the guest operating systems, applying security patches, IAM permissions, security groups, and access policies.

As we know, AWS provides several managed services which make understanding the shared responsibility model sometimes confusing. From a security standpoint, those services can be broken up into three categories:

- **Infrastructure services**: Those services tend to require the most amount of work as they live at a low level. They are typically virtualized resources such as virtual machines (EC2), network components, and storage like EBS.
- **Container services**: Container services will often live just on top of infrastructure services. The main difference is that Amazon will administrate the operating system and most functionalities of the services. These services include RDS, ElastiCache, and other services that get created through the creation of instances.

- **Abstracted Services**: This last category of services abstracts completely the notion of server or instance. You use those services through a layer of abstraction which puts most of the burden of securing such services on AWS's shoulders. Some of the services we previously saw that live in that category are S3 and DynamoDB.

You may refer to the following diagram to understand better what's required to secure a given service and who is responsible for each layer:

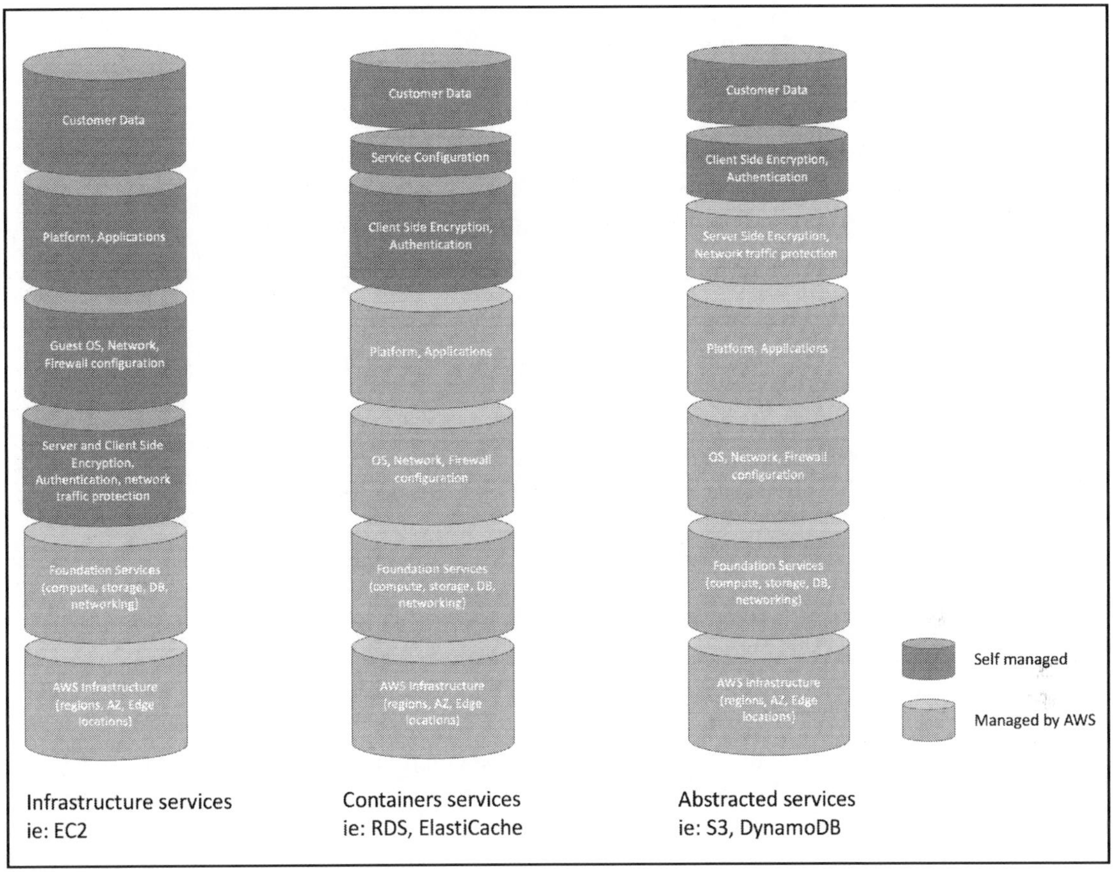

Customer Data	Customer Data	Customer Data
Platform, Applications	Service Configuration	Client Side Encryption, Authentication
Guest OS, Network, Firewall configuration	Client Side Encryption, Authentication	Server Side Encryption, Network traffic protection
Server and Client Side Encryption, Authentication, network traffic protection	Platform, Applications	Platform, Applications
Foundation Services (compute, storage, DB, networking)	OS, Network, Firewall configuration	OS, Network, Firewall configuration
AWS Infrastructure (regions, AZ, Edge locations)	Foundation Services (compute, storage, DB, networking)	Foundation Services (compute, storage, DB, networking)
	AWS Infrastructure (regions, AZ, Edge locations)	AWS Infrastructure (regions, AZ, Edge locations)

Self managed

Managed by AWS

Infrastructure services	Containers services	Abstracted services
ie: EC2	ie: RDS, ElastiCache	ie: S3, DynamoDB

You can read more on the topic of shared responsibility at `http://amzn.to/2l6irFV`. In addition, AWS provides very detailed documentation with best practices on securing each service they offer. One of the best ways to audit those layers to secure is to rely on tools to run the inspection.

Auditing the security in your cloud

Auditing each layer of security in AWS isn't an easy task. The best way to not miss anything is to rely on auditing tools to help us with that exercise.

The first tool we will look at is called **trusted advisor**.

AWS trusted advisor

Available at `https://console.aws.amazon.com/trustedadvisor/`, trusted advisor is a tool that makes several recommendations around the topic of security but also cost optimization, performance, and fault tolerance.

Specifically, on the topic of security, you will be able to validate your security groups, your IAM usage, and make sure that MFA is enabled on the root account:

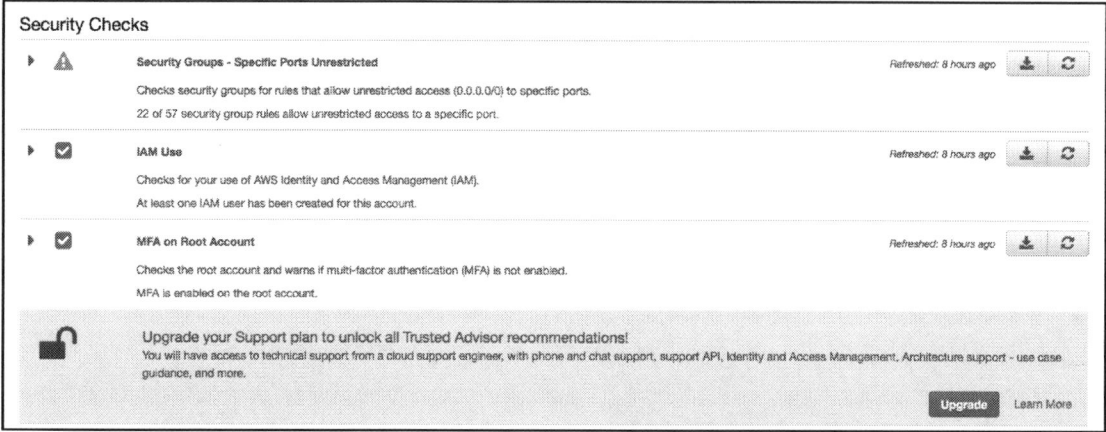

If you have a support plan, this tool will offer a few more insights on the resources mentioned earlier and on other AWS services including Route53, RDS, S3, CloudFront, and ELB.

The tool is free and easy to use but doesn't provide as much information as our next tool, AWS Inspector.

AWS Inspector

AWS Inspector is an automated security assessment service like AWS trusted advisor but it provides a much more detailed report. The service works by installing and running the AWS inspector agent on your EC2/ECS instances. This allows AWS Inspector to gain visibility of your services, your applications, and detailed information about the network, file system, and process activity. You can configure AWS Inspector to run on a regular schedule or/and make it part of your deployment workflow and have it audit your security after each production deployment for example. You can access the service at `https://console.aws.amazon.com/inspector`:

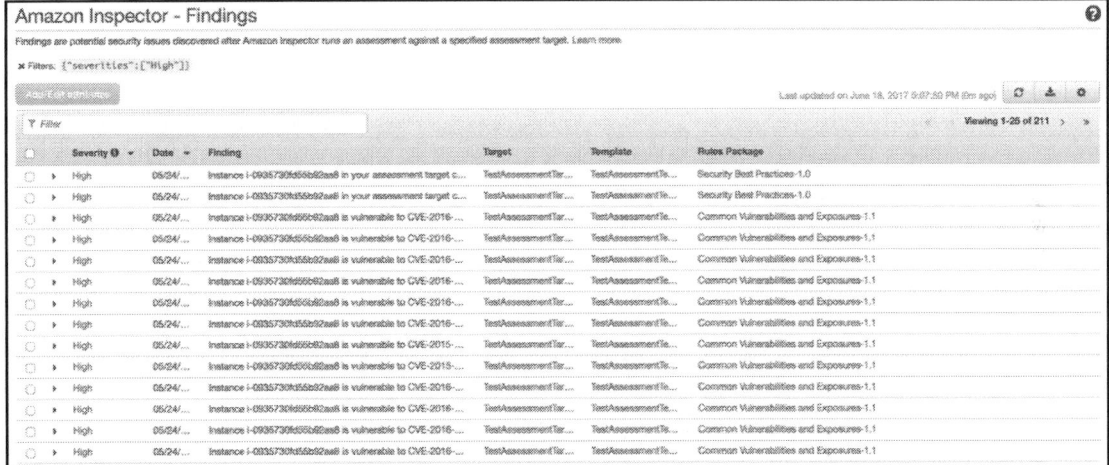

Unlike trusted advisor, AWS Inspector isn't free. You pay on a per assessment per host basis and while it's much cheaper than similar SaaS provider offers, it is still something to factor in. There is one more option that we will explore. It's using a free and open source tool, Scout2.

Scout2

Scout2 (`https://nccgroup.github.io/Scout2/`) is an open source tool that lets you audit the security of your AWS account. It produces reports similar to trusted advisor but only focuses on the area of security. With around 100 different checks, Scout2 produces a very complete solution to assess the level of security of your account.

We will use it to better comprehend some of the changes needed.

To do so, we will first clone the repository:

```
$ git clone https://github.com/nccgroup/Scout2
```

We will then cd into the directory and install the packages needed to use the tool:

```
$ cd Scout2
$ pip install -r requirements.txt
```

We can now use the tool to generate our security report as follows:

```
$ python Scout2.py
```

The tool will collect several pieces of information on your account and finally generate an HTML report that you can open with your browser, as shown in the following screenshot:

The report is organized around the different categories. Because our application is very simple, most of the interesting insights this report will produce will be around IAM which you can find in the **Security** section of the report.

Aside from the IAM issues which we will address later in the chapter, Scout2 alerts us that CloudTrail isn't enabled in any of our regions. We will first look into this.

AWS CloudTrail

CloudTrail is a service that records all API calls made to the AWS from your account. The tool is very useful to troubleshoot operational issues and, of course, is a key component of managing the security and compliance of an AWS account. The tool articulates around a concept of "trail". Each trail lets you log any API activity done on your account. Pricewise, the first trail created is always free and therefore, using this service is a no-brainer.

In the following section, we will create a CloudFormation stack using troposphere to log all API activities. CloudTrail stores up to seven days of activity, in order to extend that duration, we will take advantage of its ability to also export the data to an S3 bucket.

Enabling CloudTrail using CloudFormation

We will create a new script in our EffectiveDevOpsTemplates repository and call it `cloudtrail-cf-template.py`.

We will start with our script with our usual boilerplate:

```
"""Generating CloudFormation template."""

from troposphere import Join

from troposphere import (
    Ref,
    Template
)

from troposphere.s3 import Bucket

from troposphere.s3 import BucketPolicy

from troposphere.cloudtrail import Trail
```

```
t = Template()

t.add_description("Effective DevOps in AWS: Turn on CloudTrail and log to
S3")
```

Out-of-the-box, CloudTrail will retain seven days of activity. In order to keep the data for longer, we will configure the service to log any activity to S3. In order to do that, we will first create an S3 bucket. We will use the `DeletionPolicy` attribute to preserve the logs if/when the stack is deleted:

```
t.add_resource(Bucket(
    "S3Bucket",
    DeletionPolicy="Retain"
))
```

By default, S3 bucket resources are private and only the resources from the AWS account that the created the bucket can use the bucket. The CloudTrail needs to be able to read and write data to that bucket. In order to allow more than a given AWS account to interact with S3, AWS offers the ability to create S3 access policy resources. We will create one that will provide just enough permission to CloudTrail to read and write to the target location. You can read more about S3 `BucketPolicy` at `http://amzn.to/2l2gd7j`.

The policy we are going to create is the translation in Python of the default policy that gets created when you use the GUI to manage the service. You can refer to `http://amzn.to/2l2mnUY` for more details on that policy.

We will first create the resource and specify which bucket to apply the policy to:

```
t.add_resource(BucketPolicy(
    "BucketPolicy",
    Bucket=Ref("S3Bucket"),
```

We will now create the policy. There will be two statements, we will first grant CloudTrail the ability to read the access control list of the bucket (`http://amzn.to/2l2p3Sd`). The second statement will allow CloudTrail to write specifically to the location `AWSLogs/myAccountID`:

```
PolicyDocument={
    "Statement": [{
        "Action": "s3:GetBucketAcl",
        "Effect": "Allow",
        "Principal": {
            "Service": "cloudtrail.amazonaws.com"
        },
        "Resource": Join("", [
            "arn:aws:s3:::", Ref("S3Bucket")
```

```
            ])
    }, {
        "Action": "s3:PutObject",
        "Effect": "Allow",
        "Principal": {
            "Service": "cloudtrail.amazonaws.com"
        },
        "Resource": Join("", [
            "arn:aws:s3:::",
            Ref("S3Bucket"),
            "/AWSLogs/",
            Ref("AWS::AccountId"),
            "/*"
        ]),
        "Condition": {
            "StringEquals": {
                "s3:x-amz-acl": "bucket-owner-full-control"
            }
        }
    }]
    },
))
```

Next, we will create the `Trail` resources. We will call it `Trail`. The first thing we will do is reference the bucket we previously created:

```
t.add_resource(Trail(
    "Trail",
    S3BucketName=Ref("S3Bucket"),
```

We will now enable the logging of AWS API calls by setting the `IsLogging` attribute such as:

```
IsLogging=True,
```

We will ask CloudTrail to validate the integrity of log files with the following option. With that option enabled, CloudTrail will produce digest files in addition to our trails which allow us to make sure that the files aren't tempered. We will see how to validate those logs after creating our trail:

```
EnableLogFileValidation=True,
```

Depending on the level of information you would like to collect, you can turn on the `IncludeGlobalServiceEvents` flag to include logging of AWS global services such as IAM:

```
IncludeGlobalServiceEvents=True,
```

We will want our trail to be multi-region, meaning that it will log API calls from any AWS region. Our infrastructure might only be located in one region but it is important to collect data from every possible region to have as much data as possible and be able to monitor unusual activity in the regions not used by your service for example. To turn on the multi-region setting, you will need to use the following attribute:

```
IsMultiRegionTrail=True,
```

Lastly, we will want to set a `DependsOn` setting to make sure that the S3 policy is created by the time CloudFormation tries to create the CloudTrail resource:

```
DependsOn=["BucketPolicy"]
))
```

Our `Trail` resource is now complete. As always, we will end our script with a call to `print`:

```
print(t.to_json())
```

We can now save, commit and execute the script as follows:

```
$ git add cloudtrail-cf-template.py
$ git commit -m "Adding template to configure CloudTrail"
$ git push
$ python cloudtrail-cf-template.py > cloudtrail-cf.template
$ aws cloudformation create-stack \
      --stack-name cloudtrail \
      --template-body file://cloudtrail-cf.template
{
    "StackId": "arn:aws:cloudformation:us-east-1:511912822958:stack/cloudtrail/612c42a0-f80e-11e6-8d9b-50d5ca6326ba"
}
```

From that point on, every call made to any AWS service will be logged.

Validating CloudTrail logs integrity

When we created our CloudFormation template, we enabled the creation of digest files. Thanks to those files, we can make sure that no CloudTrail log files (and digest files) were modified or deleted. To do so, we first need to get our resource name (ARN). We can get it using the following command:

```
$ aws cloudtrail describe-trails
{
    "trailList": [
        {
```

```
            "IncludeGlobalServiceEvents": true,
            "Name": "cloudtrail-myTrail-X85D48OAI8Q4",
            "TrailARN": "arn:aws:cloudtrail:us-
 east-1:511912822958:trail/cloudtrail-myTrail-X85D48OAI8Q4",
            "LogFileValidationEnabled": true,
            "IsMultiRegionTrail": true,
            "HasCustomEventSelectors": false,
            "S3BucketName": "cloudtrail-s3bucket-ce4vw655vhku",
            "HomeRegion": "us-east-1"
        }
    ]
}
```

We can now validate the integrity of our trail for a given period of time like the following
example:

```
$ aws cloudtrail validate-logs \
      --start-time 2017-02-23T23:30:00Z \
      --end-time 2017-02-24T00:00:00Z \
      --trail-arn arn:aws:cloudtrail:us-
east-1:511912822958:trail/cloudtrail-myTrail-X85D48OAI8Q4
Validating log files for trail arn:aws:cloudtrail:us-
east-1:511912822958:trail/cloudtrail-myTrail-X85D48OAI8Q4 between
2017-02-23T23:30:00Z and 2017-02-24T00:00:00Z
Results requested for 2017-02-23T23:30:00Z to 2017-02-24T00:00:00Z
Results found for 2017-02-23T23:30:00Z to 2017-02-24T00:00:00Z:
1/1 digest files valid
32/32 log files valid
```

Now that we know that our data hasn't been tampered with, we can use it to answer
different questions around activities on the account.

Using CloudTrail logs

We just saw how to validate that our logs haven't been tampered with. We can now take
advantage of the service to answer specific questions.

The first way to use the tool is to simply use the web interface at `https://console.aws.am`
`azon.com/cloudtrail/`:

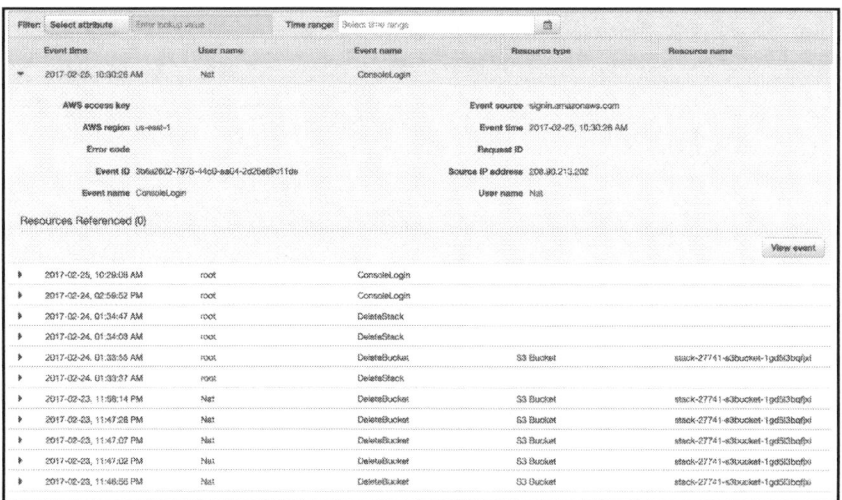

Of course, for more flexibility, you can use the command-line interface and, in particular,
the lookup-events option.

For instance, did a user log in to the console on February 25 between 18:30 and 19:30
UTC?:

```
$ aws cloudtrail lookup-events --lookup-attributes
AttributeKey=EventName,AttributeValue=ConsoleLogin\
    --start-time 2017-02-25T18:30:00Z \
    --end-time 2017-02-25T19:30:00Z
{
    "Events": [
        {
            "EventId": "3b6a2602-7975-44c0-aa04-2d26e89c11de",
            "Username": "Nat",
            "EventTime": 1488047426.0,
            "CloudTrailEvent": "{[...]}",
            "EventName": "ConsoleLogin",
            "Resources": []
        }
    ]
}
```

What did that user do around that time?

```
$ aws cloudtrail lookup-events --lookup-attributes
AttributeKey=Username,AttributeValue=Nat\
    --start-time 2017-02-25T18:30:00Z \
    --end-time 2017-02-25T19:30:00Z
[...]
```

Which security groups were deleted and by who?

```
$ aws cloudtrail lookup-events --lookup-attributes
AttributeKey=EventName,AttributeValue=DeleteSecurityGroup
        {
            "EventId": "bf8e4c26-fbb9-42c3-a44d-162ee4cf7c71",
            "Username": "foo",
            "EventTime": 1487921631.0,
            "CloudTrailEvent": [...]
    "EventName": "DeleteSecurityGroup",
            "Resources": [
                {
                    "ResourceType": "AWS::EC2::SecurityGroup",
                    "ResourceName": "sg-2091f65c"
                }
            ]
        },
```

We can run Scout2 again and just ask it to update the state of the CloudTrail service as follows:

```
$ python Scout2.py --service cloudtrail --update
```

Once the report is refreshed we can reload the report. This time, everything is green:

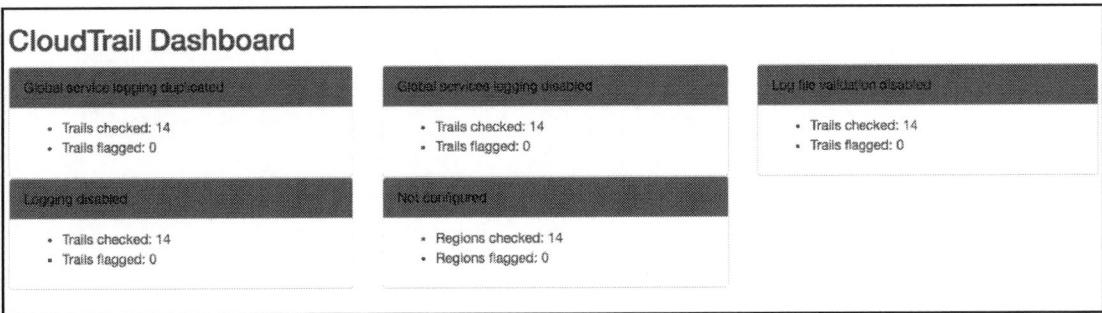

In addition to its very valuable forensic capability, CloudTrail can be used more proactively to monitor in almost real-time, any unusual activity.

For that, we will reuse the ElasticSearch and Kibana Domain we created in `Chapter7`, *Monitoring your infrastructure and services*.

Sending CloudTrail logs to ElasticSearch using Lambda

We previously created our Lambda function using the Serverless framework starting from scratch. The Serverless frameworks can also be used to download existing functions from GitHub and other code management repository systems. We will use it to install a function that downloads a `CloudTrailgizip` file, unzip, and send the records to ElasticSearch using the following command:

```
$ serverless install -u
https://github.com/EffectiveDevOpsWithAWS/serverless-cloudtrail-to-es -n
cloudtrail-aws-es
```

We will now navigate to the directory:

```
$ cd cloudtrail-aws-es
```

Previously, the Lambda function we created was written in node.js. AWS Lambda supports a few more languages including Python. We will showcase it with this function.

As before, we need to download all the dependencies locally before uploading our function to AWS. The easiest way to do that is to use Python `virtualenv`:

```
$ virtualenv -p $(which python) venv
$ source venv/bin/activate
```

To make it easy to package our requirements, we are going to use the npm package `serverless-python-requirements`. This package is already listed in the `package.json` file present in the directory, therefore we can use npm to install it:

```
$ npm install
```

Once the command has run, we can `deploy` our function:

```
$ serverless deploy
```

Once the function is deployed, we need to configure it as shown in the following steps:

1. With your browser, go to the Lambda service at `https://console.aws.amazon.com/lambda`.
2. Click on the **cloudtrail-aws-es-dev-lambda_handler** function to access its configuration.

3. In the **Code** Tab, configure ES_HOST and ES_REGION variables to point to the Domain you previously created in Chapter 7, *Monitoring your infrastructure and services.*

4. Once those two variables are configured, click on **Save** then go to the **Triggers** tab and select **add a trigger**.

5. Select the **Service S3** as the source of your trigger.

6. In the **Bucket** menu, find the bucket containing the CloudTrail logs that was generated in the previous section.

7. In the **Event** type, select **PUT**.

8. Make sure the **Enable Trigger** checkbox is set and click on **Submit**.

Shortly after the function is enabled, you should be able to see it processing logs.

 Here too, you will need to use a tool like Elastic Curator to prune your indices and avoid the ElasticSearch Domain from running out of space.

Creating a Kibana Dashboard for our CloudTrail logs

Now that our CloudTrail logs are streamed into ElasticSearch, we can really search through CloudTrail logs. In addition, we can create a dashboard to highlight some of the important events occurring on the AWS account.

To illustrate this point, we will simulate login attempts. Log out and log in a few times to the AWS console. Try to also log in using a wrong password to generate login failures in the logs.

Wait a few minutes for the data to be generated and sent to ElasticSearch then go through the following steps to create a new index pattern:

1. Open Kibana in your browser and go to the **management** menu.

2. Click on **Index Patterns**.

3. Click on **Add New**.

4. In the **Index name or pattern**, give the name logstash-cloudtrail-*.

5. In the **time-field name**, select **@timestamp**.

6. Finally, click **create** to complete the creation of the index pattern.

The next step will be to create the visualizations that will populate our dashboard:

1. Click on **Visualize** to access the visualization menu.
2. Click on **Create a visualization**.
3. Click on **Vertical bar chart**.
4. Click on **logstash-cloudtrail-***.
5. Under **Select buckets type**, click on **X-Axis**.
6. In the **aggregation** menu, select **Date histogram**.
7. Select the **@timestamp** for the Field value.
8. Click on **Add sub-bucket**.
9. Select **Split Bars**.
10. Select **Terms** as our Sub Aggregation.
11. Select the **Field responseElements.ConsoleLogin**.
12. Click on the **Apply change** icon at the top. You should end up with a visualization looking as follows:

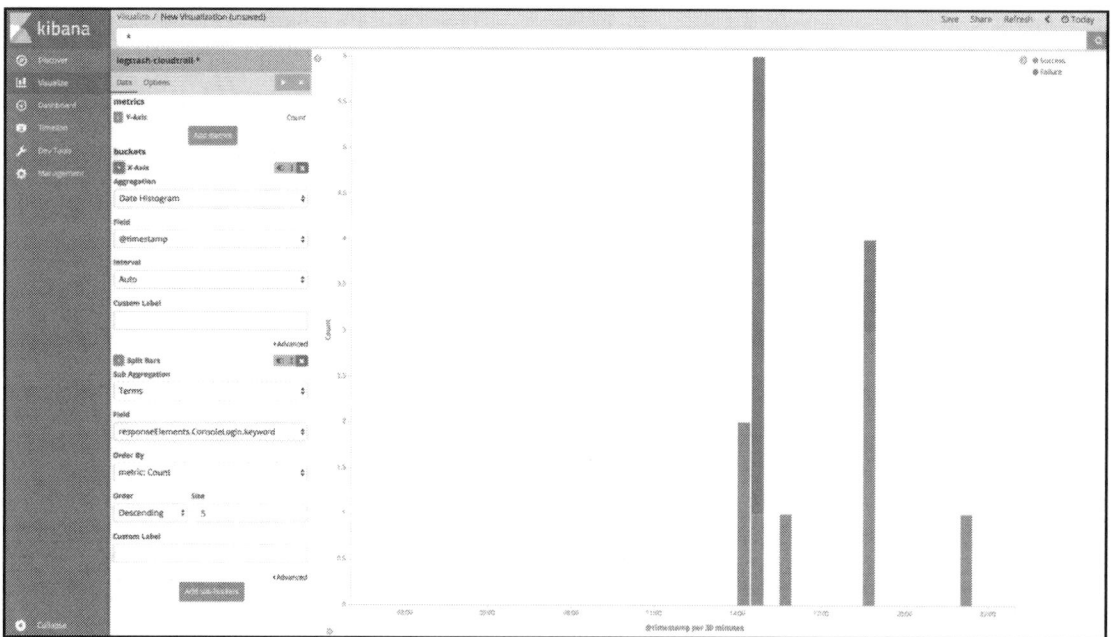

13. Click on **Save** at the top and give it the name `CloudTrail - login timeline`.

Another useful bit of information is to group login failures by IP. For this, we will create a new visualization as given in the following steps:

1. Click on **Visualize** to access the visualization menu.
2. Click on **Create a visualization**.
3. Click on **Data Table**.
4. Click on **logstash-cloudtrail-***.
5. Click on **split rows**.
6. Select **Filters**.
7. Set the **Filter1field** to `responseElements.ConsoleLogin.keyword:Failure`.
8. Click on **Add sub-bucket**.
9. Select **Split Rows**.
10. Select **Term**.
11. Use `SourceIPAddress.Keyword` as your Field and as before, click on **Apply**. You should end up with a visualization as follows:

12. You can now save the new visualization under the name `Cloudtrail - login failures by IP`.

You can continue this exercise and add a few more visualizations that are important to you. You can, for example, graph all deletion events, user activity (as shown in the following screenshot), and so on:

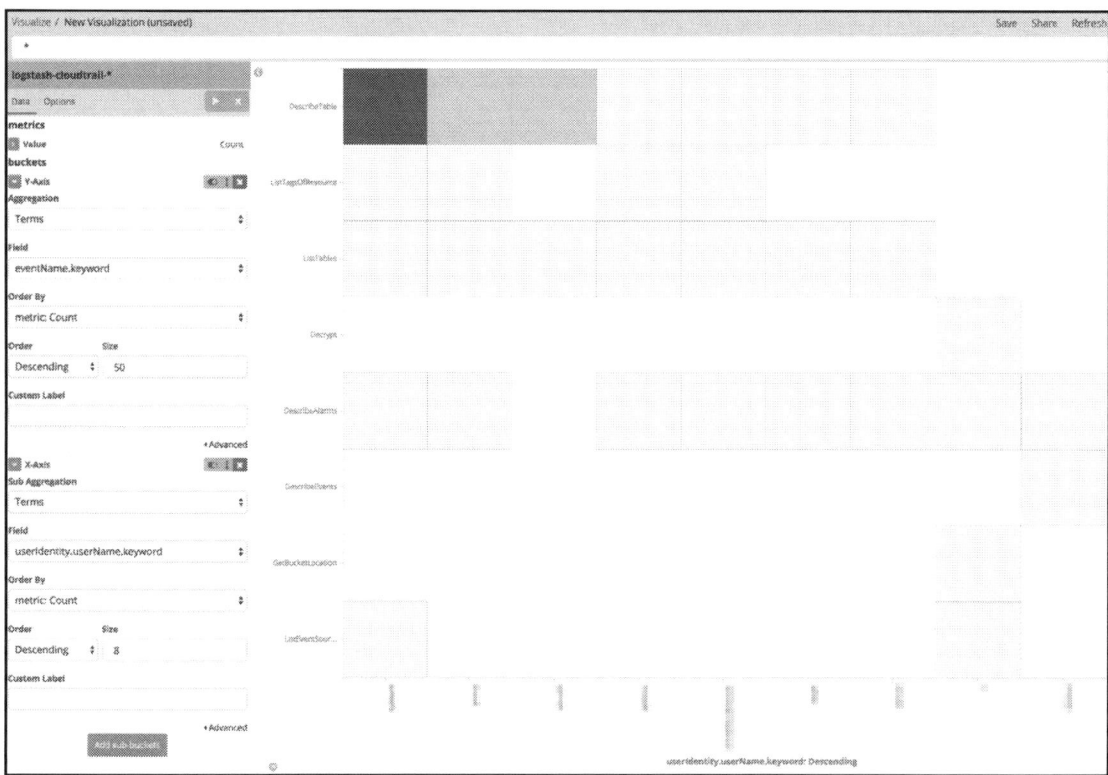

Once you have everything you need, go to the **Dashboard** menu and create a new Dashboard:

1. Go to the **Dashboard** menu in Kibana.
2. Click on **create dashboard**.
3. Click on **Add** in the top menu.
4. Select all relevant visualizations.

5. Click on **Save** and give your new dashboard a name such as `CloudTrail`:

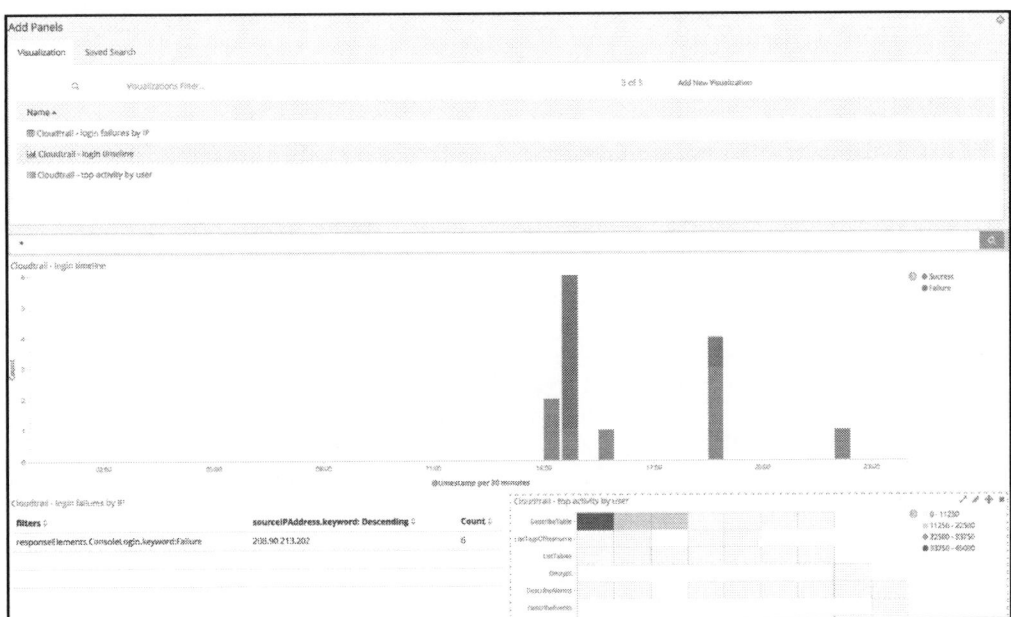

Thanks to the work we just did, we can quickly analyze any API activity. This puts us in a very good spot to start making changes to the security of our infrastructure. The first and most important service we will look at is the IAM service.

Improving the security of the IAM layer

The IAM service is at the heart of the security management of AWS. By defining users, groups, and security policies, the IAM service lets you configure your different resources such that only the right individuals and services can access the right resources.

We will first look at user management.

Managing users in AWS

In `Chapter 2`, *Deploying Your First Web Application*, we created our first IAM user. We generated its access key and gave the user full access to the AWS account by assigning the Administrator access policy to that user.

This worked great as we managed to get through most of the book using that user but from a security standpoint, there are a number of concerns that this action caused:

- There is no policy around enforcing the use of a strong password.
- We didn't put our user in a group. On a small scale, that's fine but if you ever expect to have to manage a bigger pool of AWS users, having your users be a part of a group and granting the permissions to the groups instead is a better pattern.
- We turned on MFA to access the AWS console with our users but the access key provides the same level of permissions and currently has no restriction.

We will address those three points starting with creating a password policy.

Configuring a user password policy

AWS supports the enforcement of password policies. We can ask for example passwords to be at least 16-character long and include numbers, symbols, lowercase, and capital letters. We will create one using the AWS CLI.

The easiest way to create (or update) such a policy is to use the `--generate-cli-skeleton` option to generate the JSON template of the parameters that the policy takes. We will run the command and redirect its output to a file called `password-policy` as follows:

```
$ aws iam update-account-password-policy \
        --generate-cli-skeleton > password-policy
```

We can now edit the file which at first looks like this:

```
{
    "MinimumPasswordLength": 0,
    "RequireSymbols": true,
    "RequireNumbers": true,
    "RequireUppercaseCharacters": true,
    "RequireLowercaseCharacters": true,
    "AllowUsersToChangePassword": true,
    "MaxPasswordAge": 0,
    "PasswordReusePrevention": 0,
    "HardExpiry": true
}
```

The default policy already requires the use of symbols, numbers, uppercase, and lowercase characters. We will simply increase `MinimumPasswordLength` value to `16`, `MaxPasswordAge` to `90` to force users to change their password every quarter, and `PasswordReusePrevention` to `3` to encourage users not to reuse their old passwords.

Once the changes are made, we can save the file and update the account password policy as follows:

```
$ aws iam update-account-password-policy \
      --cli-input-json file://password-policy
```

Finally, we can validate that the new policy is present and reflect the data present in the file as follows:

```
$ aws iam get-account-password-policy
{
    "PasswordPolicy": {
        "AllowUsersToChangePassword": true,
        "RequireLowercaseCharacters": true,
        "RequireUppercaseCharacters": true,
        "MinimumPasswordLength": 16,
        "RequireNumbers": true,
        "PasswordReusePrevention": 3,
        "HardExpiry": true,
        "RequireSymbols": true,
        "MaxPasswordAge": 90,
        "ExpirePasswords": true
    }
}
```

From that point on, new user accounts or existing ones changing their passwords will have to comply with the preceding policy.

We will now look into creating groups to better organize our users.

Creating groups for users and operators

In AWS, the management of permissions is done through the creation of security policies. Those policies can then be assigned to service roles like we saw throughout the book, users, and user groups. Managing security policies at the user group level, as opposed to the individual user level, offers some benefits. By managing permissions at the group level, you can easily make sure that all users from a given team have the same permissions and that if a change is needed, you don't need to repeat the change for every user in that team.

The management of users and groups can be driven either natively in AWS or, if you have an Active Directory server (either on-premises or through the AWS Directory Service) through the AD connector.

In our case, we will use the native AWS interface and with the help of CloudFormation manage our groups. For the purpose of this book, we will only create one group and call it Admins but, as you can imagine, in a real-world scenario, you will probably want to have multiple groups with specific permissions.

We will create a new script in our EffectiveDevOpsTemplates repository and call it `iam-groups-cf-template.py`. We will start with our usual boilerplate:

```
"""Generating CloudFormation template."""

from troposphere import (
    Template,
)

from troposphere.iam import (
    Group,
)

t = Template()

t.add_description("Effective DevOps in AWS: User Groups")
```

We will now create a new source of type `Group`, as shown following. We will give it the name Admins and assign the managed policy `AdministratorAccess` that we used previously with the user we created in Chapter 2, *Deploying Your First Web Application*:

```
t.add_resource(Group(
    "Admins",
    GroupName="Admins",
    ManagedPolicyArns=[
        "arn:aws:iam::aws:policy/AdministratorAccess"
    ],
))
```

Finally, we will end our script by printing the resulting JSON output:

```
print t.to_json()
```

Our script is now complete, it should look like this `http://bit.ly/2v1oO2o`

We can save it, commit it and execute it as follows:

```
$ git add iam-groups-cf-template.py
$ git commit -m "Adding template to managage user groups"
$ git push
$ python iam-groups-cf-template.py > iam-groups-cf.template
$ aws cloudformation create-stack \
      --stack-name iam-groups \
      --template-body file://iam-groups-cf.template \
      --capabilities CAPABILITY_NAMED_IAM
{
    "StackId": "arn:aws:cloudformation:us-east-1:511912822958:stack/iam-
groups/9ac717f0-0214-11e7-90a5-50fae9826c99"
}
```

This will create a new IAM group called `Admins`:

```
$ aws iam list-groups
{
    "Groups": [
        {
            "Path": "/",
            "CreateDate": "2017-03-06T02:32:47Z",
            "GroupId": "AGPAI352HLJMPCFQRWNQA",
            "Arn": "arn:aws:iam::511912822958:group/Admins",
            "GroupName": "Admins"
        }
    ]
}
```

We will now move our existing user to that group:

```
$ aws iam add-user-to-group --user-name johndoe --group-name Admins
```

And finally, because the user is now getting its access permission through the group policies, detach the policy attached to the user:

```
$ aws iam detach-user-policy \
      --user-name johndoe \
      --policy-arn arn:aws:iam::aws:policy/AdministratorAccess
```

We successfully created an `Admin` group with administrator permission and moved our user into that group. Obviously, this group is a bit particular and should be restricted to just a handful number of users. In the next section, we will create a more generic group that any user should be part of to be able to manage their account.

Creating proper IAM policies to empower users to do their work securely

As mentioned, we created our administrator group but we would like to restrict access to that group. Other users should be part of a group with more restrictive permissions. For this, we will take the opposite approach and create groups with minimal permissions and then add permissions through groups to only grant users enough permission to get their job done.

The first thing users need to do is be able to manage their own account. We want our users to be able to self-manage certain aspects of their account such as passwords, access keys, and multi-factor authentication devices.

We will first focus on granting sufficient permissions for that.

 When using access keys for service to service communication, the general consensus is that you need to be very careful about how you manage them and should not share keys with too many permissions. In addition, it is important to rotate them frequently to reduce the chance that a compromised key could be used against you. Both CloudTrail and Scout2 will monitor the age of your keys and let you know if you have keys that haven't been rotated for over 90 days. CloudTrail also monitors popular code repositories such as GitHub to see if one of your keys has been exposed publicly and used "irregularly" against EC2 for example.

Empowering users to manage their accounts

IAM is a very resourceful service. When used properly, the combination of user groups and security policies lets you implement very complex rules. We will create a new managed policy to grant the necessary permissions and attach it to a new group that all users should be part of.

We will do that in the `iam-groups-cf-template.py` script we just created in the previous section:

1. Reopen the script in your editor.
2. We will first need to import a number of classes. At the top of the script, at around line five, we are going to add to the troposphere import section, the import of `Join` and `Ref` as follows:

```
from troposphere import (
    Template,
    Join,
```

```
        Ref,
    )
```

3. In addition, at around line 11, we are going to add a new class in the troposphere.iamimport to create a managed policy as follows:

```
from troposphere.iam import (
    Group,
    ManagedPolicy,
)
```

4. We also import a number of classes from the **Amazon Web Access Control Subsystem (awacs)** library previously used with our Jenkins template. After the troposphere.iam import section, add the following:

```
from awacs.aws import (
    Action,
    Allow,
    Policy,
    Statement,
)
```

5. We can now create a new IAM managed policy. We will add a new resource of type ManagedPolicy. We will call it CommonIamPolicy as in the end, every human user should have it. In addition to defining its name, we will provide a description and start our policy document which contains the list of permissions to add to the specified users or groups. After the creation of the admin group resource, add the following:

```
t.add_resource(ManagedPolicy(
    "CommonIamPolicy",
    Description="Common policy to manage IAM resources",
    PolicyDocument=Policy(
```

6. The first parameter of that policy is the specification of the version:

```
Version="2012-10-17",
```

7. The next parameter of the policy document will be the definition of the different statements. Because admins don't want to be in the business of managing every aspect of the user accounts, our policy will give enough permissions for any user to self-manage their credentials, MFA devices, and access keys. For that, we will create a first statement that will give anyone the permissions to read the password policy defined in the previous section, list MFA devices (physical and virtual), and users. After the definition of the version of the policy document, add the following:

```
Statement=[
    Statement(
        Effect=Allow,
        Action=[
            Action("iam", "GetAccountPasswordPolicy"),
            Action("iam", "ListUsers"),
            Action("iam", "ListMFADevices"),
            Action("iam", "ListVirtualMFADEvices")
        ],
        Resource=["*"]
    ),
```

8. Our next statement will allow users that don't have any MFA devices configured to create one. In that particular case, we want to restrict the resource to only the user who is making the change. For that, we will use the policy variable `${aws:username}` and the pseudo `parameterAWS::AccountId`. You can read more about policy variables at `http://amzn.to/2mYsltz`. After the previous statement, add the following:

```
Statement(
    Effect=Allow,
    Action=[
        Action("iam", "CreateVirtualMFADevice")
    ],
    Resource=[
        Join(
            "",
            [
                "arn:aws:iam::",
                Ref("AWS::AccountId"),
                ":mfa/${aws:username}",
            ]
        )
    ]
),
```

9. We will now add a third statement. This statement will allow users to self-manage their passwords, MFA, and access keys. Here too, we will restrict those actions to the current user. Once that statement is complete, we will have all the permissions needed, we can complete the creation of that resource. After the previous statement, add the following:

```
Statement(
    Effect=Allow,
    Action=[
        Action("iam", "ChangePassword"),
        Action("iam", "CreateAccessKey"),
        Action("iam", "CreateLoginProfile"),
        Action("iam", "DeleteAccessKey"),
        Action("iam", "DeleteLoginProfile"),
        Action("iam", "EnableMFADevice"),
        Action("iam", "GetAccessKeyLastUsed"),
        Action("iam", "GetLoginProfile"),
        Action("iam", "GetUser"),
        Action("iam", "ListAccessKeys"),
        Action("iam", "UpdateAccessKey"),
        Action("iam", "UpdateLoginProfile")
    ],
    Resource=[
        Join(
            "",
            [
                "arn:aws:iam::",
                Ref("AWS::AccountId"),
                ":user/${aws:username}",
            ]
        )
    ],
)
))
```

10. Now that our managed policy is completed, we are going to create a group and reference this policy. The group will be called `AllUsers` and, as its name suggests, should contain all human users. After the creation of the managed policy resource, add the following:

```
t.add_resource(Group(
    "AllUsers",
    GroupName="AllUsers",
    ManagedPolicyArns=[
```

```
                    Ref("CommonIamPolicy")
        ]
    ))
```

Our updated script is ready. It should look like this: `http://bit.ly/2uHdsOk`.

We can save the changes.

If you don't have the `awacs` library installed, you can install it with the following command:

```
$ pip install awacs
```

We can now update our CloudFormation stack as follows:

```
$ python iam-groups-cf-template.py > iam-groups-cf.template
$ aws cloudformation update-stack \
      --stack-name iam-groups \
      --template-body file://iam-groups-cf.template \
      --capabilities CAPABILITY_NAMED_IAM
```

As before, we can add users to that group with the following command:

```
$ aws iam add-user-to-group --user-name johndoe --group-name AllUsers
```

Our user, John Doe, is now a member of both the `AllUsers` and `Admin` groups. In practice, at that point, being a member of both groups doesn't make a lot of sense since Admin John can already do everything he wants. This will change in the next section as we start incorporating restrictions on what users can do without a recent MFA authentication.

Enforcing the use of MFA devices

At this point, users who are part of the `AllUsers` groups have enough permission to manage their account. We can now restrict the permissions of users who don't have their accounts configured to use an MFA device or didn't refresh their sessions in a certain amount of time. To do that, we will add two new statements to the `CommonIamPolicy`policy as follows:

1. Reopen the script in your editor.
2. We will first add a few extra classes in the `awacs.aws` import section around line 18. We will add:

   ```
   from awacs.aws import (
       Action,
       Allow,
       Condition,
       NumericGreaterThan,
   ```

```
        Deny,
        Null,
        Policy,
        Statement,
    )
```

3. Now that this is in place, we can add our new entries in the statement array of the `CommonIamPolicy` managed policy. At the end of the third statement, around line 95, add the following statement:

```
Statement(
    Effect=Deny,
    NotAction=[
        Action("iam", "ChangePassword"),
        Action("iam", "CreateVirtualMFADevice"),
        Action("iam", "EnableMFADevice"),
        Action("iam", "GetUser"),
        Action("iam", "ListMFADevices"),
        Action("iam", "ListUsers"),
        Action("iam", "ListVirtualMFADEvices")
    ],
    Resource=["*"],
    Condition=Condition(
        Null("aws:MultiFactorAuthAge", "true"),
    ),
),
```

The statements we created previously were allowing certain actions to be performed. To do that, we were using the effect `Allow` and specifying a list of actions. Here we are doing the opposite, we are denying access to any resource if `aws:MultiFactorAuthAge` is set to null meaning that the user didn't set their MFA device. `Deny` actions are the default and have priority over `Allow` actions therefore if we want to give permissions to our users to configure their account, we need to whitelist certain actions from the `Deny` statement. This is done with the `NotAction` section.

4. We now need to add one more statement after this last one to also deny access to almost everything if the MFA sessions expired after 12H (or 43200 seconds). We will do that by duplicating the preceding statement and only change the condition as follows:

```
Statement (
    Effect=Deny,
    NotAction=[
        Action("iam", "ChangePassword"),
        Action("iam", "CreateVirtualMFADevice"),
        Action("iam", "EnableMFADevice"),
        Action("iam", "GetUser"),
        Action("iam", "ListMFADevices"),
        Action("iam", "ListUsers"),
        Action("iam", "ListVirtualMFADEvices")
    ],
    Resource=["*"],
    Condition=Condition(
        NumericGreaterThan("aws:MultiFactorAuthAge", "43200")
    ),
),
```

5. Our updated policy is now complete; we can save the file. It should look like this:
   `http://bit.ly/2uHaRnq`

6. We can update our existing CloudFormation stack by running the same command as previously:

```
$ aws cloudformation update-stack \
    --stack-name iam-groups \
    --template-body file://iam-groups-cf.template \
    --capabilities CAPABILITY_NAMED_IAM
```

At this point, our users, even administrators, can't run most commands. We can, for example, try to list all the s3 buckets to validate the restriction we just added:

```
$ aws s3 ls
An error occurred (ExpiredToken) when calling the ListBuckets operation:
The provided token has expired.
```

We now need to use a script to refresh our MFA session.

Using a script to create an MFA session

To create our sessions, we are going to use an open source script created by the same author as Scout2, we will clone the repository and install the dependencies as follows:

```
$ git clone https://github.com/nccgroup/AWS-recipes
$ cd AWS-recipes
$ pip install -r requirements.txt
```

The script we want to use is in the Python directory:

```
$ cd Python
```

The script we want to run is called aws_recipes_init_sts_session.py:

```
$ aws_recipes_init_sts_session.py
Saved STS credentials expired on 2017-02-12 10:28:48+00:00
Enter your MFA code (or 'q' to abort):
446054
```

 We assume here that you previously went through the MFA initialization steps as asked in Chapter 2, *Deploying Your First Web Application*. If you haven't done it yet, you can use the AWS console to initialize your MFA device or use the script aws_iam_enable_mfa.py present in that folder.

Once the script has run, this script will create a new session giving you a 12H window to work with the AWS CLI.

At that point, you can start creating more groups, and move users to those new groups. For example, you may create a group for accounting and give the finance team access to billing information by creating a policy with the following statement:

```
{
    "Version": "2012-10-17",
    "Statement": [
        {
            "Effect": "Allow",
            "Action": [
                "aws-portal:ViewUsage",
                "aws-portal:ViewBilling"
            ],
            "Resource": "*"
        }
    ]
}
```

Giving AWS users admin access to staging but not to production
With the system we created, we can enforce permissions on a per service basis. Depending on the development workflow you want to provide for the different groups of developers, you may need to provide admin access to your staging resources. The problem with that system is that IAM is a global service and therefore if you give a user the ability to make IAM changes, for example, you give them the ability to be administrator of all environments as they can make changes to the policy. For a more granular approach to IAM user permissions, you can rely on a feature called Cross-Account Access. At a high level, the idea consists of creating a new AWS account for your staging environment and giving administrator permissions to every engineer in that account. Then on your production AWS account, you will use the IAM service and its AssumeRole feature to grant a different set of permissions to those users coming from your staging account. You can read more on that topic at
`http://amzn.to/2rGeSdC`.

Now that we know how to manage users and user groups, we will focus on service permissions.

Managing service permissions in AWS

As you have probably realized by now, we are already using IAM extensively. Every system and CloudFormation template we created in the book included one or more IAM resources. Until now, we tried to minimize the complexity of that section to focus on the other resources, our templates, but tightening these rules is one of the most effective ways there is to improve the security of our architecture.

We will take the example of our `helloworld` application running on top of EC2 to demonstrate how we can tighten the permissions on our role.

When we worked on our CI/CD pipeline, we started to use CodePipeline and CodeDeploy to deploy our application. Whenever someone merges a change in our application, CodePipeline takes the new code and puts it on S3. After that, the CodeDeploy agent takes it from S3 and installs it on our EC2 instance. To make that possible, we had to change our role to allow our instances to communicate with S3.

We did that by creating the following policy:

```
t.add_resource(IAMPolicy(
    "Policy",
    PolicyName="AllowS3",
```

```
PolicyDocument=Policy(
    Statement=[
        Statement(
            Effect=Allow,
            Action=[Action("s3", "*")],
            Resource=["*"])
    ]
),
Roles=[Ref("Role")]
))
```

In plain English, we said that our EC2 instances are allowed to do any S3 operation on any S3 bucket. Since our application inherits these permissions, if someone manages to find an exploit in your application and do some remote code execution, they will be able to do many non-desirable actions. This includes accessing all our S3 buckets including the ones with our load balancer logs and your application artifacts. They will also be able to create new S3 buckets either to store their own content or even try to create a phishing attack by storing a virus with the hope that someone finds the bucket and try to open the objects it contains.

To be able to install the new artifacts, CodeDeploy only needs read access to S3 therefore, we could change the statement in the preceding policy to the following:

```
Statement(
    Effect=Allow,
    Action=[
        Action("s3", "Get*"),
        Action("s3", "List*")
    ],
    Resource=["*"])
)
```

In addition, we can restrict the resources to only allow those actions to target the S3 buckets used by CodeDeploy. Since the service uses one bucket per region, your new statement would look as follows:

```
Statement(
    Effect=Allow,
    Action=[
        Action("s3", "Get*"),
        Action("s3", "List*")
    ],
    "Resource": [
        "arn:aws:s3:::codedeploydemobucket/*",
        "arn:aws:s3:::aws-codedeploy-us-east-2/*",
        "arn:aws:s3:::aws-codedeploy-us-east-1/*",
        "arn:aws:s3:::aws-codedeploy-us-west-1/*",
```

```
            "arn:aws:s3:::aws-codedeploy-us-west-2/*",
            "arn:aws:s3:::aws-codedeploy-ca-central-1/*",
            "arn:aws:s3:::aws-codedeploy-eu-west-1/*",
            "arn:aws:s3:::aws-codedeploy-eu-west-2/*",
            "arn:aws:s3:::aws-codedeploy-eu-central-1/*",
            "arn:aws:s3:::aws-codedeploy-ap-northeast-1/*",
            "arn:aws:s3:::aws-codedeploy-ap-northeast-2/*",
            "arn:aws:s3:::aws-codedeploy-ap-southeast-1/*",
            "arn:aws:s3:::aws-codedeploy-ap-southeast-2/*",
            "arn:aws:s3:::aws-codedeploy-ap-south-1/*",
            "arn:aws:s3:::aws-codedeploy-sa-east-1/*",
            "arn:aws-cn:s3:::aws-codedeploy-cn-north-1/*"
    ]
)
```

With the hardening of IAM, we can efficiently restrict what our systems and users can do when interacting with AWS. We will now look at improving our network.

Strengthening the security at the network level

When using AWS, you can imagine your infrastructure as being contained in your own virtual data center. This is called a VPC. Each VPC is then subdivided into multiple subnets. So far, we have used the default VPC and subnets. We take the example of `us-east-1`. As we can see on the following image, our default VPC is using the `173.31.0.0/16` network. Within this network, we have a subnet for each availability zone.

In addition, each AZ is directly connected to an internet gateway:

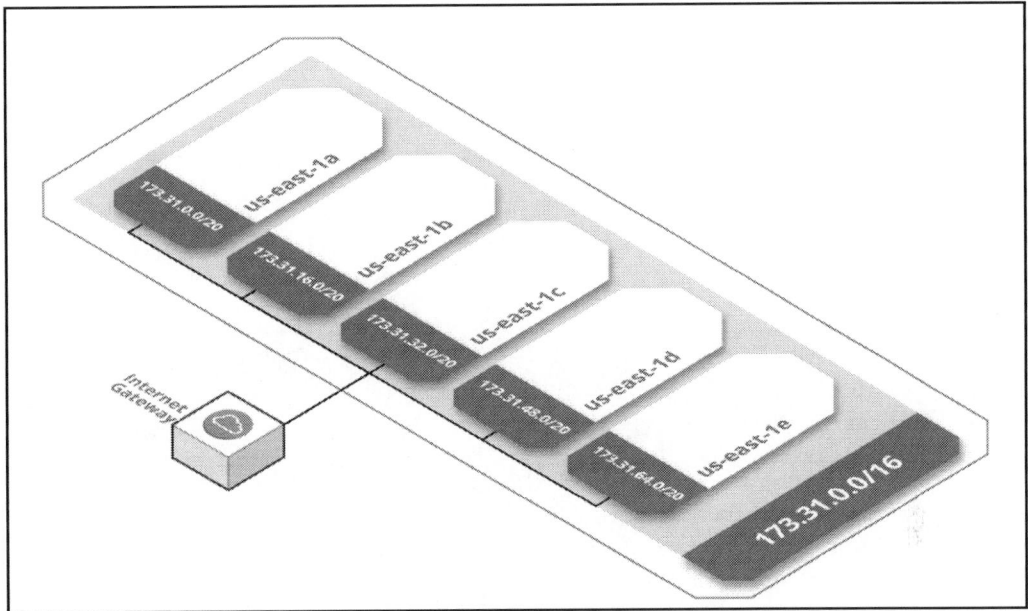

This gateway is what makes it possible for our EC2 instances to have both a public and private IP. This is also what we want to change. One of the common best practices in security is to minimize the attack surface. As services and applications become more and more complex, the likelihood of opening a security group too much also increases. What we want to create is an architecture where our EC2 instances are for the most part in a private subnet and only a handful number of resources will be on our public subnets.

We will also add an optional resource called a NAT Gateway. A NAT Gateway is a managed service that does not require administration effort and allows instances from the private subnet to connect to the internet from a unique IP. This way, our instances in the private subnets will still be able to connect to the internet but no one will be able to create a connection directly to those instances from outside of our network.

Right now, we are accessing our different instances and internal tools (if you are still using Jenkins for example) using their public IP and HTTP endpoint. The traffic is completely unencrypted. Even if we configured the security group to limit access to those services to our public IP, we are still vulnerable to some attacks, such as sniffing where the attacker will be able to capture the communication between your computer and AWS. To address this issue, we are going to create a VPN connection such that the entire communication between AWS and our computer will be encrypted.

In the end, the new architecture should look as follows:

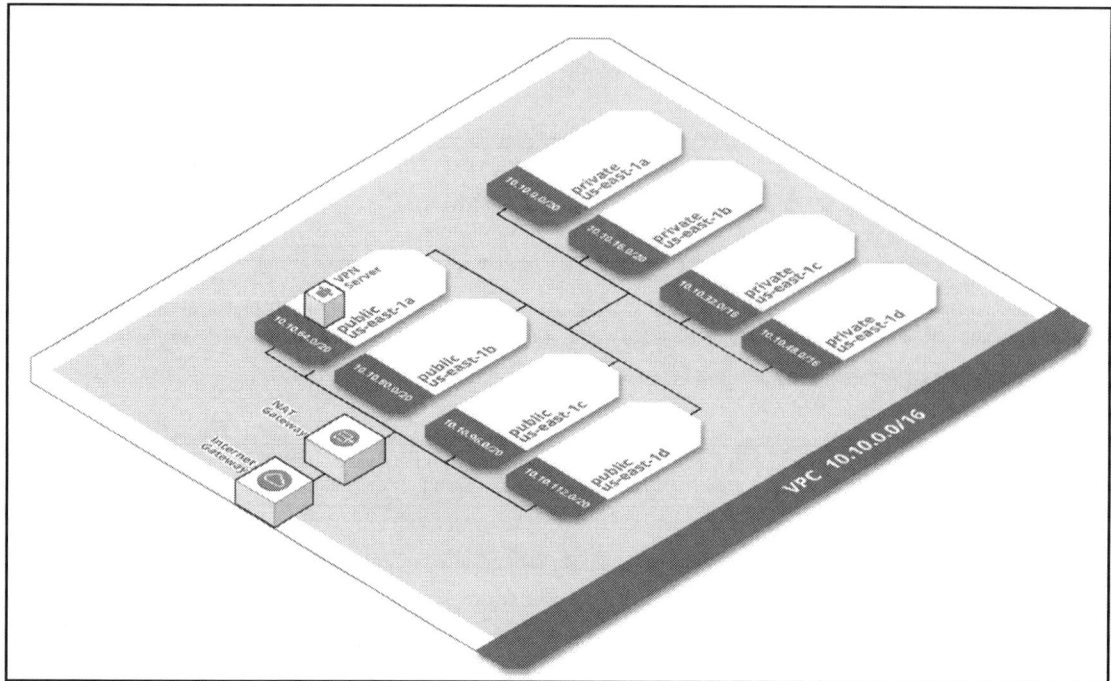

We are going to implement this new network architecture.

Creating a VPC with public and private subnets

We will create a new script in our EffectiveDevOpsTemplates repository and call it `vpc-cf-template.py`.

We will start with our usual boilerplates:

```python
"""Generating CloudFormation template."""

from troposphere import (
    GetAZs,
    Output,
    Parameter,
    Ref,
    Select,
    Sub,
    Tags,
```

```
        Template,
        GetAtt
)

from troposphere.ec2 import (
        VPC,
        InternetGateway,
        NetworkAcl,
        NetworkAclEntry,
        Route,
        RouteTable,
        Subnet,
        SubnetNetworkAclAssociation,
        SubnetRouteTableAssociation,
        VPCGatewayAttachment,
        EIP,
        NatGateway,
)

t = Template()

t.add_description("Effective DevOps in AWS: VPC, public and private
subnets")
```

This template will require providing a parameter for the CIDR. We will create our subnets on the private (non-publicly routable) IP address ranges `10.0.0.0/16` as specified in RFC 1918. Since we want to have the possibility to create multiple VPC and have private subnets for each, we will limit our VPC to a/16 network which in most cases is enough as it gives the ability to manage up to `65534` IPs:

```
t.add_parameter(Parameter(
        "ClassB",
        Type="Number",
        Description="Class B of VPC (10.XXX.0.0/16)",
        Default="0",
        MinValue=0,
        MaxValue=255,
        ConstraintDescription="Must be in the range [0-255]",
))
```

We will now create our resources. The first resource we will create is the VPC itself. The VPC resource has two optional attributes. The first one, `EnableDnsSupport` enables the ability to do DNS resolution through the AWS native DNS server at `169.254.169.253`. `EnableDnsSupport`, the second attribute, makes it so that AWS will default to assigning DNS entries to instances launched in the VPC.

In addition to those attributes, we will also create a name tag such that when we list all the VPCs either with the command-line or using the AWS console, it will be easier to differentiate the different VPCs created:

```
t.add_resource(VPC(
    "VPC",
    EnableDnsSupport="true",
    EnableDnsHostnames="true",
    CidrBlock=Sub('10.${ClassB}.0.0/16'),
    Tags=Tags(
        Name=Ref("AWS::StackName"),
    )
))
```

The next resource we will create is an internet gateway. Internet gateways are used to proxy traffic between the instances in the VPC and the internet. Internet gateways are horizontally scaled, redundant, highly available, and completely managed by AWS making it a no-brainer to have if you want your instances to be able to reach outside of your VPC. Here too, we will tag them with the name of our stack to easily identify them in the list of `InternetGateway`:

```
t.add_resource(InternetGateway(
    "InternetGateway",
    Tags=Tags(
        Name=Ref("AWS::StackName"),
    )
))
```

We defined our VPC and internet gateway, now we need to join the two together with a `VPCGatewayAttachment` resource as such:

```
t.add_resource(VPCGatewayAttachment(
    "VPNGatewayAttachment",
    VpcId=Ref("VPC"),
    InternetGatewayId=Ref("InternetGateway")
))
```

We will now configure our network. Often when dealing with network configuration, this means instantiating and configuring a number of resources. Configuring our VPC will require creating the following:

1. Subnets, which are a range of IP addresses in the VPC which will be used to launch instances.
2. Routing tables, which makes it possible to configure where network traffic is directed in the subnets.

3. `SubnetRouteTableAssociation`, which is, as its name suggests, the piece that connects subnets and routing tables together.
4. **Network Access control lists (NACL)**, which let you control the traffic in and out of the subnets for an added layer of security.
5. `SubnetNetworkAclAssociation`, which is similar to `SubnetRouteTableAssociation` but in that case, allows the association of NACL with subnets.
6. `NetworkAclEntry`, which defines the rule inside the network ACL.

The minimum required by AWS is to have one subnet per availability zone. In addition, we want to break out our hosts into publicly accessible or private. We need one subnet for each combination of availability zones and accessibility (public or private). Since `us-east-1` has four availability zones this means creating two routing tables, two NACL, eight subnets, `8SubnetRouteTableAssociation`, `8SubnetNetworkAclAssociation` resources, and four network ACL entries. If we were using CloudFormation, this would translate into a very lengthy repetitive and error prone process to create those 32 resources. Fortunately, since we are creating a script to generate the CloudFormation template, we can take advantage of our situation and create several loops to minimize the work. We will first create three variables: an array called accessibility to break out private and public resources, names to help us differentiate with the different availability zones and finally, a simple counter:

```
accessibility = ["Private", "Public"]
names = ["A", "B", "C", "D"]
count = 0
```

We will now create a loop through both accessibility values and create the routing tables and network ACL. We will proceed similarly as we did previously and add a tag `Name` for each of them to make their identification easier. For the purpose of our template, we will also programmatically generate their name and call them `PrivateRouteTable`, `PublicRouteTable`, `PrivateNetworkAcl`, `PublicNetworkAcl`, as such:

```
for a in accessibility:
    t.add_resource(RouteTable(
        "{}RouteTable".format(a),
        VpcId=Ref("VPC"),
        Tags=Tags(
            Name=Sub("${{AWS::StackName}} {}".format(a)),
        )
    ))
    t.add_resource(NetworkAcl(
        "{}NetworkAcl".format(a),
        VpcId=Ref("VPC"),
```

```
            Tags=Tags(
                Name=Sub("${{AWS::StackName}} {}".format(a))
            )
    ))
```

We will now nest another loop inside the accessibility loop to list out each availability zone and create the subnets. Aside from the name that we will generate programmatically like we did for the previous resources, the creation of subnets requires specifying a number of parameters including the `AvailabilityZone`, the `CidrBlock`, and specifying if the subnet is public or private. In order to provide the `AvailabilityZone` value, we will take advantage of the function `GetAZs()` which returns an array of all availability zones available in a region (`http://amzn.to/2nAtmsl`), the function select which extracts a value from an array, and the counter variable previously initialized. This will allow us to evenly distribute the different subnets we create to each availability zone. For the CIDR block, we will use the class B parameter provided at the template creation time and also take advantage of the counter variable. We will multiply it by `16` such that we can create continuous blocks of `4094` hosts. Finally, to specify the value of the last parameter `MapPublicIpOnLaunch`, we will take advantage of the conditional statement functions (`http://amzn.to/2oijikU`). After the creation of the `NetworkACL` resources, add the following:

```
    for n in names:
        t.add_resource(Subnet(
            "{}Subnet{}".format(a, n),
            VpcId=Ref("VPC"),
            AvailabilityZone=Select(count % 4, GetAZs()),
            CidrBlock=Sub("10.${{ClassB}}.{}.0/20".format(count * 16)),
            MapPublicIpOnLaunch="true" if a == "Public" else "false",
            Tags=Tags(
                Name=Sub("${{AWS::StackName}} {} {}".format(a, n)),
            )
        ))
```

We can now increase the value of the counter and create the two remaining resources, `SubnetRouteTableAssociation` and `SubnetNetworkAclAssociation` as follows:

```
        count += 1
        t.add_resource(SubnetRouteTableAssociation(
            "{}Subnet{}RouteTableAssociation".format(a, n),
            SubnetId=Ref("{}Subnet{}".format(a, n)),
            RouteTableId=Ref("{}RouteTable".format(a)),
        ))
        t.add_resource(SubnetNetworkAclAssociation(
            "{}Subnet{}NetworkAclAssociation".format(a, n),
            SubnetId=Ref("{}Subnet{}".format(a, n)),
```

```
            NetworkAclId=Ref("{}NetworkAcl".format(a)),
    ))
```

This completes the creation of our biggest loop and through it, the creation of most resources needed for our subnets. We just need to add our network ACL entries. For that, we will create another nested loop. This time, we will loop over the same accessibility and the network traffic origination. We will create a new array and call it directions as follows:

```
directions = ["Inbound", "Outbound"]
```

From there, we will create our two for loops and add the NetworkAclEntries as follows:

```
for a in accessibility:
    for d in directions:
        t.add_resource(NetworkAclEntry(
            "{}{}NetworkAclEntry".format(d, a),
            NetworkAclId=Ref("{}NetworkAcl".format(a)),
            RuleNumber="100",
            Protocol="-1",
            Egress="true" if d == "Outbound" else "false",
            RuleAction="allow",
            CidrBlock="0.0.0.0/0",
        ))
```

At that point, most of the complex resources are created. We need to add a few more things. We will first create a new route table to link our public route table to the internet gateway as follows:

```
t.add_resource(Route(
    "RouteTablePublicInternetRoute",
    GatewayId=Ref("InternetGateway"),
    DestinationCidrBlock="0.0.0.0/0",
    RouteTableId=Ref("PublicRouteTable"),
))
```

We will now create our NAT gateway. Since it's preferable to always keep the same IPs for these types of service, we will first create an ElasticIP (http://amzn.to/2oi7v64) which will provide us the ability to keep the same IP and reassign it to other resources if we need to rebuild our NAT gateway, for example:

```
t.add_resource(EIP(
    "EIP",
    Domain="VPC"
))
```

We will now create the NAT gateway and provide it the allocation ID from the EIP created just before. We will arbitrarily assign our gateway to our first public subnet:

 For redundancy and performance purposes, it is a common practice to create a NAT Gateway for each public subnet, but since this service isn't free unlike the other resources we are creating in this template, we are just going to demonstrate the minimum viable solution.

```
t.add_resource(NatGateway(
    "NatGateway",
    AllocationId=GetAtt("EIP", "AllocationId"),
    SubnetId=Ref("PublicSubnetA")
))
```

With the creation of the NAT gateway, our private subnets now have a way to reach the internet. To complete this operation, we need to configure our route. We will do that by adding a new route table as we did a few lines before for the public route table as follows:

```
t.add_resource(Route(
    "RouteNat",
    RouteTableId=Ref("PrivateRouteTable"),
    DestinationCidrBlock="0.0.0.0/0",
    NatGatewayId=Ref("NatGateway")
))
```

Our template is done, we will simply list our VPC ID in our CloudFormation template output and, as always, conclude the creation of the script by printing the JSON output of our template:

```
t.add_output(Output(
    "VPCId",
    Description="VPCId of the newly created VPC",
    Value=Ref("VPC"),
))

print(t.to_json())
```

We can now commit our changes and generate the template and create a stack. We will pick the 10.10.0.0 network to create our VPC. As such, the command-line to run is the following:

```
$ git add vpc-cf-template.py
$ git commit -m "Creating a new VPC with public and private zones"
$ git push
$ python vpc-cf-template.py > vpc-cf.template
$ aws cloudformation create-stack \
      --stack-name vpc-10 \
```

```
--capabilities CAPABILITY_IAM \
--template-body file://vpc-cf.template \
--parameters ParameterKey=ClassB,ParameterValue=10
```

Our new VPC is now created. We will now redeploy our `helloworld` application to illustrate how to take advantage of this new architecture.

Recreating our helloworld stack using our new VPC

The default VPC we used so far had only public subnets. Now that we have public and private subnets, we can adapt our applications to take advantage of it. Our `helloworld` application and its 3-tier architecture fits perfectly in that design.

For our application to be accessible on the internet, we will need to keep the ELB in the public subnets but the EC2 instances can be moved to the private zone. This won't be an issue as resources in the public zone can reach resources in the private zone.

Recreating our application to take advantage of private subnets

1. We will duplicate the `nodeserver-cf-template.py` updated previously in `Chapter 5`, *Scaling Your Infrastructure*, and make a version optimized for our new architecture.

   ```
   $ cp nodeserver-cf-template.py nodeserver-vpc-cf-template.py
   ```

2. We will now open the `nodeserver-vpc-cf-template.py` script in our editor to start making changes. The EC2 instances won't have a public IP therefore, we can change our security group to not allow SSH traffic from our public IP. This means that we can remove the code that gets our public IP

   ```
   from ipaddress import ip_network
   from ipify import get_ip
   PublicCidrIp = str(ip_network(get_ip()))
   ```

3. Now that our infrastructure will run using a private IP, we can open the full range of possible IPs by changing our SSH security group rule from the following:

```
ec2.SecurityGroupRule(
    IpProtocol="tcp",
    FromPort="22",
    ToPort="22",
    CidrIp=PublicCidrIp,
),
```

To the following:

```
ec2.SecurityGroupRule(
    IpProtocol="tcp",
    FromPort="22",
    ToPort="22",
    CidrIp="10.0.0.0/8",
),
```

4. Lastly, we need to change our subnetting. Right now, as we create the template, in the parameters section, we are requesting the list of public zones to use. We will also need to request the list of private zones and then use those for our Auto Scaling Group. Add after the `PublicSubnet` parameter section, the following:

```
t.add_parameter(Parameter(
    "PrivateSubnet",
    Description="PrivateSubnet",
    Type="List<AWS::EC2::Subnet::Id>",
    ConstraintDescription="PrivateSubnet"
))
```

5. Then, change the `VPCZoneIdentifier` option of the `AutoscalingGroup` resource to use that new parameter as follows:

```
t.add_resource(AutoScalingGroup(
    "AutoscalingGroup",
    DesiredCapacity=Ref("ScaleCapacity"),
    LaunchConfigurationName=Ref("LaunchConfiguration"),
    MinSize=2,
    MaxSize=5,
    LoadBalancerNames=[Ref("LoadBalancer")],
    VPCZoneIdentifier=Ref("PrivateSubnet"),
))
```

The new template is ready to be used. The code should look as follow `http://bit.ly/2v1Z 5qw`.

We can save it in git as follows:

```
$ git add nodeserver-vpc-cf-template.py
$ git commit -m "Creating a simple a HelloWorld application to run in the
private zone"
$ git push
```

Creating our helloworld application in the new VPC

We are now going to redeploy our application in the new VPC. We will start by generating the new template as follows:

```
$ python nodeserver-vpc-cf-template.py > nodeserver-vpc-cf.template
```

We will use the web interface of CloudFormation to create our new stack:

1. Open the CloudFormation service in your browser by accessing the following URL:

   `https://console.aws.amazon.com/cloudformation`

2. Click on **Create Stack**
3. On the next page, click on **Browse** to select the file `nodeserver-vpc-cf.template` we just generated and click on **Next**.

4. This will bring us to the following screen:

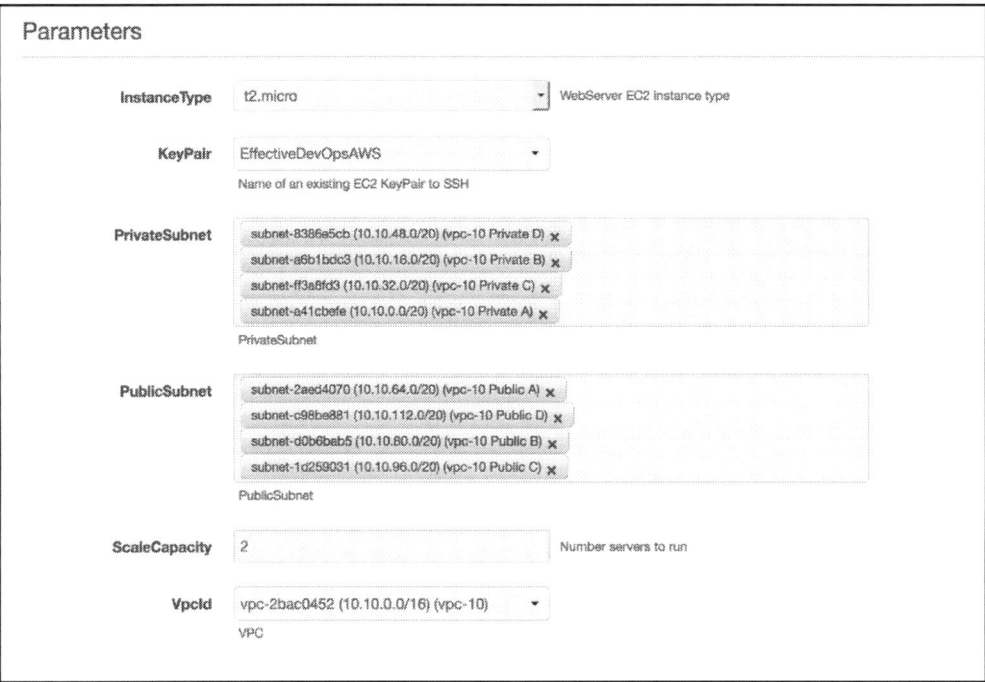

Start by Providing a name to the stack such as `helloworld-vpc-10`, select **t2.micro** as your instance type, **EffectiveDevOpsAWS** as your Keypair and set the **ScaleCapacity** to 2. Next, we will want to set the **PrivateSubnet**, **PublicSubnet** and the **VPCId** such that our application will now run on our custom VPC. Fill up those fields as shown on the preceding screenshot.

5. Complete the creation of the stack by clicking **Next** on the next two screens, acknowledge that you are aware of the IAM changes by clicking on the checkbox and, finally, click on **Update**.

When CloudFormation is done updating our stack, the most notable change will be that our EC2 instances will now have only private IPs:

Public DNS (IPv4)	ec2-54-221-43-80.compute-1.amazonaws.com
IPv4 Public IP	54.221.43.80
IPv6 IPs	-
Private DNS	ip-172-31-62-32.ec2.internal
Private IPs	172.31.62.32
Secondary private IPs	
VPC ID	vpc-f7dc4093
Subnet ID	subnet-4decfe66
Network interfaces	eth0
Source/dest. check	True
EBS-optimized	False
Root device type	ebs
Root device	/dev/xvda
Block devices	/dev/xvda

Public DNS (IPv4)	--
IPv4 Public IP	--
IPv6 IPs	--
Private DNS	ip-10-10-14-60.ec2.internal
Private IPs	10.10.14.60
Secondary private IPs	
VPC ID	vpc-2bac0452
Subnet ID	subnet-a41cbefe
Network interfaces	eth0
Source/dest. check	True
EBS-optimized	False
Root device type	ebs
Root device	/dev/xvda
Block devices	/dev/xvda

The instances launched into a virtual private subnet can't communicate with the outside network, the only way those instances can be accessed now is through other resources in the public subnet or by attaching a virtual private gateway to the VPC. If you are working from an office equipped with customer gateway supporting IPSEC hardware VPN such as a Cisco ASA, you can refer to `http://amzn.to/2rKAQMA` to configure them to create a direct connection to the VPC. If you don't have such infrastructure or want a disaster recovery backup mechanism, you can create a VPN server in your public subnet.

Creating a VPN connection to our VPC

The goal of our VPN connection is to have a direct and secure connection between our computer and the resources in the VPC. Depending on your work environment, there might be multiple options available. You may have the ability to create an IPsec connection using a hardware VPN, your internet provider might have an option to use AWS Direct Connect provides a dedicated private connection from a remote network to your VPC and so on. What we will demonstrate here is the most rudimentary approach. We will install a VPN server in our infrastructure and use the VPN client available on our operating system to connect. We will start with the VPN server.

Deploying a VPN server to AWS

As you would expect, there are several good options to do that. You can use a commercial product such as a virtual appliance from CISCO or Juniper or use an open solution such as OpenVPN. In addition, we also need to decide how to deploy our VPN. We can use an EC2 instance or a container and an ELB.

For these kinds of off-the-shelf solutions, one of the fastest ways to get going is to use the AWS marketplace (`http://amzn.to/2snWDXn`). If you look at the different solutions offered in terms of VPN, you will see one for `SoftEther` which is completely free (`http://amzn.to/2rDDDqF`):

`SoftEther` is an open source VPN server which supports many protocols including L2TP/IPsec. The good thing about this protocol is that Windows, Mac, Linux, and most switches and routers will support this protocol natively so you don't have to install a custom VPN client to establish the VPN connection.

We will install this appliance by creating a CloudFormation template for it. Using a product from the marketplace such as `SoftEther` is easy, you simply need to point to the correct AMI ID to start using it.

We will create a new script and call it `vpnserver-cf-template.py`:

1. The script starts as always with our boilerplates: `import`, `template variable`, and `description`:

```
"""Generating CloudFormation template."""

from troposphere import (
    ec2,
    GetAtt,
    Output,
    Parameter,
    Ref,
    Template,
    Select,
)

t = Template()

t.add_description("Effective DevOps in AWS: SoftEtherVPN
Server")
```

2. Next, we will add the different parameters needed to correctly deploy our VPN. We will request an `SSHkeypair`, the VPC ID, and the public subnets since our VPN needs to be accessible from the internet:

```
t.add_parameter(Parameter(
    "KeyPair",
    Description="Name of an existing EC2KeyPair to SSH",
    Type="AWS::EC2::KeyPair::KeyName",
    ConstraintDescription="must be the name of an existing
EC2KeyPair."
))

t.add_parameter(Parameter(
    "VpcId",
    Type="AWS::EC2::VPC::Id",
```

```
            Description="VPC"
    ))

    t.add_parameter(Parameter(
        "PublicSubnet",
        Description="PublicSubnet",
        Type="List<AWS::EC2::Subnet::Id>",
        ConstraintDescription="PublicSubnet"
    ))
```

3. We will now configure our security group. We need to open UDP 4500, UDP 500, and TCP 443. Note that we aren't opening the SSH port. If you ever need to SSH to that instance, you can update the template to also open TCP 22. In addition, we are setting the VpcId parameter so that the security group gets created in the proper VPC:

```
    t.add_resource(ec2.SecurityGroup(
        "VPNSecurityGroup",
        GroupDescription="SoftEther security group",
        SecurityGroupIngress=[
            ec2.SecurityGroupRule(
                IpProtocol="udp",
                FromPort="4500",
                ToPort="4500",
                CidrIp="0.0.0.0/0",
            ),
            ec2.SecurityGroupRule(
                IpProtocol="udp",
                FromPort="500",
                ToPort="500",
                CidrIp="0.0.0.0/0",
            ),
            ec2.SecurityGroupRule(
                IpProtocol="tcp",
                FromPort="443",
                ToPort="443",
                CidrIp="0.0.0.0/0",
            )
        ],
        VpcId=Ref("VpcId")
    ))
```

4. The only other resource we need is the EC2 instance that will run our VPN. We will specify the image ID of the `SoftEther` appliance and create a network interface on one of the public subnets provided. In this case, we are keeping the code fairly simple so we will simply extract the first public subnet provided at creation time to configure our network interface:

```
t.add_resource(ec2.Instance(
    "server",
    ImageId="ami-a4c7edb2",
    InstanceType="t2.micro",
    KeyName=Ref("KeyPair"),
    NetworkInterfaces=[
        ec2.NetworkInterfaceProperty(
            GroupSet=[Ref("VPNSecurityGroup")],
            AssociatePublicIpAddress='true',
            SubnetId=Select("0", Ref("PublicSubnet")),
            DeviceIndex='0',
        )]
))
```

5. The last portion of our template will contain information to configure the VPN client. To prevent anyone from connecting to the VPN, the VPN server will by default, use the `instance-id` as a password and pre-shared key for authentication:

```
t.add_output(Output(
    "VPNAddress",
    Description="VPN address",
    Value=GetAtt("server", "PublicIp")
))

t.add_output(Output(
    "VPNUser",
    Description="VPN username",
    Value="vpn"
))

t.add_output(Output(
    "VPNPassword",
    Description="VPN password",
    Value=Ref("server")
))

t.add_output(Output(
    "VPNL2TP",
    Description="L2TPpreshared key for authentication",
```

```
                    Value=Ref("server")
            ))

            t.add_output(Output(
                "VPNAdminPassword",
                Description="Password to connect administration mode",
                Value=Ref("server")
            ))
```

6. Lastly, we will print out the template, using the code:

```
        print t.to_json()
```

Our template is ready to be used. It should look as follows: http://bit.ly/2v1UJQ0.

You can commit the changes:

```
$ git add vpnserver-cf-template.py
$ git commit -m "Adding a template for the SoftEther VPN server"
$ git push
$ python vpnserver-cf-template.py > vpnserver-cf.template
```

We can now deploy it. We will do it using the CLI. We will first extract our VPC ID and the first public subnet id as we will need those ID to create our stack:

```
$ aws ec2 describe-vpcs --query 'Vpcs[].[VpcId,CidrBlock]' --output text
vpc-f7dc4093 172.31.0.0/16
vpc-2bac0452 10.10.0.0/16

$ aws ec2 describe-subnets --query 'Subnets[].SubnetId' \
        --filters 'Name=tag:Name,Values=vpc-10 Public A' --output text
subnet-2aed4070
```

We can now create our new CloudFormation stack as follow (adapt the ID using the output of the previous commands):

```
$ aws cloudformation create-stack \
        --stack-name vpn \
        --capabilities CAPABILITY_IAM \
        --template-body file://vpnserver-cf.template \
        --parameters \
        ParameterKey=KeyPair,ParameterValue=EffectiveDevOpsAWS \
        ParameterKey=VpcId,ParameterValue=vpc-2bac0452 \
        ParameterKey=PublicSubnet,ParameterValue=subnet-2aed4070
```

Once the template is deployed, you can look at the template output to get the information needed to configure your computer to connect to `SoftEther`, as follows:

```
$ aws cloudformation describe-stacks \
    --stack-name vpn \
    --query 'Stacks[0].Outputs'
[
    {
        "Description": "VPN username",
        "OutputKey": "VPNUser",
        "OutputValue": "vpn"
    },
    {
        "Description": "VPN address",
        "OutputKey": "VPNAddress",
        "OutputValue": "54.234.114.241"
    },
    {
        "Description": "VPN password",
        "OutputKey": "VPNPassword",
        "OutputValue": "i-04cc709357306118e"
    },
    {
        "Description": "L2TPpreshared key for authentication",
        "OutputKey": "VPNL2TP",
        "OutputValue": "i-04cc709357306118e"
    },
    {
        "Description": "Password to connect administration mode",
        "OutputKey": "VPNAdminPassword",
        "OutputValue": "i-04cc709357306118e"
    }
]
```

Configuring your computer to use this VPN

We will provide the instructions to configure Windows 10 and macOS to connect to the VPN:

On Windows 10:

1. From the Windows 10 Start Menu, type the word **VPN** then click on **Change virtual private networks (VPN)**:

2. On the next menu, click on **Add a VPN connection**.

3. This will open a new window to configure your connection. Select **Windows (built-in)** as your **VPN provider**, give your VPN a connection name such as **EffectiveDevOps**, provide the IP address of your VPN as your server name (you can get it from the `awsdescribe-stacks` command as shown in the previous section), select the **L2TP/IPSec with pre-sharedkey** VPN configuration and give the instance-id value as a pre-shared secret and finally, click to **Save**:

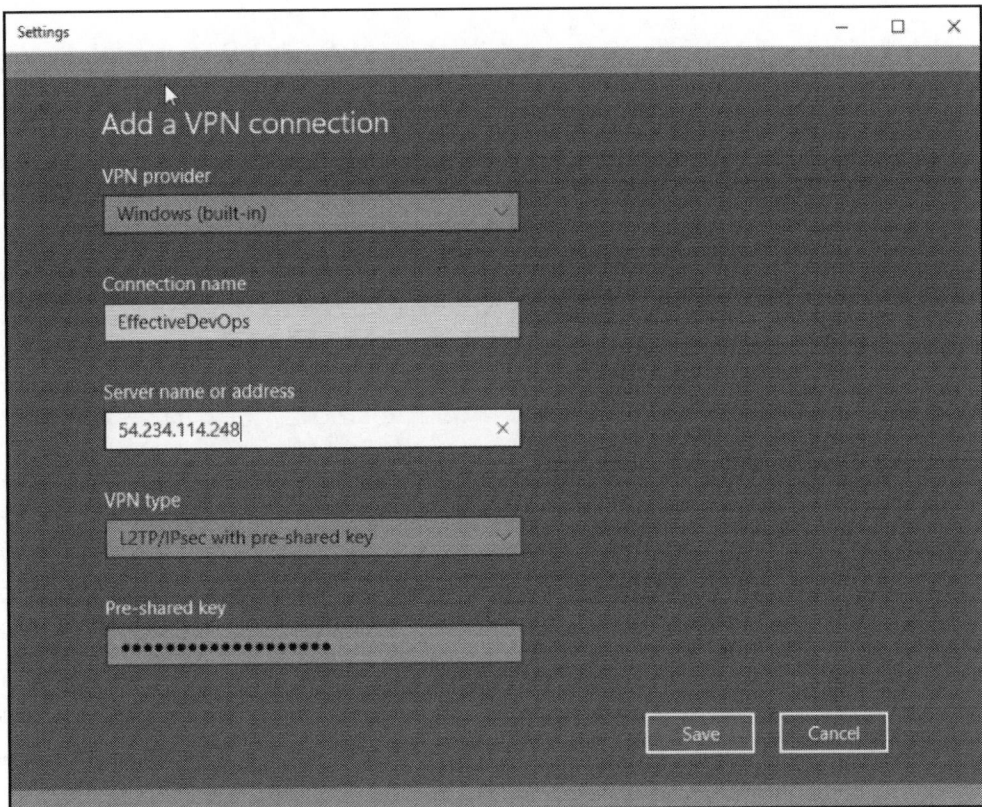

4. Once you are back on the previous menu, click on **Connect**. The first time you connect to your VPN, you will need to provider a username and password. The username is vpn and the password, the instance id. Once you have provided that information, you will be able to SSH instances on the private subnet:

On macOS:

1. Open the system preferences of your mac and select **Network**.
2. Click on the plus icon to create a new entry, a new menu should pop up.
3. Select the VPN interface, **L2TP over IPSec VPN Type** and provide a name for your VPN connection entry:

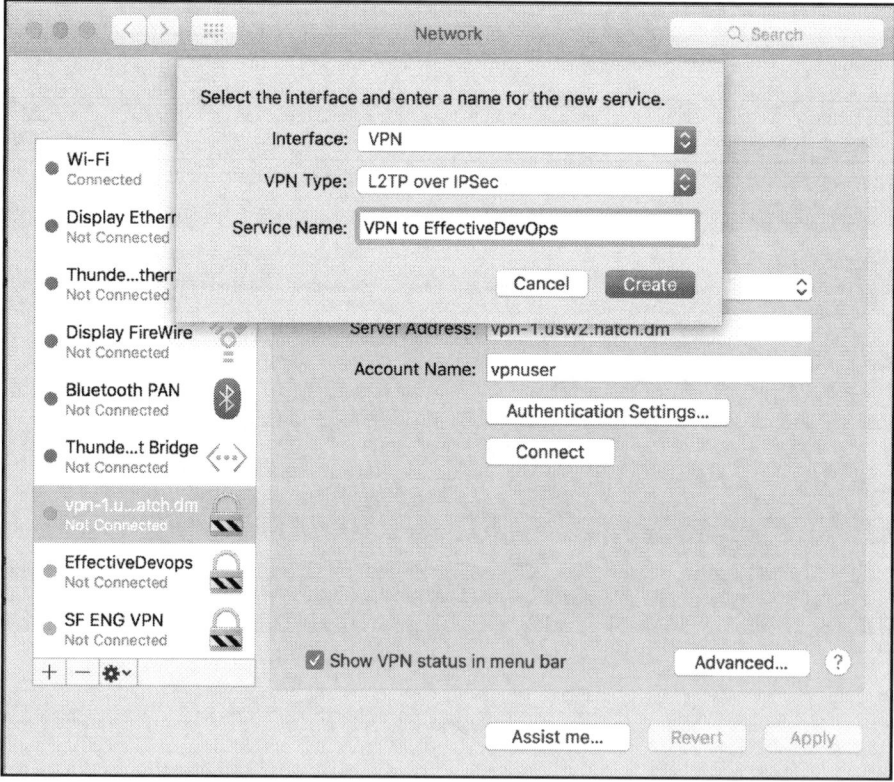

4. By looking at the output of the `aws describe-stacks` command as shown in the previous section, you will be able to find the server address and account name. Provide that information then click on **Authentication Settings**:

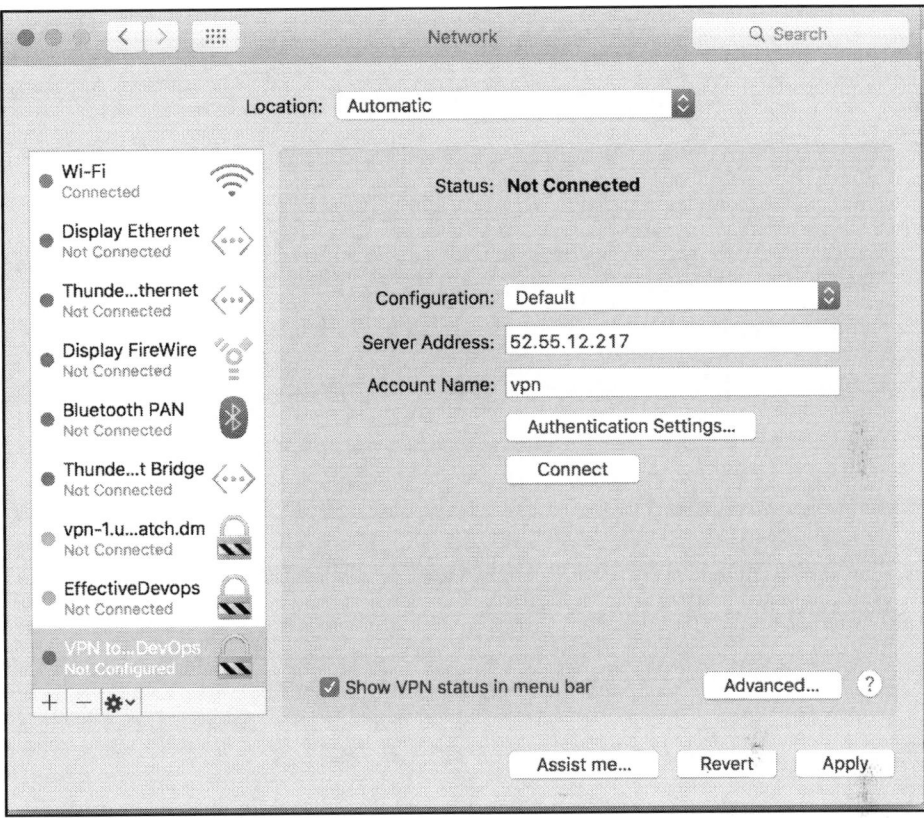

5. In this next menu, provide the password and shared secret (also provided in the `aws describe-stacks` command output) and click on **OK**:

6. Finally, click on **Advanced** at the bottom of the **Network** menu and select **Send all traffic over VPN connection**:

7. Once done, click on **connect**. You will be able to ssh the hosts in the private subnets.

Isolating staging from production

We saw in a previous tip, in the IAM users section, that we can break-out the environment using different AWS accounts, which can solve the most advanced user permission issues someone may encounter. If you don't need this kind of granularity in your user permissions management but still wish to prevent services in your staging environment from accidentally hitting resources in your production environment, you can rely on VPCs to solve that problem. Now that we can easily create VPCs, we can isolate the different environments present in our account. For instance, we can create the VPC `10.10.0.0/16` we just created for staging and add a new VPC on `10.20.0.0/16` for production. Thanks to the nature of VPC, these environments will not be able to reach one another directly.

In the last section of the chapter, we will talk about some services and strategies to avoid being hit with a successful targeted attack.

Protecting against targeted attacks

Throughout this chapter, we saw many tools and strategies to better secure our infrastructure against standard attacks. In some situations, like when someone purposefully tries to take your service down using **Denial of Service (DOS)** attacks or a **Distributed Denial of Service** (DDOS) attack, this might not be enough.

Protecting against DOS and DDOS attacks

In some cases, an attacker may try to target your service with a sophisticated attack.

The two most common attacks are:

- **Volumetric attacks**: where an attacker takes advantage of a botnet and overloads your servers with thousands and thousands of concurrent requests to the point that your servers are saturated.
- **Layer 7 attacks**: where an attacker tries to find a vulnerability in your application code and exploit it. The most common examples of layer 7 attacks are SQL injection and **cross-site scripting (XSS)** attacks.

To protect your application against these types of attack, AWS provides a **web application firewall (WAF)** which monitors the requests sent to your ALB and Amazon CloudFront distribution. On top of that, AWS also offers a service called AWS Shield which protects your service against volumetric attacks.

 AWS Shield comes standard with AWS for no additional cost but you may be in some situations where you need a more advanced layer of protection. For that, AWS provides another service called Advanced Shield. Advanced Shield pricing is slightly different and is usually more geared toward medium to larger size companies. It includes some extra features such as an application traffic monitoring system, additional DDoS mitigation capacity for large attacks, more reporting, and the support from a dedicated security team.

At a high level, AWS WAF works as follows:

1. You define a certain number of conditions which describes the requests you want to watch. This includes filtering based on HTTP header information (like user agent for example), content based conditions like malicious-looking SQL code, cross-site scripting, specific IP ranges, and so on.
2. You combined those conditions under a concept of rules. *Requests coming from this set of IPs AND with that particular http header* or *Requests with a body greater than 8192 bytes*.
3. You then create a Web ACL that describes the default action (allow traffic) and the different actions to perform when your other rules are matched (reject, count, or allow) for each rule matched.

You can read more about the service and the different conditions and actions available in the AWS documentation at `http://amzn.to/2suvS3R`.

To turn on AWS WAF, we can once again use CloudFormation. If you are interested in deploying a standard set of rules for AWS WAF, you can use the following template:

`http://bit.ly/2v2ybyI`

The template takes two arguments, a name (WebACLName) and the ARN of your ALB. It protects against the most common attacks.

The last topic we will cover is protecting against ransomware.

Protecting against ransomware

Ransomware has gained popularity in recent years. The idea is that a hacker or a group of hackers will try to find and exploit a vulnerability in your infrastructure or services. If they manage to gain enough permissions to take over the control of your AWS account then it will provide them access to not only all your computing instances but also all the data present in your databases. Since your services are now managed using CloudFormation and Ansible, you will be able to quickly redeploy your infrastructure. The bigger issue is the data. In these kinds of hacking events, it is common for hackers to encrypt all your data and ask for a ransom in exchange for the decryption key.

If you are cautious about your data, you are likely to create regular backups but it is also likely that your backups are stored on S3 which is now out of reach for you and at the mercy of the hackers who can easily delete those backups.

To protect your service against this type of attack, it is important to not keep your backups only on your main AWS account. One of the most straightforward ways to avoid that situation is to create another AWS account and replicate all your backups to that account. You can easily implement this using the S3 cross region replication mechanism as described at `http://amzn.to/2suGfo1`.

Summary

In this very last chapter of the book, we covered one of the more complex aspects of a Cloud infrastructure: its security. After understanding what an AWS customer is expected to secure, we looked at different ways to audit and assess the security of our infrastructure.

We then started to make changes to some of the most critical components of our infrastructure with the help of the IAM service. We put in place policies for users to enforce the use of complex passwords and MFA devices. Still relying on IAM, we also looked at how to better limit the AWS permissions of our resources.

Once we had IAM under control, we started to make changes to our network to only expose to the internet what needs to be internet-facing. For that, we created a new VPC with public and private zones.

Finally, in the last section of the chapter, we saw ways to protect ourselves against targeted attacks by taking advantage of the AWS Web Application firewall and replicating our backups to another account.

Index

Made in the USA
San Bernardino, CA
25 August 2017